DANGER
OVER PANAMA

DANGER
OVER PANAMA

by Jules Dubois

THE **BOBBS-MERRILL** COMPANY, INC.
A SUBSIDIARY OF HOWARD W. SAMS & CO., INC.
Publishers • INDIANAPOLIS • NEW YORK

To my wife Lucille

First Printing, 1964
Copyright © 1964 by Jules Dubois
All rights reserved
Library of Congress catalog card number 64:23196

Printed in the United States of America

Contents

Contents

Introduction

In an article requested by the *American Mercury* magazine in March, 1953, I wrote:

"There is a monument in the Republic of Panama which honors the French who failed to build the Panama Canal. There is no monument to honor the Americans who did build the canal.

"If our National Security Council, our Joint Chiefs of Staff, our State, Defense, and other departments of our national administration have never given that poignant fact some thought, it is appropriate for them to do so now."

This book gives some detailed, historical thought to the above poignant fact, to the tragic events of January, 1964, and to what the future might hold for us there.

JULES DUBOIS

Coral Gables, Florida
February, 1964

1. The Communist Strategy

When World War II ended, there was only one power in the world capable of waging war against the United States in the foreseeable future. That power was Soviet Russia. Soviet Russia was already preparing itself confidently and actively in the Western Hemisphere for the eventuality of such a war.

There was little, if any, difference between the Soviet plan of operation and that which was employed by the Nazis before and during World War II. Adolf Hitler's master plan called first for propaganda to win the people over to the Nazi organization, after which the organization was charged with the responsibility for the continuation of propaganda, so that the existing conditions would be destroyed by propaganda and minds would be permeated with the new doctrine. After this was accomplished would come the fight for power and the ultimate success of their doctrine, which would enable their agents to seize Western Hemisphere governments or at least to influence policy to such a degree that it would be tantamount to control. The Soviets and their agents revived Hitler's plan, which had in fact been part of the Kremlin's master strategy in Latin America since the early 1920's.

Even before the end of World War II, when the United States and

3

Russia were still allied in the fight against Nazi Germany, the Communists dusted off the ancient charge of "Yankee Imperialism" and began to flaunt it daily at the United States.

The Soviet international propaganda policy in Latin America after World War II can be stated briefly:

1. Stress that the U.S.S.R. won the war unaided and that it is the dominant power in international affairs.

2. Exploit the democratic progressive elements so that they will exert pressure on their governments to accept the policies advocated by the U.S.S.R.

3. Encourage the unionization of all unskilled, skilled, and professional labor groups so that the working class can dominate policies.

4. Stress reestablishment of diplomatic relations with the U.S.S.R.

5. Denounce every negotiation with the United States as a betrayal of national interests to Yankee imperialism.

6. Denounce Inter-American Military Cooperation as intention of the United States to gain control of the military forces of the hemisphere.

7. Denounce the control of the Panama Canal by the United States; stress that the Canal should be internationalized or nationalized.

8. Stress that the U.S.S.R. wants peace and that only Anglo-Saxon imperialism wants war.

There was no more fertile field in the world for the propagation of the Communist doctrine than among the masses of Latin America. The twenty republics, nominally a predominantly Roman Catholic sphere of influence, numbered only 133,000,000 inhabitants in 1946, but exploded into a restless population of 200,000,000 by the start of 1964, at a time when Fidel Castro was entrenched as Cuba's Communist dictator and as Moscow's mainspring in its plans to drive the United States from the Panama Canal.

Moscow's plans were at least forty years old when the "flag war" erupted on the banks of the Canal on the night of January 9, 1964. That night the citizens of the United States were to be shocked into an awakening about Panama that was long overdue. The direct role of Fidel Castro and the global Communist conspiracy in Panama are thoroughly documented. Despite denials by Castro, by Soviet Premier

Nikita S. Khrushchev, by other spokesmen for Russia and Communist China around the world, and by the Panamanians themselves, the hand of Castro's Communist Cuba—where the model university for communist subversion is based—was, as the evidence will show, definitely behind the war that raged on the Panama Canal Zone boundary.

This does not mean that there did not exist a situation, and conditions, that provided a ready target for those who were expertly trained and quickly mobilized to execute their plan of action. Neither does it mean that there is no need for remedial measures by both parties—the United States and Panama—to correct inequities and to improve the state of mind of their citizens both in the Republic and in the Zone so that the security of the Canal and of the Western Hemisphere will not be jeopardized. The adroit enemy tried to smash the defenses of the Western Hemisphere at its weakest link. The Panama Canal proved, early in January, 1964, to have been softened up by the propaganda offensive that was launched by the Communists in a ceaseless bombardment around the world, and especially throughout Latin America.

The timetable of Communist Cuba's role in attempting to weaken the defenses of the Panama Canal follows:

April, 1959. An expeditionary force, composed of ninety-one Cubans, sailed from that island for Panama, allegedly commanded by three Panamanians who were lost at sea before landing. The force was commanded by Major Cesar Vega, a Cuban, and landed on the beach at Nombre de Dios (where Christopher Columbus, who gave the village its name, had landed on his fourth voyage in 1502). Panama protested the invasion to the Organization of American States, and a committee was flown from Washington to investigate and end the conflict. When other American republics lent units of their armed forces to help Panama crush the invasion, Castro sent orders to the Cubans to surrender. They surrendered on the beach on May 1. Vega refused to deliver his weapon to the OAS representatives who were on the beach. Instead, he insisted on surrendering it to me, and it is in my journalistic museum. It was a United States Army Colt .45 automatic. Vega, since in exile, has admitted that Castro authorized the expedition. It was supposed to be part of a coordinated assault to overthrow the constitutional government of President Ernesto de la Guardia, Jr., in which

Roberto Arias, son of the late President Harmodio Arias and husband of ballerina Dame Margot Fonteyn, participated on the Pacific Coast. A planned pincer operation against the Panama Canal had been frustrated.

November, 1959. Gregorio Ortega, a Cuban Communist and special correspondent of the newspaper, *Revolucion,* of Havana, was arrested in the province of Chiriqui with Rogelio Caparrós, a correspondent for the magazine, *Bohemia.* Ortega and Caparrós were sent to Panama as a team, ostensibly to report on the flag riots of November 3, 1959. Their mission, apparently, proved to be to foment the flag riots of November 28, 1959. They were observed inciting the peasants in Chiriqui to mobilize for a motorcade march of protest into the Canal Zone. Ortega and Caparrós had been supplied by the Castro government with diplomatic passports to facilitate their travel and their mobility in Panama. The government of Panama ordered them to leave the country, but they had already accomplished most of their mission.

June, 1960. The Cuban Embassy in Panama was caught training Panamanian labor leaders in the techniques of agitation and sabotage. In the same month, subversive propaganda, shipped from Cuba by two known Panamanian Communist agitators who were working and training there, was confiscated by the government.

November, 1960. The Panama government demanded the withdrawal of the Cuban Consul, Adolfo Marti Fuentes, after it obtained evidence of his direct participation in seditious activities. This was under President Robert F. Chiari, who assumed office on October 1, 1960.

January, 1961. Castro was asked by the government of Panama to withdraw Ambassador José Antonio Cabrera for his flagrant intervention in the internal affairs of the country.

July, 1961. The Cuban *chargé d'affaires* in Panama fired from the embassy window on a demonstration that protested the executions in Cuba. He was ordered out of the country.

December, 1961. After Fidel Castro insulted President Chiari again in a radio broadcast, Panama broke diplomatic relations with Cuba.

January, 1963. Marcos A. Robles, Minister of Government and Justice (Interior) of Panama, accused Castro agents of instigating peasant riots in the province of Chiriqui.

February, 1963. Castro agents burned several railroad cars on the Chiriqui Railroad.

October, 1963. Castro agents tossed "Molotov cocktails" into the United States Information Service office of the American Embassy.

November, 1963. The *Guardia Nacional* of Panama (the only armed force, which also serves as a police force) arrested Juan Bautista Chavarría, a Costa Rican Communist, when he tried to smuggle Castro propaganda into the country. The police also found a cache of explosives, weapons, and money that had been smuggled into the country the same day from Cuba.

January 9, 1964. Panamanian Communists, trained in Cuba, played a major role in the flag war on the Canal Zone boundary and in the uneasy truce of the treaty that followed immediately.

January 10, 1964. The Panamanian Committee for the Defense of the Cuban Revolution, whose officers include David Turner and his brother Jorge, Deputy Thelma King, Alvaro Menendez Franco, and other Castro Communists who have frequently traveled to Cuba and have undergone training there, was one of two organizations that distributed inflammatory handbills and took credit for the flag riots in the Canal Zone. The other organization was the Partido Izquierdista Socialista, the Communist faction of the Socialist Party of Panama. The text of the handbill of the Panamanian Committee for the Defense of the Cuban Revolution is both a boastful and a threatening document, as these excerpts show:

The Panamanian Committee for the Defense of the Revolution declares that it was present in the heroic protests of the Panamanian students against the troops of Yankee imperialism in the Canal Zone. It addresses itself to the Panamanian people through this means in order to make known that the generous blood spilled by the students and worker youth will not have been spilled in vain.

Panama will be very soon, like Cuba, a Marxist-Leninist state and will have leaders like the Comrade Fidel Castro, Great Captain of the Second Latin American independence.

Then the Canal Zone will be Panamanian, as in effect it is, and there will be no mass assassination of students and men and women of our people. Very soon that supreme revolutionary movement will arrive. Everything is ripe for the conquest of our fatherland.

Panama will be a Socialist country that will count, as Cuba now counts, with the atomic, economic, and moral support of the fatherland of the proletariat, which is the U.S.S.R. (Soviet Union).

Panamanians: We should follow the example of Cuba: to every Yankee demand, a Panamanian demand. To each Yankee outrage, a Panamanian protest. To each Yankee assassination, a Panamanian act of vengeance. Let us confiscate the Yankee properties in the entire national territory. Out with the Zonians and other imperialists from Panamanian national territory.

This Committee for the Defense of the Cuban Revolution, which seconded and led the students from the Eagle's Nest* toward the heroic antiimperialist battle, reports today to all the Panamanians that Socialist Cuba is on our side, corresponding to our cause as we correspond to theirs. Castro will send us more arms and more experienced leaders so that we can make revolutionarily viable the demands of our government. For that it is indispensable that President Chiari break relations with the United States and reestablish them with Cuba. Also it is necessary that our government denounce the treaties of 1903, 1936, etc.

With the support of Socialist Cuba we will have support from the Socialist world.

Let us be faithful to the mandate of our martyrs. Let us make ourselves worthy of their memory as fighters for the territorial integrity of the fatherland, expelling all the Yankee assassins from Panama.

That afternoon, Foreign Minister Galileo Solis cabled Secretary of State Dean Rusk and formally advised that Panama had broken diplomatic relations with the United States.

Soviet Russia's planting of the seed for the internationalization of the Panama Canal dates back to 1924. It was accomplished by Alexander Lossovsky, head of the Profintern, which was the precursor of the Comintern. He received Victor Raul Haya de la Torre of Peru, who then was a young firebrand, a rabble-rousing student-politician on an invited visit to Moscow. Haya swallowed the seed and wrote the plan into the major program for his *Alianza Popular Revolucionaria Americana* (American Popular Revolutionary Alliance, called APRA) party. The internationalization of the Panama Canal thus became Point Four of the APRA program. Explaining it, Haya wrote:

*The National Institute (Panama's largest high school).

The Panama Canal in the hands of the United States is one of the most serious dangers for the sovereignty of Latin America. The international program of APRA proclaims frankly the internationalization of the Panama Canal as a continental objective.

The internationalization of the Panama Canal is the libertion of the means of circulation of the wealth indispensable for the free economic life of our people. The motto of the coat of arms of that small republic [Panama] is "Pro Mundi Beneficio." But the Latin apothegm of its resplendent heraldry has not been fulfilled by acts.

The Panama Canal for the benefit of imperialism is an instrument of domination over our countries and a great danger in case of war. Its internationalization would be, then, imperative for a complete victory over imperialism. That is why it constitutes for us an Indo-American economic and political principle.

The above was written in Haya's first published book, *El Anti-Imperialismo y El APRA*, which spelled out his party's domestic and foreign policies. On June 8, 1962, in an interview I had with him in Lima, Peru, a day before the presidential election, Haya modified the above view and advocated placing the Canal under the control of the Organization of American States.

For years, another rabble rouser spoke out not only against United States control and operation of the Canal, but also against any attempt to build another canal elsewhere in Latin America. He is Vicente Lombardo-Toledano, who, until he was displaced by Fidel Castro, was the No. 1 Voice of Soviet Russia in Latin America. Lombardo was Moscow's main labor stooge for all the countries south of the Rio Grande. He organized the Latin American Confederation of Workers (CTAL) in 1938, and ten years later organized the *Partido Popular Socialista* (Socialist Party) in Mexico. Writing in the Mexican leftist magazine, *SIEMPRE,* on January 24, 1964, Lombardo parroted the line that has been echoed by the Sino-Soviet propaganda machinery with increased cadence since the flag war erupted. He announced that his party, which is a Soviet front,

. . . was born in 1948 in order to fight for the full independence of the Mexican nation. It supports without reservations the demand of the Panamanian people that the Canal be delivered to them. In this way there will not only disappear the military government within the heart of the Republic of Panama, which the Pentagon operates from Washington, and the civilian government of the Canal Zone, which the Department of State operates,* but also the principal political espionage center of North American imperialism in the Continent, the training camps for other ranks and officers who must crush the mobilizations of our people who fight for their liberty, and other series of institutions which watch the march of our nations and dictate the necessary measures in order to prevent them from some day achieving the full independence to which they have a right.

Lombardo revealed something that has been known for some time: that the Panamanian Federation of Students has been Communist dominated and has been used as a spearhead in all movements to weaken the defenses of the Panama Canal and to blacken the image of the United States in the Canal Zone. Lombardo's article continued:

> The Panamanians have become conscious of what it signifies to have military bases and the United States Southern Command encrusted in their territory. Nationalization and neutralization appear as two inseparable demands, and although the jurists begin to make precisions, the entire people discuss obtaining the maximum in their government's negotiations. Victor Avila, Secretary General of the Panamanian Federation of Students—6,000 university, 40,000 high school—told me in the University [of Panama]: "The Zone is a base for aggression against Cuba as it was for Guatemala in 1954. That constantly endangers Panama. We will fight until we achieve the demilitarization of the Canal and the withdrawal of all the American troops who are in the Zone."
>
> In the classroom where we talked there was this inscription: "If the oligarchy plays the game of imperialism, the oligarchy and imperialism will be crushed by the furor of the people."

It is quite obvious from the above quotes that Lombardo's mission to Panama in 1963, after Avila, a Cuban-trained Communist had won

---

*Incorrect. It is an autonomous organization that reports to the President of the United States. President Theodore Roosevelt directed the enterprise personally but President Taft, while continuing to hold the authority, designated the Secretary of War as his representative. This has never been changed except that the Secretary of the Army (not the Department of the Army) now is the President's representative. The Governor communicates direct with the Secretary of the Army and not through military channels.

the Students' Federation election at the university when the new term began in the month of May, was to urge them to pursue the battle for the Canal.

For some months in the fall of 1963 it was reliably reported in diplomatic quarters in Havana that Fidel Castro had been admonished by the Kremlin that further Russian aid would be contingent on his ability to produce another victory in Latin America for the Soviet master plan. This is why Castro intensified the smuggling of arms into Venezuela and why he encouraged the attempt by the Armed Forces of Liberation in that South American republic to prevent the citizens from voting on election day. Both offensives failed, and Castro was further discredited as a man who could produce for Moscow in other countries.

The then President Romulo Betancourt of Venezuela filed charges of aggression against Castro as soon as he verified the origin of a cache of arms—six tons of them—which had been found on the beach near Coro, northwest of Caracas, on November 2. Betancourt had an iron-clad case against Castro, and the bearded dictator of Communist Cuba knew it. He planned two diversionary actions, both designed to relegate the Venezuelan charges into the background before the Organization of American States. An investigating committee of the OAS council had flown to Caracas and ascertained the veracity of the accusations by Venezuela. It was preparing a report for the council, but first decided to give Castro a chance to defend himself, although in January, 1962, Cuba had been excluded from the OAS at the Eighth Emergency Meeting of Consultation of the Foreign Ministers of the American Republics at Punta del Este, Uruguay.

There was another country that was ripe for an explosion that could serve to blacken the image of the United States and possibly compel the OAS to give priority to the newer case and defer action on Venezuela's charges against Castro. That country was Panama. All the elements for a successful diversionary operation that would appear to be primarily nationalistic in origin were available there. Waiting to fall on the prey was a numerically small but efficiently organized Communist party, with allied fellow-traveling organizations, whose activists had been skillfully trained in Cuba, Prague, Moscow, and Peking for that purpose. That explosion, as has been noted, occurred on the night of January 9, 1964. The Venezuelan charges against Castro were immediately given a lower priority, for Panama filed accusations against the United States before both the United Nations Security Council and the Council of the Organization of American States.

Within a few days, Fidel Castro was on his way to Russia to collect from Khrushchev for services rendered. The Soviet master plan for Panama, which had been drafted so many years earlier, was being implemented in an adeptly executed offensive. There had been cemented immediately a Nationalist-Communist alliance, amid the emotional frenzy that had been generated to wrest control of the Canal from the United States and shatter with red hammers the vital link in the chain of defense of the Western Hemisphere.

Chief Minister Nikita S. Khrushchev gave Castro a hero's welcome and a hug in Russia. He accompanied the Cuban on a visit to Kalinin on January 17 where he spoke at a textile factory and referred to the Panama crisis as follows:

> So now Comrade Castro is in Kalinin, and there is blood flowing in Panama. The United States imperialists are screaming till they are hoarse that the events in Panama are the handiwork of Castro. But Comrade Fidel is on holiday here, shooting wild boar. These events in Panama were not organized by Comrade Castro. These events are the result of the predatory policy of the United States imperialists. The imperialists are saying that the Communists took an active part in the Panama events. But we know well that the people of Panama, the workers of Panama, are struggling for the freedom of their country. They want to free themselves from the oppression of the United States imperialists. This is a legitimate desire and we are on the side of the people of Panama.

Naturally, no one expected Khrushchev to confess publicly that Castro's red hand had dipped deeply into the banks of the Canal to produce the crisis. Neither was it politic for Castro to make such an admission, one which would only aggravate the Venezuelan case that was pending against him. The Soviet propaganda drums beat out, in a ceaseless staccato, their message to the world; Communist parties all over, including Red China and Latin America, whipped up anti-American demonstrations and burned American flags "in solidarity with Panama."

On January 10, *Pravda* and Moscow Radio hastened to disseminate the Party line: "Progressive forces in the National-Liberation Movement in Latin America have rallied to support the Panamanian patriots." Three days later *Pravda* commented:

> The crude, arbitrary answer of American power to the just demands of the Panamanians convinces over and over again that United States policy toward their countries is a policy of force and plunder.
>
> That is why the front of solidarity is growing and broadening throughout Latin America. The secretary of the Brazil Peace Workers' Movement said that if today we do not put an end once and for all to this policy, then tomorrow, after Panama, the turn will come to every other Latin country.
>
> In Havana the National Directorate of Committees for the Defense of the Revolution said: "We say to the people of Panama, its workers, its women, its students, that those who are dying today, like those who died at the Bay of Pigs, are dying for absolute independence."

Then, on January 14, *Pravda* revealed a coordinated strategy for Panama and Cuba as follows:

> January 9, 1964 will be entered in the history of American imperialism as one of the most infamous dates. On that day American military forces, entrenched on territory that they had seized from Panama, began the bloody repression of Panamanian patriots. The echo of the shots has been resounding around a world shaken by the monstrous crime. The Panamanian people want their land freed of the heel of the foreign soldier so that he will not be able to suppress the National Liberation Movement of the fraternal peoples of Latin America through a military base on Panamanian territory.
>
> The bloody events in Panama show that the American imperialists are trying to suppress the Latin National Liberation Movement with fire and sword. Aggression against Panama is a direct continuation of aggression against Cuba, the main target of all recent American actions in Latin America.
>
> The United States refused the demand of the Cuban people, freed from the yoke of American monopolies, that the seized Guantanamo territory be returned, saying that the base on foreign soil is an indispensable defense against communism. Now it refuses the demand of the Panamanian government which, by no means Communist, is a bourgeois government. Nikita Sergeyevich Khrushchev last December again emphasized that United States imperialism, carrying a policy of colonial

expansion in Latin America, Africa, and Asia, is the mainstay of contemporary colonialism. The Soviet Union always has been on the side of the peoples fighting for freedom and independence, and it always will be.

All of the above was echoed in a radio roundtable in Moscow by Soviet international commentators. They were Victor Shragin, Nikolai Yevgenyevich Polyanov, and Leonid Ivanovich Zavyalov. Here is what they had to say:

Shragin: The Press stresses in particular that part in Comrade Khrushchev's speech wherein he spoke of the support of the Soviet Union for the courageous struggle of the working people of Panama for the freedom of their country and against the oppression of the United States imperialists. The stormy events in Panama continue profoundly to agitate the world public. I ask you, Leonid Ivanovich, to deal with these events.

Zavyalov: Our radio listeners know what has happened in Panama. We have already had much comment about these events in our broadcasts. But I would like now to dwell on the history of this question, insofar as the events which have been played out in Panama reflect the struggle of the people of Panama against the United States imperialist policy. The legal status of the Panama Canal is regulated by a treaty concluded in 1903, when Theodore Roosevelt was in power in the United States. It is he who is spoken of as the "father of the 'big stick' policy."

Shragin: Or, as it is also called, the "policy of the iron collar."

Zavyalov: That president imposed on the Panamanian state a shackling treaty, according to which the United States got permanent concessions for the building of the Canal and for the right to exploit it subsequently. In fact, the treaty tore away from Panama a part of its legitimate territory. According to this treaty, Panama granted the Canal Zone to the United States only on lease and thus Panama rightly considers the Zone its own state territory.

Shragin: Yes, but the United States pays Panama a high rent for the use of the Canal.

Zavyalov: It is a miserly rent in comparison to the income which the United States gets from the exploitation of the Canal, which passes through the territory of Panama.

Polyanov: Just in the last fiscal year, the United States, according to official figures, got more than $58 million net profit from the exploitation of the Canal.

Zavyalov: But now the subject is a different one. It is not so much the distribution of the income and profit from the Canal and its exploitation as the return to the State of Panama of its legitimate territory. That is the subject now, because United States troops have, in essence, occupied the Panama Canal Zone and have torn it from the territory of the State of Panama, thereby in fact committing aggression against Panama.

Polyanov: It is not only the international legal aspect of the matter which is important. The United States also maintains a military base in Panama. The United States makes use of the territory of Panama also for the training of deviationists, spies, and various other thugs, who are then sent into the countries of Latin America—for instance, to combat the Venezuelan partisans—and they are also sent to the territory of Free Cuba.

Shragin: Also in Panama is Howard Air Force Base. Every morning from its runways U-2 planes take off and spy on Cuba from a high altitude.

Zavyalov: I would say they use it as a springboard for their penetration into Latin America and for their struggle against the National Liberation Movement in Latin America.

The Party line had reached Panama earlier. The Communists began quickly to organize fronts through which they would press for their objectives. One of the first such fronts was the Committee for the Redemption and Defense of National Sovereignty. On the night of January 15, meeting in the auditorium of the Sindicato de Periodistas (Newspapermen's Association) in Panama City, this group adopted a Declaration of Principles and two resolutions. One resolution urged the immediate printing of banners to be displayed in all stores and on all buses with these words: NATIONALIZATION OF THE CANAL. The other insisted that all negotiations for a new treaty be conducted in Panama and not in Washington. The Declaration of Principles read:

The Committee for the Redemption and Defense of National Sovereignty declares:

1. The need to strengthen before the Security Council of the United Nations and the Council of the Organization of American States the denunciations in connection with the aggression of the North American Armed Forces in the Canal Zone.

2. The need to reiterate the recognition of the constitutional principle

according to which the government, exercising its sovereign rights as a Panamanian state, can take diplomatic steps for the establishment or severance of diplomatic relations in accordance with the nation's interest.

3. Denunciation of the 1903 Canal treaty and complementary agreements.

4. The nationalization of the Panama Canal as the aspiration of the republic, a concept which should be incorporated in the text of the new treaty, assuring the republic the conditions and benefits it deserves as a territorial sovereign.

5. The neutralization of the Panama Canal as an aspiration of the republic which should be obtained in accordance with the procedures and norms most convenient to the republic's interest.

Another instrument promoted by the Communists was the First Extraordinary Congress of Municipal Councils that met in Panama City on January 18 and 19. Delegates from sixty-three municipal councils in the republic converged on the capital for the sessions. Alvaro Menendez-Franco, Havana- and Moscow-trained Communist member of the Panama City Municipal Council (and its former president), made the closing speech. Several resolutions were adopted. All of them were significant, but the most comprehensive one, approved on the night of January 18, embodies the points emphasized by Moscow. The text of that resolution reads:

WHEREAS, The United States Army stationed in the Panamanian territory of the Canal Zone, during the ninth, the tenth, and the eleventh of January, cowardly massacred hundreds of defenseless and unarmed Panamanians for the sole reason that they loved their motherland and firmly supported its sovereignty, and

WHEREAS, The United States Army stationed in the Panama Canal Zone has become an element of grave public and international disturbance and has carried out an unspeakable military aggression against the nation's sovereignty and integrity, and

WHEREAS, By virtue of the events which have occurred, the presence of United States armed units in that territory is undesirable and constitutes an offensive humiliation of national dignity and a factor that destroys sentiments of peace in this area of the continent, and

WHEREAS, Panama is and will continue to be sovereign throughout its territory in spite of the savagery, the economic power, and the great brute force of the United States Army, and

WHEREAS, The national government, in a worthy action and in defense of the people's aspirations, has severed diplomatic relations with the United States government, determined not to renew them until that government gives assurances of its decision to negotiate a new canal treaty,

Resolves,

1. To demand that the national government negotiate with the United Nations the withdrawal of the armed forces from the Canal Zone and their replacement with police units of that highest organization.

2. To support the national government's step of severing diplomatic relations until the 1903, 1936, and 1955 treaties are abolished in accordance with the Panamanian people's aspirations, and a new document concluded that embodies Panama's legitimate rights and clearly and completely establishes a deadline for the abandonment of the Canal Zone by the United States.

3. To demand from the national government, in the event the United States does not agree to negotiate, that it call, within a peremptory period, an urgent meeting of the United Nations General Assembly so that the international organization may fully recognize Panama's absolute sovereignty in the Canal Zone territory, and act—in accordance with its pronouncement against colonialism and for the judicial equality of states, and within international law—to settle the Panamanian demands and aspirations.

Every major crisis between the United States and Panama since World War II occurred while the Isthmian republic was on the eve, or in the midst, of a presidential campaign. Elections were scheduled for May 10, 1964. President Chiari's own Liberal-Republican party coalition as well as a six-party Opposition Alliance were alarmed by the display of strength of former President Arnulfo Arias when he was nominated on January 4. An estimated thirty thousand persons, including those brought into the capital from the provinces, paraded. It was the largest political demonstration in the history of the sixty-year-old republic. The eruption of the flag war five nights later, and Chiari's firm stand against the United States, was to lessen the impact of the Arnulfo Arias demonstration, at least temporarily. But pressure on Chiari was not to subside. He had been criticized for a year and a half because he had returned from a visit to Washington, in June, 1962, without a firm commitment from the late President John F. Kennedy to negotiate a new treaty. The attacks did not all emanate from the Communists.

At 1:40 A.M. on January 15, 1964, the Inter-American Peace Committee, which had been striving to reach a formula to end the flag war, announced that its work was finished. The flag war had ended, but the "treaty war" was about to begin. There was pressure on Chiari from all sides, and the Federation of University Students led the agitation. Chiari had no intention of wavering from his original stand, he assured the students. There would be no resumption of relations with the United States until and unless there was an airtight commitment from Washington to negotiate a new treaty. The Opposition Alliance, which did not include the Communist fronts, issued a statement on January 16, the text of which read:

> The Alliance, fully aware that during the trying days which the country experienced it should refrain, for the sake of national unity, from taking a stand which could be interpreted as a unilateral action by the political parties comprising it, denounced only the unjustified North American aggression against our people. After having taken that patriotic position, and in the face of official reports that are at a variance with the national aspirations, the Alliance can no longer sidestep its duty of informing the nation that it is dissatisfied with the turn events have taken. Therefore it declares:
>
> 1. The severance of diplomatic relations with the United States was originally announced but no steps were taken to formalize this.
>
> 2. It was announced that our country would bring the charge of aggression before the United Nations Security Council, but on making it, our government inexplicably agreed that the charge be tabled until the Organization of American States rendered its report.
>
> 3. It was announced that the charge of aggression would be brought before the OAS, but the government did not even reach the point of sustaining this charge. Instead it contented itself with accepting the intervention of the Inter-American Peace Committee to look into the matter.
>
> 4. It was announced that the 1903 treaty would be denounced, but on the following day the report was denied, and
>
> 5. It spite of the fact that the President announced several times that diplomatic relations with the United States would not be resumed until

that government agreed to open negotiations for a new treaty, the Inter-American Peace Committee issued—with the acquiescence of the government—a communiqué that was susceptible to the unilateral interpretations, which, as is the tradition, has been detrimental to the national interests.

In the face of the state of affairs thus outlined, the Opposition Alliance reiterates its position that the Panamanian negotiators should sit down to negotiate with the United States representatives only if they agree, without doubts or dilatory tactics, that a new general treaty to replace the unjust and unworthy treaty currently regulating our relations will be negotiated. Otherwise, the heroic endeavor of 9 January 1964 could be flouted.

The above was signed by the *Partido Renovador, Partido Civico Nacional, Tercer Partido Nacionalista, Partido Dipal,* Liberal Civil Resistance, and *Coalicion Patriotica Nacional.*

That same night Arnulfo Arias' *Panameñista* party issued a discreet and dispassionate communiqué in which it reiterated the nationalistic posture of the candidate, at the same time criticizing the Chiari regime for bungling. Yet, the fear of Arnulfo Arias' political strength was not dispelled, for Radio Tribuna, partially owned by Fidel Castro's admirer, Deputy Thelma King, in an effort to discredit Arias in the heat of the nationalistic hysteria, referred to him as "the only pro-Yankee candidate."

Thus the United States was caught in a vise: the vortex of the global Communist conspiracy on one side, and the ambitions of the politicians seeking to win a most important and most historic presidential election. The U.S. government had been placed in the anomalous position of operating the world's most strategic waterway and occupying a ten-mile-wide zone in the middle of a country with which we had three treaties but whose leaders, bowing to emotional and intentional pressure, severed diplomatic relations with us.

The move against Panama was not an isolated one. The Canal was one of the important pawns in the strategy of the Soviet Union to control all of the world's strategic interoceanic passages. Turkey's own military might, and its membership in NATO, make it difficult for the Soviet to try a power grab for the Dardanelles at this time, although Russia has had its designs on those straits for more than a century. Yet, in the third month of 1964, the box score already showed the following in favor of the Soviet Union:

1. The Suez Canal was in the hands of Abdal Gamal Nasser, dictator of Egypt, unfriendly to the West.

2. Cuba was under the Communist dictatorship of Fidel Castro. The island looks north to the Florida Straits and along the chain of islands that are the Bahamas; the Windward Passage is to the east, although the naval and military might of the United States can be alerted at a moment's notice to erase that threat.

3. The Communist seizure of Zanzibar altered the control of the Straits of Madagascar.

4. Ahmed Ben Bella, a friend of Moscow, was the dictator of Algeria, which had the Straits of Gibraltar under its guns.

5. The delivery of the Sakhalin Islands to the Soviet Union as a World War II prize flanked the Bering Straits further, even though the Russian continent is not too far away from the tip of Alaska.

6. Sukarno, the pro-Moscow dictator of Indonesia, threatened the Malayan Straits with an invasion and seizure of Malaysia.

7. A possible victory of a Communist-Leftist alliance in the September presidential election in Chile could threaten the Straits of Magellan.

8. The Panama Canal was under a many-pronged attack to wrest its control from the United States.

The man who officially encouraged the secession of Panama from Colombia, and who ordered the most expeditious construction of the Canal, warned against internationalization of that waterway in an article written for the Kansas City *Star* on December 2, 1918:

> The Panama Canal must not be internationalized. It is our canal; we built it; we fortified it, and we will protect it, and we will not permit our enemies to use it in war. In time of peace all nations shall use it alike but in time of war our interest at once becomes dominant.

That man was Theodore Roosevelt.

2. The Problem Is Born

The cornerstone that was laid in 1903 to construct relations between the government of the United States and the newborn Republic of Panama was conceived erroneously and cemented improperly. Therein repose the reasons for the structural deficiencies that have continued to mar relationships between the two governments for sixty years. Any house that is built on a false foundation is bound to cause trouble during its lifetime, necessitating continuous readjustments and maintenance. Unless rapidly and adequately reinforced, it is eventually doomed to collapse.

The history of the United States association with a transit route in Panama dates back to the year 1846, when there were no transcontinental railroad routes. Colombia had been for more than twenty years assessing differential duties which made trans-isthmian travel prohibitive even under normal circumstances. The trip from coast to coast across the United States took eight or nine months and included encounters with scalp-hunting Indians. The voyage around Cape Horn required four or five months and carried with it all the dangers of the seas. The American *chargé d'affaires* in Bogotá, Benjamin A. Bidlack, acting without instructions from the Department of State and entirely on his own responsibility, signed a commercial and navigation treaty with Foreign Minister Manuel María Mallarino of the Republic of New Granada on December 12, 1846.

In transmitting this treaty to the Senate for ratification in the Fifty-eighth Congress, Second Session, President Polk said:

It will be perceived by the thirty-fifth article of this treaty that New Granada proposes to guarantee to the government and citizens of the United States the rights of passage across the Isthmus of Panama, or by the natural roads, and over any canal or railroad which may be constructed to unite the two seas, on conditions that the United States shall make a similar guaranty to New Granada of the neutrality of this portion of her territory and her sovereignty over the same. The reasons which caused the insertion of this important stipulation in the treaty will be fully made known to the Senate by the accompanying documents. From these it will appear that our *chargé d'affaires* acted, in this particular, upon his own responsibility and without instruction. Under such circumstances it became my duty to decide whether I would submit the treaty to the Senate; and, after mature consideration, I have determined to adopt this course.

The importance of this concession to the commercial and political interests of the United States cannot easily be overrated. The route by the Isthmus of Panama is the shortest between the two oceans; and, from the information herewith communicated, it would seem to be the most practical route for a railroad or canal. The vast advantages to our commerce which would result from such a communication, not only with the west coast of America, but with Asia and the islands of the Pacific, are too obvious to require any detail. Such a passage would relieve us from a long and dangerous navigation of more than 9,000 miles around Cape Horn, and render our communication with our own possessions on the northwest coast of America comparatively easy and speedy.... The guarantee of the sovereignty of New Granada over the Isthmus is a natural consequence of the guarantee of its neutrality, and there does not seem to be any other practicable mode of securing the neutrality of this territory.

The Senate ratified the treaty on June 10, 1848, and ratifications were exchanged the same day. On June 12, 1848, the treaty was finally proclaimed. In December, 1849, an American corporation, the Panama

Railroad Company, was chartered by the legislature of the State of New York, and a few months later the company had signed a contract with the Foreign Minister of the Republic of New Granada in Bogotá for the construction of a railroad across the Isthmus of Panama. Construction of this railroad began in the same year. In 1851 a train was run to Gatun and in 1855 the railroad was formally opened between Colón— then Aspinwall—and Panama.

In 1863 the Republic of New Granada changed its name to the Republic of Colombia, without affecting the territorial limits over which it exercised sovereignty. In 1865 there was a revolution in the State of Panama and the Department of State refused to invoke Article XXXV of the treaty with New Granada, which guaranteed the Isthmus against seizure or invasion by a foreign power only. In 1867 the contract between the company and the government of Colombia was revised. By virtue of the new contract, no company could build another road or canal across the Isthmus without first reimbursing the Panama Railroad Company for the rights. Also, Colombia ceded the railroad to that company for a period of ninety-nine years in exchange for a million dollars in cash and an annuity of $250,000, retaining its reversionary rights.

In 1868 Secretary of State William H. Seward entered into diplomatic relations with the Republic of Colombia for the construction by the United States of an interoceanic ship canal across the Isthmus of Panama. This treaty was signed in Bogotá on January 14, 1869, and it was communicated to the Senate of the United States in secret session for ratification by President Andrew Johnson on February 15, 1869. In Article III, Colombia stipulated and agreed not to undertake or allow the opening of any other interoceanic canal or any other new railway through or across their territory. In Article V, the United States agreed to construct the canal, the political sovereignty of Colombia, however, being retained by the latter government. Article XIII provided that the United States of America could devolve all the rights contained in the treaty upon any individual citizen or association of citizens of the United States of America. The treaty gave to the United States of America all possible control of the Panama Canal except that which pertained to the political sovereignty of Colombia. The Senate refused to ratify the treaty.

Two protocols had to be signed with Colombia to interpret Article

XXXV of the treaty of 1846. The first was signed on February 22, 1869, by Foreign Minister Pablo Arosemena and American Minister Ernest Dichman. This clarified the right of transit of American troops and federal prisoners over the Isthmus. The second was signed by Foreign Minister Luis Carlos Rico and Dichman on October 23, 1879. This clarified the right of dual custody of federal prisoners transported across the Isthmus. It was agreed that a Colombian civilian officer would accompany United States civilian officers and that, whenever necessary, help would be provided by Colombia which would assign national or state soldiers.

In 1870 a second treaty was entered into between the United States of Colombia and the United States of America, a treaty which granted identical privileges to those of the treaty of 1869 but in addition contained a broader clause in Article X, which read: "As soon as the canal, its appendages, and appurtenances shall be completed, the entire possession, inspection, direction, and management of the same shall appertain to the United States of America." The government of Colombia ratified that treaty but the Senate of the United States again rejected it. The Republic of Colombia had granted to the United States the entire control, protectorate, and management of the canal and again surrendered everything except her own political sovereignty.

In 1876 the Congress of the United States abolished the diplomatic mission in Bogotá. The Colombians, who had done all in their power to place themselves under the guardianship and control of the United States, had been disappointed by the failure of the Senate to ratify the two treaties, and, conversely, so was the U.S. government. In 1878 diplomatic relations were restored, but it was too late to mend the damage. On March 20, 1878, the Republic of Colombia granted a concession for the construction of an interoceanic ship canal to Lieutenant Lucien Napoleon Bonaparte Wyse, an officer of the French Navy. This contract was approved by the Colombian Congress by Law 28 of May 18, 1878. In 1879 the Wyse contract was purchased by the Compagnie Universelle du Canal Interoceanique de Panama (the old French Canal Company) for the sum of $10 million.

The reason for the Senate's rejection of the two treaties is not quite clear. However, it may well have been the case that the Senate considered it inadvisable to accept a treaty that contained reversionary rights for Colombia after a period of one hundred years. Or it may have been because of the Clayton-Bulwer treaty with Great Britain, which prevented the United States from constructing a canal without the consent of Great Britain. It may also have been that the financiers who had plans for the construction of transcontinental railroads were instrumental in lobbying against an interoceanic ship canal which would have enabled oceangoing freight to compete with the land lines. Whatever other reasons may have existed, the United States lost its opportunity to build the canal in the nineteenth century.

The French Canal Company failed, and on October 20, 1894, it was reorganized into La Compagnie Nouvelle du Canal de Panama, or the *New* French Canal Company. This company also failed, and its chief engineer, Ferdinand de Lesseps, who had built the Suez Canal, was scorned by the people who had deified him a few years earlier. The result of this failure was that American public opinion considered it not only a disaster from a financial standpoint, but also a scandalous affair from an engineering standpoint. Therefore, in 1896 the Congress officially recognized the Nicaraguan route as the one for an American canal and granted a charter to a company formed for its construction. It was in that year that the New French Canal Company contracted the services of the New York law firm of Sullivan and Cromwell, and William Nelson Cromwell undertook the lobbying task to swing American interest from Nicaragua to Panama.

In a brief to the New French Canal Company, which he submitted to justify his fee, Mr. Cromwell wrote: "We had personal interviews with members of Congress; we employed, as assistants, Washington lawyers instructed to follow, day by day, the evidence then being taken by a House committee on the subject, studying reports and giving instructions." From then on, there was carried out one of the greatest and most effective campaigns of lobbying in the history of the Congress of the United States.

Public opinion in the United States was electrified by the voyage of the battleship U.S.S. *Oregon* from the Pacific around Cape Horn to join Admiral Sampson's fleet in battle against the Spanish fleet off Cuba in 1898. The *Oregon* reached Admiral Sampson's fleet only just in time to participate in the last naval engagement of the Spanish-American War, the Battle of Santiago. There was no further procrastination. It was agreed that an interoceanic ship canal was a vital necessity for the national defense.

On June 15, 1899, President William McKinley appointed the Isthmian Canal Commission for the purpose of studying all possible canal routes, including that of Panama. Without receipt of the report of the commission, the House of Representatives approved the Nicaraguan Canal bill by a vote of 234 to 36 and sent it on to the Senate. On May 14, 1900, the Senate Committee on Interoceanic Canals and Waterways reported the bill favorably and asked for the immediate discussion of the bill. Mr. Cromwell tells how the attempt to bring it up for discussion was defeated in the Senate:

> One, at least, of our partners was busy with this matter night and day for several weeks conferring with senators and members of the commission, preparing arguments, and giving them publicity, and pleading insistently for the defeat of the bill passed by the House. Without going into details, we merely note the fact that Senator Morgan's motion was put to a vote on May 14, 1900, and defeated by a small majority of 7 votes—28 nays, 21 ayes.

With President McKinley assassinated and Theodore Roosevelt sworn in as President, the supporters of the Nicaraguan Canal route demanded immediate passage of a bill when Congress reconvened on December 2, 1901.

On May 25, 1900, Cromwell promoted the organization of a financial syndicate to buy the worthless stock of the Compagnie Nouvelle du Canal de Panama at a price not exceeding 20 per cent per share of a par value of $100. The syndicate included J. P. Morgan and Company, James Stillman, Isaac Seligman, J. Edward Simmons, Douglas Robinson, Henry W. Taft, J. R. Delamar, Vernon H. Brown, George J. Gould, Chauncey M. Depew, E. C. Converse, Clarence H. Mackay, Winslow Lanier and Company, Charles R. Flint, and Edward J. Hill. Later they were joined by H. J. Satterlee, Nelson P. Cromwell, G. W. Young, F. L. Jeffries, and J. R. Hill. The Nelson P. Cromwell was believed to have been William Nelson Cromwell, and the F. L. Jeffries was believed to have been Dr. Manuel Amador Guerrero. The agreement called for the stock to be held by a committee of three and to be sold at not less than 55 per cent of par value of $100 a share, a clear profit of 35 per cent over the original purchase price. Simmons was then president of the Panama Railroad. The Isthmian Canal Commission having recommended the Panama route under pressure by President Roosevelt, Cromwell enlisted the help of Senator John Colt Spooner, a staunch advocate of that route, to push a bill through the Senate.

On January 9, 1902, the House of Representatives had already voted overwhelmingly, by 309 to 2, on the Hepburn Bill, which called for the construction of the canal in Nicaragua. In the meantime, Cromwell was covering his flank and conferring with the Colombian minister in Washington, José Vicente Concha, who was succeeded later by Dr. Tomas Herrán, about the prospective sale of the Panama Canal Company rights to the United States. Joined with Cromwell in this work was M. Philippe Bunau-Varilla, a Frenchman and an official of the canal company, a man who was destined to play a most historic and important role in the decisions bearing on the fate of the canal problem, and on the future relations of Panama with the United States.

At the end of 1901, Nicaragua issued new postage stamps that showed its volcanoes, and there was a special one of Mount Momotombo, situated in the lake along the proposed canal route. The stamp showed smoke puffing out of the crater of the volcano. Cromwell, his lobbyist aids, and Bunau-Varilla judiciously sent those stamps to each senator, but still there was no majority assured to reverse the decisive vote by the House. Then, on May 8, 1902, Mount Pelée, on the French island of Martinique in the Caribbean, erupted. The volcano spewed forth flames and fiery lava that devastated one-tenth of the island and took a toll of 40,000 lives in and around St. Pierre. That disaster clinched the vote for Spooner. His bill was passed by only eight votes, 42 to 34. The date of the vote was June 19, 1902. Spooner waved the Nicaraguan postage stamp in the face of his fellow senators to underscore his argument that a catastrophe like that of Mount Pelée might destroy a canal built in the Central American republic.

President Roosevelt favored the Panama route, and as the Spooner Bill had to go back into conference to be married into the Hepburn Bill, there was a protracted debate. The Senate conferees stood pat on their bill. They would make no compromise. The House had to accept Panama or no canal at all. The White House applied pressure to persuade the adamant congressmen to acquiesce to the wishes of the senators. Thus the Panama route was officially and finally accepted by the Congress of the United States, and the Spooner Bill was approved on June 28, 1902.

Cromwell prepared a draft of a proposed treaty with Colombia which he submitted to Secretary of State John Hay. On November 18, 1902, Minister Concha transmitted the draft to Bogotá, and ten days later, without waiting for his letters of recall, he left for home. In conversations with Minister Tomas Herrán, Secretary Hay offered a maximum of $10 million cash to the government of Colombia and an annuity of $100,000 for the canal rights. On December 31, 1902, Colombia upped its annuity demands to $600,000, a sum that was unacceptable to the United States. With negotiations about to break off, a compromise of $250,000 per annum was suggested by Cromwell, accepted by Hay and Herrán, and on January 22, 1903, the Hay-Herrán Treaty was signed between the United States and Colombia. President Roosevelt sent it to the Senate for ratification the next day.

There was considerable doubt in official Washington that Colombia would ratify this treaty. This doubt was fully justified; Colombian public opinion was definitely opposed to it. The Colombians wanted indemnification from the French Canal Company for the relinquishment of their reversionary rights in the Hay-Herrán Treaty. The French Canal Company, with Cromwell acting on one side and M. Bunau-Varilla on the other, refused to accede to the wishes of Colombia. Behind the scenes a separatist movement was being plotted that was to make Panama an independent nation. On May 12, 1903, Dr. Juan B. Perez y Soto, Senator from the Department of Panama, wrote an article in a Bogotá newspaper in which he said: "The Herrán Treaty will be rejected by a unanimous vote in both chambers."

The State Department, alarmed by reports from Bogotá and Panama that the Hay-Herrán Treaty would be rejected, cabled American Minister A. M. Beaupré in the Colombian capital on June 9, 1903:

> The Colombian government apparently does not appreciate the gravity of the situation. The canal negotiations were initiated by Colombia, and were energetically pressed upon this government for several years. The propositions presented by Colombia, with slight modifications, were finally accepted by us. In virtue of this agreement our Congress reversed its previous judgment and decided upon the Panama route. If Colombia

should now reject the treaty or unduly delay its ratification, the friendly understanding between the two countries would be so seriously compromised that action might be taken by the Congress next winter which every friend of Colombia would regret.

The above message was classified as confidential, but Minister Beaupré was informed to communicate it orally to the foreign minister and, if he so requested, to furnish him with a copy of the admonition.

Perez y Soto proved to be very right. On May 18, 1903, the Senate of the United States had already ratified the treaty without amendment. But Colombia rejected the treaty on August 12, 1903, disregarding the warning sent by Hay.

The separatist movement of Panama got underway with increased fervor and was encouraged by Cromwell and Bunau-Varilla, who, as interested parties in the French Canal Company, had developed a plan to sell the rights of that company to the government of the United States for the sum of $40 million in cash. Bunau-Varilla laid the plan for the revolt with Dr. Manuel Amador Guerrero, a prominent Panama physician, in a New York hotel. Another senator from the Department of Panama, José Augustin Arango, became a leader in the separatist movement "because I had complete conviction that the Hay-Herrán Treaty would be rejected; consequently I saw only one means of saving the Isthmus from the ruin toward which it was heading: our separation from Colombia."

The government of Colombia was aware that a separatist movement was afoot, and consequently embarked on the S.S. *Cartagena* troop reinforcements for Panama. The transport reached Colón on November 3, 1903, the day the Panamanians declared themselves independent. Five hundred Colombian troops disembarked that morning. At 6:00 P.M., the popular uprising occurred in Panama City and a *de facto* government was established with a provisional junta composed of José Augustin Arango, Federico Boyd, and Tomas Arias.

Having notified the general superintendent of the Panama Railroad Company that night that the revolution had been successful, the junta also sent the following historic telegram:

HONORABLE SUPERINTENDENT OF THE RAILROAD, COLON:
This junta of government has knowledge that the military forces

brought to Colón by the steamship *Cartagena* have asked you to transport them to this side, and as this act would be of grave consequence for the company you represent, we urge you not to accede to such request, because the junta of government would see itself obliged to use its armed forces to attack the trains bringing over soldiers at whatever point on the railroad line. We hope that you will inform us of your decision on this most important matter.

(Signed) J. A. ARANGO
FEDERICO BOYD
TOMAS ARIAS

The Colombian troops were not transported to Panama City.

The Acting Secretary of the Navy, Charles Hial Darling, had sent the following message to the U.S.S. *Nashville* which was anchored off Colón on November, 1903: "In the interests of peace, make every effort to prevent government troops at Colón from proceeding to Panama. The transit of the Isthmus must be kept open and order maintained. Acknowledge."

In order to be certain that Commander John Hubbard, Captain of the *Nashville,* had received the message, a duplicate was cabled by the Department of State to the American Consul General in Panama, with instructions to "secure a special train if necessary" to Colón to get it aboard the warship.

The U.S.S. *Dixie,* which had joined the *Nashville* in Colón on November 5, 1903, landed two companies of marines under command of Major Lejeune. The commander of the Colombian troops, General Tovar, journeyed over to Panama where he was immediately arrested by the rebels. Meanwhile, the Colombian troops faced the American marines over barricades in Colón, but not a shot was exchanged between them. After General Tovar was released and permitted to return to his ship, he reembarked the troops and sailed for Colombia.

The revolution was consummated, and the junta issued a manifesto which stated in part:

In separating from our brothers of Colombia we do so without hatred and without joy. Just as a son withdraws from under the paternal roof, the Isthmian people in adopting the course they have chosen have done so in sorrow, but in obedience to the supreme and inevitable duty they owe to themselves and to their own welfare. We therefore begin to form a nation, one of the free nations of the world, considering Colombia as a sister nation by which we shall stand whenever circumstances so require and for whose prosperity we make the most fervent and sincere wishes.

The cornerstone that laid the wrong foundation for relations between the United States and Panama was to undergo a constant cracking as Panamanian historians narrated only their biased versions of how they achieved their independence. Convenient omissions led the schoolchildren to consider, from the earliest ages, that our country was the villain. There is no balanced study in Panama of the independence, and President Theodore Roosevelt didn't help matters much when he boasted in a speech at a University of California Charter Day celebration on March 23, 1911: "I took the Isthmus and left Congress to debate." Nor when he said in a speech in Buenos Aires, Argentina, two years later: "I took Panama."

The United States played a definite role in Panama's independence and enacted a law to pay Colombia $25 million in reparations for the secession in 1922. But the Panamanians are not taught the role Americans played to help them gain their independence—a role undertaken at the invitation and the insistence of the leaders of the secessionist movement.

For example, President Roosevelt dispatched five United States Army officers to Panama in October, 1903, on a cloak and dagger mission. They were to observe and report on the situation within the Colombian Department and to prepare plans for both offensive and defensive operations should it become necessary to commit United States troops there. The officers traveled under assumed names and an assumed variety of occupations. There was one medical major, three captains, and one lieutenant.

To prevent a fight between Colombian troops and United States Marines in Colón on November 3, 1903, the Americans accepted a proposal from Colonel Eliseo Torres, who became commander of the Colombian troops in Colón after General Juan B. Tovar and Ramon G. Amaya were tricked into traveling without their soldiers by rail to Panama, where they were arrested. Torres offered not to fight if he were paid $8,000 in cash, and if the passage of the remainder of his troops back to Cartagena would be guaranteed. Unable to get any funds from the already bankrupt secessionist leaders, Herbert G. Prescott, Assistant Superintendent of the Panama Railroad, authorized the money for Torres to be disbursed from the company safe at Colón. The passage for the troops to be taken by the Royal Mail Line steamer *Orinoco* to Cartagena was guaranteed by a promissory note signed by Colonel J. R. Shaler, Superintendent of the Panama Railroad, Commander John Hubbard of the U.S.S. *Nashville*, and Porfirio Melendez, a prominent citizen of Colón, who acted for the provisional government that was established that night. In November, 1910, the National Assembly of Panama adopted a resolution in which it declared Shaler a "Hero of the Republic" for his role in aiding the independence, but that resolution has long been stricken from the history books of the young nation.

An American adventurer and soldier of fortune, who was to dig his spurs deep into the internal affairs of Central America for years to come, also figured in the movement. He was "General" Herbert Ottley Jeffries, who appeared on November 3, 1903 as commander of a gunboat that silenced the loyal Colombian gunboat *Bogotá*, whose captain had not been invited to join the rebellion. The *Bogotá* lobbed several shells into the Chiriqui Fort, the parapets of which protected a landing from the Bay of Panama. Jeffries was rewarded with a grant of 200,000 acres of timberland along the Bayano River, almost forty miles east of Panama City.

Panama's independence was assured when General Esteban Huertas, the army commander in Panama, was brought over to the movement for $30,000 in silver. After Amador became the country's first constitutional president, he retired Huertas for life with a pension of $50,000 in gold.

Meanwhile, Maria de la Ossa de Amador, who inspired her husband to follow through with the independence plans when everything appeared gloomy, enlisted the help of members of her family to give birth to the new republic. A brother, Jeronimo de la Ossa, composed the national anthem. The latter's wife Angelica and their daughter Maria Emilia were the "Betsy Rosses" of the country. They designed and sewed Panama's first flags. It was one of these flags that was raised for the first time in Colón on November 5, 1903, by Major William Murray

Black of the United States Army. Another of Señora Amador's brothers, Francisco de la Ossa, was for many years Mayor of Panama City. In the opinion of M. Bunau-Varilla,

> . . . the government of Mr. Roosevelt would have had the moral right publicly to tear up its agreements with Colombia, owing to the intolerable abuse she was making of them. It had the good fortune to escape this necessity, which the domestic policy of the United States would have most probably prevented it from realizing. It was able to dispense justice, while keeping rigorously within the limits of its international obligations, thanks to the courageous determination of the people of Panama. On the evening of the 3rd of November, when the dispatch from Amador reached me announcing the explosion of the long-expected revolution, President Roosevelt was free to act and his action was untrammeled. He was hampered by no secret intrigues with the confederations. He took Panama, as he said later, because Panama offered herself, and because he was at liberty morally to accept the offer. The liberty of which Mr. Roosevelt was to make such fruitful and brilliant use was as complete as possible.

It is necessary to go back to the month of September, 1903, to understand the part that M. Bunau-Varilla played in the revolution at Panama. At that time a grave question of conscience confronted him. "Had I a moral right to take part in a revolution and to encourage its development?" he asked himself. Immediately he answered in the affirmative, "because I had twice warned President Marroquin, in November, 1902, and in June, 1903, of the grave risks of which its anti-canal policy exposed Colombia. Yes, because I had again notified these risks to the Vice-President of the Senate, General Nel Ospina, in August, 1903. . . . I certainly had the moral right to annul, by political action at Panama, the fatal effect which political action at Bogotá was bound to have on the gigantic French interests of which I was the sole defender."

M. Bunau-Varilla was interested primarily in recovering the money which he, as brother of the influential publisher of *Le Matin* of Paris, had invested in the French Canal Company, and with a substantial profit at that. He says that he gave Dr. Amador "up to the 3rd of November as a final limit for action. If you have not accomplished the revolution on that day or before I shall consider myself free of all re-

sponsibility for further events." This was on October 19, 1903, in a
New York hotel.

Amador, of course, acted quickly. He sailed from New York on
October 20, pursuant to Bunau-Varilla's insistence. Therefore, the
Frenchman was able to boast: "The military and diplomatic situation,
which I had conceived and dreamed of realizing when returning from
Washington on the 9th day of October preceding, had been completely
established twenty-six days afterward." Bunau-Varilla succeeded in
having the provisional government of Panama designate him as Envoy
Extraordinary and Minister Plenipotentiary of Panama to the United
States. This was one of the most curious and opportunistic developments in the foreign affairs of any nation, and is cause and effect of the
false foundation on which was to be erected the new republic's diplomatic association with the United States. The *de facto* government was
wholly dependent on Bunau-Varilla for financial support, which he had
promised Amador to the extent of $100,000. The new government had
merely appointed him as confidential agent. An ultimatum which he
sent to the unstable government on November 6 brought the result he
desired, and he was elevated to the rank of minister.

But other complications were to arise for Bunau-Varilla. Two delegates had been dispatched to Washington to join him in the negotiations
for the drafting of a treaty that would permit the construction of the
Panama Canal. These delegates were Dr. Manuel Amador and Don
Federico Boyd. They carried with them written instructions to be delivered to Bunau-Varilla which read in part: "You will have to adjust
a treaty for the canal construction by the United States. But all the
clauses of this treaty will be discussed previously with the delegates of
the Junta, Señores Amador and Boyd. And you will proceed in everything strictly in accord with them. . . ."

On November 9 Bunau-Varilla was invited to an informal luncheon
by Secretary of State Hay. Writes Bunau-Varilla in his book, *Panama*:

> After the luncheon with Mr. Hay, we discussed the situation. I con-
> densed my views in the following terms: "Mr. Secretary of State, the
> situation harbors the same fatal germs—perhaps even more virulent
> ones—as those which caused at Bogotá the rejection of the Hay-Herrán
> Treaty. The same elements will be found at Panama; but the passions of
> parties and of contradictory interests at Washington will add other per-

nicious elements still more active. The situation can be saved only by firmness of decision, and lightning rapidity of action. It is necessary to leave the enemy no time to perfect his plans. It is necessary to strike, to strike again, to keep on striking, and to win the victory before the foe has time to block the way."

"By the way," said Secretary Hay, "what is this commission, which according to the press despatches is going to leave the Isthmus to make the Treaty?"

"So long as I am here, Mr. Secretary," I [Bunau-Varilla] answered, "you will have to deal exclusively with me."

M. Bunau-Varilla says he "nipped this intrigue in the bud" by the following cablegram which he sent to the Minister of Foreign Affairs of Panama at 4:30 P.M. on November 9, and which crossed with the one advising him of the trip of the delegates "carrying your letters of credence":

I have explicitly denied rumor to the effect that a special commission is coming to discuss and sign the treaty, which produced a very bad impression, as it would be contradictory to my mission. I have given the assurance that nothing on our side would be done to provent the rapid drafting of the treaty. I shall submit to the approval of Your Excellency all the articles in succession, as they are agreed upon. It is eminently necessary to act rapidly in order to paralyze the formation of an obstructionist group supported by Nicaraguan and Colombian intrigues."

The Frenchman narrates how he accelerated the treaty negotiations in order to accomplish the signing before the arrival of the two delegates from Panama. He says:

I was thus led to the conclusion that the indispensable condition of success was to draft a new treaty, so well adapted to American exigencies that it could challenge any criticism in the Senate. The only things that I resolved to defend were first, the principle of neutrality of the interoceanic passage; secondly, the rigorous equality and perfect justice in the treatment of all flags, whether American or non-American, from the point of view of the charges and conditions of transit; thirdly, the attribution to Panama of an indemnity equal to that agreed on with Colombia; fourthly, the protection of Panama. By way of compensation I had decided to extend widely the share of sovereignty attributed to the United

States in the Canal Zone by the Hay-Herrán Treaty. . . . To cut short
any possible debate I decided to grant a concession of sovereignty *en
bloc*. The formula which seemed to me the best one was to grant to the
United States in the Canal Zone "all the rights, powers, and authority
which the United States would possess and exercise if it were the sovereign of the territory; to the entire exclusion of the exercise by the Republic of Panama of any such sovereign rights, power and authority."

At 10:00 P.M. on November 17, 1903, Bunau-Varilla addressed a
note to Secretary Hay urging that he "would like very much to terminate
the negotiation and sign the treaty tomorrow." Secretary Hay replied
immediately, and Bunau-Varilla rushed over to his residence that same
night. The Frenchman goes on:

> I condensed my impressions as to the necessity of acting rapidly in
> the following words: "So long as the delegation has not arrived in Wash-
> ington, I shall be free to deal with you alone, provided with complete
> and absolute powers. When they arrive, I shall no longer be alone. In
> fact, I may perhaps soon no longer be here at all."

At 6:40 P.M. the next evening, the treaty was signed. Amador and
Boyd had left New York by train at 4:50 P.M. the same day.

It will be recalled that on November 9 Bunau-Varilla had informed
the Foreign Minister of Panama that "I shall submit to the approval of
Your Excellency all the articles in succession, as they are agreed upon."
He neglected to comply with this on his own responsibility, because of
his zealousness to sign the treaty, expedite its ratification, and collect
$40 million as compensation to the New French Canal Company for
sale of its franchise to the government of the United States. When
Amador and Boyd reached Washington, they were received at the
Union Station by Bunau-Varilla, who presented them with a *fait
accompli*. "Amador was positively overcome by the ordeal," Bunau-
Varilla reports. "He nearly swooned on the platform of the station."

Bunau-Varilla tried in vain to get Amador and Boyd to exercise their
authority as delegates in order to ratify the treaty then and there in
Washington. It was necessary for the treaty to be shipped to Panama
for ratification by the junta. On November 25, 1903, Bunau-Varilla
cabled an ultimatum to the government of Panama to ratify the treaty
else he would resign. "It was, therefore, necessary at all costs to prevent

the treaty I had signed from being discussed by ignorance and blindness in the marketplace," he says. "To secure the desired results there was but one method for the government, the method which is always the same; namely, prompt and decisive action." On December 2, 1903, the treaty was ratified by Panama.

The ratification, though, was not by the constitutional congress of Panama but by the provisional junta of government and the six cabinet ministers. Bunau-Varilla had accomplished his objective. The text of the ratification decree follows:

Considering

1. That in this treaty the Republic of Panama has obtained a guarantee of its independence.

2. That for reasons of foreign security it is indispensable to consider this treaty with the greatest celerity so that the United States can begin to comply with that principal obligation with efficiency.

3. That the aspiration of the people of the Isthmus, which is the opening of the canal, and its service in favor of the commerce of all the nations, has been realized with this treaty; and

4. That the Provisional Junta of Government formed by unanimous will of the people of the Republic possesses all the powers of sovereign in the territory.

Decrees

Only Article. Approve the treaty celebrated in Washington, Capital District of the Republic of the United States of America, the 18th day of November of the present year between His Excellency Philippe Bunau-Varilla, Envoy Extraordinary and Minister Plenipotentiary of this Republic, and His Excellency John Hay, Secretary of State of the Republic of the United States of America.

Publish it.

Dated in Panama, the second of December of 1903

(*Signed*) J. A. Arango—Tomas Arias

Manuel Espinosa B.

The Minister of Government	Eusebio A. Morales
The Minister of Foreign Relations	F. V. De La Espriella
The Minister of Justice	Carlos A. Mendoza
The Minister of Finance	Manuel E. Amador
The Minister of War and Navy	Nicanor A. de Obarrio
For the Minister of Public Instruction the Undersecretary	Francisco Antonio Facio

On February 23, 1904, the Senate of the United States ratified the treaty by a vote of 75 to 17 and it was proclaimed by President Roosevelt on February 25. The ratifications were exchanged on February 26, 1904.

Senator Money, in the Senate treaty debate on February 20, expressed, according to Bunau-Varilla's interpretation,

> . . . the singular moral coercion to which he and his friends [opponents of the Panama route and proponents of the Nicaraguan route] were obliged to succumb.
>
> So this treaty comes to us negotiated by a *de facto* government; perhaps the people there having no voice in it whatever. Perhaps the people, if a vote were taken, would be exceedingly hostile to it. But it comes to us more liberal in its concessions to us and giving us more than anybody in this Chamber ever dreamed of having. We have approved over and over again treaties with Costa Rica and Nicaragua and other countries for a canal, but we have never had a concession so extraordinary in its character as this. In fact it sounds very much as if we wrote it ourselves; and I should believe that we did write it ourselves, except for the fact that the Administration had before, having "carte blanche," written such very bad ones that I do not believe it could write such a good one for us.

Bunau-Varilla cabled the news of the ratification to the government of Panama and concluded with the following words: "While defending the great French enterprise, which was almost killed by falsehood and calumny, I acted in the capacity of a French citizen defending a great moral interest in France. This excludes all idea of material remuneration." He then asked the government of Panama to withhold the salary of his office and with it form the nucleus of a fund for the erection of a monument to Ferdinand de Lesseps "whose genius has consecrated its territory to the progress of the world for the honor of Panama and for the glory of France and of the United States."

Immediately after the exchange of ratifications Bunau-Varilla went to the telegraph office and cabled the government of Panama that he had accomplished his task as Minister Plenipotentiary and that he considered his services for that government had ended. "I had fulfilled my mission," he writes, "the mission I had taken on myself; I had safeguarded the work of the French genius; I had avenged its honor; I had served France."

Bunau-Varilla had served France and not the Republic of Panama. And the Roosevelt Administration had recognized him as the Envoy Extraordinary and Minister Plenipotentiary of Panama before he had received his Letters of Credence which were in the possession of the two delegates, Amador and Boyd. Bunau-Varilla had laid a cornerstone with the haste of avarice. It was bound to be unstable, to cause apprehension in the hearts of the founders of the new republic, and eventually to germinate animosity against the United States.

It was not long before dissension and misunderstanding began to make itself felt in Panama, and the situation became so acute that President Roosevelt dispatched Secretary of War William Howard Taft to the Isthmus on October 18, 1904, with the following letter of instructions:

> There is no ground for believing that in the execution of the rights conferred by the treaty, the people of Panama have been unduly alarmed at the effect of the establishment of a government in the canal strip by the commission. Apparently they fear less the effect be to create out of a part of their territory a competing and independent community which shall injuriously affect their business, reduce their incomes, and diminish their prestige as a nation.
>
> The United States is to confer on the people of the State of Panama a very great benefit by the expenditure of millions of dollars in the construction of the canal. But this fact must not blind us to the importance of so exercising the authority given us under the treaty with Panama as to avoid creating any suspicion, however unfounded, of our intentions as to the future.
>
> We have not the slightest intention of establishing an independent colony in the middle of the State of Panama, or of exercising any greater governmental functions than are necessary to enable us, conveniently and safely, to construct, maintain, and operate the canal under the rights given us by this treaty. Least of all do we desire to interfere with the interest and prosperity of the people of Panama.
>
> The exercise of such powers as are given us by the treaty within the geographical boundaries of the Republic of Panama may easily, if a real sympathy for both the present and the future peace of the people of Panama is not shown, create distrust of the American government.
>
> This would seriously interfere with the success of our great project in that country.

You will advise the President of the Republic what the policy of this government is to be and assure him that it is not the purpose of the United States to take advantage of the rights conferred upon it by the treaty to interfere with the welfare and prosperity of the State of Panama or the cities of Colon and Panama.

(*Signed*) THEODORE ROOSEVELT

Secretary Taft gave the government and the people of Panama the assurance they were anxious to hear, and a few months later President Roosevelt issued an executive order which limited duty-free importations into the Canal Zone to merchandise in transit to other countries, construction materials, coal, and fuel oil. Tariffs on articles brought into the Zone from the Republic of Panama were removed; one hospital in the Zone was made available for patients from Panama; the United States undertook to build a highway to a distance of six miles outside of the limits of Panama City; currency was regulated; the delimitation of the Zone boundary was set provisionally. Other minor adjustments were made to better relations.

Shortly after Secretary Taft left the Isthmus, however, Governor Charles E. Magoon found it necessary in 1905 to establish commissaries in the Zone in order to provide essential foodstuffs for the laborers at prices within their reach. Canal employees were paid twice a month, and on each payday merchants in the cities of Panama and Colón would skyrocket their prices 300 to 500 per cent in excess of the normal sales price. Complaint after complaint was recorded, and the merchants were warned publicly to correct their malpractices else stores would be established in the Zone. The merchants refused to pay heed.

The commissary situation has been one of the many thorns in relations with Panama ever since. In August, 1905, Don Ricardo Arias, a prominent businessman, predicted in an exchange of open letters with Governor Magoon all the evils that have come to pass in the conflict between the Canal Zone and Panama over the commissaries.

Governor Magoon's reply failed to satisfy the merchants. Soon the commissaries began to branch out into the big business of general merchandising, including the sale of luxuries. The government of Panama made five demands in 1908:

1. that the privileges on the commissary be restricted to employees on the gold roll;
2. that the semi-monthly payday be restored;
3. that the use of coupon books be discontinued;
4. that the use of coupon books, if continued, be safeguarded and made good in trade with Panama merchants;
5. that European importations be discontinued.

The five demands were rejected.

"There is no sorer point in Panamanian-American relations," Undersecretary of State Sumner Welles pointed out years later, "than the use by the United States of territory within the Republic." The original treaty, negotiated in 1903, before the independence of Panama was even consolidated, by which the United States was granted the right to construct, protect, and maintain the Canal, gave this country sweeping authority. It included the right of intervention in Panama. It gave this government power to take over any land or water within the Republic which the United States might declare was needed for the protection or the maintenance of the Canal. As a Panamanian once said to me, this right was equivalent to the possession by the United States of a mortgage over all the territory of the nation, and a mortgage which might be foreclosed without prior notice and at any moment. Our authorities in the Canal Zone all too often exercised this right with little discretion and with even less regard for the susceptibilities of the Panamanian people.

"As the years passed, and the Republic of Panama reached maturity, enforcement of the terms of the original treaty severely strained relations between the two countries. Some of the provisions became anachronistic. Others were patently unjust. Moreover, it was obvious that one of the greatest assurances that the United States can have that the Canal will be adequately safeguarded lies in a friendly disposition on the part of the Panamanian people and in their realization of their own interest in protecting the Canal.

"In 1936 a new treaty was concluded. It abrogated those provisions of the old treaty which impaired the sovereignty of Panama, and abolished the right of American intervention. It was based upon the principles that while the ability of the United States to protect and maintain the Canal should not be weakened, both countries were jointly concerned, and that Panama should be a partner with the United States in insuring the effective defense of the Canal and its efficient maintenance. The treaty of 1936 terminated an era during which Panama had been obligated to submit to almost any unilateral decision which this government saw fit to take. The new treaty was an outcome of the Good Neighbor Policy."

By the treaty of 1936, Panama accepted joint responsibility in the defense of the Canal. In 1945 the Department of State failed to challenge the unilateral interpretation made by the government of Panama of the Defense Sites Agreement of May 18, 1942. It also failed to advise the government of Panama sufficiently in advance of the date of expiration of the agreement—according to the unilateral interpretation of Panama—of the postwar defense requirements for the Panama Canal so that the Panamanian government might have complied willingly with its treaty obligation in the joint defense of the Canal.

The first negotiations to revise the basic Canal treaty of 1903 were completed in Washington on June 28, 1926. The new treaty was signed by Secretary of State Frank B. Kellogg for the United States and Francis White, as Chief of the Latin American Affairs Division. Minister Ricardo J. Alfaro and Eusebio A. Morales (the latter, as Minister of Government, had ratified the 1903 treaty) were negotiators for Panama. Rodolfo Chiari, father of the man who was chief executive when the flag war erupted in 1964, was president of Panama. The Panama National Assembly rejected the new treaty because the United States failed to make the concessions that the legislators desired.

President Harmodio Arias sent a team of negotiators to Washington in 1934 to discuss a new treaty, and one was signed on March 2, 1936, together with a Trans-Isthmian Highway Convention. The major accomplishments by Panama were the abolition of the guarantee by the United States of the independence of Panama and the U.S. right to intervene in Panama's internal affairs; an increase in the Canal annuity from $250,000 gold to $430,000 devalued; and a statement by the United States that no additional lands or waters were needed for the defense of the Canal. But there was a "safeguard" in Article X that opened the door for a request for such lands if the United States invoked it in the event of an "international conflagration." This, as will be seen later, was to become necessary.

Still dissatisfied with the existing treaties, in 1953 President José Antonio Remon requested President Dwight D. Eisenhower to agree to new treaty negotiations. These were begun in the same year and ended in late December, 1954. Remon was assassinated on the night of January 2, 1955, but the new treaty was formally signed later that month. This, too, was not to satisfy the Panamanians.

The past and the present diplomatic relations of the government of the United States with the government of the Republic of Panama have a tremendous bearing on the future. Also, the establishment in the Canal Zone of a bureaucratic and autocratic administration that has made little or no effort to orient American employees to the fact that they are literally in the heart of a foreign country and should make attempts to understand the psychology of the natives has been one of our cardinal diplomatic and administrative mistakes in the Canal Zone.

3. Panama and Pearl Harbor

For nearly seven hours on the morning of April 21, 1934—from 5:05 A.M. until 11:50 A.M., to be exact—the Blue Army defending the Panama Canal battled against the overwhelming forces of the Brown Fleet in the most unusual and concentrated attack ever made against any land defenses. When the smoke of battle had drifted away, both sides claimed success in their maneuvers, each registering considerable damage by spectacular air bombardments and counterattacks with shells from antiaircraft guns and "Big Berthas" of the Panama Coast Artillery Corps.

The feature of this then extraordinary and thrilling warlike show— the first of its kind ever tested in Panama—was the surprise aerial bombardment of Albrook Field, the Pacific side bulwark of the air defenders, and of the harbor at Balboa, by three hundred dive bombers from the giant aircraft carriers of the Brown Fleet, including the U.S.S. *Saratoga* and the U.S.S. *Lexington*. This attack occurred between 8:20 A.M. and 8:35 A.M. Swooping down from the skies like rockets, the planes were protected from observation by the blinding tropical sunlight, and the defending forces were caught napping, with almost every fighter plane of the 16th Pursuit Squadron parked on the runways and ramps. The airplanes of the 16th Pursuit Squadron, the only fighter force defending the Canal, were blown to bits before the defenders could halt the onslaught. The surprise attack occurred but a little more than thirty minutes after the first air attack when more than fifty dive bombers destroyed not only the hangars at the Albrook Field Air Base but also smashed shipping at anchor in Balboa Harbor.

After this attack, during which the antiaircraft gunners trained their weapons on the speedy planes, the attackers turned southeast to return to their carriers. In their stead there appeared level bombardment airplanes, flying at a higher altitude, and these dropped bombs over department headquarters at Quarry Heights, forcing Major General Harold B. Fiske, commander of the defending forces, to move his GHQ to the post of Corozal, about three miles away. It was after the second attack that three giant Martin bombers from the army air base at France Field, near the Atlantic entrance to the Canal, theoretically dropped six five-hundred-pound bombs on the deck of an aircraft carrier, believed to be the U.S.S. *Lexington*, while it was cruising in Panama Bay, about one hundred miles south of Balboa. The airmen claimed destruction of more than three-quarters of the *Lexington's* planes on the flight deck and asserted that the fighting lady was so disabled that she would sink.

Admiral David F. Sellers' attacking fleet had slipped into the Bay of Panama shortly after dark on the night of April 20, 1934. With the aid of a natural screen provided by clouds, and poor visibility from the coast, an advance guard composed of destroyers was able to approach to within fifteen miles of Otoque Island—about fifteen miles due west of the Canal entrance at Balboa—before dawn on April 21. The aircraft carriers moved in unobserved and unreported to a point within ninety nautical miles of Panama. The first wave of attacking airplanes took off from the carriers at 5:30 A.M., upon the command of Admiral J. V. Reeves, commander of the Battle Force, and headed toward Albrook Field from the southeast by way of the island of Chepillo and the town of Chepo, forty miles from Balboa. The main objective of this joint Army and Navy exercise was to catch the defense planes on the ground at the stronghold, to destroy them, to destroy the hangars and base engineering shops, and to destroy any shipping that might be encountered in the harbor. This mission was accomplished by the Brown Fleet in Panama on the morning of April 21, 1934.

The Japanese accomplished the same mission seven years later, but with real bombs and bullets, at Pearl Harbor, Hawaii, on the morning of December 7, 1941.

But there was no Pearl Harbor in Panama—neither on December 7, 1941, nor thereafter.

Many military men who served in Panama from September, 1939, to December 7, 1941, are still puzzled over the complete surprise of the attack with which the Japanese struck at Pearl Harbor on that fatal day. Not that they expected the Japanese to select Pearl Harbor as the particular target of attack, but many of them did consider Pearl Harbor as *one* of the possible points of attack along with the Panama Canal. For years the war games in the Canal Zone included a simulated attack by enemy airplanes from carriers approaching from the vicinity of the Galapagos Islands, about a thousand miles southwest from the harbor at Balboa. Suicidal attacks were considered not only feasible but quite probable, should the Canal have been included in the enemy's war plans.

At Pearl Harbor the mission was to defend that naval base against enemy attacks. That mission was not accomplished. The mission of the Commanding General of the Panama Canal Department was to defend the Canal against enemy attacks from without and from within. That mission was accomplished. There were no enemy attacks.

One of the costliest mistakes made by the Japanese when they instigated the war against the United States was that of failure to attack the Panama Canal, either simultaneously with or very soon after the attack against Pearl Harbor. Damage to the Canal could have, and would have, delayed the buildup of our war effort in the Pacific to a very dangerous point. It would have delayed the flow of supplies to Great Britain and to Russia. It would have delayed the sending of essential war materials from South America to the United States, such as tin from Bolivia, where Eastern and Gulf States ports and plants could have ready access to them. It would surely have had an adverse effect on the war in Europe. Failure to block the Canal must be recorded in the annals of history as a grave error by the Japanese and the Germans.

The defenses of Panama on December 7, 1941 could not have withstood as blistering an attack as was inflicted on Pearl Harbor. Nevertheless, the defenses of Panama, weak as they were, would not have been caught napping.

It was on November 27, 1941 that General George C. Marshall, Chief of Staff, sent a war warning to Lieutenant General Frank Maxwell Andrews, who was commanding the Caribbean Defense Command and the Panama Canal Department. Two days later, on November 29, 1941, General Andrews reported to General Marshall by letter that the defenses of Panama had been fully alerted.

"Fully alerted" in Panama meant an alert not only against sabotage but against all possible enemy attack. Fighter planes—what few were available then—were out on dawn patrol every day. Antiaircraft positions were manned twenty-four hours a day. Ammunition—all that was available—was stocked at every position. Bombardment aircraft were armed, and combat crews were already functioning as well-knit teams. And, despite the scant field forces that were present at that time, the equivalent of one division of infantry troops was strategically deployed along the two coasts.

On that same day he transmitted his report to General Marshall, General Andrews dispatched his Assistant Chief of Staff for Military Intelligence in the Panama Canal Department, Colonel James K. Cockrell, Sr., in a special Army transport plane to Guatemala, Honduras, El Salvador, Nicaragua, Costa Rica, Colombia, and Ecuador to alert the American military attachés in the capitals of those republics and to establish a closer and more effective liaison with his headquarters in the wake of an emergency. As Chief of the Intelligence Branch in Colonel Cockrell's office, I accompanied him and the fine officer he was replacing, Colonel Leslie D. Carter, on this mission. When Pearl Harbor was attacked we were in Quito, Ecuador, on the last leg of our trip, having reached there at noon from Bogotá, Colombia.

When the Japanese attacked the fleet at Pearl Harbor, work was being expedited to enlarge and improve the defenses of the Panama Canal. The locks at Miraflores, Pedro Miguel, and Gatun were being reinforced against air attack. Revetments had already been constructed for the dispersal of aircraft. Plans were executed without delay to disperse aircraft from the main bases along the Canal to tactical satellite fields and strategic intermediate bases scattered throughout the Republic of Panama. Guards were patrolling vital installations and the locks areas with full battle gear and with orders to shoot first and to ask questions afterward. Strategic trails and other approaches were covered by foot and mechanized patrols. Aircraft and beach warning stations (what few there were at the time) were operating on a permanent twenty-four-hour basis.

The salient fact was that the Axis powers wanted Panama and planned to get it the easy way, an accomplishment which was on the road toward realization. But there was no Pearl Harbor at Panama, because the people of Panama were, on the whole, friendly to the cause of the United States, and the Allied war effort.

4. The Keys to the Canal

Of most direct military significance to the United States on September 1, 1939, when Adolf Hitler marched his Nazi troops into Poland, was Latin America. Here was a potential stepping-stone of bases for Germany, bases that might well encircle the Panama Canal and endanger the security of the United States. Latin America's position and importance in the defense of the Western Hemisphere was well defined by Major General George V. Strong when, as Assistant Chief of Staff War Plans in 1939, he said that under the conditions existing, and in view of the development of weapons at that time, this hemisphere would be safe from aggression from abroad just as long as two conditions obtained: (1) that the Panama Canal be open for transport to the United States fleets, and (2) the aggressors from abroad have no bases in this hemisphere from which to operate.

This analysis by General Strong formed the basis of planning the United States military policy for Latin America in the pre-Pearl Harbor days.

The global character of modern warfare brought renewed emphasis upon the length and security of supply lines over which the material required for a nation to wage a successful war depends, as well as over

51

which weapons of war, food and supplies, and replacements must travel. Since the focal point of our wartime, or peacetime, line of communication is the Panama Canal, the continued and uninterrupted operation of this waterway is vital to our commerce. Its obstruction by an enemy would seriously curtail our preparation for war and, in time of war, hamper our entire war effort. In the event of such obstuction the next available route is around Cape Horn, a voyage which involves many weeks of travel. An enemy in possession of the Straits of Magellan at such a time would be in a position to sever our sea communications between the Atlantic and the Pacific.

Of secondary importance to our lines of communication in the Southern Hemisphere is the passage in the South Atlantic Ocean between Dakar in Africa and Natal at the eastern tip of the bulge of Brazil. Through this passage sails all the shipping between our East Coast and Gulf Coast ports and the eastern seaboard of South America. Domination of this passage by any potential enemy, like damage to the Panama Canal, would constitute a great menace to our security. Immediately after the fall of France in 1940, the great eastern bulge of Brazil placed South America only 1,800 miles from that part of the African coast which was under the domination of the Nazi boot, Dakar. This region of Brazil, except for a narrow strip along the coast that has sufficient rainfall for permanent agriculture, suffers from periodic droughts. These droughts make it necessary at times for a large part of the population either to be fed by the government or to be evacuated to the more fertile interior regions. Because of its sparse population, its narrow margin of food supply, and its isolation from the country's principal fertile areas, this Bulge is virtually a military liability for defense purposes. But its accessibility to four-engine aircraft from Africa, and the availability of its coves and unused natural harbors to ships, made it attractive to Nazi Germany and Fascist Italy.

The thousands of miles of coastline, from the Gulf of Mexico to the Caribbean and thence to the South Atlantic and from the Pacific Ocean off California down to the Straits of Magellan, touched all but two of the republics of Latin America. The two landlocked republics are Bolivia and Paraguay. Every world power, therefore, has a water-route access to the eighteen South American republics and is capable, unless the nations are sufficiently alerted to the danger, of establishing bases in those republics. Just north of the Brazilian bulge is the colony of French Guiana, and further northeast, almost midway between Trinidad, a British possession, and Puerto Rico, a United States possession, is the French island of Martinique. Ruled by administrators who were dependent on Vichy France for their subsistence, these colonies also constituted a potential danger to the United States.

The Nazis, Fascists, and Japanese had been crying for *Lebensraum*. The Tripartite Alliance that was to create the Axis partnership before the end of September, 1939, the same year that Hitler and Stalin marched into Poland, had already resulted in a division of enemy spheres of influence around the world. The Nazis had arranged their sphere of influence in Eastern Europe and, with Soviet Russia and Red Army troops, had moved into half of Poland. With the totalitarian nations of the world lined up either in battle or alliance against the democratic powers, the natural consequence was for their eyes to turn to the hemisphere that has its greatest wealth in unexploited natural resources, the southern half of the Western Hemisphere. With their sights trained on Latin America, the Axis powers began to groom puppets and sympathetic groups in every republic to seize the reigns of their governments' machinery. This circumvention, and ultimate violation, of the Monroe Doctrine had to cause considerable concern to the American people.

When President James Monroe declared on December 2, 1823, that the United States would consider any effort by a European nation to extend its system to any part of this hemisphere as "dangerous to our peace and safety," he established a doctrine that was to be the foundation of our Latin-American policy. The Monroe Doctrine has passed through several stages since 1823, from active U.S. intervention in the internal affairs of the Latin-American republics to the enunciated Good Neighbor Policy of the Roosevelt Era. At each of the evolutive stages the United States policy has been maligned constantly, both at home and abroad, either as one of "imperialism" or one of "dollar diplomacy." But no matter how mistakenly it may have been applied at times, policy toward Latin America had always had one basic tenet: the peace and security of the United States.

A scant twelve years after President Monroe enunciated his doctrine, the United States made little effort to enforce it. When Guatemala appealed in 1835 for help against British encroachment, we turned the other way, thus British Honduras was founded. Today this dispute is still pending. However, in 1881, the position of our government changed, and we invoked the Monroe Doctrine to justify our position that the frontier conflict between Great Britain and Venezuela over the territory of British Guiana should be arbitrated. The United States indicated clearly at that time that it regarded any further extension of British territory into Venezuela not only as a threat to its security but, in the words of the doctrine, as a "manifestation of an unfriendly disposition toward the United States." The issue was settled to our satisfaction. Now Venezuela claims an area of British Guiana as far south as the Essequibo River.

With the advent of the twentieth century and the materialization of plans for the construction of the Panama Canal, the strategic importance of the Caribbean and Central American countries increased for the United States. It was deemed expedient then to adopt certain protective devices, which ranged from customs receiverships in those countries to outright military action and intervention. In one form or another the United States intervened in Mexico, Venezuela, Cuba, Haiti, Panama, Nicaragua, and the Dominican Republic. These interventions would hardly fall within the literal scope of the Monroe Doctrine, but they were the result of expedient interpretations advanced by Presidents Theodore Roosevelt and Woodrow Wilson. It was the Roosevelt corollary that put the United States on record as declaring that adherence to the Monroe Doctrine required our exercise of an international police power throughout the Western Hemisphere. Under this corollary, which was to reappear in 1945 in the plans for the United Nations Organization, the United States intervened to forestall forcible collection by European nations of payments due from defaulting Latin-American republics.

President Wilson's interpretation was that unstable Latin-American regimes were a threat to our security. He was the father of the policy of nonrecognition of governments that are established by force and against the will of the people. While the interpretations of the Monroe Doctrine by Presidents Theodore Roosevelt and Woodrow Wilson were based on the presumptive right of American self-interest and self-defense, the Latin-American people, having witnessed American expansions in the

Spanish-American War, were strongly suspicious of our plans and motives. It has been a difficult task to erase these suspicions, and although they have not completely disappeared, considerable progress was made on the credit side of the ledger after World War I.

But these earlier interventions furnished the Axis with the fuel they needed for their political warfare drive to undermine the prestige of the United States in Latin America. However, they overlooked the fact that the United States had begun long before to develop a gradual recognition that its security depended on both United States respect for the Latin-American nations and their respect and good will toward us.

When Charles Evans Hughes was Secretary of State in 1922, he sponsored a Central American conference which negotiated thirteen treaties of amity and peace. A year later a revolution broke out in Honduras and U.S. Marines landed there, but then, adhering to the new treaties, the United States immediately went into consultation with the other Central American republics and worked out a mutually satisfactory solution. In 1924, U.S. Marines were removed from the Dominican Republic, giving evidence of the desire of our government to withdraw from its previous role of professor of government by military intervention. President Calvin Coolidge tried to withdraw the Marines from Nicaragua in 1925, but the turbulent situation there precluded the move at that time. Just before President Herbert Hoover turned his office over to Franklin Delano Roosevelt in 1933, the Marines were removed from Nicaragua, and at the same time an announcement was made that they would soon abandon Haiti.

Thus the foundation had been laid by Hoover for President Roosevelt to state in his first inaugural address on March 4, 1933:

> I would dedicate this nation to the policy of the good neighbor, the neighbor who resolutely respects himself, and, because he does so, respects the rights of others, the neighbor who respects his obligations and respects the sanctity of agreements in and with a world of neighbors.

The enunciation of this new policy, at least its baptism with an attractive name, and its subsequent translation into reality by the Roosevelt Administration, began to yield profitable fruit. Almost every Latin-American republic, with the threat of Axis incursion facing it, began to express a definite responsibility for collective as well as unilateral action against any non-American state that might endeavor to violate American territorial integrity and political independence. Under the Roosevelt Administration steps were taken to strengthen hemispheric solidarity by diplomatic and economic means.

It was not until 1939 that the threat of foreign military missions in Latin America was brought out in bold relief, especially as the motives of the Nazi agents in the Western Hemisphere became more apparent.

Hitler planned, with his Axis partners, to dominate the world politically and economically. To achieve this goal it was necessary, first, to conquer it militarily. His speeches were replete with references to his plans for conquest in Latin America. Political unrest is constant in Latin America, and nobody knew this better than the agents of the Axis who were dispersed to stimulate unrest at strategic points throughout the Southern Hemisphere. To assist them were the agents of Franco's Spanish Falange. The Consejo de Hispanidad, organized by the Falangist party for the sole purpose of restoring the influence of the old Spanish empire in the Western Hemisphere, was in active operation, working closely and effectively under the direction of the more sagacious organizers, the Nazis.

"If there ever was a place where democracy is senseless and suicidal," said Adolf Hitler, "it is South America. . . . Our youth must learn to colonize. If we had Mexico we could solve all our difficulties. Mexico is a country that cries out for a capable master. . . . The Argentine and Bolivia are now in the front line of interest. . . . We shall create a new Germany in Brazil."

In 1940 a plot was discovered by an investigating committee of the Uruguayan congress which was designed to overthrow the democratic government, install a German-controlled puppet regime, and transform Uruguay into an agricultural colony of the Nazis. The plot was nipped in the bud. Brazil shipped rifles to Uruguay, and President Roosevelt dispatched the cruisers U.S.S. *Wichita* and U.S.S. *Quincy* to the harbor at Montevideo. Dr. Edwin C. Wilson, United States Minister to Uruguay, who one year later as Ambassador to Panama was to deal with President Arnulfo Arias, announced that our government was prepared to crush any activity that tended to endanger the economic or political freedom of the Americas, especially when the activity was encouraged by non-American sources.

In his broadcast to the American republics on Columbus Day, October 12, 1940, which is celebrated south of the Rio Grande as the "Day of the Race," President Roosevelt stated that the "core of our defense is the faith we have in the institutions we defend. The Americas will not be scared or threatened into the ways the dictators want us to follow." President Roosevelt had very much in mind when he made that speech —Germany's swift economic and attempted political and military penetration in Latin America.

By 1939, Germany's infiltration in Latin America assumed what was tantamount to an invasion. There were approximately three million Axis nationals residing in Latin America then, each of whom could have been made available to form part of a militant striking force capable of implementing the plans of the Axis at the appropriate time. In addition to these men, there were more than six million naturalized citizens of Axis origin and first-generation descendants of Axis nationals who retained their Old World ties and sympathies for the Axis powers and who were then among the most articulate supporters of Axis ideologies. Of these, the largest numbers were residing in Brazil and Argentina.

In Brazil there were more than 1,500,000 Germans, 2,500,000 Italians, and approximately 345,000 Japanese. In Argentina, the Italian colony and its first-generation descendants, including naturalized citizens, numbered 4,780,000, and there were also resident more than 100,000 Germans and about 8,700 Japanese. Bolivia, which was advised during the Chaco War against Paraguay in the 1930's by a German military mission, had 18,000 Germans resident but it also had 23,070 Italians and 900 Japanese. Paraguay had 45,000 Germans, 5,600 Italians, and 509 Japanese. Uruguay's 13,000 Germans worked to encourage the leaders of the Herrerista (pro-Nazi) party to overthrow the democratic regime. Also living in Uruguay were 100,000 Italians and 94 Japanese.

Included among Colombia's 7,090 Germans were pilots, ground crewmen, and technical experts of the Nazi-controlled Scadta Airline Company. Scattered through Colombia also were 3,012 Italians, while 365 Japanese were allegedly cultivating cotton fields on large plains in the rich Cauca Valley, just a few hundred air miles south of the Panama Canal. In Peru there resided 4,035 Germans, some of whom were employed by Lufthansa Airlines, another Nazi-controlled company, and

Axis activities there were reinforced by the presence of 11,560 Italians and 52,728 Japanese or descendants thereof. In Venezuela there were 7,000 Germans, 1,500 Italians, and 45 Japanese, whose presence caused concern among the operators of the Allied-controlled, essential oilfields.

While Panama itself could boast of only 1,175 Germans, 1,369 Italians, and 658 Japanese, most of whom resided in the espionage-infested terminal cities of Panama and Colón, north in Costa Rica were 5,000 Germans, 6,800 Italians, and 92 Japanese. Many of the Germans and Italians possessed influence and, as in the other countries of the Americas, they had intermarried with natives of those republics, some of whom were related to the most prominent and powerful families.

Mexico had 16,501 Germans, 11,808 Italians, and 22,310 Japanese, while to the south, Guatemala, with its critical chicle and coffee plantations, had 5,700 Germans, 420 Italians, and a handful of Japanese. Honduras reported 953 Germans, 398 Italians, and three Japanese; El Salvador had 465 Germans, 523 Italians, and eight Japanese. Further south, in Ecuador, with the Galapagos Islands a strategic link in the Canal defenses, there were 3,366 Germans and a Nazi-controlled domestic airline which used trimotor Junkers aircraft and was then only five hours flying time away from the Canal. In addition, in Ecuador there were 7,625 Italians and 610 Japanese.

The Caribbean islands of Cuba, the Dominican Republic, and Haiti had their share of Axis nationals, too. Cuba accounted for 8,044 Germans, 2,672 Italians, and 819 Japanese. Haiti had 355 Germans and 75 Italians, while in the Dominican Republic lived 139 Germans, 1,302 Italians, and 769 Japanese.

The Axis powers had in their hands in 1939 the keys with which to close the locks of the Panama Canal to the United States Fleet and to all Allied shipping. The average citizen in the United States at that time was little aware of the potential danger that existed, just as he was unfamiliar with the fact that there was a new danger over Panama as 1964 drew near.

As soon as Hitler marched into Poland and President Roosevelt decreed on September 5, 1939, the existence of a limited national emergency, the Department of State issued a hurried call for the first Emergency Meeting of Consultation of the Council of Foreign Ministers of the American Republics, a meeting to convene before the end of that same month. Heading the United States delegation was Sumner Welles, Under Secretary of State, assisted by Dr. Edwin C. Wilson, Minister to Uruguay. Welles's fluency with the Spanish language, his understanding of the people of the Americas and their problems, and his firsthand knowledge of the menace that was confronting the free peoples of the world, made him the ideal man to represent American interests at this emergency meeting, while his chief, Secretary of State Cordell Hull, was occupied in Washington with the more immediate problems of the conflict that had set Europe, and that was soon to set the world, aflame.

At this Panama Conference, the Nazis appeared in force as observers for the first time at a Pan-American Conference. Kurt Sell of DNB, German News Agency correspondent in Washington, and Dr. Manfred Zapp, who in 1938 establishd the Trans-Ocean News Agency in New York to service the entire Western Hemisphere as a propagandist and as an espionage agent, flew down from the United States and were duly accredited as correspondents at the conference. But despite his request for credentials, Zapp failed to file a single story during his entire stay of more than a month in Panama. Otto Reinbeck, German Minister to Panama and Central America, flew in from Guatemala to direct operations of the Nazi diplomatic and espionage corps. Reinbeck brought with him a native Guatemalan who was in the employ of the German Legation in Guatemala City. This influx caused a local newspaper to report that "the increased attendance of German diplomats, scribes, and observers found mingling more and more in the gathering of delegates and local and foreign press representatives had not been well received by the latter and has been the subject of no little interest on the part of the American authorities in the Canal Zone and the authorities of the Republic of Panama." Reinbeck told the local press that it was only natural for him to put in an appearance as the conference dealt with a war in which Germany was very much concerned, and that he "hoped the consultations would result in agreements and understanding leading to the peace and welfare of the entire world." A year later he was to return to Panama in full diplomatic regalia to attend the inauguration of Dr. Arnulfo Arias as President of Panama.

The agenda for this meeting of the foreign ministers, which opened on the afternoon of September 23, 1939, included "steps to be taken in common, or individually, to suppress violations of neutrality and subversive activities by nationals of belligerent countries or others seeking to promote the interests of belligerent powers in the territory and jurisdiction of any or all of the American republics." Desirous then of keeping the war away from the Americas, and the Americas away from the war, the conference agreed to the tightening of a security belt around a three-hundred-mile zone extending seaward from the shores of the Western Hemisphere. This security belt, of course, was devised primarily to keep the Nazi submarines and agents away from this hemisphere. But this declaration did not deter the Nazis, who were well aware of the inability of the nations of this hemisphere, including the United States, to carry out effective neutrality patrols along the thousands of miles of ocean which were included in the safety belt. Therefore, the Nazis considered it perfectly safe to send one of their prize pocket battleships, the *Admiral Graf Spee*, on a raiding mission in the South Atlantic Ocean to destroy British and Allied shipping that was transporting critical foodstuffs from Argentina and Uruguay to the United Kingdom. Early in December, 1939, the *Admiral Graf Spee* was damaged in a running battle with a British cruiser squadron comprised of the 9,000-ton H.M.S. *Cumberland,* H.M.S. *Ajax,* and H.M.S. *Achilles,* each 7,500 tons, and fled into the harbor of Montevideo, Uruguay, for safety and necessary repairs.

The government of Uruguay set a time limit for the completion of the repairs, and that hour expired on the night of December 17. Deployed in strategic positions at a battle distance off the coast were the three British cruisers, waiting for the Nazi man-of-war. But Herr Hitler had other plans; he was not going to permit the British to claim a naval victory so early in the war. Following the World War I tactics of the German Admiralty, which had ordered the cruiser *Dresden* destroyed in Chilean waters and the famous raider *Emden* scuttled in the South Seas, the Fuehrer ordered Captain Hans Langdorff, commander of the *Admiral Graf Spee,* to scuttle the ship in Montevideo harbor. The order was executed on the afternoon of December 17.

The Nazis accused Uruguay of yielding to British pressure, which was true, but Uruguay was also acting under the security decisions of the Panama Conference. The ship could have been interned, but Nazi psychology was not ripe for such procedure in December, 1939. The sympathetic government of Argentina immediately extended "provisional hospitality" to the 1,055 surviving officers and men of the *Admiral Graf Spee*. They were transported from Uruguay across the Rio de la Plata and were interned in the naval barracks in Buenos Aires.

The addition of 1,055 rabid Nazis already trained to perfection in warfare to the millions of Axis nationals living in the Americas accentuated the possibilities of increased German subversive activity, especially as it was a foregone conclusion that many of the *Graf Spee* officers and crew would be able to escape from confinement and make their way to other republics in the Western Hemisphere. And gradually they did succeed in making good their escape.

Secretary of State Cordell Hull told the House Foreign Affairs Committee on January 15, 1941, that "the control of the high seas by law-abiding nations is the key to the security of the Western Hemisphere in the present-day world situation. Should that control be gained by the partners of the tripartite pact, the danger to our country, great as it is today, would be multiplied manifold." Then he added, very significantly: "Subversive forces are hard at work in many American countries, seeking to create internal dissension and disunion as the now familiar prelude to armed invasion." The latter was to be more graphically true at the start of 1964, but this time it was to be from Soviet Russia and Red China and their base in Cuba.

When Hitler declared unrestricted submarine warfare against the United States, President Roosevelt told the people of the world in a fireside chat on September 11, 1941:

> This Nazi attempt to seize control of the oceans is but a counterpart of the Nazi plots now being carried on throughout the Western Hemisphere—all designed toward the same end. For Hitler's advance guards —not only his avowed agents but also his dupes among us—have sought to make ready for him footholds and bridgeheads in the New World to be used as soon as he has gained control of the oceans. His intrigues, his plots, his machinations, his sabotage in this New World are well known to the government of the United States. Conspiracy has followed conspiracy. Last year a plot to seize the government of Uruguay was smashed by the prompt action of that country which was supported in full by her American neighbors. A like plot was then hatching in Argentina, and

that government has carefully and wisely blocked it at every point. More recently an endeavor was made to subvert the government of Bolivia. Within the last few weeks, the discovery was made of secret landing fields in Colombia, within easy range of the Panama Canal. I could multiply such instances.

Thus it became increasingly evident that the Nazis were laying the groundwork for the day when, under orders from the Fuehrer, they could turn the keys in the Western Hemisphere and acquire the Republic of Panama, and with it the vital link in the defense of the United States and the American republics, the Panama Canal. This was not to happen, but, instead, a latent enemy was to surface after World War II to try to accomplish the same objective.

5. The Nazi Air Plans

When Adolf Hitler marched into Poland, the Germans had control of almost all the domestic airlines in South America, and were operating across the South Atlantic. Only the Japanese had confined their aerial activities in the Western Hemisphere to the role of observant passengers on the commercial routes. In Colombia alone there were 134 trained military pilots and other German technical personnel operating within only a few hundred miles of the Panama Canal. Until the middle of 1939, airplanes piloted by Germans landed at frequent intervals at France Field, the military air base on the Atlantic side of the Canal Zone.

To appreciate the strategic planning of air operations in South America by the German high command in Berlin, a mere glance at a map will illustrate in bold relief the corresponding threat against the Panama Canal. The treaty at Versailles had prohibited the Germans from building up an air force. This treaty was burned to all intent and purposes, by Hitler's march into the Rhineland in 1936, and it was apparent that the war which had loomed as a possibility when the Fuehrer's program became understandable in 1934 had now entered the realm of probability. The German high command, then, assumed direct

63

guiding control of all airline operations in South America. A program of organization, expansion, and training was ordered.

In South America the Germans were able to train their nationals in real airplanes, in addition to sponsoring and encouraging the formation and operation of glider sports clubs, the membership of which consisted mostly of young Germans. Air General Ernst Udet, whose post-World War I record included stunt flying in the United States and practical experience of commercial air service in Colombia, was designated by Marshal Hermann Goering as chief planner and director of air operations in South America. Another phase of these operations, that of espionage and subversion, was under the direction of Admiral Canaris, chief of the Nazi overseas intelligence service.

The keystone of the tactical organization of the Nazi airlines in Latin America was the Lloyd Aereo Boliviano, which had been given a contract by the government of Bolivia that was so strong that it could stand up even in the event Germany went to war. Lloyd Aereo Boliviano ingratiated itself with the people of Bolivia by playing a direct role in the Chaco War between Bolivia and Paraguay. Bomb racks and portable machine guns were installed in the airplanes of this commercial transport line, and the German pilots were given military status, thus forming Bolivia's air arm in that war. These Germans flew many sorties against the Paraguayans, bombing and strafing supplies, transport, and troops.

Lloyd Aereo Boliviano was perhaps the most predominantly Junker-owned airline in South America. The Germans had invested more than three million reichsmarks in this line, or approximately $1,200,000. Its General Manager was a loyal Nazi named Emil Schroth, who was also the agent in Bolivia for the United Aircraft Corporation and other American aircraft companies. This enabled him to buy American equipment at list price, less 40 per cent, less 5 per cent, and then less another 2 per cent for a cash discount. Although on paper 55 per cent of the stock appeared to be owned by Bolivians, this was merely a subterfuge.

While Lloyd Aereo Boliviano was the keystone of the Latin American organization, the financial structure revolved around a holding company founded by the Lufthansa interests in Berlin, which was also Junker-controlled. This holding company also controlled airlines in

Argentina, Brazil, Chile, Peru, and Ecuador. In only one country did it fail to control a German-dominated company outright. This was in Colombia, where Peter Paul von Bauer, a native of Austria and a World War I pilot for Germany, had founded the Scadta Airline in 1921. Scadta, however, was an important spoke in the wheel of the Nazi strategic plans to seize the Panama Canal either in collaboration with their Axis partners, Japan and Italy, or independently. Von Bauer had been a member of Udet's squadron in World War I.

Aeroposta Argentina, the Lufthansa affiliate in Argentina, operated a transport line from Buenos Aires to Comodoro Rivadavia to Tierra del Fuego and the strategically important Straits of Magellan.

In Brazil, Lufthansa had two affiliates. One, the Condor, was an international line that operated schedules from Rio de Janeiro to Porto Alegre, to Montevideo, Uruguay, to Buenos Aires and Mendoza, Argentina, and to Santiago, Chile, and return. The other, a domestic line known as VASP, operated exclusively in Brazil. Nearly all the personnel engaged by VASP were German nationals or first-generation descendants of Germans.

In Peru the Lufthsansa-Peru airline operated between Lima, the capital, and La Paz, capital of Bolivia, where it made connections with Lloyd Aereo Boliviano.

The Condor airline operated in Chile between Santiago, Buenos Aires, and Rio de Janeiro, where it connected with its Condor affiliate, Cruzeiro do Brasil.

In Ecuador the Sindicato Ecuatoriana de Transportes Aereos, known as SEDTA, operated domestically, and occasionally made chartered flights to neighboring countries.

In Colombia the Scadta Airline provided both a domestic transcontinental service and an international service. It operated both land planes and hydroplanes. It maintained airfields, shops, hangars, and technical schools, as did the other German lines in South America, and it produced photo maps of the entire republic of Colombia, not for the government of Colombia but for the war ministry in Berlin. It produced photo maps of the Republic of Panama from the Colombian coast to the Panama Canal Zone. It sent mosaics to Germany of all strategic areas of Colombia and the approaches to the Panama Canal. Early in 1939 it was confirmed that photo murals of the Panama Canal Zone of a scale of 1:100,000 were on the walls of a planning room of the German high command in Berlin. An apparently sympathetic visitor from the Canal Zone to Berlin was shown these murals late in 1938, and it was intimated to him that plans were materializing for an eventual acquisition of the Panama Canal.

Looking again at a map of Latin America, it will become apparent that the Germans had a potential military air force strategically dispersed throughout South America, so that at the given moment staging operations could be undertaken preparatory to the launching of a full-scale attack against the Panama Canal.

In Europe, before the Nazis launched any full-scale drives to annex or conquer adjacent countries, such operations would be preceded by a softening-up process that required assistance not only from their own ethnic groups in Austria, in the Sudetenland, and in Danzig, but also from symphatetic natives. The situation in Latin America before Pearl Harbor was no different. The Nazis poured in military organizers, trained leaders and *agents provocateurs*, under the guise of tourists. Some of these people operated in large centers, but others went into the sparsely inhabited hinterlands to influence the attitudes of the natives residing there. In some of these latter areas the Nazis undertook to construct fabulously large strips, which, had they been designed for legitimate commercial operations, would have been a financial liability. These landing strips were built on lands that were owned by Germans either outright or through the medium of friendly native intermediaries. Some of these strips were being cleared near the Caribbean and Pacific littorals of Colombia.

Anyone familiar with military planning could see in 1938 that the Germans were preparing for long-range aerial operations in the Western Hemisphere. SEDTA airlines were operating Junker F-13's and Focke Wulfe 34's in Ecuador in addition to two Ju-52's, trimotor airplanes. In the latter part of 1938 there was delivered to this airline a more modern Ju-52 which came from the Condor Airlines by way of Brazil, Argentina, and Chile after having been flown across the South Atlantic Ocean. In 1939 a Bloch-Blenheim was flown across the South Atlantic for Lloyd Aereo Boliviano, which was already using Ju-86's, the progenitor of the dread trimotor Stuka.

In Argentina the Germans built Quilmes Airport, spending more than $200,000 for the construction of a hangar. In Bolivia they built the best maintenance base in South America at Santa Cruz and another maintenance base at Trinidad. From Brazil to Cochabamba, Bolivia, they built landing strips all the way across the continent, along a normally good-weather route that would permit low-altitude flying and allow the pilots to maintain a 5,000-foot ceiling. They were advancing plans for the construction of a seaplane hangar at Iquitos, Peru, on the Amazon River, as a part of their over-all strategic plan for a network of seaplane bases throughout the Americas. They were the first to land and take off with a four-engine airplane at an altitude higher than 10,-000 feet; they did this in 1940 at La Paz, Bolivia, from an airport that is almost 15,000 feet high.

It was in 1937 that the Nazis began their large-scale expansionist operations in South America with the establishment of a Condor-operated Berlin-to-Rio airline. The S.S. *Westphalen* was anchored midway in the South Atlantic Ocean to serve as a mother ship for these airplanes and to effect rescue operations in the event of an accident. This service continued until war broke out and the Nazi high command decided to suspend these operations.

Envisaging that war would compel them to suspend operations, because of their need for pilots in combat theaters, the Germans in 1939 sponsored the organization of the Linea Americana Transporte Italiana, known as LATI, to operate between Rome, Africa, Brazil, and Argentina. This was done because the Nazi high command was dissatisfied with the effective progress of Axis propaganda in Latin America, and also because it needed a means to send and receive men and materials and yet circumvent the British blockade. Among the significant passengers on the round-trip flights of this airline to Germany and Italy at varying times were Peter Paul von Bauer of Scadta Airlines; General Wilhelm von Faupel, head of the Ibero-American Institute of Berlin, who, in addition to being in charge of East coast military sabotage in Latin America, carried special assignments from Hitler himself; General Hans Kundt, in charge of the West coast of South America, military sabotage; General Gunther Niedenfuehr, chief military leader for South America; General Otto Kriesche, assistant to General Niedenfuehr, who also carried with him credentials signed by Marshal Hermann Goering designating him as Goering's military air minister for

South America; General Eberhardt Bonstedt, who carried credentials designating him as "military leader for South America," and whose assistant was Eric O. Cerjack-Boyna, diplomatically accredited to the German legation in Panama, of whom more will be heard later; Major Otto von Dippelius, Professor of Military Tactics for Chilean Army schools and propagandist; Julius Holzer, chief storm trooper; Arnulf Fuerggman, *Gauleiter* for all South America and specialist in anti-Semitic propaganda; Arthur Deitrich, Nazi propaganda chief for South America; Alfredo Mueller, leader for Argentina and specialist in military clubs, organizations, and reserve corps; Hans Voigt, chief of the German State Railroad Bureau for Chile; Kazue Kuwajima, Japanese Ambassador in Brazil; and many others.

In addition to flying Nazi spies to and from the Western Hemisphere, LATI also imported into Latin America more than five thousand pounds of horror-filled war films designed to frighten the Latin Americans away from cooperation with the United States. Furthermore, the Italians flew out of Brazil almost seven thousands pounds of mica, without which the Germans could not continue to fight the war. Few German and Italian passengers on LATI ever paid for their tickets; they traveled on passes.

It was not until October 1941, when the Department of State in Washington threatened to place the Brazilian subsidiary of the Standard Oil Company of New Jersey on the Proclaimed List of Blocked Nationals (a black list) that LATI had to cease operations. The position of the Standard Oil Company prior to this action was that it could not refuse to sell aviation fuel and lubricants to LATI and the Condor airline in Brazil without being liable to a damage suit for breach of contract.

And while these long-range operations were being undertaken in other parts of South America, the Germans were consolidating their operations in Colombia. It is of interest to note here that as early as 1928 Scadta had conducted an aerial survey flight through Central America as far north as Guatemala. A Dornier Wahl flying boat landed in all the lakes of Central America. In 1929, applications for permits for operations in Central America were filed by Scadta. Pan American World Airways was just beginning to operate, and with the assistance of the State and War Departments in Washington, influence was exercised by American diplomats in Central America to freeze out the German company. So Von Bauer was compelled to confine his activities to Colombia, but, having been frozen out of Central America, he offered to sell out Scadta to Pan American World Airways for 11 million pesos, about $10 million. Juan Trippe, president of Pan American, sent a survey party down to Colombia to appraise the Scadta properties. After a complete and most thorough inspection, the American experts reported back to Trippe that Scadta was then worth only one-third of Von Bauer's price. Von Bauer rejected Trippe's natural counter-offer and effected a stock manipulation which produced for him enough capital to continue operations.

Trippe's investigators did discover one very interesting thing, however, and that was that the German personnel of Scadta were far ahead of the Americans in that early day of commercial aviation in the improvisation of solutions for maintenance and operational problems. For example, encountering difficulty because of condensation, and rain, on flights through thermal squalls, which reduced the operational hours of engines, the Germans prepared a mixture of beeswax, mentholatum, and high-consistency grease which they used to tropicalize or waterproof ignition systems of the motors. With early operations in Colombia being along the all-water route of the Magdalena, Atrato, and San Juan rivers, Scadta used Dorniers, Junkers, and Fokker-13's with pontoons for these flights. They made frequent flights from Barranquilla and Cartagena to Folks River in Cristobal, on the Atlantic side of the Panama Canal, as early as 1928. All these water operations involved quite serious maintenance and operational difficulties.

Scadta engaged in normal operations throughout the year 1936. But in 1937 the company began to train 70 per cent more personnel than was necessary for its existing or projected schedules. The additional personnel consisted of enthusiastic young Nazis brought into Colombia from Germany. The turnover in pilot personnel alone for the years 1937, 1938, and 1939 averaged 150 pilots annually. Late in 1936, responding to instructions from General Udet, Scadta established its *Seccion Tecnica* (Technical Section) which was charged with the training of all ground crews in maintenance and engineering duties.

Every German ship that docked at the ports of Cartagena and Barranquilla unloaded scores of young Germans for duty with Scadta, and

German ships that sailed from those Colombian ports took aboard an equal number of young Nazis fully checked out and trained by the Scadta specialists. Chief Pilot Selbstaedt personally checked out each trainee in instrument and high-altitude flying. He was assisted by Hans Hoffman and Fritz Hertshauser. Later, the latter two broke away from Scadta to organize Aerovias Ramales in competition, but Nazi party discipline cut short their venture. Hoffman married a daughter of General Arango, from one of Colombia's most prominent families, and managed to remain in Colombia throughout the war.

The *Seccion Tecnica* had another important mission, and that was the mosaic mapping of the entire coastlines of Colombia and the Canal Zone. Using multiple-lens cameras, the Scadta aerial photographers were furnished the best equipment that money could buy, a good bit of it of American manufacture.

In 1939 and early in 1940 there began a heavy movement of engines and spare parts into Colombia for Scadta. The airline did not need this exorbitant amount of replacements. Furthermore, in 1939 Scadta built a pilot's club at Puerto Colombia, the port for Barranquilla, the membership of which was so exclusive that only high German officers in Colombia and pilots of the company were admitted. The boathouse had a marine railway. Late in 1939 Scadta also purchased two sailboats, which were delivered from Germany by Hamburg-American Line steamers. The boats, Scadta explained, were for the purpose of teaching the pilots seamanship, and with them came an abundance of radio direction-finding equipment.

The Almacenes Helda at Barranquilla, a Nazi-owned shipyard, was capable of taking care of any repairs—of ships or airplanes. Ernest Wilhelm Schnurbusch, chief engineer for Almacenes Helda, was also its Nazi party leader. He militarized not only the employees of his firm but also those of Scadta who came under his jurisdiction in Barranquilla. Schnurbusch was a naval architect. The machine shops under his orders were capable of building anything; he designed and built industrial gas factories in Colombia and was manufacturing oxygen, hydrogen, and gasoline. Thus Scadta had a very potent ally in Almacenes Helda and, working in combination, they were capable of tackling and conquering any maintenance problems that might have arisen in the event the Nazis had decided to launch a military operation against Panama with Colombia as a base.

Few Americans knew in 1939 that Juan Trippe had years before managed to buy up 40 per cent of the stock of Scadta and with it an option which stipulated that he could purchase controlling interest before 1939, but it was known that Peter Paul von Bauer was no longer anxious to sell, especially as the Nazis were beginning their forward march to conquest and glory. Besides, Scadta was very important in 1939 to German plans.

Gonzalo Mejia, a millionaire from Medellin, Colombia, and a Harvard graduate, had founded the Uraba, Medellin, and Central Airways (UMCA), employing mainly American pilots. This strapping, six-foot, four-inch pro-American flew to New York in the fall of 1939 to confer with Juan Trippe and to propose the purchase of Scadta by Colombian capital in association with Pan American World Airways. His conferences at that time were unsuccessful; Pan Am failed to evince immediate interest in Scadta, and Gonzalo Mejia returned to Medellin and UMCA.

With highly trained Nazi military pilots flying airplanes but a few hundred miles from the Panama Canal, considerable concern was beginning to be felt by military staffs in the Canal Zone. The War Department was urged to take up the matter with the Department of State, with a view toward indicating diplomatically to Colombia that a danger existed if those pilots could be used for a bombing attack against the Panama Canal. One hundred thirty-four pilots could man as many airplanes for attacks against the Panama Canal, for the flight from Barranquilla on the northern Caribbean coast to the Gatun Locks or the Gatun Dam on the Atlantic side of the Canal could be completed in round-trip fashion in four hours. The round-trip flight from Medellin to Miraflores or the Pedro Miguel locks could be made in similar time. Furthermore, German pilots could also attack Allied shipping off the Colombian and Panamanian coasts.

Of course, Scadta pilots did not do any of these things, and neither did the German pilots on the other Nazi-controlled airlines in South America. But it could have been done if the United States had assumed a complacent attitude of watchful waiting. When you see a rattlesnake poised to strike, you do not wait until he has struck before you crush him—not if you want to survive. The State Department, responding to the urgency expressed by the War Department, instructed Ambassador Spruille Braden to make representations to the government of Colombia to neutralize the activities of the German pilots. Similar instructions went to every legation and embassy in South America. On June 10, 1940, the government of Colombia removed the last of the Nazi pilots from Scadta, but not before Pan American World Airways was convinced by the Department of State that it should exercise its option to purchase Scadta, and thus Avianca Company, a Pan Am subsidiary, was organized in Colombia in substitution for the German company.

American pilots had been sent to Colombia at the behest of the Department of State, to assume the controls of the airplanes in the Scadta service. But there had been considerable procrastination on the part of Pan American World Airways to take up the option Juan Trippe possessed, notwithstanding the fact that the government of Colombia had expressed its approval of the move to Ambassador Braden. George Rile, Executive Vice-President of Pan Am, flew to Bogotá to handle the entire deal. There were many heated sessions in the American Embassy between Ambassador Braden and Mr. Rile, which culminated on June 10, 1940, with Mr. Braden pounding his desk and telling Mr. Rile in the most forceful, and at times the most undiplomatic application of the English language that Pan Am must take over Scadta immediately. The Scadta operation ceased at five o'clock that afternoon. Avianca operations began the next morning.

As soon as Pan Am took over, every German in the employ of Scadta, except one accountant, was fired. Then the most startling discoveries were made by Pan Am engineers. Scadta had started to build airfields at strategic places in Colombia, places where neither traffic warranted them nor subsidy (from Colombia) provided for them. At Cienaga, several miles inland on the northeastern coast near Santa Marta, there was found already under construction a runway 8,000 feet long by 3,000 feet wide. At Necocli on Anachacuna Bay, also on the north coast, was another fantastically large airfield under construction, of dimensions equal to the one at Cienaga. Coincidentally or not, Japanese in that area were always clearing away jungle brush while busy with their gardening activities.

The diplomatic *démarche* was on throughout South America to crush the Axis airlines before they struck at the Panama Canal. Representations were made to the government of Bolivia to halt operations of Lloyd Aereo Boliviano. John Shannon was sent to La Paz by Pan American Grace Airways to arrange for the acquisition of the Nazi airline interests there, but it was not until 1941 that the Nazis could be ousted. Shannon was made Vice-President of Panagra when he consummated the deal and remained in Bolivia to direct operations there. But the Bolivians had been educated to Nazi ways, and it took considerable time for Shannon and his assistants to de-nazify them. They were biased and much passive resistance was encountered by Shannon. Here, Schroth had done a superb job for the Nazis.

To the success of the elimination of Scadta, Lloyd Aereo Boliviano, and others must be attributed the fact that the Panama Canal was not attacked on or before December 7, 1941, by a fleet of Nazi bombardment airplanes operating from bases in South America.

6. The Fifth Column

In his Navy Day address on October 27, 1941, President Franklin Delano Roosevelt made public for the first time the fact that Adolf Hitler's plan of conquest included the Panama Canal.

"Hitler has often protested," said President Roosevelt, "that his plans of conquest do not extend across the Atlantic Ocean. His submarines and raiders prove otherwise. So does the entire design of his new World. Order. For example, I have in my possession a secret map made in Germany by Hitler's government—by the planners of the new World Order. This map refers to South America and part of Central America as Hitler proposes to recognize it. Today, in this area [on the secret map] there are fourteen separate countries. The geographical experts of Berlin, however, have ruthlessly obliterated all existing boundary lines and divided South America into five vassal states, bringing the whole continent under their domination. And they have also arranged it that the territory of one of these new puppet states includes the Republic of Panama and our great lifeline—the Panama Canal. This map makes clear the Nazi design not only against South America but against the United States itself."

The Russians, meanwhile, then at war with the Nazis, were to inherit the above plans and with better conspiratorial skill put them into execution.

Any military man will tell you that the best defense is a good offense. Therefore, a war, or a preparation for war, which looks to defense alone is a lost one. But during the years 1934-1941 the United States was not at war, and consequently the people were in a purely defensive state of mind. This enabled the Axis to spend millions of dollars in the Western Hemisphere, to build up a great force of sympathizers to lay the groundwork for the execution of Hitler's plans. Some of this money was spent very wisely and effectively, overtly in many places, covertly in still others. This force of sympathizers became to be known as the "fifth column," because in the Spanish civil war of 1936-1939 four columns attacked Madrid from the outside, while the Nazi-Fascist sympathizers worked inside the city to disrupt communications, spread dissension, and undermine the morale of the Republic's defenders in order to expedite General Francisco Franco's capture of the capital of Spain. Although the Falangist propagandists christened this form of warfare, the term became common throughout the hemisphere, as the Nazis had used the identical technique with their own national minorities in the Sudentenland, in Austria, and in Danzig long before they had applied and dramatized it in the Madrid campaign.

The constant agitation on the part of German minorities in Czechoslovakia, Austria, and Poland had produced one domestic crisis after another, seriously impairing the stability of the governments of those republics. The fifth columns in those countries concentrated their activities among the masses of the population, in order to develop a state of mind favorable to the approved Nazi plans of action. Therefore, when the moment arrived when those nations should have been united against German pressure, there was much disunity caused by procrastinating individuals whose opinions had been formed by the Nazis. The same pattern was to unfold throughout the Western Hemisphere.

The fifth column in Latin America was not composed of a single entity but comprised five separate units, each interlocking and each performing an equally important service for the Axis powers. These units were the diplomatic, economic, political, psychological, and, not of least importance, the military. The organizational work of the fifth columns started early in 1931 with the preliminary psychological phase.

Hitler's advance agents, acting under the guise of correspondents for the *Völkischer Beobachter,* the Nazi party newspaper being published in Munich, circulated their propaganda freely throughout all newspaper offices, and their initial objective was a campaign for the abolition of the Versailles Treaty. The Japanese began similar psychological operations preparatory to, and during the Mukden incident of the same year. But it was near the end of 1934 that the vast Axis psychological plan really started to roll, as Hitler began to lay the groundwork for his reoccupation of the Rhineland while Mussolini was devising plans for the capture of Abyssinia.

It was no coincidence that the pro-Nazi and anti-American propaganda began to increase throughout Latin America in 1934. Early in that year Adolf Hitler had appointed General Wilhelm von Faupel as director of the Ibero-American Institute of Berlin. Founded in 1930 by a German scholar, Dr. Otto Boelitz, this institute had developed a cultural link with the Western Hemisphere, with thousands of volumes of books donated by universities, colleges, and governments. In General von Faupel, Hitler had picked the right man for the right job. Von Faupel had been an instructor at the Argentine War College before World War I, returning to Buenos Aires in 1921 as technical adviser to the Inspector General of the Argentine Army, after having served at the front and having tasted defeat on the battlefield. In 1926 he transferred to Brazil as military adviser for the Brazilian Army, and a year later he became chief of the military mission in Chile. Von Faupel knew all of Latin America, for he had traveled with Frau von Faupel from the Rio Grande to Patagonia. He had mingled with the masses and with the aristocracy. He was familiar with the political forces in the republics and, what was most important to Hitler, he could organize and direct an army of shock troops that could number in the millions, the ranks of which would be available for propaganda, subversion, sabotage, and espionage in behalf of the Nazi state.

General von Faupel chose some talented lieutenants to assist him in his so-called cultural activities. There was Professor Otto Quelle, editor of the *Ibero-Amerikanisches Archiv*, and Dr. Hans Richert, who were jointly charged with the Portuguese and Brazilian sections. There were Frederico Nielsen-Reyes, who had seen diplomatic service in Latin America, and Fritz Berndt, who had served as Berlin correspondent for some Latin-American newspapers, both of whom directed the Bolivian and Chilean section; there were Dr. Karl von Hagen and Hans Bock, who were responsible for all operations from Mexico to Panama; and there were Professor Gustav Freiberg, formerly head of the Botanical Gardens at Asunción, Paraguay, and Frau Simons Erwin Hoene, who handled the Rio de la Plata nations of Argentina, Uruguay, and Paraguay. To Frau Edith von Faupel, a Doctor of Philosophy, was charged the responsibility of the states that had once formed part of Gran Colombia—Venezuela, Colombia, Ecuador, and Peru. General von Faupel reorganized the functional operations of the Ibero-American Institute along military lines. Dr. Otto Boelitz, the founder of the Institute, faded into oblivion.

The *Wilhelmstrasse* directed operations of the diplomatic unit, which was later to centralize most of the Nazi activities under its wing. With the psychological phase already under way, people were being won in Latin America for the future Nazi organization as the diplomats entered into the picture in full swing to win over the masses. Influential officials of governments were cultivated so that the propaganda could continue unmolested, and thus there could be undertaken the destruction of any doctrine inimical to Axis interests preparatory to the fight for power and the achievement of the final success of the Nazi doctrine.

In Germany, Italy, and Japan ranking diplomats and attachés of Latin-American countries were also being won over. As many Latin Americans possess an overwhelming awe of what military force and power can accomplish, having resided for years under dictatorial reigns in their own countries, they marveled at the advances made by Hitlerian rule not only inside the Reich but also beyond its frontiers, in accordance with the nefarious doctrine of *Mein Kampf*. These Latin Americans overlooked the fact that the Italians had raped Ethiopia and had invaded Albania on a sanctimonious Good Friday. And they also had little sympathy for the weak Chinese, then fighting bravely against the Japanese expansionists of the Co-prosperity Sphere for Asia. They overlooked all these points because the fifth column kept them busily occupied with other thoughts, thoughts of the grandeur of the Reich and the New World Order, and thoughts against the United States.

Latin America was a fertile field for General von Faupel and the

Axis fifth column. There had festered in the Western Hemisphere for almost a century many sores, the results of several imperialistic incidents in which the United States had played a major role. But, since 1933, the United States had been committed to the Good Neighbor Policy, and in implementing this policy it had entered into Pan-American treaties embodying the principles of nonintervention in the domestic affairs of the other American republics. The United States had also abandoned the Platt Amendment, which gave it the right to intervene in the internal affairs of Cuba; the U.S. Marines had withdrawn from Haiti and Nicaragua; many trade agreements of mutual profit had been entered into with the other American republics; the U.S. had helped settle various boundary disputes between nations; a new general treaty with Panama upon a mutually satisfactory basis had been signed; several Pan-American conferences productive of many agreements of mutual advantage had been held. The United States was at last embarked on a policy that was destined to establish solidarity in the Western Hemisphere on a peaceful basis, and the Axis partners tried hard to destroy the effectiveness of this policy with their fifth column.

The diplomatic phase of Axis operations worked hand in glove with the psychological phase, because with the latter the enemy-to-be had already commenced political warfare against the United States. Propagandists such as Herr Augusto Dziuk were hard at work in Panama receiving their orders from Berlin and their money from the German legations or consulates. Dziuk had resided in Panama for almost thirty-five years. He was familiar with the minutest details about the country and the people. He was a business associate of a son of former President Belisario Porras. As one illustration of the early effectiveness of his propaganda activities, when he published a pamphlet about "The Satanic War and the Internationalization of the Panama Canal" in September, 1934, the foreword was written by J. Rivera Reyes, a prominent attorney who at the time was also President of the Panamanian Society of International Action. Among other objectives, Dziuk's pamphlet was designed to plant the seed of the idea that the Panama Canal should be internationalized, that the neutralization of the Canal's defenses was the only way to preserve peace.

And Señor Rivera Reyes unwittingly assisted Herr Dziuk in his program, for he wrote in his foreword:

These pages which are offered to us today by Mr. Augusto Dziuk, German geologist and engineer, relate in a novel and pleasing manner apparently fantastic deeds relative to the realization of these two great principles: that of the internationalization of the Panama Canal and that of the real, effective, and perpetual neutrality of the Panama Canal, which may be achieved only by virtue of a catastrophic world war. This pamphlet can contribute to the awakening of the American public conscience concerning the great problem of the fortifications of the Panama Canal. God grant that these predictions contained in his work, which are so interesting for the Panamanians and the entire world, may be translated soon into adventurous reality. The world shall thus have removed from its path one of the greatest causes of resentment and hatred, and to Panama then will be done justice.

And Herr Dziuk in his own introduction had indicated that the fifth column would propagate this theme constantly, for he wrote under the ominous title of "The Day Will Come" the following: "Let us all work without surcease, diplomats and politicians, newspapermen and editorial writers, novelists and authors, and with all the means within our reach in order that this magnificent day of great benefit for humanity may draw nearer." Herr Dziuk delivered a copy of this pamphlet to every member of the diplomatic and consular corps in the Republic of Panama, to prominent officials of the government, and to members of the press. He placed it on sale at the newsstands for twenty-five cents.

The pamphlet was replete with perfidious remarks intended to inflame the spirit of national resentment of the Panamanians against the United States. There were such passages as:

For the Republic of Panama, the country most interested in this matter, the Canal has not brought the benefits that the founders of the Republic had expected as a result of their sacrifices . . . but [by] this tyrannical power the United States year by year took over more and more of that small and weak country, placing an apparently formidable chain of fortifications along the route of the Panama Canal and within a perimeter of more than one hundred and fifty kilometers around the two entrances of the Canal, *threatening in this manner the commerce of the maritime nations.* [The italics belong to Herr Dziuk, and what follows he took pains to publish in capital letters.] This Panama Canal had already become with the years a menace for all nations and by now it was not only a project to aid world commerce but, better still, a project for the maintenance of a military hegemony, paid for by all the inhabitants of the entire world who bought the merchandise that the ships carried through the Canal, paying tolls—very high for certain—for the transit through this Canal route not only to defray the costs of its construction and operation but also to pay for the maintenance of the military force and of the fortifications that are useful only to this military and imperialistic power.

The above observations by Herr Dziuk served their multiple purpose. They ignited the nationalistic spirit of many Panamanians in the same manner that the Germans had been successful in kindling extreme nationalistic fires against the British in Egypt, where the Suez Canal was the Empire's life line. And they spread the germ of anti-Americanism, just as the Germans had spread anti-British sentiment in Egypt. Herr Dziuk needed no additional encouragement from General von Faupel, but when the General visited Panama in July-August, 1934, Dziuk was among the more prominent members of the local German colony to hold long conferences with the chief of Hitler's cultural activities in Latin America. The germination of extreme nationalism and anti-Americanism were part and parcel of these activities. The propagandists had to win the people over to the organization first, and the Nazis had hit upon the right theme in Panama.

Herr Dziuk's contribution was but a minute one in comparison to the over-all picture. Yet it was a valuable one that the Nazis had decided to implement because of its long-range advantages. Just at the time Dziuk published his pamphlet, he scored a psychological victory. It was Herr Dziuk who earlier in 1934 had offered his services gratuitously to the government of Panama to organize the *Semana Nacional,* or National Week. This *Semana Nacional* was a miniature Leipzig Fair, and all products of the country were placed on display. Herr Dziuk also set up a booth to display German machinery. The *Semana Nacional* was a tremendous success, something that Panama had badly needed. But Herr Dziuk's purpose in organizing the fair was not altrustic: his motives were to improve the nationalistic patrimony, to ingratiate himself, and to propagandize and sell German products. And he made a great hit with the Panamanians, as was to be expected. He had done them a service, but at the same time he performed a greater service for the *Fuehrer.*

Ewald Banse, a German psychologist, wrote in his *Raum und Volk im Weltkrieg*:

Applied psychology as a weapon of war means propaganda intended to influence the mental attitudes of nations toward war. It is essential to attack the enemy nation in its weak spots [and what nation has not its weak spots?], to undermine and break down its resistance, and to convince it that it is being deceived, misled, and brought to destruction by its own government. Thus, the people will lose confidence in the justice of their cause so that the political opposition in those nations [and what nation is without one?] will raise its head and become a more powerful troublemaker. The enemy nation's originally solid, powerful, and well-knit fabric must be gradually disintegrated, broken down, rotted, so that it falls apart like a fungus trod upon in a forest.

This precisely is the course the Germans followed in Latin America from 1934 on, and the one which the Russians were to imitate after the Nazi surrender. Troublemakers, however, could not operate without troubleseekers. Herr Dziuk was both a troubleseeker and a troublemaker. Troubleseekers were those members of the many Nazi fact-finding agencies who ferreted out the kernels of disturbance, which the Nazis called *störurungskerne,* such as those political parties and minority groups badly divided by differences of opinion, the frustrated politicians who were out of office, petty political and personal jealousies and rivalries, racial controversies, and economic inequalities. The troublemakers spread the Nazi ideology; they utilized the facts that the troubleseekers had unearthed, committed material and psychological sabotage, exploited and publicized obvious and latent frictions in the interest of demoralization and eventually complete disintegration.

The Spanish Falangists had organized the fifth column in Madrid under the guidance of General Wilhelm von Faupel, who was assisting General Francisco Franco in one phase of the Nazi over-all strategic plan for the domination of the Western Hemisphere. Just before the Spanish civil war, incited by the Germans and the Russians in 1936 to convert Spain into a puppet state, General Hermann Goering looked at maps of Europe and South America and declared: "Spain is the way to two continents."

Two years later, in an address before the German Academy in Berlin while the Pan-American Conference was meeting in Lima, Peru, General von Faupel said: "A victory for Falangist Spain will cement our relations with Latin America and will be a rude shock to the Good Neighbor Policy of President Roosevelt."

The Nazis thus were cutting the pattern for the conquest of Latin America, utilizing Franco and his supporters as mere tools to construct the machinery to be used in the execution of the master plan. Meanwhile, the coast had been cleared for the Japanese invasion of China on July 7, 1937. The Japanese possessed the self-assurance that the only opposition that would be encountered besides the weak Chinese forces would be the equally feeble protests by the U.S. Department of State. The United States was not thinking of war.

The Spanish Falange was organized, again with Nazi guidance, and with this came the announcement of the National Syndicalism Program of the Traditionalist Spanish Phalanx of the Juntas Ofensivas Nacional-Sindicalista (National-Syndicalist Offensive Boards). Although "syndicalist" is a peculiarly Spanish word, used to signify the organization of groups of working and professional classes, a freer translation would approximate socialism.

In the program published in Panama by local Falangists immediately after the outbreak of the Civil War in 1936, there was a most striking resemblance to the party programs published previously by the Fascists and the Nazis. In fact, except for the alteration of the geographical name of the country, the programs were almost identical. Of particular interest was the reference made to the Western Hemisphere nations. "Regarding the Latin-American countries," it said, "we intend to tighten the links of culture, of economic interest, and of power. Spain claims to be the spiritual axle of the Spanish World as a recognition of her universal enterprises."

While the Nazis were engaged in organizing quietly at first, they soon began to grow more articulate and bothersome. German nationals were being organized throughout Latin America as members of the National Socialist Party's *Auslander* faction.

In Brazil, just as in Panama, the Nazis wanted native sons of Germany to fight for Hitler's cause, to acquire influence themselves, or cultivate influential friends, in the policy-making positions of those republics. They launched in 1939 an intensive drive to knit the Brazilian

German colony into one solid, strong, and menacing force. One can
well imagine what might have happened had the German and Japanese
elements of Brazil been able to join forces to gain control of that vast
territory for the Axis. Happily, there was no close liaison between the
Nazis and the Japanese in subversive operations on the lower levels in
Latin America.

Thus we see that the Axis grand strategy began to unfold itself from
the maze of the pieces of the international puzzle picture into a clear
and understandable portrait of planned conquest and destruction of
human liberties the world over.

From 1934 on, the Germans had set about with methodical precision
to build up a militant Nazi organization throughout Latin America. In
every capital a branch of the National Socialist party of Germany was
founded, and as a new organization was born in Germany its counterpart was established without delay in Latin America. Native nationalist
groups, Italian Fascists, Spanish Falangists, members of the diplomatic
corps, and businessmen were used whenever considered advantageous.
There were veterans' organizations, SA shock troops (Hitler's storm
troopers, or Brownshirts), Hitler Youth organizations, German Boy
Scouts, German Girl Scouts, National Socialists' Women's party, German labor unions, "Strength Through Joy" contingents, amateur theat-
rical groups, mutual aid societies, German seamen's homes, German
sports clubs, German glee clubs, societies for the protection of German
immigrants, German Teachers' Association, German orphans' homes.
In addition there were, of course, the Gestapo, the secret service, and
the S. S. Blackshirts.

In coffee and banana plantations from Guatemala to Panama, many
Germans were employed as overseers or foremen. Buried deep in the
jungle, these loyal Nazis took advantage of their isolation and militarized their laborers. The laborers were awakened by the call of a
bugle, they ate at a militarized mess, and they were marched off to the
fields in military formation. When there was insufficient work in the
fields, their time was occupied in drilling and absorbing basic infantry
training. From Panama southward similar practices were followed. In
Panama itself there were no German foremen employed at coffee and
banana plantations. But there were plenty of Nazis on hand for other

duties that enabled them to engage in espionage and subversive activities.

The offices of the Hamburg-American Line, Nazi Germany's steamship organization, were centers of espionage and propaganda. Four Nazis employed by that company in Cristobal, Canal Zone, were tried and convicted of espionage in the Canal Zone District Court early in 1939. One of the four, Gisbert Groos, was the son of Admiral Otto Groos, a writer on naval strategy and military politics and an honorary doctor of several German universities. While his son was trying to pry into the secrets of the fortifications and approaches to the Panama Canal, Admiral Groos was delivering conferences on Grand Sea Strategy at Nazi military and naval schools.

The quartet of Nazis was arrested on the Front Randolph military reservation, which fronts the Caribbean entrance to the Canal. They were hiking on a Sunday morning, under the pretext of seeking a trail leading along the coast to Panama's undefended natural harbor of Puerto Pilon, an area of immense strategic importance. But on the way they took photographs of coast defense guns, antiaircraft batteries, and searchlight installations. Puerto Pilon, lying but a mile and a half by the seacoast route from Galeta Island, the terminus of the Atlantic cable lines, which was fortified by carefully guarded installations, could be reached by a secret channel that cuts the distance to half a mile. Half a mile through a recently dredged channel, deep and wide enough to permit the navigation of submarines—that was the distance between the strategic military reservation of Fort Randolph and the unfortified deep-water Panamanian port. And it was along this route that the four Germans were avowedly seeking a trail, their objective being the little port which they could have located less laboriously by road straight from the Canal Zone boundary. This fact, the judge said in pronouncing sentence after the jurors had handed down their verdict, constituted one of the most serious aspects of the Nazi case.

Another Hapag-Lloyd employee in Panama, Hans von Appen, was the principal actor in a comic-opera performance that ended the war for him in December, 1939. He boarded the Hapag-Lloyd liner S.S. *Dusseldorf* in Valparaiso harbor on December 13 for Hamburg, Germany. He was shaving on the the morning of December 15 when the ship's alarm sounded. He rushed on the deck and noticed a flaming shell fall across the bow of the ship. A short time later, the cruiser H.M.S. *Despatch* pulled alongside and captured the S. S. *Dusseldorf* as a war prize. Von Appen, who could speak English well, overheard the British crew comment a few days later that they would soon approach the Panama Canal. He devised what he thought was a cunning plan to gain asylum in the Republic of Panama. For three days and three nights he restrained himself from visiting the ship's head (toilet) and he also abstained from brushing his teeth or from washing his mouth. So he developed acute stomach pains, a fever, a repulsive breath, and a coated tongue, all of which compelled the British commander aboard the S.S. *Dusseldorf* to radio to Balboa for an ambulance to remove the sick passenger upon the ship's arrival.

A quarantine doctor boarded the vessel out in the bay, diagnosed Von Appen's illness as possible acute appendicitis, and ordered his removal to Gorgas Hospital in Ancon, Canal Zone. As he was removed, Von Appen boasted to the press: "Both the Americans and the Panamanians will grant me the asylum they have given all refugees." A member of the German Legation staff rushed to Gorgas Hospital and protested against the hospitalization of Von Appen in the Canal Zone and insisted on his transfer to Panama Hospital, a privately-owned institution staffed by American and Panamanian doctors.

Blood tests and other examinations disclosed that all Von Appen was suffering from was a self-imposed constipation. He was administered a purge and very shortly his fever disappeared and he returned to normalcy. By arrangement with the government of Panama, and over the protest of the German Legation, Von Appen was transferred from the hospital to the Quarantine Station in Balboa for safekeeping. Soon, the Department of State ruled that Von Appen should be returned to the British as a prisoner of war, and he was shipped from the Canal Zone for internment in Jamaica right after the New Year of 1940. The diplomatic representative of the German Legation who handled the Von Appen case was Erik O. Cerjack-Boyna.

Operating at an early date in the service of the Nazi cause were businessmen, such as Cerjack-Boyna, a native of Austria and a commission agent in the Republic of Panama, who had wed a Panamanian. Cerjack-Boyna had been an officer in the Aline Chasseurs Regiment in World War I. On September 2, 1939 he was announced by the German Legation as "Civil Attaché" of the legation. Thus his emergence from the economic unit of the fifth column into the diplomatic unit permitted him more freedom of action under the ample protection of diplomatic immunity, and he brazenly took every advantage of it.

But as intelligence representative of the Berlin Ministry of Economics in Panama since Hitler's rise to power Cerjack-Boyna had already managed to place a firm finger on Panama's commercial life. When Hitler marched into Poland, some of Cerjack-Boyna's grandiose commercial plans were smashed. He had been greasing the skids for the exclusive sale of Diesel-powered German trucks and passenger vehicles to the government of Panama and in addition he entertained hopes of flooding the local market with his products. His connections with the Ministry of Economics naturally made him an influential man in Nazi circles in Panama.

Economic, diplomatic, psychological, and political penetration was all part of a carefully conceived plan for the conquest of Latin America in which the Japanese, too, had their interested role.

7. The Mikado's Marionettes

He was a barber and he operated a two-by-four shop in the congested slum district of Calidonia which was inhabited mostly by descendants of West Indians who helped dig the Canal and who now are employed on the maintenance and operation of the waterway. They were his best customers. His hole-in-the-wall barber shop was spotlessly clean. He shaved black beards, cut black hair six days a week. Early in the year 1939 I walked into his shop one morning for a haircut. I was known to the barber, having had him cut my hair on several occasions.

"Americans are installing big guns on west bank of Canal, aren't they?" asked the barber shortly after he began to clip my hair.

"I don't know about that," I replied as another lock of hair was removed.

"Sure you do," replied the barber. "Aren't they?"

"I don't know," I repeated, although I did, and then I added politely, "sorry."

"Oh, but they are," insisted the barber. "I know they are."

"If you're so sure you know," I parried, "then why ask me?"

"Well, you always get around in the Zone," said the barber, "I thought you'd know."

"How do you know about this?" I countered.

"Oh, very simple," answered the barber. "One of the Negroes who is working on the emplacements gets his haircut and his shaves regularly here. He told me."

This same barber was also interested in tropical fishes. I next heard of him from Señora Clotilde de la Guardia de la Ossa, a distinguished Panamanian matron whose hobby was the collection and sale of tropical fishes. The barber visited her one day at her Acuario Sonny Boy in the Las Sabanas District overlooking the swank Panama Golf Club. He bought several prize tropical fishes from her.

"Can you use some fish aquariums?" he asked of the matron.

"Sure, I can use plenty of them!" she replied.

"Well, I have quite a few from Japan and I shall be pleased to sell them to you."

"Fine, I shall be glad to buy them."

"Come to my room above the barber shop any time and I shall let you have them."

"I shall come on Monday afternoon."

"No. Do not come on Monday afternoon because I do not work on Mondays. Every Monday I go to the pier at Balboa to watch the arrival of one of the Maru ships from Japan. Come on Tuesday."

"Very well, then, I shall come on Tuesday."

On the next Tuesday Señora de la Ossa was driven to the barber shop by her chauffeur. She directed the chauffeur to accompany her to the room of the barber, as the latter was not in his shop when they arrived. They walked up to the second story. The barber's room was another two-by-four, barely furnished with a cot and a wardrobe. Señora de la Ossa bought her aquariums at the fantastically cheap price of twenty cents each, later selling them, with her tongue in her cheek, for from $1.00 to $1.50, according to their sizes, notwithstanding the fact that they were easily worth $3.00 each. On a hanger on the wall of the barber's room she noticed a formal dress suit of tails and white tie. Protruding from the tie was a large diamond. The breast links also displayed diamonds.

"Hey, what is that doing here?" Señora de la Ossa asked with customary Panamanian curiosity and a jovial inflection.

"That is mine," replied the barber.

"Yours?" the matron gasped in astonishment.

"Yes, mine," said the barber complacently. "I wear it when I have to attend functions at the Japanese Legation."

Later that afternoon, Señora de la Ossa was back at her *acuario* puttering around her aquariums when an attaché of the Japanese Legation arrived.

"Señora," he said. "The minister would like you to fix for him a beautiful aquarium which he would like to use as a centerpiece for a table at a dinner he is giving this evening. Spare no cost, but please fix one up and deliver it to the legation as soon as it is ready. He has just received a shipment of fishes from the Maru that is now docked at Balboa, and he wants a nice aquarium for them."

"Very well," said the matron, and she prepared the aquarium, using one which she had just purchased from the barber. As the sudden night was beginning to fall on Panama her car rolled up to the Japanese Legation in Bella Vista. She was ushered inside to deliver the aquarium. The minister showed her the collection of newly arrived fishes, which was really an admirable one. The dinner was in honor of the officers of the *Tatsuta* Maru. In the midst of the spotlessly clean officers, in his tails and diamond-studded shirt, was the same barber who had sold her the aquariums. He recognized the matron and gave her a salute and a smile of recognition.

Later that night the barber returned to his small shop, removed his white tie and tails and diamond-studded shirt, and stored them in his wardrobe. The next morning he picked up his shears once again and resumed his work in the barber shop. And so did forty-seven other Japanese barbers in the cities of Panama and Colon.

Like Mixu Watanabe, the barber, Commander in His Imperial Majesty's Japanese Navy, there were many others in Panama City and Colón and the rest of Latin America who formed an army of marionettes for the Mikado, ready to follow the orders which were issued in the name of the "Son of Heaven" in Tokyo.

The Canal Zone was wide open for Japanese to move about as they wished—until early in 1940. Every Japanese ship that arrived, and there was at least one or two each week, brought more Japanese to Panama. Some of the older Japanese residents would suddenly disappear, and a new face would replace the departed one. As most of them looked alike to the Panamanians, the unsuspecting natives could detect no difference.

At No. 8 Avenida Pablo Arosemena, near Panama's main public market and in the heart of the waterfront area, the Japanese rented the entire second floor of one building for their fishermen. From dawn till dusk the fishermen would sail in their sampans along the coast of Panama and return without any fish for sale. If they had wanted charts of the depths of channels at the Canal approaches, they could have purchased them at the office of the Captain of the Port at Balboa. But they wanted a little more than that. They wanted the exact soundings of the depths of the close-in approaches to the port of La Chorrera, the Bayano River, the Pacora River, the Rio Chico, the Juan Diaz River, the port of Aguadulce, Bahia Hondo, Puerto Pedasi and Rio Pedregal. When the distance became too great for their sampans to negotiate, the tuna fishermen took over with the Diesel-powered fishing vessels.

The Japanese began to increase their espionage operations around Panama in 1935, and the increase continued on a noticeable scale up to Pearl Harbor day. Takahiko Wakabayashi was Japanese Consul General in Panama, then the senior foreign office representative. He was a genial, affable, squarely-built Japanese with a choppy mustache and a sly smile. His consulate offices were situated in his residence in Bella Vista where he lived with Mrs. Wakabayashi and their two children, a girl and a boy. In 1934 the lighter-than-air dirigible *Akron* was joining the fleet in Panama and was to fly over Albrook Field to be moored to the mast of the U.S.S. *Patoka*. Wakabayashi had purchased a Graflex camera similar to the one used by press photographers. He drove to the Canal Zone in his Packard limousine with Mrs. Wakabayashi and the children and parked on Gaillard Highway at the end of the North-South runway at Albrook Field shortly before the scheduled time for the *Akron* to pass by. He focused his camera and as the *Akron* came along took enough pictures to empty an entire film pack.

But Wakabayashi's day of duty was not ended. It was a Saturday afternoon, and the fleet was tied up in Balboa Harbor for the weekend. Wakabayashi drove to the dock area, parked his Packard in front of Dock 17, reloaded his Graflex and had a field day taking photographs of our warships. In 1934 there were no restrictions against taking photographs in the Canal Zone. But every Japanese merchant ship that sailed through the Panama Canal carried charts of prohibited areas at Japanese ports with admonishments thereon that the taking of photographs were strictly *verboten*, offenders being subject to arrest and imprisonment.

The Japanese foreign office must have been pleased with Wakabayashi's work. They also were laying plans for future expansion to the south, so the Consul General was immediately promoted to Bogotá and elevated to the rank of *chargé d'affaires*. The Japanese had had no legation in Colombia, and Wakabayashi, who spoke fluent Spanish and had done so well in Panama during his four-year tour, was commissioned by his government to place the cornerstone in Bogotá with the Colombian foreign office for the establishment of a legation for the Mikado.

Before Wakabayashi departed from Panama, to which place he was to return quite often, he helped his nationals expand their businesses there. Yoshitaro Amano, who was the chief of Japanese intelligence for Central and South America, had started operations some years before with a very small store on Central Avenue, near Santa Ana Plaza. Before Wakabayashi departed, Amano had branched out toward the center of the city and had opened a large store known as the Casa Japonesa at the corner of East 17th Street and Central Avenue. Most of the merchandise sold at these stores was cheap Japanese goods which met the demands of the limited pocketbooks of the masses of the natives. It didn't matter that the merchandise they bought was so poorly made that they would have to resupply themselves soon. The products satisfied their immediate needs, and thus Amano did a land-office business that permitted him to turn over his inventories every sixty days, perfectly content with a very small margin of profit. But Amano was hardly ever in his store. He was almost always on the road, traveling by plane or by boat between Guatemala and Chile. In Chile Amano had acquired a cattle ranch estimated to be worth $750,000.

Amano in some respects personified the worst of Oriental stereotypes. He made it a practice to send lavish gifts to newly-appointed native government officials, but one such gesture backfired in 1935. José Isaac Fabrega, then the editor of *La Estralla de Panama*, was appointed Foreign Minister of Panama early in December of that year.

Bright and early the next morning, only an hour and a half after the news reached the streets, a truck rolled up to Fabrega's residence on East 39th Street, Bella Vista. From it was unloaded a massive grandfather's clock and it was deposited on Fabrega's doorstep. The driver knocked on the door of the house, and Señor Fabrega appeared in his bathrobe and examined the clock. Upon inquiry he learned from the driver that a card of explanation was attached to it. Fabrega examined the card, and it read CONGRATULATIONS! Y. AMANO, CASA JAPONESA.

"I'm sorry," said Fabrega to the driver, "I have never met Señor Y. Amano. I do not know him. Please take the clock back and tell him I do not accept any gifts."

The driver and his helper were dumbfounded. They returned the clock to the rear room of the Casa Japonesa and not a word was said by the sphinxlike Japanese manager. Y. Amano was out of town. The manager had simply carried out standing instructions.

Allegedly to encourage amateur photography in the Canal Zone, Amano had organized a photographic club. He advertised in the newspapers and offered handsome cash prizes for the best photographs submitted every month, with the stipulation that the subjects must originate in the Zone and could include still objects such as buildings and installations. Amano obtained a very profitable return from this enterprise. Many Canal Zone photographers, unaware of Amano's motives, contributed over a period of ten years thousands of photographs to his stockpile of intelligence. There were views of naval vessels being locked through the Canal or in Gaillard Cut; photos of vessels tied up at the docks in Balboa or lying at anchorage in Limon Bay in Colón; pictures of the warehouses, refrigeration plants, and water works of the Canal Zone. Amano's prizes ranged from cash to costly Leica and Zeiss cameras, which he purchased from Antonio Lehmann, pro-Nazi owner of the Foto Sport in San José, Costa Rica. Lehmann, having been born in San José, had been admitted into membership of the NSDAP (the Nazi Party) on October 1, 1934. Because Germany was trading with Costa Rica on the barter system, the best German cameras could be purchased at comparatively cheap prices at the Foto Sport and other Costa Rican stores.

Soon, Lehmann was doing a lucrative business with army post exchanges in the Canal Zone, shipping German cameras and photographic utilities to them for cash payment. The post exchanges, in turn, sold the cameras and equipment to the Army and Navy personnel authorized to purchase at those stores.

Amano, or one of his assistants, collated the photographs contributed to him, made an equitable selection of them, tacked on appropriate legends to them, and dispatched them to Japan weekly on one of the Maru ships that called regularly at the Canal. This gold mine of intelligence continued for Amano until the White House issued an executive order in June, 1941, which restricted the taking of photographs in the Canal Zone.

Amano was to all appearances a bachelor, and this permitted him to cultivate the friendship of an American lady resident in the Canal Zone. He was seen frequently with her, sight-seeing in the Zone in a taxicab, always preferring the touring type of vehicle because it offered better visibility. But his operations were not confined solely to that of a drygoods and crockery merchant. He branched out as a tuna fishing magnate and registered his most modern tuna clipper, the *Amano* Maru, under the Panamanian flag. The *Amano* made many a fishing trip out of Balboa Harbor but always returned to port without a catch. Her stern was built in a special design so that the ship could carry either mines or midget "suicide" submarines. The *Amano* began operations on an intensive scale in 1938, using Balboa as its base port. It would next be reported off the Galapagos Islands, that strategic archipelago that is owned by Ecuador and sits in the Pacific Ocean 980 miles from the Balboa entrance of the Panama Canal. The *Amano* would be reported at Puntarenas, Costa Rica, then off the Nicaraguan, Salvadorean, and Guatemalan coasts and finally back to Panama. Unlike the other tuna fishing vessels that were manned by Japanese crews and sailed out of California ports for the fishing grounds in the vicinity of the Galapagos Islands, the *Amano* never cast any fishing nets over its side. The California tuna clippers did return to port with their hauls, even though they may have had rendezvous with Japanese submarines and with other vessels on the high seas. But not the *Amano* Maru. This clipper was too busy on more important missions for the Mikado.

With acceleration in 1938 of the Japanese "fishing" expeditions by the *Amano* Maru and by the fishermen who operated from No. 8 Avenida Pablo Arosemena, the concern of the military and naval authorities in the Canal Zone began to increase.

Some months earlier the M/S *Taiyo* Maru, a tuna fishing boat whose home port was San Diego, California, had hit the rocky reefs off the Fortified Islands near Fort Amador at the Pacific entrance to the Canal at two o'clock in the morning. The *Taiyo* Maru had entered from seaward unannounced on that moonless night and had penetrated into a prohibited area where it should not have been cruising. The sounding gear was still over its port bow when Canal authorities boarded the wreckage early the next morning.

Secretary of State Cordell Hull, accompanied by Assistant Secretary Adolf A. Berle, halted briefly in Panama en route to the Pan-American Conference in Lima and made a courtesy call on President Juan Demostenes Arosemena. They had a very long conversation. What was said then only Tony Muto, the newsreel cameraman who was present, knew, but he wouldn't talk. However, several weeks later a decree was issued by the government which prohibited fishing by Japanese in Panamanian waters. The Japanese didn't like that very much. For three years the Japanese had had an envoy extraordinary and minister plenipotentiary accredited to the government of Panama, and the decree which expelled their fisherman was a serious blow to diplomatic prestige.

The registration of the *Amano* Maru was canceled, and the home port of the ship was transferred to Puntarenas, Costa Rica. Having sailed across from Japan, where she was built, without halting at any refueling points, the *Amano* Maru used to spend upwards of twenty days at sea before returning to port. She continued the practice at Puntarenas. Meanwhile, the other fishermen, those with sampans, were now in the ranks of the unemployed, and soon the Japanese Legation shipped them back home.

Like the Nazis, the Japanese believed that economic penetration was a necessary adjunct to eventual political and military penetration. So they undertook their program of expansion in Panama by establishing the Nippon Trade Agency, a commercial office, on the top floor of the National City Bank Building in Panama City. The Nippon Trade

Agency selected a site for office space which was directly across the hall from the office of the commercial attaché of the United States. This gave Tsumi Hatta, the head of the office, an opportunity to see all who entered and left the American attaché's office.

It was in 1935 that T. Yokoi arrived in Panama from Seattle, Washington. Yokoi could speak excellent English, having been, by his own admission, a language student in the United States. Now he was visiting Panama just to have a good time and to learn the Spanish language and to try to understand the people. Following that, he planned to continue his tour to Venezuela and to other parts of South America before returning to Japan. Yokoi spent his days walking around Panama City and its environs, and his nights studying Spanish. At eight o'clock every night he began his lessons with a special female tutor, and could be seen walking home to his furnished room two hours later. Soon T. Yokoi became quite proficient in Spanish and could converse freely and almost without an accent.

When that occurred, early in 1936, Yokoi suddenly appeared behind the counters of the Casa Japonesa store on Central Avenue. When questioned about his sudden desire to go to work, Yokoi replied that he was tired of loafing and, besides, the work helped him perfect his Spanish; it gave him an opportunity to converse with the natives who entered to purchase the inexpensive Japanese goods. Meanwhile, several Japanese rented the corner of East 19th Street and Central Avenue and opened up a modernized department store called Miyako. The owner, or at least the manager, was a T. Tahada. In a few months Yokoi transferred from the counters of the Casa Japonesa to the Miyako counters and spent another full year in Panama City.

In 1938 another Japanese store opened, the Casa Japonesa, on 10th Street near Bolivar in Colón. The proprietor was T. Yokoi. The store consisted of two showcases and a dozen shelves filled with merchandise of a general nature. Yokoi's office was in a little cubbyhole of an improvised balcony built into the small store. The store was just across the street from Miss Ohada's shirt shop, in the natural line of drift of the sailors from the naval base at Coco Solo. Yokoi used to receive his mail in a post-office box in Cristobal, Canal Zone, and every morning he walked on schedule at nine o'clock to pick it up or to deposit a letter. One morning he was stopped by an acquaintance, who was particularly anxious to ascertain whether or not Yokoi was a Japanese naval officer. There had been certain indications that he was, but the acquaintance decided to take a long shot that morning. Yokoi squatted down on the pavement in Japanese fashion and engaged in conversation.

"It appears to me," said the acquaintance, after the discussion had woven around general subjects of travel, "that a naval officer is more broad-minded that an army officer."

"Why do you say that?" Yokoi asked, as he broke out into a broad smile of apparent contentment.

"Because it is true," the man insisted, and Yokoi continued to smile.

"Why do you insist it is true?" he asked.

"Because naval officers travel more than army officers," the acquaintance said, and Yokoi's smile broadened a little more and his eyes sparkled. A few days later Yokoi's trunk was searched, unknown to him, and his identification card as a Lieutenant Commander of the Imperial Japanese Navy was found among his effects.

In the meantime, Takahiko Wakabayashi had continued his loyal service in the diplomatic corps of the Mikado, while an envoy extraordinary and minister plenipotentiary had replaced him both in Panama and in Colombia. He returned to Panama from Japan en route to Buenos Aires, where he was to serve as First Secretary of the Japanese embassy, and renewed some of his old contacts. Since Wakabayashi had arrived in Colombia, however, Japanese farmers had begun to settle in the rich Cauca Valley region and acquired land under the pretext of establishing large cotton plantations. They leveled vast areas that could be converted overnight into landing strips for aircraft, although they did plant some cotton. Wakabayashi had made similar arrangements with the Costa Rican government to the north, and Japanese farmers had moved into the province of Guanacaste, leveled long stretches of fertile land, and begun to plant cotton. The land for the "plantations" in Colombia and in Costa Rica had been purchased by Y. Amano.

On his way to Argentina, Wakabayashi stopped off in Brazil to visit the leaders of the Japanese colony in Sao Paulo. Three hundred thousand strong, these Japanese were being whipped up continuously into a state of frenzy for the Mikado. The *Shinto Romei*, a secret society, was working among them, and active agitators would be landed in Brazil from Japan aboard one of the Maru ships to operate among these colonists. The Brazilian authorities were constantly on the alert to prevent any fanatical uprising. There was also overland communication over the dense and almost impenetrable jungle fastness of Brazil's Amazon region with the thirty thousand Japanese residents in Peru. Messages were carried to and from the Japanese colonists in Panama and Brazil, via the Maru ships of the Nippon Yoshen Kaisha Line, the Koshen Kaisha Line, or the Mitsui Line which had regular sailings until the Japanese government began to remove them from their runs in order to convert them for war service in 1940.

Soon Wakabayashi was to leave the diplomatic service and return to Panama as Latin-American representative of the Japanese Exporters Association, with the mission of increasing Japan's economic expansion in the Western Hemisphere. Wakabayashi tried to buy up local minerals and raw materials with long-term barter agreements. Like the Nazis, he offered Japanese goods in return. Many of the Latin-American nations were unwilling to enter into the barter negotiations with the Japanese; they wanted a cash return for their sales. But they did permit merchants to purchase Japanese goods for cash if they desired. The Japanese then launched an all-out offensive to undersell United States textiles and staples. They extended credit for as long as 180 days in comparison to the United States exporters' maximum of 60 days sight draft or cash upon receipt of documents. Wakabayashi assigned to local non-Japanese merchants exclusive agency representations for certain Japanese manufactures, which enabled them to order and import merchandise directly from the manufacturer through the Japanese Exporters Association. Japanese silks and cotton textiles and manufactured goods flooded the market at prices far below United States products of similar manufacture. Furthermore, American exporters were not too anxious in the pre-Pearl Harbor days to compete for the Latin-American trade.

On January 5, 1941, Japanese Foreign Minister Yosuke Matsuoka delivered an international broadcast to the Japanese residing in North, Central, and South America: "I wish you to cooperate with the people in whichever country you reside," he said. "I pray that we may not make this year one of the fall of civilization, but that we will work for peace." Two weeks later Takahiko Wakabayashi made his last visit to Panama. He flew in from Costa Rica with eight of the best Leica cameras purchased at the Foto Sport in San José. He left them with Amano, whose traveling was becoming more infrequent.

Just about that time Matsuoka sounded a clear warning note that Japan was going to war with the United States. In an address before the diet on January 20, 1941, he said:

> The United States has evinced no adequate understanding of the fact that the establishment of a sphere of common prosperity is truly a matter of vital concern to Japan. She apparently entertains the idea that her own first line of national defense lies along the mid-Atlantic to the East, but that westward it lies not only along the eastern Pacific but even as far as China and the South Seas. If the United States assumes such an attitude, it would be to say the least a very one-sided contention on her part to cast reflections on our superiority in the western Pacific by suggesting that it betokens ambitious designs. I, for one, believe that such a position assumed by the United States would not be calculated to contribute toward the promotion of world peace . . . . The Tripartite Pact has been concluded for the purpose not only of making sustained efforts for the establishment of spheres of common prosperity throughout Greater East Asia, but of preventing, in its course, any other extension of the present disturbances. . . . Should the United States, unfortunately, become involved in the European war, and should Japan, too, be compelled to participate in the war, another great war both in name and in reality would ensue, precipitating a situation which would defy all attempts at saving it. . . . The establishment of New World order, the goal of the powerful Tripartite Pact, if only for the time being, will surely be accomplished. There is no room for doubt that it will be crowned with brilliant success."

A careful reading between the lines of the above speech by Matsuoka produced the conclusion that Japanese war plans were already set in January, 1941. Therefore, it was with mingled curiosity and also with their tongues in their cheeks that Lieutenant General Daniel Von Voorhis and other high-ranking officers of the Army and Navy command in the Canal Zone entertained three Japanese admirals and five Japanese naval captains on February 7, 1941, on direct orders from Washington. They were traveling on the Japanese naval transport *Asaka* Maru, which had formerly frequented the Canal as a cargo carrying vessel of the Nippon Wosen Kaisha Line. But General Von Voorhis had orders from the War Department to take the admirals and their party on a tour of the defenses of the Panama Canal. Admiral Sakamake, an aviation expert of the Japanese navy, was to leave the transport at Lisbon, Portugal, and return to Japan via the United States after receiving delivery in that port of complete plans of Portuguese Timor. Admiral Mito, of the Engineering Department of the Japanese naval ministry, and Admiral Irifune, Superintendent of the Gunnery School of the Japanese Navy, were to proceed on to the European continent with the five naval captains as naval attachés to Japanese legations and embassies there.

The officers were taken on a conducted tour of the Zone's defenses by General Von Voorhis. The climax of the trip was a visit to Fort Kobbe, on the west bank of the Balboa entrance of the Canal, where the Japanese were shown the sixteen-inch coastal batteries which were manned by troops of the Panama Coast Artillery Command. The admirals and their assistants sailed from the Canal Zone that night very much impressed with the preparations. Admiral Sakamake, the aviation expert, saw the hilltops along the Canal route dotted with tents, radar, and searchlights, which signified that antiaircraft batteries were manned and their personnel were on the alert.

It was in the spring of 1940 that Katalino Kobiyama "cooked his own goose" after many years of espionage activities in Panama and in the Canal Zone. There were varying stories about Kobiyama, but the most accurate was that he was piped aboard a Japanese man-of-war off the Perlas Islands many years before and accorded high naval honors. He was definitely piped aboard the Japanese gunboat *Idzumo* when it docked at Panama in 1932 on a good-will cruise. Kobiyama was Amano's chief contact man with the Japanese colony and he was also a very handy man for the Japanese minister and his staff. He had resided in Panama for more than twenty years, and he was familiar with every nook and cranny of the city and spoke the language fluently. His main means of livelihood was apparently the work of a ship's chandler, supplying all the Japanese vessels that arrived at Canal Zone ports. That, too, was an excellent cover for his operations, because it gave him free access to the vital pier area and also enabled him to contact transient Japanese personalities. One of his tasks was to ship out old Japanese agents and to import new ones without immigration authorities' tumbling to the procedure.

On the particular April, 1940, afternoon in question, Katalino Kobiyama was loitering about Pier 18 in Balboa. This wharf is the principal one on the Pacific side of the Canal. Diplomatic relations between Japan and the United States, and between Japan and Great Britain, were normal at the time, but apparently they were not so between Kobiyama and Great Britain. There was a British merchant ship docked at Pier 18 with a deck cargo of twin-engine Boston bombers. José Domingo Alzamora, a pro-American native Panamanian who was working as a cargo checker on the pier, observed Kobiyama shuffling along the dock area and approaching the armed merchantman. It was a vicinity in which, Alzamora knew, the Japanese had no business. He saw Kobiyama remove from his pocket a box of matches and a pencil. Kobiyama opened the matchbox and wrote something inside it. Kobiyama returned the matchbox and the pencil to his pocket and turned to leave the pier area. Alzamora was suspicious of this unusual act and he hastened to notify a policeman on duty at the pier entrance. As Kobiyama reached the exit he was halted by the policeman. The policeman asked him to produce the matchbox, which Kobiyama did hesitatingly. Examination of the inside of the box showed that Kobiyama had written the name of a ship on it. He was taken off to Balboa jail where he was tried and fined $25 and jailed for thirty days for loitering on the pier. Kobiyama's effects were searched, and much information was obtained which proved of value to the intelligence services in the Canal Zone. Kobiyama, a chubby man, fifty-eight years old, stockily built, and exceptionally tall for a Japanese, had met his Waterloo. He admitted that he had planned to go immediately to the office of Boyd Brothers in Panama City, who were also agents for the Japanese lines, and deliver the information about the British armed merchantman to Hans Heidelk, an ardent pro-Nazi, for transmission through channels to the Nazi submarines that would lay in wait for it in the Caribbean after it sailed through the Canal.

The capture of Kobiyama and his subsequent deportation to Japan, for he was shipped out on the first available steamer, threw Amano and the Japanese Legation into a tailspin. It was Kobiyama who had organized a vast network of agents among the natives in Panama and in the Zone, who reported to him regularly and who were an important part of the Nipponese plans for eventual sabotage operations against vital installations along the Canal route. Amano and his No. 1 assistant, Sriderara Yoshida, immediately set about trying to rebuild the fences which had collapsed when Kobiyama was captured. Most of Kobiyama's contacts, fearful that the Zone's intelligence authorities had extracted from Kobiyama information about them, were reluctant to approach any Japanese from then on.

The task of reconstructing the espionage wall that had crumbled with Kobiyama's elimination from the local scene fell to Yoshida. He worked long and frantic hours, but soon he, too, was to send the plans of the Japanese warlords askew. The Japanese, through certain Panamanian contacts, were kept well abreast of the political situation in Panama. They knew that, after the inauguration of Arnulfo Arias, Foreign Minister Raul de Roux was going to submit a bill to the National Assembly in which the Japanese were to be included under the "prohibited immigration" classification in accordance with a provision in the new constitution which the Arias regime was to put through. Yoshida asked for an audience with the foreign minister, and it was granted. He was ushered into his office while the chief of the Department of Immigration, Alberto de la Guardia, a graduate of Santa Clara University in California, was there. Yoshida told de Roux that he had asked for the interview for the express purpose of fulfilling a request made by his chief, Y. Amano, who had wished him to present to the minister a gift of a book of photographs of all Central America and Panama which Amano had taken himself and which he had printed recently. De Roux opened the book to examine the pages of photographs and out of one of the pages fell an envelope containing large bills. De Roux gasped, and so did Yoshida when he saw the expressions on the two faces. De Roux summoned a policeman and ordered the immediate arrest of Yoshida on a charge of attempted bribery of a government official. Yoshida denied all allegations and claimed that Amano, who was traveling in Chile at the time, must have left the bills in one of the copies of his book! De Roux reported the incident to President Arnulfo Arias and the latter ordered the immediate deportation of Yoshida, pointing out that an object lesson had to be made of him. Yoshida was on his way back to Japan in a few days.

The incident brought Amano back to Panama by airplane as quickly as possible, but he arrived too late to stay Yoshida's deportation order. Nevertheless, measures barring the Japanese from business in Panama were not applied during Arnulfo Arias's administration although the Chinese were ousted. Amano set to work trying to reconstruct Yoshida's organization, but the contacts with all the big politicos who manifested any friendliness toward Japan had been made solely and exclusively by Yoshida, who could be seen frequently with them in the beer gardens. One very prominent politican, later President Enrique A. Jiménez, personally attached his card as an endorsement to Yoshida's petitions for authorization to bring more Japanese into Panama before the petitions were transmitted to the immigration office.

Twice in less than one year the key men of the Japanese espionage and subversive organizations had committed faux pas which provoked their deportation from Panama. Yoshida's ouster created havoc among them. Amano's attempts to operate on the wrecked organization were not too successful. Canal Zone counterintelligence agents were watching his every move, and that of other Japanese; they had Amano and his contacts tabbed. With the potential local sabotage organization broken up, there was one very live source that the Japanese could prepare for operations designed to block the Panama Canal. That was the Japanese merchant fleet itself.

On April 12, 1941, the Japanese had signed their Neutrality Pact with Russia. That meant that they had secured their Outer Mongolian frontier for the time being; there was no necessity to reinforce their Manchurian army. It freed them for operations in the proposed East Asia Co-prosperity Sphere, in the Philippines, in Hawaii, and in the Panama Canal. A graph which the Marine Division of the Panama Canal had begun to prepare at the beginning of 1940 showed a gradual removal of Japanese ships from sailings through the Panama Canal or from calls at the port of Balboa for sailings along the west coast of South America. Now, when any maritime nation begins to remove its merchant marine fleet from normal trading activities, there is an obvious conclusion that can be drawn: that nation is readying for war.

Such was the conclusion drawn by General Van Voorhis and his staff at the end of June, 1941. General Van Voorhis' mission was to defend the Panama Canal from attacks from without and from within, and from sabotage. He could not guarantee the successful accomplishment of his mission if vessels of the Japanese merchant fleet were permitted to continue to sail through the Panama Canal. As soon as President Roosevelt had decreed the unlimited national emergency the month before, General Van Voorhis ordered military guards, armed to the teeth, to board all vessels and to sail through the Canal in them to guard the vital areas. Furthermore, the guards on the locks had been reinforced to a battalion on each of the three locks of the Canal. General Van Voorhis had a decision to make. War had not been declared between Japan and the United States, but General Van Voorhis issued an order prohibiting Japanese flagships from sailing through the Canal. Two ships were caught by the order at Balboa and three at Cristobal. The Japanese Minister in Panama, Masatoshi Akiyama, rushed to Quarry Heights to interview General Van Voorhis. The Japanese ambassador in Washington protested to the State Department. The War Department queried General Van Voorhis. He replied that he was fulfilling his mission: he was not going to take a chance and let the Japanese block the Canal by opening the sea locks of one or more of their ships and sinking in the locks or in the narrow Gaillard Cut. President Roosevelt upheld the decision. The five ships, awaiting transit through the Canal, sailed around the Horn. Japanese plans had again suffered a setback in Panama.

When the United States black list was published on July 17, 1941, no Japanese were on it. But that didn't prevent some of the key Japanese agents in Panama to begin to liquidate their properties in August, 1941, and to leave either for Japan or for other points in South America. Yaichi Otake, who operated a tire-vulcanizing shop in the populated Calidonia section of Panama City, sold out and returned to Japan to don his uniform as a major in the Japanese army. Kiyoshi Kawamanura and Yasu Mio sold their barber shops and returned to their homeland to put on their naval uniforms as first lieutenants. Miss Ohada sold her shirt shop in Colón and was shipped back to Japan.

On September 27, 1941, the Japanese minister in Panama gave his last public reception for officials of the Canal Zone and Panama. It was a very limited party and not more than a hundred persons attended. By then, Lieutenant General Frank M. Andrews had succeeded General Van Voorhis as Commander of the Caribbean Defense Command,

Panama Canal Department. He attended with members of his staff, and the Japanese minister also invited the German *chargé d'affaires* and Erik O. Cerjack-Boyna. At this party Minister Akiyama asked General Andrews if he might not tour the Pacific side of the Canal escorted by an officer from Andrews' staff. The date was set for the morning of October 9, and I was detailed to escort the Minister and his party.

At eight o'clock that morning I called at the Japanese Legation on East 43rd Street, Bella Vista, to accompany Minister Akiyama on his tour. The party included the entire legation staff and, although the Minister had wanted to use his Packard limousine, they were all herded, politely of course, into an Army staff car. The minister was particularly anxious to see only two points, one of which he could have driven to any day in his own car. They were the Cruces Trail and Howard Field, the latter a new $23 million air base under construction near Fort Kobbe. The Cruces Trail is that famous foot-and-mule trail across the Isthmus which connects Colon with Panama, over which the gold treasures of the days of the conquistadors had passed. An old Spanish cannon had been placed on a promontory where Madden Road cuts across the trail; it is distinctly marked with a sign in black and gold letters and arrows pointing in north and south directions.

An interesting conversation took place with Akiyama when the car reached the historic trail.

"May we alight from the car?" asked Minister Akiyama.

"Yes, Mr. Minister," I replied. The party alighted and stood on the highway.

"May we walk up the steps to the trail?" the Minister asked, fingering his silver-handled walking stick.

"By all means, Mr. Minister," and the entire party walked up the steps to the trail. We paused, and the Minister then pounded on the old cobblestones that had been there for almost four centuries.

"Is this trail paved like this all the way?" he asked.

"Yes, Mr. Minister, all the way."

"Very interesting, very interesting," mumbled the Minister as he pounded the cobblestones again. "You know," he resumed, "my colleagues and I like to take long walks on Sundays; that is, we like to go hiking. Would there be any objection if we should come out here some Sunday morning soon and go hiking about this trail?"

"None at all," I assured him, "but if you all wake up dead some Monday morning don't blame me."

Minister Akiyama and his staff emitted embarrassed laughs and headed back to the car. They never did make the hike. The Cruces Trail, like all the other strategic trails in the Canal Zone, was guarded by hidden infantry patrols from the Panama Mobile Force. The Minister's interest in the Cruces Trail had vanished quickly. The reconnaissance then continued to the air base at Howard Field, which could be reached either by boarding a ferry to cross the Canal or via a temporary bridge across the locks.

At Howard Field the party climbed to a hill that provided an excellent bird's-eye view of the entire air base and its installations, work on which was proceeding with feverish haste. The party entered one of the new unfinished sets of officers' quarters on the hill, and the burly Japanese commercial attaché soon illustrated the real purpose of the trip. He removed a miniature Minox camera from his pocket and tried to photograph the new runway that had just been completed to handle our heaviest bombers. I interjected myself into a position that prevented the picture from being taken. The commercial attaché returned the camera hastily to his pocket. In a few minutes he tried again, and once more his movements were caught in time and the attempt was frustrated. Minister Akiyama began to show some great concern and must have said some strong words to his subordinates because the tour ended rather abruptly right then and there. The camera was returned to the pocket of the commercial attaché for the last time.

Two weeks later, Minister Akiyama gave a dinner party for all the diplomats from Latin America who were accredited to the government of Panama. The party was held in his legation dining room. After the fine dinner and abundant wines which he always served, the guests adjoined to the reception room. They sat down, and conversation became general for about twenty minutes. Then Minister Akiyama informed his guests that he had something very important to tell them, and that what he was going to say was in complete confidence.

"Gentlemen," he began, "war between Japan and the United States may break out at any time." His Spanish was sharp, fluent, and matter of fact. "I have been requested by my government to ascertain what the attitude may be of your neutral governments in the event war does break out." The diplomats were shocked, stunned at the frank approach of Minister Akiyama.

The Costa Rican Ambassador, Enrique Fonseca-Zuñiga, who was dean of the diplomatic corps, spoke up to break the tension in the smoke-filled salon. "Mr. Minister, this is astounding news. We all regret to hear it. But in response to your question, I believe that my colleagues will agree with me that the question should be put directly to our respective governments by your government." The other guests present nodded assent.

"Thank you, gentlemen," said Minister Akiyama. "I wish to emphasize the fact that what I have just said has been in complete confidence. Perhaps there may be an eleventh-hour change to alter the situation and to save the world from disaster."

The diplomats left the Japanese Legation in a very pensive mood. Some of them could not keep the confidence long. In a few hours Army intelligence in the Zone had wind of the sensational revelation by the Japanese Minister. The information was cabled without delay to the War Department. Combat crews of the Army Air Corps were immediately alerted at their bases. The rest of the Canal Zone force had been on the alert for some time.

That storm clouds were brewing in the Pacific there was little doubt. This was crystal clear in Panama in early November, 1941. Just after Special Ambassador Kurusu reached Washington in November, 1941, a secretary of the Japanese Legation in Panama, commenting on the international situation, said: "The clouds are growing darker. I fear they will not blow away." He was right.

On the morning of December 4, 1941, there was great activity in the patio of the Japanese Legation in Panama. Smoke was belching skyward. The staff was burning confidential documents and code books. The Minister had received his orders from Tokyo. The Japanese task force was already en route to Pearl Harbor; war would break out in a few days. It did on the morning of December 7.

But Amano and other Japanese had been making their exodus steadily from Panama in small numbers. When Pearl Harbor was attacked, Amano was ensconced safely in neutral Chile.

As soon as the radio had announced the treacherous attack against our fleet, and before any official word had been transmitted to them from the Army command at Quarry Heights, the Panama police, under the command of Colonel Rogelio Fabrega, swooped down and arrested every Japanese and every member of his family, as well as every Nazi and Fascist, excepting those who were protected by diplomatic immunity. The list of dangerous agents and suspects had been delivered to Colonel Fabrega on the afternoon of December 5.

If the Japanese in concert with the Nazis and the Fascists, had had a sabotage plan, that plan was torpedoed by the prompt, unilateral, and very helpful action of the police of the Republic of Panama under the command of Colonel Fabrega.

8. Freedom for the Axis

It was a dark, rainy night in Panama in the month of May of the year 1927. The rainy season had just started and, as generally happens in the month of May, it poured down in buckets. Eight young men who had graduated from college in the United States but two years earlier were standing outside a building on Avenida A. They had a rendevous with destiny, or at least one of them thought so. They were going to organize a secret patriotic society with the ultimate aim of gaining control of the reins of government so that they could improve the national patrimony which had been jeopardized, or so they complained, by the abolition of the Taft Agreement by President Calvin Coolidge.

The job, they had agreed in their preliminary conversations, was not one that could be accomplished in one year, two years, three years, or even four years. It was a long-term, long-range project, but they were willing to give it a try. The organization meeting was a success. Each founding member was to select and recommend another candidate for membership; soon, cells were to be established. They had decided on a name. It was to be *Accion Comunal* (Communal Action). One of the organizers was Dr. Arnulfo Arias.

Meetings were held once each month on a Thursday night during the

111

early organizational days. The second meeting produced sixteen members. The third brought thirty-two, the fourth accounted for sixty-four, and the fifth landed one hundred twenty-eight. Then meetings were held once a week, again on Thursday nights. The membership was frozen at three hundred. It was still a secret society, but soon it began to publish a weekly newspaper. It was Panama's first extremely nationalistic newspaper.

Accion Comunal was neither a Nazi-designed nor Fascist-inspired organization at the time of its founding. It was a patriotic, nationalistic society with an avowed purpose of improving the national patrimony. But *Accion Comunal* became, either advertently or inadvertently, the advance guard of extreme nationalism in Panama. And this extreme nationalism had to lead eventually to the triumph of nazism-fascism at a time when it was inimical to the interests of the United States and detrimental to the security and solidarity of purpose of the nations of the Western Hemisphere.

Arnulfo Arias was young and ambitious, as most men are at the age of thirty-one. He was a promising practicing physician and surgeon with a clinic situated at one of the busy points along Avenida Central. He was a man risen from the people, having been born, like Abraham Lincoln, in the tropical equivalent of a log cabin—a thatch-roofed hut at the town of Rio Grande in the central province of Cocle, virtually in the heart of Panama's rich cattle-breeding midlands. His father was of Spanish extraction. His mother bore the features of a proud descendant of Indian and Spanish forebears. She worked hard for him and for his other brothers and sisters, hoping to raise them in a manner that would not only provide for them an enviable education but would also make them prominent and respected citizens. She had cause to be proud of two of her sons; she was able to see them inaugurated as presidents of her country in her lifetime, an achievement that few mothers could ever dream of and perhaps none may experience again.

The thirty-one-year-old physician and surgeon had catapulted to fame when he led attackers against the presidential palace on January 2, 1931, and helped overthrow the constitutional government. Yet only one of the two presidential brothers, the elder, finished his legal term of four years in office. The young and ambitious medico lasted exactly one year and eight days. He spent the remainder of what would have been his legal term in office in exile in Argentina, and in December 1945 he was in jail in Panama awaiting trial for alleged treason, a frustrated attempt again to overthrow a government by revolutionary methods. He denied all charges and was granted full amnesty on December 31, 1946.

The story of the rise and fall of President Arnulfo Arias, forty years old when he began his term of office in 1940, is considered by many to be very closely interrelated with the plans of Nazi Germany for the conquest of the Panama Canal. Perhaps President Arnulfo Arias was not, as some charge, a Nazi sympathizer, and perhaps he was not, as was reported in the New York *Herald Tribune* in October, 1941, going to be appointed *Gauleiter* of Central America by Adolf Hitler in the event of a Nazi victory. Perhaps he was, and is today, a 100 per cent pro-Panamanian. But his delay in agreeing to urgent plans of the State, War, and Navy Departments for the expansion and improvement of the defenses of the Canal within the territory of the Republic of Panama created grave doubts in the minds of many. In February, 1941, the Department of State was compelled to invoke at the request of the government of Panama Article X of the United States-Panama Treaty of 1936, a safety clause written in by the American negotiators for just such a contingency, in order to expedite occupation of the base sites.

On the afternoon of March 5, 1941, only nine months before the Japanese attack on Pearl Harbor, President Arnulfo Arias issued a very significant manifesto to his nation:

> The governments of the Republic of Panama and of the United States of America have recently exchanged views, at the latter's initiative, regarding the situation created by the present European conflagration insofar as it can affect the security of the Panama Canal. The conversations have developed within the spirit of most ample and perfect understanding and on the basis of the Arias-Roosevelt Treaty of March 2, 1936.
>
> The government of Panama, harmonizing its contractual obligations with the imperious and unavoidable duty of safeguarding its own sovereign rights, has carefully studied the requests of the North American government. These tend, concretely, to obtain the use of several sites outside of the Canal Zone and in Panamanian territory for the installation of air bases and searchlight and detector stations that the govern-

ment of Washington considers indispensable for the defense of said interoceanic waterway, basing the requests on Article X of the treaty. The government of Panama, after carefully studying the situation in different meetings of the Cabinet Council, has decided to accede to the requirements of the United States government in view of the fact that the latter "has reached the conclusion that, in accordance with Article X of the Treaty of 1936, an INTERNATIONAL CONFLAGRATION has broken out, bringing with it the existence of a threat to the security of the Panama Canal that requires on the part of the United States the adoption of measures for its defense."

The preoccupation of defending the legitimate rights of Panama as regards its territorial integrity and political independence, together with the application of the Treaty of 1936, have led the government of the Republic to subordinate the use of the lands requested to stipulated conditions, among them being: Firstly, that the North American military authorities will occupy said territories only for the duration of the present European conflagration, and therefore they will be vacated as soon as the conflict ends. Secondly, that the North American government will acknowledge in favor of Panama adequate compensations. And, finally, that the Republic of Panama will exercise jurisdiction over all civilians within the sites occupied, in accordance with procedure which, in the judgment of the two governments, is necessary for the defense of the Canal.

In view of the haste shown by the government of the United States, the government of the Republic has consented that the Canal Zone authorities initiate the necessary military preparations. The Panamanian government itself esteems that the conditions herein above indicated and the final agreements between the two parties directly interested will lead to the development of the future negotiations free of the least difficulties in accordance with the letter and spirit of the Treaty of March 2, 1936.

It is difficult, and even incredible, to conceive that there could be engendered a threat from within against the Panama Canal, but there existed concern that such might be possible during the one year and eight days in office of President Arnulfo Arias, because of the freedom with which Axis espionage agents and propagandists operated near the Panama Canal. It is also incredible because one would have believed that with the Panama Canal Zone right next door, any government of Panama would by natural choice and sound policy be cooperative and friendly with the United States. Yet the situation in Panama in 1940-

41 was almost identical with the trouble that the British government was experiencing at that time in Egypt while the Nazi armies were threatening Generals Wavell and Auchinleck. Such an analogy, nevertheless, was not a very pleasant one for the American people to contemplate; war was creeping up slowly but surely.

It was either late in 1940 or early in 1941 that Alexander T. Kirk, one of our abler diplomats and then *chargé d'affaires* in Berlin, wrote a personal letter to his long-time friend in the Department of State, Undersecretary Sumner Welles, in which he reported a story that he or one of his associates had overheard at a Berlin cocktail party that had been attended by high officers of the Nazi party. The Nazis had boasted at this party that they were "on the inside" in Panama and that the new president of Panama was a great friend and admirer of the Germans. Whether the report was actually true or not, it is difficult to say, but Kirk apparently considered it of sufficient importance and gravity to communicate it in a personal missive to Sumner Welles.

The reaction of Washington to the Kirk letter was one of watchful waiting. As early as September 25, 1940 certain ominous indications began to appear. Cerjack-Boyna boasted one week before President Arias's inauguration that there would be a moderation of the anti-Nazi press campaign in the pro-American daily newspapers of Panama City and that the moderation would be ordered from the presidential palace. He proved to be well-informed.

President Arnulfo Arias was a strong, dominant personality who enforced his will not only over his subordinates but also over many of Panama's influential capitalists. Considering the secret Nazi map to which President Roosevelt had referred, the trend in Panama in 1940 and 1941 was a very dangerous one and charged with grave potentialities for the lifeline of the United States—the Panama Canal. It was common knowledge in 1936 that Arnulfo Arias would be the administration's candidate in 1940 and thus become the next president of Panama. He was opposed by Dr. Ricardo J. Alfaro, former President of the Republic and for many years Minister in Washington, whose reputation as an international lawyer included that of being a friend of the United States. With the two major dailies in Panama City supporting Arnulfo Arias, with radio broadcasting stations reluctant to sell time to the Alfaro party for fear of future reprisals, with the government machine steam-rollering openly for Arias, Dr. Alfaro withdrew from the race two days before the polls opened, despite the fact that observers considered he would have received a majority of the popular vote if his supporters had been permitted to vote. Thus Arnulfo Arias ascended to the presidency legally in what turned out to be a "no-contest" election.

As Minister to Rome during the years when fascism was bent on restoring the old Roman Empire by conquering Ethiopia, Arnulfo Arias witnessed Europe's march toward war. In 1937 he had an audience with Adolf Hitler in the Reichchancellery in Berlin. From Rome he was transferred to Paris as Minister there. He had observed the might of the Wehrmacht and the Luftwaffe in the heyday of their formative power. He had watched the so-called democracies of Europe deteriorate, thanks to adept assists by Nazi intrigue and propaganda. And, a most important factor that cannot be overlooked, he was cultivated by Nazi and Fascist officials and diplomats. He had seen Munich, and he knew that England and France were inadequately prepared for war, and like many others he evidently expected the Rome-Berlin Axis to win a rapid victory.

With this background, the first two official addresses by President Arnulfo Arias provided Nazi propagandists throughout Latin America with a world of fuel with which to kindle the flames of anti-American sentiment. In his inaugural address on October 1, 1940, Arias voiced his distrust in democracy:

> The word "democracy," like the words "liberty" and "liberalism," have been misused and worn out, and their meaning is already so confused and vague that it is difficult for the citizens of today to penetrate their real meaning. They are pronounced by the imperialist regimes, characterized by diehard aristocracies or by enriched bureaucratic classes to explain their tyranny and their exploitations, and they are used by the popular fronts to disguise their hungerings for domination and privilege. On our part, gentlemen, we wish to preserve that elevated meaning that signifies opportunity for all Panamanians within their merits, their patriotism, their moral and physical value of their capacity for work. The demagogic concept that "all men are born equals" has no acceptance, no justification in the biologic and evolutive life which is the basis of our existence.

The nationalistic pattern of Hitler's Germany was clearly evident in the above declaration, and while in office Arnulfo Arias began to translate into effective action just what he said.

Present at his inauguration on October 1, 1940, were diplomatic missions from Germany, Italy, and Japan, as well as from all other nations of the world with whom Panama entertained diplomatic relations. This gave Arias an opportunity to enunciate his policy of the strictest neutrality:

> In view of the circumstances of our geographic position and the condition of abnormality and transition that the present international panorama presents, we are animated by the sincere conviction that our international status should be maintained on a plane of peace, of harmony, and of close cooperation and comprehension with all the countries of the globe. Eloquent proofs of this is the presence here of all the Honorable Missions which have come in representation of their respective governments, and to whom I present my cordial and effusive greetings of welcome.

The Axis diplomats received the above declaration of policy with more elation than the Allied representatives. The Nazis had sent their crack diplomat for Central America, Otto Reinbeck, as Special Ambassador at the inaugural ceremonies. The United States had sent Ambassador Spruille Braden from Colombia.

But Arnulfo Arias had never been one to hide his thoughts or to disguise his intentions. While his brother, Dr. Harmodio Arias, was president, from 1932-36, he dispatched a letter to the commanding general of the Panama Canal Department in which he recognized fully the need of the United States Army to utilize lands in the Republic for training purposes and to establish temporary bases. Bound by the treaty of 1903, President Harmodio Arias authorized the commanding general to select the areas needed, occupy them, and afterward to notify the government of Panama of the action taken.

The United States Army began to use a site at Rio Hato, sixty miles from the Canal, as a landing field. Permission for the expansion of the Rio Hato site and occupation of sites on the strategic islands of Taboga and Taboguilla, which flank the Pacific entrance of the Canal, was apparently arranged in 1939 to the satisfaction of the United States Army and the owners of the lands in question without the diplomatic formality of consulting the foreign office of the government of Panama.

On October 2, 1940, President Arnulfo Arias was invited by the Columbia Broadcasting System to address the people of the United States. He took advantage of this opportunity to challenge the government of the United States because of the occupation of lands in the Republic of Panama and thus forecast the troublesome days that were to come.

> I must state, however, my deep-felt regret of the fact that the North American authorities have on various occasions occupied among other Panamanian localities Rio Hato on the mainland, and parts of the islands of Taboga and Taboguilla, without previously obtaining from the Panamanian government the required consent, which would have been the correct procedure. These acts have profoundly disturbed and deeply hurt our citizens, who sincerely hope that such events will not be repeated. We also have the right to hope that what has occurred will be settled in a manner suitable to the highest ideals and democratic principles proclaimed by so powerful a country as the United States of North America.

It was during the tenure in office of President Arnulfo Arias that our State Department acquired the biggest diplomatic headache in the history of our relations with Latin America. The headache was to last until the very day Arias was overthrown by his own people.

With a war raging in Europe that was threatening to spread its disaster over the entire world, one would naturally feel that any head of the Panama nation would cooperate unhesitatingly with the United States in the urgent question of making available land required for the adequate defense of the Canal. One can well understand, and one should, that there would be a reluctance to grant that land in perpetuity. President Arnulfo Arias refused to permit the United States to proceed with the defense projects until he had received the tacit assurance from President Roosevelt that the sites in question would be returned to the Republic of Panama as soon as the war terminated. Writes Arias's biographer, Dr. Felipe Juan Escobar:

> It must be remembered here that Panama had already opened the door to the rectification of the injustices of the Hay-Bunau-Varilla Treaty by

means of the Roosevelt-Arias Treaty of 1936 and that the Administration of Dr. J. D. Arosemena had received evident samples that the Good Neighbor Policy also included Panama, despite our small size and despite the international insecurity of that time. But there must also be borne in mind that Arnulfo Arias had not ceased being the "comunalista" of 1931 whose anti-Americanism was constantly seen livened by the collaborationist policies of those administrations.

This situation was aggravated by a purely personal incident that became apparent from the very beginning in his inaugural speech and in almost all the private conversations that he had about the subject. This personal incident consisted in the conviction that he had that his brother, Dr. Harmodio Arias, who had carried the Roosevelt-Arias Treaty negotiations to a happy conclusion, was intimately associated with the negotiations by means whereof the Army of the United States acquired control of the lands of Rio Hato, on which there was operating at the time of his inauguration one of the largest airports of the continent, without the national government possessing official knowledge of the transaction or assurance that it would have given its consent thereto. The Rio Hato business irritated him with the mere memory of what had happened and he became obsessed with the idea that he had to rectify in some manner what he believed had been a rebuff to the dignity of Panamanian sovereignty.

Although the above analysis may be a rational explanation of what motivated President Arnulfo Arias's stand, there were some points which both the biographer and President Arias overlooked. On September 22, 1939, Major General David L. Stone, who was commanding the Panama Canal Department, made a statement in an interview to American correspondents who had accompanied Undersecretary of State Sumner Welles to the Panama Conference, which was published in the Panama *American* as follows:

> General Stone gave the visitors a brief description of one of his pet projects, the immense natural landing field at Rio Hato which is connected with the Canal Zone by the Panama national highway. He explained how the United States was giving $1.5 million toward the concreting of the road and was also arranging to lend Panama some millions of dollars for completion of the highway as far as Rio Hato.
>
> For the benefit of the newspapermen who were not familiar with developments here, the general explained that at first great difficulty had

been experienced in finding some formula which would enable the United States to acquire the use of the land at Rio Hato, since Panamanians are determined not to cede the jurisdiction over any more of their territory.

"I consulted on this matter," the General said, "with Dr. Harmodio Arias, one of the most brilliant men in this part of the world, who is a personal friend of mine and a good friend of the United States. Dr. Arias was most helpful to me in finding a solution of the problem and we finally found the answer by arranging to lease the land for the Rio Hato airfield for a number of years. Now we are going ahead with the developments of the field which, when we are finished, will be one of the finest military airfields in the world."

It will be seen, therefore, that General Stone used the good offices of Dr. Harmodio Arias, the former President of Panama, to find a solution which would enable the United States Army to continue to occupy the Rio Hato base.

Shortly after President Arnulfo Arias's inauguration, Ambassador Dawson requested an appointment with him at the earliest practicable date (as he desired to bring with him Lieutenant General Van Voorhis, the military commander in the Zone) to explain the urgency of acquiring the lands needed for the construction of defense bases to protect the Canal. Although the request was made the first week in October, President Arias replied through his foreign minister that he could not possibly see Ambassador Dawson until November 7, 1940. This delay, coming on the heels of public boasts by Cerjack-Boyna that President Arias would not long tolerate attacks in the press against officials of the Axis powers in Panama, and his inaugural speech in which he emphasized Panama's complete neutrality with all nations of the world, caused considerable apprehension.

The citizens of Panama began to look at their governmental machinery with bewilderment and wondered what would come next. They saw the Axis agents spreading their propaganda freely and with delight; they read anti-American editorials in the afternoon newspaper, La Tribuna, which President Arias had purchased just before he assumed the presidency. They saw the names of Cristobal Rodriguez, Arias's Secretary-General, as the editor of that newspaper and of Antonio Isaza, Arias's private secretary, as the city editor. They heard the local Nazis and the

Fascists sing the praises of Arnulfo Arias and his Administration and they began to ask themselves questions. The newspapers and the radio brought reports every day of the advances being made by Hitler's forces and of the devastation being caused by Marshal Hermann Goering's Luftwaffe bombers over England. The Nazi armies were poised on the English Channel, all of Europe was overrun, the Japanese were rattling sabers in the Orient. Thousands upon thousands of laborers were working day and night in the Canal Zone on projects of reinforcement of the Canal's locks, the defense sites, and the construction of additional and modernized bases. But almost every afternoon *La Tribuna* reiterated with unmistakable emphasis that Panama was at peace and in harmony with all the nations of the world and that she would remain as such. Perhaps the report that Alan Kirk had made to Sumner Welles contained some basis of fact. Perhaps the Nazis were "in" in Panama as they had boasted in Berlin.

The big problem, then, for our State Department and our naval and military authorities when Arnulfo Arias became president was to obtain authorization to occupy sites for the construction of defenses in the territory of the Republic of Panama outside the five-mile strip on each side of the Canal which had been leased to the United States in perpetuity. It is interesting to read what Arias's Foreign Minister, Raul de Roux, had to say about the early negotiations for these sites. "Here is the History," he wrote:

In June of 1940 with Dr. Augusto S. Boyd at the head of the Administration of the State in his character of First Designate in Charge of the Executive Power, the Ambassador of the United States of America visited the Secretary of Foreign Relations, Dr. Narciso Garay, in his office and stated to him, confidentially, that the adequate protection of the Canal made the use on the part of the North American armed forces of new "lands and additional waters" on the Isthmus of imperious necessity, and that, in accordance with the dispositions in the General Treaty of March 2, 1936, the Government of Washington had ordered him to request the delivery of these "lands and addditional waters" and to submit to the consideration of the government of Panama a draft of a Contract of Rental, in which it was stipulated, among other things, that said lands and waters would pass to the unrestricted jurisdiction of the United

States for a term of nine hundred ninety-nine years (or to be it IN PER-PETUITY), without other compensation than the intrinsic value of the same.

No reference is made of this negotiation, neither in the "Report" presented by Secretary Garay to the Legislative Chamber in its Ordinary Sessions of 1940 nor in any publications, for which reason we are unacquainted with the official reaction. We only know that the transaction was started in the office of the Chief Executive.

Months later, as soon as Dr. Arnulfo Arias took possession of the presidency of the Republic, the United States renewed its previous request in the same terms and with like confidential character.

Here Dr. de Roux makes reference to page 297 of the biennal report of the Minister of Foreign Relations to corroborate his statement. The first article of the proposed draft Rental Contract reads: "The Republic of Panama by these presents rents to the United States for a period of nine hundred ninety-nine years, from the date of the issuance of the Decree-Law to which Article X refers, the following areas of land situated in the Republic of Panama and which are described as follows. . . ." and then the land in question is described. Professor de Roux continues:

On this occasion, giving the North American request all its importance and transcendence, the President disposed to pass it immediately to the study of the Council of Ministers, which, after ripe and thorough examination, agreed to communicate to the government of Washington that the Panamanian Executive had positive pleasure in offering his most effective cooperation in the defense of the hemisphere and that he found himself in the best disposition to facilitate without delay the necessary areas for the protection of the Canal, on the following essential basis:

1. The occupation of the "lands and additional waters" shall be TRANSITORY and limited to the time that the war emergency that has placed in danger the security of the Continent will last;

2. Panama shall preserve her sovereignty and complete civil jurisdiction over all the lands, waters, and air space, and the United States shall have exclusive jurisdiction over its military service personnel; and

3. Panama shall receive adequate compensation.

In order to adopt this resolution, the Cabinet Council took into account the traditional Panamanian spirit of solidarity and Inter-American cooperation and the obligation acquired by the Republic in Article X of the General Treaty of March 2, 1936, as well as the inevitable obligation of the government "to defend the legitimate rights of Panama in regard to its territorial integrity and political independence."

"In case of an international conflagration, or the existence of any threat of aggression which would endanger the security of the Republic or the neutrality or security of the Panama Canal, the government of the Republic of Panama and the United States of America will take such measures of defense as they consider necessary for the protection of their common interests. Any measures in safeguarding such interests which shall appear essential to one government to take and which may affect the territory under the jurisdiction of the other government will be the subject of consultation between the two governments."

The above treaty had been ratified by the National Assembly of Panama in 1938 but had not been ratified by the United States Congress until July, 1939, because there was considerable opposition among members of the Senate Foreign Relations Committee to relinquishing the blanket right given to the United States in the Treaty of 1903 to acquire additional lands and waters in the Republic of Panama should same be required for the adequate maintenance, operation, and protection of the Panama Canal. The Treaty of 1936 carried the stipulation that the government of the United States did not consider that additional lands and waters would be required from the Republic of Panama for the defense of the Canal. The opposition in the Senate was so strongly against the ratification of the new treaty before the summer recess of 1939 that Secretary of State Hull summoned Ambassador Augusto Boyd to his office and explained the gravity of the situation to him.

Dr. Boyd related the story to me of how the support of Senator Key Pittman, chairman of the Foreign Relations Committee at the time, was enlisted to obtain quick ratification of the treaty. Dr. Boyd offered to deliver his signed note to Secretary Hull in which he would state that in the event additional lands and waters were necessary for the adequate protection of the Canal, the government of Panama would not object to their immediate occupation and the two governments could negotiate afterward. Secretary Hull accepted the offer, and Dr. Boyd sat down right there and then in Secretary Hull's office, wrote the note, signed it, and handed it to Secretary Hull. The latter dictated his reply immediately, signed the note, delivered it to Ambassador Boyd, and left for the Senate Building to testify before the Foreign Relations Committee with the two notes in his hands. The Senate then ratified the treaty in July, 1939. The assurances given by Dr. Boyd, an uncle of Aquilino Boyd, who was later to figure in conflicts with the United States, were not to be honored by future governments of Panama.

An objective and thoroughly comprehensive analysis of Arnulfo Arias's foreign policy at the time was furnished by his biographer. After referring to the Rio Hato problem, the biographer wrote:

This emotional attitude in the face of a problem of such transcendence, especially in the hour of world unrest in which we lived, made him lose all sense of proportion. In reality, he demonstrated that he had the idea that he was the head of an American power, that he could haggle roughly with the War and Navy Departments of the United States who were, in truth, the ones who had the last word in questions regarding the Canal Zone and the defenses of the same.

Two facts appear to have escaped his perception: first that the threat to the American continent by the Axis nations was seen in all America as possible, and provoked an instinctive movement of common defense; and secondly, by the act of considering said threat as a common danger almost all the American republics had already demonstrated their solidarity with the United States and were on the roads of frank and enthusiastic collaboration with them. Even Mexico, so disconsolate and resentful, which had problems of such grave domestic importance to settle with the United States, was one of the first to offer not only passive cooperation but active cooperation as well in the policy of unification and defense of the continent led by the United States.

But Arnulfo Arias, by an erroneous deviation of his *Panameñismo*, started to place little obstacles and delays in the way of the matter of the demands for a rapid understanding for base site concessions that were being requested by the military authorities of the Canal Zone to such an extent that he even used to boast with delight about his highhanded treatment of some of those authorities.

The Army and the Navy were convinced that war was inevitable. They didn't know when or where it would break out, or better said, how or when the United States would enter it. Therefore, the criterion that they had to adopt with respect to every delay, to every difficulty of procedure, to every objection that had stamps of the illogical, was that he [Arias] was deliberately trying to block the indispensable preparations to fortify the Canal Zone. This was a great responsibility for them, for the defense of the Canal could be considered as the Achilles heel for the maritime and even land power of the United States and in that period its uninterrupted operation was a valuable contribution for England, the last remaining bastion in the fight against the Nazis.

One cannot but recall the concepts emitted by Arnulfo Arias in his important speeches with regard to this point and feel a great strangeness that his official deportment would not have been at the level that his words demonstrated. The mutual understanding, the mutual respect, the continental solidarity, those and others similar were the terms with which Arnulfo Arias referred to the international relations of Panama with the United States, and when they touched the specific ground of our difficulties, his "Panamananism" was emphatic for the recognition of our dignity as an independent State, but he was understanding about the obligations that the character of our joint responsibilities for the Canal imposed on us. To forget this in the precise moments in which this work acquired an incalculable strategic value was inconceivable. But his attitude of just that gave margin to the most fearful conjectures.

When a little country negotiates with a big one, the two extremes are equally dangerous: collaborationism without measure provokes scorn, and systematic opposition at least irritates and under trying conditions can be taken as an excuse for drastic proceedings.

But Panama did not need to adopt either of the two attitudes. On the contrary, to my way of seeing it, it was an era of the best period of international weight and the scale would have tipped in her favor, obtaining incalculable benefits of material and political character in her relations with the United States.

The effort the United States was making to erase the relative unpopularity that its former aggressive policy toward our people had given it in the nations of Latin America was notorious. The Good Neighbor Policy had transformed into a policy of unification of the two Americas, not on the basis of hegemony but on a basis of understanding. The effect that the experiences of other peoples had produced on the present leaders of the United States was also notorious, experiences from which arose as an appreciable fact the value of an alliance based on sympathy, cordiality, and sound understanding for the same ends for all the operations of importance in the modern war.

The United States was, then, in its different directing spheres, in a state of mind to carry its condescending to extremes never before dreamed of. The reconciliation with Mexico, the tolerance of the impertinences of Argentina, the rectifications of its policy with Cuba, its economic assistance distributed liberally to other peoples of America, were practical examples that they wanted the Americas to take into account and thus convince themselves of the sincerity of the new course adopted.

Panama, in addition to this, had the symbolic support of the Americas. Panama, as the smallest republic in population and the youngest in existence as an independent State, had the advantage of seeing itself the weakest of the nations with interests in conflict with the interests of the most powerful of the republics of the world.

The conduct that the United States adopted toward us was the concrete index of its international prestige. According to the manner in which it took into account equity, justice, the principle of nonintervention in the internal affairs of the States and the respect of the national dignity of a friendly country so would the value of its word as a democracy and the weight of its principles of international conduct be judged abroad. We could say that all America and that part of the world that still believes in these things would look at Panama as a mirror in order to know what they could expect from the United States.

It was an enviable position that Arnulfo Arias was deteriorating little by little by means of ineffective but irritating pinpricks inflicted upon the patience of a powerful government like the United States, which knows that in the long run in vital questions in Panama it could obtain what may be necessary and indispensable for its plans. When I compare this attitude with what later happened in Chile, for example, when a single speech by Sumner Welles caused a cabinet crisis in that powerful and distant southern republic, I marvel in retrospect that among us there had not previously occurred more spectacular things.

The tension of this position was accentuated as the inevitable entrance of the United States into the war became more evident. In this period still of indecision and uncertainty, the United States granted important concessions. The construction of the Trans-Isthmian Highway at its expense; the credit with the Export-Import Bank for the national highway; the acknowledgment of a rate of rental for the defense sites; very pleasing quotas of agricultural materials, and others. All these compensations had without doubt a military value for the United States but they were, nevertheless, benefits for Panama which appeared to have forgotten that the defense of the Canal is the defense of our own existence and that, therefore, we have as many obligations as the United States to contribute proportionately to safeguard it.

But this in itself was but of passing mention, while it was kept within the domestic boundaries. From the moment in which it passed the territorial frontiers in order to invade the field of the international policy of the Americas, from this moment the *Panameñismo* of Arnulfo Arias, interpreted by him as a constant hostility to the American government, undermined the foundations of his authority and prepared his consequent violent overthrow. His refusal to arm the ships that sailed with the Panamanian flag was a public ostentation of his disagreement with the policy of the United States and was the culminating and explosive note.

Many say that this was hands-down proof that Arnulfo Arias was at the service of the Axis nations and that they had seduced him with the promise of making him *Gauleiter* of all Central America the day that nazism triumphed over the democracies. Even the press took up these rumors and similar accusations are made in a book written by an American author who was in Panama only four days. It is extremely difficult for me to believe such a fantasy.

Of all the actions of Arnulfo Arias it can be inferred that he was "well inspired," we can put it that way, by the spectacular methods and results of the totalitarians, but from that inference to say that his conduct implied a deliberate complicity in the programs of world conquest of Germany, Italy, and Japan there is much difference. I cannot reconcile the deep *Panameñista* sentiment of his policy in general with the total renunciation that a submission to the Axis demanded. Arnulfo Arias loved himself too much to feel tempted to cease being the supreme chief of his country, even though it were a small and weak country, in order to convert himself into an executor of orders in the role of a subordinate of any other nation for all the sympathy that he may have had for it or for all that he admired the practical results of its doctrines, its methods, and its organizations.

One interpretation that does him more honor and that may not be very far from reality is that his foreign policy with regard to the United States was based on a bad guess. A bad guess that started with his belief that Germany would win the war and that the United States would keep out of it. A bad guess that terminated in a mistaken appreciation of the tactics of negotiations between a big and strong country and a small and weak country that had only as support the moral force of its just aspirations.

In effect, it could very well have been that Arnulfo Arias, taking into account the fact that the United States had to proceed with kid gloves in the matter of political pressure or open military intervention, at least in America and especially in Panama, was using this card as a trump in order to obtain the greatest number and extent of concessions that the United States would have been willing to make in order to be assured of the collaboration of Panama in the preparation of its war plans.

On the other hand, the specific concessions that the United States requested for the Canal Zone should have had for Arnulfo Arias the character of a mutual necessity and even to the point of a material advantage for Panama, because the country was going to be stimulated by a material and economic boom that signified work disseminated throughout the national territory and paid for with the resources of another State. In addition to this, it is possible that Arnulfo Arias was not very certain that Europe could invade America and in this event, at least during his term in office. He would have obtained all the benefits without risking a single sacrifice by his machine-made anti-Americanism.

In any way, it is clear how he analyzed the international situation of Panama with regard to the United States with the criterion of a simplist. It is seen that there did not enter into his estimates the reaction that could be expected from the impatient and determined military element and he didn't have the slightest notion that in times of international unrest in which we were living, military strategy always has the last word in matters of diplomacy.

This capital error of Arnulfo Arias and the lack of civic firmness of those called to approve and to support his acts in order to warn him of the magnitude of his aberration, caused the ruin of his government. Neither in the Republic of Panama nor in any other country of America could there be sustained a government which out of sincere sympathy or out of tactics of that of an international negotiator, permitted itself the luxury of placing obstacles in the united march of the Americas for the defense of democracy.

From this moment his destiny was sealed.

During the negotiation for the base sites, Ambassador Dawson had some personal conversations with Foreign Minister de Roux during which the latter made the observation that the United States had given Great Britain fifty destroyers in exchange for bases in the Caribbean islands and that the government of Panama felt that it should receive some comparable recompense because, as was pointed out by de Roux in a note of December 3, 1940:

The installations that the Army of the United States planned to distribute throughout the Republic of Panama will be considered, without doubt, in the event of a war emergency, as military objectives and the entire territory of the nation will become, without discrimination, a battlefield. Furthermore, the enemy attacks will be directed almost from preference, in the initial moments to destroy such installations with serious and incalculable damages for the inhabitants and the richness of the country. The facts enunciated are not, then, as the statement of General Van Voorhis appears to suggest *possible* but *certain*, and they preoccupy the Panamanian President in a very special manner.

This prompted an *aide-mémoire* from the American Embassy to Minister de Roux on December 30, 1940, in which it was explained that the arrangement "between the United States and Great Britain that involves the over-age United States destroyers and the rental of bases in possessions of the British in the Western Hemisphere was based on considerations of general hemispheric defense of which Panama is a beneficiary. The only cash payment that can be made is for the equitable value for any privately-owned land within the rented areas. It must be pointed out again that the bases are available for the use of all the American republics for the hemispheric defense plan, as has been stated by this government."

In this *aide-mémoire* the United States government invoked for the first time, at the request of the government of Panama, Article X of the General Treaty of 1936 in the following words: "It is the considered point of view of the Department that the present situation justifies the application of Article X of the General Treaty." And on that same day the American Embassy delivered a second *aide-mémoire* in which it was pointed out that the Mixed Commission was visiting the proposed base sites and that General Van Voorhis had stated that the task would require at least four months "in order to visit all the five auxiliary landing fields, eight emergency landing fields, seven antiaircraft sites, forty-six searchlight positions, and sixty-five miles of main road with right of way." The embassy went on to say: "General Van Voorhis has chosen from the different requirements the following sites that are considered of immediate importance," and then listed four auxiliary landing fields, six emergency landing fields, seventeen searchlight positions, and twenty miles of main road. Again Ambassador Dawson urged that the Government of Panama take immediate steps to contract those sites, most of which were private property, and that permission be granted to the American military authorities to effect preliminary preparation of those sites. *"In view of the extreme urgency of the measures that are contemplated for the defense of the Canal,"* Dawson concluded, *"the embassy is certain that the government of Panama will accede to the request from General Van Voorhis so that the rental contract of the abovementioned sites may receive prior considerations and that the authorization may be granted for their preliminary preparation."*

Replies were received to both *aides-mémoires*. In one de Roux wrote:

> Panama is ready to cooperate in the general defense of the hemisphere; but it must necessarily follow the interpretation that all the American nations have given to this obligation, according to which much cooperation cannot include any obligation that affects the sovereignty of the political independence of an American State. . . . The plan of defense of the Canal, prepared by the War and Navy Departments of the United States, represents practically the military occupation of the Isthmus by the American armed forces and this fact cannot be considered and acquiesced to by the Republic of Panama as a result of the obligation that falls on her in the defense of the hemisphere. No Panamanian citizen would sign an obligation that would have such scope, nor would any Latin-American nation, if they should be consulted, ask such sacrifice of Panama.

In the other *aide-mémoire*, de Roux rejected the request made by General Van Voorhis to occupy the sites immediately in the following language:

> The government of Panama has considered with especial sympathy the wishes of General Van Voorhis that "as soon as the sites referred to are visited a contract or contracts will be negotiated immediately on the spot without awaiting that the inspection of the other sites be finished," and sees no objection in acceding to his request as soon as the general basis of such contracts are agreed upon which are at present being discussed informally between the governments of Panama and the United States. When said condition is fulfilled, the government of Panama will proceed to authorize the preliminary preparation of the sites referred to.
>
> The fact that the National Assembly is meeting makes it impossible for the President to grant the authorization requested by General Van Voorhis without consulting the opinion of the Congress. And for that it

is indispensable to make known in advance the conditions agreed upon between both governments.

It is felt that the rapidity with which the rental contracts can be dispatched does not depend alone on the government of Panama, which declares that it finds itself in the best disposition to hurry the study and agreement of the aforesaid general bases for its part.

It would be appreciated if the Embassy of the United States would make known to General Van Voorhis this good disposition of the government of Panama and the just causes that prevent it from pleasing him today."

The fact that the National Assembly was in session could not possibly have been the governing factor in the rejection by President Arnulfo Arias; the majority of the legislators responded to his every beck and call.

Panamanian Ambassador Carlos N. Brin had requested in January, 1941, an audience with President Roosevelt, but the latter was too busy to see him. Dr. Brin delivered to Undersecretary of State Sumner Welles, at his request, a copy of a memorandum which he had been instructed to deliver in person to President Roosevelt. Minister de Roux, by transmitting twelve demands for compensation to his ambassador in Washington, by-passed Ambassador Dawson in Panama and did not furnish him with a copy of the demands. In short, negotiations in Panama had been summarily broken off since January 7. Dr. Brin reported the results of his conference with Welles to his government at once by cable and by diplomatic note:

Regarding the principal demands, Undersecretary Welles told me today that President Roosevelt refuses to consider them at the same time that negotiations are on for the establishment of the bases in territory under Panamanian jurisdiction. It is the opinion of the President, Sumner Welles informs me, that the present situation, which they consider of an emergency nature, demands the immediate and independent negotiation of those bases; that the government of Panama is obligated by the Treaty of 1936 to cooperate in every manner in the defense of the Canal and this would constitute a definite proof of said cooperation. He added that perhaps later, when the matter of the bases was already settled, they could consider the demands that our government has presented.

Also Undersecretary Welles told me that the government of the United

States wishes urgently that the government of Panama concede, as soon as possible, the necessary permission to start the preliminary work on the lands already indicated and that the Army believes that it is losing much time.

Mr. Welles told me that he would like the negotiations to be concluded in Panama instead of in Washington, for the American Ambassador and General Van Voorhis were fully familiar with their needs.

This diplomacy had been successful, for on February 5, 1941, Ambassador Brin informed Sumner Welles at luncheon that the government of Panama expected to resume negotiations in Panama. At 11:30 the next morning, Ambassador Dawson and General Van Voorhis were again received in audience by President Arias. After Ambassador Dawson had read to him the gist of a cablegram that he had received from Sumner Welles and that summarized the conference with Dr. Brin and asked that the government of Panama cooperate in the defense of the Canal, President Arias said that he wanted to renew the "desires of the government of Panama to cooperate with the United States in the defense of the Canal." He added that he considered it only fair that the United States government first contract some promise of compensation other than the mere rental for the lands. The discussion continued for thirty minutes and finally President Arias said that he would accept a memorandum from Ambassador Dawson as soon as possible, so that he could submit it to the cabinet and to the Foreign Relations Committee of the National Assembly "for consideration."

Ambassador Dawson had several more conversations with Minister de Roux, and on February 18, 1941, on the same date that Ambassador Brin was granted an audience with President Roosevelt, the American Embassy submitted to the government of Panama the memorandum requested by President Arias which invoked Article X of the General Treaty of 1936 and solicited immediate permission to occupy the sites. It is well to remember here that in his *aide-mémoire* of December 30, 1940, Ambassador Dawson also invoked Article X of that same treaty. Two more *aides-mémoires* were exchanged before the final one from Minister de Roux on March 5, 1941, which read in part:

So sincere and feeling is the wish of the government of Panama to cooperate in the effective defense of the Canal, and so firm are its plans to respect and comply with its obligations and with the entire Western

Hemisphere that "in view of the urgency with which, according to the American government, these defense sites are needed" it is ready to authorize immediately the military preparations required in the certainty that, with ample spirit of understanding and of justice, its aspirations may be duly consulted and considered sympathetically in the contracts that have to be signed later.

The government of the Republic of Panama will get together with the military authorities of the Canal Zone in order to provide the steps that may be pertinent to the indicated ends.

That afternoon President Arias issued a manifesto to the nation in which he advised the people of Panama that the base sites had been granted to the United States. What hurried Arias to his decision was the fact that the pressure from the State Department was increasing, and that President Roosevelt had emphasized to Ambassador Brin that a definite peril existed from the Nazi aviators who were still in Latin America and not very far from the Canal. Further delay was extremely dangerous.

The military high command, and the State Department, heaved a long and happy sigh of relief and work was commenced immediately on round-the-clock shifts, using both ordinary labor and soldiers because of the emergency. Pearl Harbor was only nine months away.

In April, 1941, it was announced that the Honorable Edwin C. Wilson, Ambassador to Uruguay, who had smoked out the pro-Nazis in Montevideo the year before, was to be transferred to Panama. Ambassador Dawson was to return to his old post in Montevideo. The Nazis began feverish activity because they expected Ambassador Wilson to come in with two chips on his shoulders and demand that President Arias clean them out of Panama. Cerjack-Boyna was the most surprised German one ever saw when this failed to materialize. As Ambassador Wilson presented his credentials to President Arias, the latter accepted them with thanks and entered into an explanation of Panama's desires to receive just compensation for the sacrifice which it was making for continental defense. The next morning Foreign Minister de Roux departed for Washington to attempt to negotiate in person twelve points that had been submitted to President Roosevelt on February 18.

And while Minister de Roux was in Washington, President Arias took three more steps which did not serve to dispel the totalitarian atmosphere that had enveloped him. He ordered the organization of the

Cachorros de Urraca (Cubs of Urraca), a youth organization patterned after the Hitler Youth or the Fascist *Ballila*, which was also to receive military training; and he submitted a bill to the National Assembly which virtually abridged the freedom of the press. The new press law said in part: "The press is not only a medium of expressing thought but also a means of expressing news, and it is necessary to regulate it to prevent the dangers of false and insidious news." The law provided that a bond of $1,000 had to be posted by daily newspapers, and a lesser amount posted by weeklies, in order to guarantee that the law would not be violated. Also Dr. Karl Brunner, the pro-Nazi city planner, had recommended that all roofs be painted red so that the aerial view of the city would be uniform. It was so ordered. There was suspicion that this measure was designed to guide Nazi airmen to the Canal Zone and to save Panama City from aerial bombardment.

At about this time a group of pro-American Panamanians had organized the Society of Friends of the United States. Its president, Dr. Horacio F. Alfaro, former Foreign Minister and former Minister to Washington, invited President Arias to accept the honorary presidency of the society. President Arias declined with thanks, replying that such an organization was absolutely unnecessary in Panama because every Panamanian was by force of circumstances a friend of the United States.

On July 4, 1941, the administration of Arnulfo Arias was to demonstrate its greatest affection for the United States. Foreign Minister de Roux gave a reception at the Club Union in honor of Ambassador Wilson. It was the first time in the history of Panama that such a gesture had been made by a foreign minister. Minister de Roux had returned from Washington without any definite agreement on the twelve demands that his government had made.

But soon Panama was to reaffirm her full neutrality. President Arnulfo Arias's sister, Doña Josefita Arias de Lueders, who had been married to a German formerly employed in the Hapag-Lloyd office in Panama, was appointed as Consul General in New York, being the first woman to hold that post. On August 15, 1941, she cabled her brother as follows: I BEG YOU TO INFORM ME URGENTLY WHETHER PANAMANIAN SHIPS MAY BE EQUIPPED WITH DEFENSE ARMAMENT.

That was the first time that Arias's Administration had been asked to take a stand on this matter. On August 19 Minister de Roux cabled Ambassador Brin in Washington the following instructions:

Please advise Consul General in New York by telephone that government cannot authorize that Panamanian flagships justify such procedure. Any measure taken by Panamanian ships that falls within dispositions of Article XII of Second Section of Maritime Neutrality Convention signed at Sixth Pan-American Conference is of exclusive responsibility of owners, Panamanian government not assuming any obligation as a result thereof. Ships entering belligerent zone do so under own responsibility and likewise damages they may suffer for disobeying dispositions international Maritime Neutrality will be at their own risk.

The Nazis continued to sink Panama's flagships because they were carrying munitions to Great Britain and to other Allies.

In August, 1941, the German government had requested the government of Panama and other nations of the Western Hemisphere to close their consulates in the occupied countries of Europe on the grounds that they were in zones that were subject to military activity. Costa Rica and other governments refused to close the consulates on the juridical grounds that the military occupation was but a transitory thing. On September 11, 1941, Minister de Roux announced that Panama was withdrawing its consuls from Germany and the occupied territories.

Minister Villalaz received instructions on September 16, 1941, to protest to the German government against the sinking of the S.S. *Sessa* and the S.S. *Montana*, two Panama flagships. On September 24, he sent the following apologetic report by air mail to Minister de Roux:

BERLIN, September 24, 1941

Legation of Panama, Berlin
No. 245
MR. MINISTER:

As soon as I received the cable of September 16 from Your Excellency in which you ordered me to protest and file a claim before the German government because of the sinking of the ships *Sessa* and *Montana* by a German submarine, I requested an audience of the Undersecretary of State in the Office of Foreign Affairs (because the Secretary of State was absent) who received me the following day at six in the afternoon.

After having spoken with him some moments about the matter that had brought me to see him, I delivered to him the note in which is contained the protest of the government of Panama and the claim for adequate indemnification for the sinking of the ships in question.

Yesterday he gave me the first reply which I communicated by the following cable:

"FOREIGN OFFICE PANAMA

I presented protest and claim. German foreign office will study and will investigate matter and reserves till later. Writing—VILLALAZ."

I suspended, then, my efforts for now until the German foreign office delivers to me its definitive reply and Your Excellency sends to me the documents needed to continue my action.

However, I can convey for the knowledge of Your Excellency today that the German government laments any incident that might hinder in the least bit the good relations existing between the two countries, with greatest reason because Panama has assumed a strictly neutral attitude in the face of the present European conflagration.

I promise Your Excellency that I will not abandon this matter and that I shall always make every effort to protect Panamanian interests.

I take advantage of this opportunity to subscribe myself to Your Excellency with the assurances of my highest consideration and esteem.

(*Signed*) F. VILLALAZ C."

On the same day that Villalaz wrote the above letter Ambassador Brin notified his foreign office the S.S. *Pink Star* had been sunk on September 19. On October 5 he advised that still another Panama flagship, the *I. C. White*, had been torpedoed on September 27.

Foreign Minister de Roux laid Minister Villalaz's note before a special cabinet session which President Arnulfo Arias had summoned for the morning of October 6, 1941. The cabinet reiterated the neutrality of the Republic of Panama in the following language:

The Cabinet Council has been unanimous in declaring that it cannot in any way authorize that Panamanian ships be equipped with armaments of any kind because the condition of neutrality which is maintained up to the present time by the American republics would not justify such a procedure.

From then on, the destiny of President Arnulfo Arias's first term in office was sealed. He was overthrown on October 9, 1941, while he was on an unauthorized holiday in Havana. He had traveled there secretly to keep a rendezvous with his mistress, one Anita de la Vega.

9. Overthrow of Arnulfo Arias

It was with deep pain that we who formed part of the old regime had witnessed how the noble program of social reforms that we had defended as sane principles had become in practice a system of persecutions that was undermining the foundations of our social and economic structure, which in the hands of irresponsible officials, had reached the extremes of human cruelty. The people felt in the living flesh the expressive whiplash of exorbitant fines, of arbitrary imprisonments, of unscrupulous abuses which kept the country in a state of constant anxiety incompatible with public peace and with the free exercise of the duties and rights of the citizen. Such was the painful development of events in recent months that even those of us who formed part of that regime were victims of the oppressive machinery to the extent that we felt ourselves impotent to remedy the evil by the common means of persuasion, nonconformity, and resistance. The situation was unbearable. The crisis became more acute every day.

In the above statement by Ricardo Adolfo de la Guardia, Minister of Government and Justice, ranking cabinet officer in President Arnulfo Arias's government, is contained a considerable portion of the background of the causes that led to the overthrow of the champion of *Pa-*

nameñismo on October 9, 1941. Dr. Arnulfo Arias's neutralism toward the Allied war effort also angered some political leaders and inspired the underground opposition to plan to overthrow him. Had not Ricardo Adolfo de la Guardia taken advantage of the opportunity that was handed to him on the morning of October 9, Arnulfo Arias would have found himself ousted by a bloody and decisive revolt on the night of October 11, one that had been planned to the minutest detail and that was destined to produce a political house-cleaning in the Republic. Instead, a bloodless coup catapulated de la Guardia into the presidency.

"The effect of the fall of Arnulfo Arias and consequently of *Panameñismo* was electrifying," wrote Dr. Felipe Juan Escobar:

> The Republic was shaken with a quaking of surprise and exhaled a sigh of relief. It was a purely emotional attitude that didn't halt to analyze methods, individuals, or legal consequences. There was a feeling that a tremendous load had been removed and that everyone was able to walk with the same freedom as he had normally been accustomed to. To that extreme had the national atmosphere been charged with unrest, uncertainties, and fears by the extravagances and mistakes of *Panameñismo*, or, better said, of the policy of Arnulfo Arias which he cherished with his primitive idea of the *Panameñista* creed. Business once again acquired confidence in its stability, which it had almost lost; the citizen lost that intolerable state of irritation that had been caused by an excess of domestic regimentation; and relations with the Zone authorities entered the easy path of rapid and unblocked official assent.

Between October 1, 1940, and October 6, 1941, President Arnulfo Arias made one of many grave mistakes. He sought in vain to gain financial control of the two major daily newspapers of Panama City, one of which was owned by his elder brother, former President Harmodio Arias. The latter was no adversary to belittle, and his subtle counterattacks devastated.

The new constitution, which had been proclaimed on January 2, had barred Chinese, Japanese, West Indian Negroes, Syrians, Arabs, and others as undesirable and under prohibitive immigration. President Arias immediately undertook the nationalization of commerce; his friends raided the shops and *cantinas* of Chinese merchants who were intimidated, fined, jailed, and sometimes deported after being forced to sell their holdings for virtually a pauper's penny. The Japanese, on the other hand, remained untouched. By including as undesirable the West Indian Negroes, President Arias had deprived approximately 70,-000 persons of citizenship.

A group of prominent politicians and capitalists organized an active underground bloc early in August, 1941, to overthrow Arias. They plotted with great caution and were very careful that no word should reach the ears of those loyal to Arnulfo Arias. Money was contributed to the cause by the local capitalists in liberal quantities. They needed arms and ammunition and none could be obtained locally. So they dispatched an emissary to Colombia to contact a notorious smuggler and gun runner, "El Cojo" (Gimpy) Gomez, to sound him out about leading an armed assault against the constituted authority in Panama. Gomez accepted, and the plotters continued their secret conclaves, finally setting the revolt date for the night of October 11.

Included in the plan of these revolutionists was the designation of a provisional president and the calling of a general election three months after the revolt to elect a constitutional president. Either Colonel Manuel Pino or Licenciate Victor Florencio Goytia, the attorney who had been a director of Pancho Arias's Partido Renovador since 1932, was to be the provisional president. Don Pancho Arias was to be the popular presidential candidate. But fate played an important part to alter these plans. Don Pancho's elder daughter, Pachis, was being married on October 3, 1941 in Lima, Peru, to one of the Miro Quesadas, a family that owned the newspaper, *El Comercio*. Don Pancho went to Peru to give his daughter in marriage and was not due back in Panama until October 11.

In the meantime, Arnulfo Arias announced his government's decision against the arming of merchant vessels. This decision gave increased encouragement to the plotters. "El Cojo" Gomez had already sailed for Panama from the Pacific coast of Colombia with ten men aboard his auxiliary sloop and a supply of arms and ammunition to await the signal to strike.

The senior Panamanian officers of the police force learned that President Arias had left Cristobal on the morning of October 7, aboard a Pan American World Airways plane destined for Havana, Cuba, under the name of "A. Madrid." They learned this through an officer of their own police force who had been at the Folks River landing when the plane took off. They decided to take the situation into their own hands. On the morning of October 8, they convinced Colonel Fernando Gomez Ayau, their Guatemalan adviser, that it was most expedient that he make an inspection trip to the northeastern province of Bocas de Toro on the Caribbean Sea and near the frontier of Costa Rica.

On the night of October 8 the active revolutionary committee met and conferred for hours, trying to reach a definite decision as to who should become provisional president, as the Panamanian officers had accepted the movement and were ready to participate in a bloodless coup. Tired of what appeared to them to be procrastination, they decided to call on their immediate superior, Minister of Government and Justice Ricardo Adolfo de la Guardia, advise him that President Arias had left the country illegally, and tell him that they felt someone with authority should take over the reins of government. De la Guardia, who never lacked personal courage, sped to police headquarters on Avenue A and assumed command of the police and the government about midnight, still acting as Minister of Government and Justice.

Leaders of the revolutionary committee called on de la Guardia and explained to him that the country was ripe for a revolution; that it was fed up with the abuses by Arnulfo Arias and the pro-Nazi clique surrounding him; that he should act without delay. The remainder of that night was one of grave decision for de la Guardia.

At eight o'clock the next morning he paid a spontaneous, unsolicited, and surprising call on United States Ambassador Edwin C. Wilson at the latter's residence and informed him that Arnulfo Arias had left the country without legal authority. He stated that he had assumed command of the police and that he was going to pave the way to assume the presidency himself before the day would end. He said further that his government would cooperate with the United States in the defense of the Canal. Ambassador Wilson listened, thanked him for the information, and then immediately telephoned Undersecretary of State Sumner Welles in Washington to report the latest developments. To say that Ambassador Wilson was displeased with the news he received would be a voluntary distortion of the truth, for Axis spies, potential saboteurs, and propagandists were still operating freely throughout the Republic of Panama. Besides, the reaffirmation of Panamanian neutrality, based on an article of the International Maritime Neutrality Convention which was signed in Havana and which the United States never had accepted or ratified, had not been considered by Americans as a very friendly act, especially after President Roosevelt had declared that an unlimited emergency existed and American naval vessels had been ordered to destroy Nazi submarines.

"The moment called for action," said de la Guardia, "decisive and rapid action. With the measure of civic patience overflowing, the country was able to witness with astonishment the unprecedented spectacle of a ruler absenting himself from his country without prior consultation, without the constitutional permission required, leaving the supreme command of the nation without a directing head at a time when anxiety, fear, uncertainty, and protest were in full evolution. Accompanied by the present Commandant of the National Police [Colonel Rogelio Fabrega], we assembled the highest officers and members of the valorous corps, and making a sacred invocation of their patriotism, their valor, and their manliness, I ordered them to comply with their duties. To this call these self-sacrificing servants of the nation responded immediately, making possible this bloodless victory without casualties."

De la Guardia summoned his colleagues in the Arias cabinet to a meeting at police headquarters and told them, to their surprise, that President Arias had departed for Havana. De la Guardia added that he planned to take over the government and invited the others to join him. Minister of Education José Pezet, who as First Designate was the constitutional successor, refused to join. So did Enrique Linares, Jr., Minister of Treasury and brother-in-law of Arias. And so did all others, except Minister of Agriculture and Commerce Ernesto Fabrega, a cousin of the chief of police. De la Guardia ordered the imprisonment of the rest of the cabinet. "El Cojo" Gomez, whose sloop had been lying at anchor in Panama Bay for three days, was no longer needed. The Second Designate, Minister to Mexico Ernesto Jaen Guardia, was on leave of absence in Panama. De la Guardia summoned him, his brother-in-law, to assume the presidency temporarily, appoint a cabinet, resign, and then let de la Guardia as Minister of Government and Justice become Provisional President. He did this because the Third Designate, Minister to Peru Anibal Rios, was in Lima. Besides, Rios was going to be forced to resign anyway.

Ernesto Jaen Guardia was sworn in as President just before noon. He appointed his cabinet, which included de la Guardia as Minister of Government and Justice; Dr. Octavio Fabrega, a cousin of the chief of police, former editor of *El Panama America*, and law partner of Dr. Harmodio Arias, as Minister of Foreign Affairs; Colonel Manuel Pino, ex-Chief of Police, as Minister of Public Works; Licenciate Victor Florencia Goytia as Minister of Education; Don José A. Sosa as Minister of Treasury; and Don Ernesto Fabrega as Minister of Agriculture and Commerce. Ninety minutes after he was sworn in, Ernesto Jaen Guardia resigned. De la Guardia, elected by the new cabinet, was sworn in by the supreme court. He immediately appointed Jaen Guardia as Ambassador to Washington.

The American press, radio, and public received the overthrow of President Arnulfo Arias with as much elation as did the people of Panama. De la Guardia enunciated the foreign policy of his government in the following terms:

> Our foreign policy will be one of peace with all the foreign powers but with this very important exception: that this peace is at present threatened throughout the world by the overwhelming forces of those governments which, in tragic Europe, have proclaimed conquest as a legitimate right and after absorbing and enslaving entire nations of the Old World, now threaten to extend their radius to the Western Hemisphere. Our attitude of peace, therefore, must be a watchful and alert peace, filled with foresight and caution, avoiding the destruction of the efficiency of our defense by the orthodox concept of a neutrality which, if strictly applied, would keep us lethargic and defenseless to awaken only when it was too late, when moral and material slavery had substituted the precious gift of freedom that should be dearer to us than life itself.

Arnulfo Arias was profoundly shocked when he received the news in Cuba. He told the press he had left Panama to visit an oculist in Havana; the press knew that the "oculist" was Anita de la Vega, a girl friend. Arias tried to obtain passage on the first airplane from Cuba to Panama, but Pan American World Airways replied that they were booked to capacity for weeks. He finally booked a slower passage on the S.S. *Cefalu* of the Standard Fruit and Steamship Company. When the steamer arrived in Cristobal less than a week after his overthrow,

Arnulfo Arias was welcomed on board by his father-in-law, Don Enrique Linares, Sr., and two friends and was urged to resign as president. He refused to do so. Then followed a series of incidents that culminated in Arias's rapid and involuntary exile from the country. As he was escorted from the steamer by Canal Zone police to the city limits of Colón, he was apprehended by Panamanian police and taken across the Isthmus to Panama City by special railroad motor car, and imprisoned at once.

Dr. Escobar omits the foregoing details from his biography of Dr. Arias, as well as the habeas corpus proceedings he filed to obtain the release of Dr. Arias. However, the government authorities let Arias languish in jail for five days before chartering a special Pan American World Airways plane to fly him to Nicaragua. He was not even issued a passport. In Nicaragua, President Anastasio Somoza kept Arias under constant surveillance. From Nicaragua he traveled to Mexico, then to Cuba, then to Venezuela, then to Brazil, and finally to Argentina, where he spent most of his exile (until October, 1945) and established a close friendship with Colonel Juan D. Peron, soon to become Argentina's president.

On the night of October 9, Berlin Radio broadcast the news of the overthrow of Arnulfo Arias and commented that "he was overthrown at the instigation of the United States government."

The *Wilhelmstrasse*, the *Palazzo Venezia*, Franco's foreign office, and Tokyo were among those who also asserted erroneously on October 9, 1941, that the government of the United States was responsible for Arias's removal from office.

The Nazis, of course, received the news of the change with extreme displeasure. They knew that their days of freedom of action in Panama were numbered.

Nine days after the overthrow of Arnulfo Arias, Cerjack-Boyna was declared *persona non grata* by the government of Panama. He was not handed his passport because Panama had been his legal residence for many years and because his wife was a Panamanian.

Cerjack-Boyna had to turn over the direction of his network of spies to someone else and go underground. He had already made such plans, so the action of the government of Panama came neither as a surprise nor as a shock to him. On December 7, 1941, Cerjack-Boyna fled to the diplomatic immunity of the German Legation to avoid his internment as an enemy alien. He was shipped out of Panama with the Axis diplomats to the United States for repatriation to Germany in a diplomatic exchange. His wife and children accompanied him. When Cerjack-Boyna arrived in Germany and saw the condition of the Reich late in 1942, he broke into tears and admitted to his wife that he was afraid Germany was going to lose the war. He was assigned to Trieste as chief of Nazi propaganda operation there, and his family resided in the resort city of Bled in Yugoslavia. The Panama government helped to obtain the return of Mrs. Cerjack-Boyna and her children to Panama late in 1945. Cerjack-Boyna later died, and one of his daughters married Harmodio Arias, Jr. The diplomatic representative of Vichy in Panama, Pierre Henri de la Blanchetai, who also was very pro-Nazi, departed for Argentina of his own volition shortly after the removal of Arnulfo Arias.

The pro-Nazi radio commentator, Julio Argain, was ordered to leave Panama promptly and to return to his native Chile, which he did posthaste. Later, Argain was to work as a journalist in Argentina and was a very competent one.

But there was another diplomat who did not leave Panama of his own accord. He was Don Carlos Arcos y Cuadra, Count of Bailen, who was the Spanish Minister. While the Panamanians were celebrating the thirty-eighth anniversary of their independence from Colombia on November 3, 1941, at the Union Club, the Count of Bailen walked in and was invited by a group of men to participate in a toast at their table. He declined the invitation with a slurring remark that "Panama is dominated by the Yankee boot." Present was Roberto de la Guardia, a brother of the President. Together with another countrymen, Ricardo Acevedo, de la Guardia escorted the Count of Bailen to the door and urged him to leave the club before an irate Panamanian bashed his face. The action by the Count of Bailen created an international diplomatic scandal, especially since it had occurred on Panama's independence day. Acting swiftly on November 10, 1941, the government declared the Count of Bailen *persona non grata* and handed him his passport. He eventually departed for Havana, Cuba, whence he was ousted for pro-Nazi activities. He finished the war at the Spanish Embassy in Berlin.

The Japanese, too, were soon to feel the effects of the foreign policy of the regime that replaced Arnulfo Arias. Some of the Japanese had sold out their businesses voluntarily before the exodus of Arnulfo Arias, but the larger stores had been assured by him that they would be permitted to remain in business. Between October 9, 1941, and October 28, 1941, the last of the Japanese stores had shut their doors.

On November 5, 1941, the Ministry of Agriculture and Commerce announced that the forty-six Japanese barbers who were still operating shops in the cities of Panama and Colón would either have to close their establishments or sell out. The decision was based on Article III of Law 24 (1941) on the Nationalization of Commerce and Industry, which article had been applied months before to the Chinese but had not been made applicable to the Japanese.

Japanese Minister Akiyama filed a note of protest at the Panama foreign office, which was promptly rejected by Foreign Minister Octavio Fabrega as "an insulting note." The Japanese closed shop. The mimeograph machine in the German Legation in Panama ceased operation by order of the government of Panama.

The Axis could no longer operate freely on the banks of the Panama Canal. Arnulfo Arias was by no means a finished man in Panamanian politics. He had developed a fanatical following; he had managed to produce a mystique around his personality; he had become the most controversial figure in the country. Waving the banner of *Panameñismo*, in 1948 he was one of three presidential candidates. His opponents were Domingo Diaz Arosemena and José Isaac Fabrega. It was a very close, hotly contested campaign; it was so close that the National Electoral Jury took three months, in the slowest count in history, to declare Domingo Diaz the winner by a narrow margin. Arnulfo Arias and his partisans were not to take what they considered to be a fraudulent election in silence. The seeds of political subversion began to blossom and were well watered for many months. Diaz, who was past seventy, became gravely ill and died in August, 1949, less than a year after taking office.

Diaz's death produced a series of dramatic developments that were to return Arnulfo Arias to power, and, later, to blast him out of the palace. Dr. Daniel Chanis, Jr., a highly respected surgeon, constitutional First Vice President, assumed the presidency. Chanis ruled without difficulty until November, 1949, when he clashed with Colonel José Antonio Remon, the Chief of Police. He signed a decree in which he fired Remon, but the latter declared himself in rebellion and fired Chanis instead.

Roberto F. Chiari, constitutional Second Vice President, was installed to replace Chanis. Chiari lasted four days, from November 20 to November 24, 1949. He refused to accept any dictation on appointments from Remon. Arnulfo Arias was then escorted to the palace and sworn in on the grounds that the election had been stolen from him. Thus, from November 19, 1949, to November 24, 1949, Panama achieved the undistinguished record of having three presidents.

Arnulfo Arias governed in relative peace for more than a year. His views on Panama's relationship with the United States and the Canal Zone had softened, and there was a friendly approximation on both sides. He accepted honors in the Zone, being the guest at military reviews and at receptions. But he was still impatient with the democratic processes of government, and in the spring of 1951 he had again irritated many people. He climaxed this with the issuance of a decree in which he declared himself dictator. The liberal opposition united and, under the leadership of Temistocles Diaz, son of the late Domingo Diaz, assembled the majority of the National Assembly to meet in the editorial offices of Diaz's newspaper, *La Nacion*. There, on the night of May 9, 1951, the legislators unanimously voted to oust Arias and summoned Don Alcibiades Arosemena, constitutional First Vice President to assume office.

Arias was not going to be ousted so easily. He entrenched himself in the presidential palace. The supreme court held an emergency session in the early morning of May 10, 1951, to hear a petition to rule on the action by the unusual meeting of the legislators the night before in the newspaper office. By a four-to-one vote it ruled the action *inobjetable,* or unobjectionable. Thus the ouster of the Arnulfo Arias had the support of the highest court of the land. There was pressure on Remon to force Arias out. Remon was undecided until just before noon, when he ordered the police to open an attack against the palace. After a four-and-a-half-hour battle Arias was finally blasted out of the palace, but not before Lieutenant Colonel Alfredo Lezcano Gomez, Commander of the palace guard, was killed trying to arrest Arias inside the palace, and not before a farewell orgy of drinking and destruction of furniture and fixtures. Arias's official photographer was also killed in the fighting.

As Arias was being escorted out of the palace under guard, the trousers of his white sharkskin suit were stained with blood. He waved at a small crowd outside and shouted: *"Volveremos"* (We shall return!). He was escorted to jail to face an impeachment trial. It was a picturesque trial by the National Assembly, for Arias nonchalantly entered the legislature carrying a copy of the book, *Kon-Tiki,* which he feigned reading while the trial progressed. His prosecutor was the same man who wrote a biography of him in 1941, Dr. Felipe Juan Escobar, who was appointed by the assembly. Arias was impeached and divested of all powers and of all his civil rights.

He retired to his coffee *finca* in Boquete in the highlands of the province of Chiriqui, near the Costa Rican frontier. There he devoted his energies to improving his profitable coffee crop, while his still-loyal partisans campaigned ceaselessly to obtain a restoration of his civil rights. His wife, Ana Matilde Linares, was to die from cancer before those rights were restored by a law enacted by the National Assembly that was elected in 1960. The law was signed by President Roberto F. Chiari, who won over two candidates in what was generally accepted as having been the most honest election ever held in Panama. The voters went to the polls with ballot boxes they could see were empty when voting started. The boxes had plastic sides, leaving no opportunity for double-voting; President Ernesto de la Guardia, Jr., had contracted the services of a Canadian mission to establish a fraud-proof electoral identity-card system. The defeated candidates were former President Ricardo Manual Arias Espinosa, who served from January 13, 1955, until October 1, 1956, and Victor Florencio Goytia, of the Civil Resistance party, and an ex-Chief Justice of the Supreme Court.

In the interim, on January 2, 1955, Remon was assassinated at the Juan Franco Race Track. Standing next to him a few minutes before the assassin's bullet snuffed out his life was Thelma King. It was suspected that she may have been the "finger girl" for the assassin, should he have been an imported trigger man. José Ramon Guizado, constitutional First Vice President, was arrested and imprisoned on an alleged confession by Ruben Miró Guardia, a nephew of former President Harmodio Arias, that he had killed Remon on order from Guizado.

The Remon assassination never was resolved to anybody's entire satisfaction. Miró repudiated his confession but he and other alleged accomplices were not brought to trial for more than two years. Guizado received a political trial before the National Assembly, which formally indicted him as an accomplice of the murder and impeached him, thus legalizing "Dicky" Arias's succession as constitutional Second Vice President. After a protracted public trial, Miró and the other alleged accomplices were acquited by a jury by a four-to-three vote. Guizado was then released from prison.

10. The Defense Bases Fiasco

There were wide holes in the defenses of the Panama Canal in 1941 and 1942. The gaps were so great that an enemy air task force could have slipped through the flimsy screen then cast by our air reconnaissance patrols and attacked and destroyed vital installations. The attackers would have met the most concentrated and devastating barrage of antiaircraft fire in military history, but some planes would undoubtedly have succeeded in penetrating the barriers of defense within the five miles of land on each side of the Canal. To plug these holes and to endeavor to make them as impregnable as possible against enemy attacks, it was necessary to extend the defenses of the Canal into other republics—to the south, to the north, to the east, and to the west—and also to scatter 134 bases and other sites throughout the territory of the Republic of Panama.

Work was being pushed day and night on the completion of a landing strip and other utilities on Seymour Island in the Galapagos archipelago, almost one thousand miles from the Canal. The government of Ecuador let the United States build an air base on the mainland at Salinas. Consequently, four-engined patrol planes could fly from Salinas to Galapagos and then proceed north-northeast to Guatemala and return. Peru had also made available the El Pato airport at Talara, which had been operated by the International Petroleum Company, and which was expanded under United States Army Air Force supervision.

The official negotiations for the sites in the Republic of Panama, which had started prior to the inauguration of President Arnulfo Arias, terminated on the morning of May 18, 1942, with the signing in the foreign office in Panama City of the Defense Sites Agreement. Foreign Minister Octavio Fabrega announced to the citizens of Panama that the government of the United States had agreed to compensate the government of Panama in exchange therefor as follows:

1. The United States will transfer to Panama, free of cost, the property and dominion over the waterworks and sewerage systems in the cities of Panama and Colón, renouncing the right to acquire new land or buildings for the purpose of sanitation in the cities of Panama and Colón.

2. The United States will transfer to Panama, without cost whatever, the virtual totality of the lots of land of the Panama Railroad Company in the city of Colón, and the totality of the lots of said company in the city of Panama. The value of these lots has been fixed at approximately twelve million balboas (B/12,000,000). In the exchange of notes an exact description is made of the area comprised in the lots to be transferred.

3. The two governments shall intensify their effort for preventing the contraband traffic from the Canal Zone and with this purpose in view, the government of said Zone shall appoint a representative to be in contact with the government of Panama for continuously adopting the necessary measures.

4. The United States agrees to build a bridge or tunnel across the Canal as soon as the present emergency ends. In the meanwhile, the United States agrees to improve, as far as possible, the present ferry service.

5. As expressed in the lease agreement, the United States agrees to contribute one-third of the total annual cost of reparation and maintenance of the roads used by the military forces of the United States in Panama. These repairs shall be made by Panama.

6. The United States agrees to cooperate insofar as possible in carrying out the Panamanian policy in matters of immigration tending toward the immigration of healthy, hard-working elements capable of contribut-

ing toward the ethnic, economic, and demographic improvement of the country.

7. The government of the United States agrees that the military police and the Canal Zone police shall use only their clubs when in Panamanian territory.

8. The government of the United States agrees that whenever there is an excess of electric energy from the Panama Canal's generating plants at the Madden Dam, said energy shall be furnished at the request of the Panamanian government, to the cities of Panama and Colón, at the prices agreed upon between the two governments.

9. The United States agrees to assume, free of obligations for Panama, the total cost of the concrete highway to Rio Hato, and consequently it will cancel the debt of two-and-a-half million dollars ($2,500,000) which was contracted for the purpose by Panama with the Import and Export Bank of the United States.

10. The United States agrees to transfer the Panama railroad station and its dependencies to another site to be furnished by the government of Panama and which may be satisfactory.

11. The United States shall give favorable consideration to the claims which Panama may present in regard to serious interruptions of traffic in Panama caused by troop movements in Panamanian territory, and

12. The United States shall grant to Panama the right-of-way for the construction of an oil pipeline connecting Panama with the Port of Balboa at a point agreed upon by both governments. The United States also agrees to give facilities for unloading petroleum products from vessels anchored in Balboa and for the transmission of said products over the aforementioned pipeline at a reasonable cost. Panama will pay the cost of said pipeline.

On August 13, 1942, President Roosevelt asked Congress for legislation to enable him to implement the above concessions, stating in his message that Panama's cooperation in the current international crisis was tangible evidence that relations between the two countries were based firmly upon "the recognition of mutual interest and the disposition to assume common responsibilities."

"In my opinion," he added, "the time has come for this government to make certain concessions which have been desired by the Republic of Panama over a period of years and in this manner correct certain factors in the relation between the two countries which do not make for confidence and friendship between our two countries." He explained that it was expedient to return all real estate holdings in Panama and Colón acquired under agreements for the Panama Railroad Company "through concessionary contracts with the Republic of New Granada signed in 1850, 1856, and 1867, and as an element of such ownership the Panama Railroad Company has of course over a period of years rented property to Panamanian citizens—merchants, businessmen, and residents—and is in fact the principal landlord in Colón. For obvious reasons, this is unsatisfactory. I think, therefore, that this government should promptly withdraw from the real estate business in the Republic of Panama and convey to that country its rights, title, and interest as well as its reversionary rights to all Panama Railroad Company lands in the cities of Panama and Colón which are not needed for the operation of the railroad or for the operation, maintenance, sanitation, or protection of the Canal.

The Congress approved President Roosevelt's request and Panama thus benefited to the extent of almost $20 million in outright compensation for the lease of the defense sites, over and above the annual rentals to be paid for the land occupied by United States forces. The diplomatic hurdles on the defense sites question had, at long last, been overcome, at least for the period of actual hostilities. Thus it was possible to increase the iron ring of defenses around the Panama Canal.

The foregoing twelve points, it is well to remember, were substantially the same demands that President Arnulfo Arias had submitted to President Roosevelt early in 1941.

Little was it thought on that morning of May 18, 1942, with the United States' participation in World War II only five months old, that the Defense Sites Agreement would be the subject of a protracted international dispute four years later between Panama and the United States. But such a conflict was destined to arise, due largely to the lack of militant, alert diplomacy on the part of our Department of State. President Ricardo Adolfo de la Guardia gave way to political pressure in December, 1944, abolished the constitution of 1941, and summoned national elections for a constitutional assembly, which elected his successor—Don Enrique A. Jiménez, who had been Ambassador in Washington—on June 15, 1945. The main task of the constitutional assembly was to draft and approve a new constitution, one more democratic than that of 1941.

On October 31, 1945, the newspapers in Panama City announced that Foreign Minister Alfaro and former Foreign Minister Octavio Fabrega had been summoned by the constitutional assembly to enlighten the legislators on Panama's interpretation of the Defense Sites Agreement. Three questions were prepared in writing by Deputy José Isaac Fabrega, another former Foreign Minister. The gentlemen cited were requested to be prepared to answer this interrogation on November 6, 1945. The questions arose from a debate governing an article on jurisdictional rights of the Republic which was being written into the new constitution. The pertinent part of the article is headed:

JURISDICTIONAL LIMITATIONS ARE RECOGNIZED AS STIPULATED IN PUBLIC TREATIES EFFECTED PREVIOUSLY TO THIS CONSTITUTION.

The questions submitted were:

1. What is the interpretation given by the Panama government to the provision in the Defense Sites Agreement of May 18, 1942, which states that the defense sites will be vacated and their use suspended one year after the final peace treaty becomes effective? What is the government's interpretation of the final peace treaty ending the armed conflict?

2. Are all defense sites to be vacated by the United States forces one year after the final peace treaty becomes effective or are there certain sites which, under special agreement, must be vacated prior to that time? If the latter applies, what defense sites are involved and when must they be vacated?

3. What is the expiration date for the authority given to the United States for using the section of the national highway when air activities so require?

On November 1, 1945, Brigadier General Frank T. Hines, former Director of the Veteran's Administration, presented his credentials as Ambassador to Panama, a post which had been vacant since early January, 1945, when Avra Warren left to become Director of the Office of American Republic Affairs in the Department of State. Foreign Minister Alfaro appeared before the constitutional assembly with a prepared statement which read:

Article I of the agreement covering the rental of the defense sites in the Republic of Panama, celebrated between the government of Panama and the United States the 18th day of May, 1942, referring to the lands comprised within said sites, says as follows:

"These lands shall be evacuated and the use thereof by the United States of America shall terminate one year after the date on which the definitive treaty of peace which brings about the end of the present war shall have entered into effect."

The Executive Power is of the criterion that the expression "definitive treaty of peace which brings about the end of the present war" refers to any pact, agreement, act, or instrument celebrated between the belligerent countries, in virtue whereof the hostilities inherent to the state of war have ceased definitively. Consequently, the Panamanian Executive considers that treaties which successively brought about the end of the war were: (1) the divers instruments signed by the German military commanders and the Allied military commanders, by virtue whereof the land, naval, and air forces that were found in Germany and in some of the occupied countries surrender unconditionally; and, (2) the instrument of unconditional surrender signed aboard the battleship *Missouri* in Tokyo Bay the 1st of September of 1945 by the representatives of the Emperor of Japan and the military and naval commanders of the United States, Great Britain, China, France, Russia, Australia, Holland, and New Zealand.

Now, then, as the capitulation aboard the *Missouri* was the last to be held and was therefore the treaty that put an end to the hostilities existing between the Axis countries and the United Nations, said capitulation must rightly be understood as the definitive peace treaty that brought about the end of the war.

The general text of the agreement covering rental of the defense sites and the negotiations that preceded it, demonstrate that said agreement had in mind two contrary situations, to wit: the existence or nonexistence of hostilities, or, in other words, the existence or nonexistence of war or war emergency; and it also had in view that one year after the cessation of war, of hostilities, or of emergency, the defense sites should be evacuated. The third clause of Article I shows that when, referring to the expressed period of one year from the date of definitive treaty of peace it says the following:

"If within that period the two governments believe that, in spite of the cessation of hostilities, a state of international insecurity continues to exist which makes vitally necessary the continuation of the use of any of the said defense bases or areas, the two governments shall again enter into mutual consultation. . . ."

As can be seen, tied as the clause is with the anterior one, the expression "cessation of hostilities" is used with the equivalent significance of the expression "definitive treaty of peace which brings about the end of the present war." It also should be observed that in Article V the stipulation is repeated relative to the abandonment of the defense sites one year from the end of the emergency and that, as in Article I, there is employed in the second clause the expression "definitive treaty of peace that brings about the end of the present war," while in the third the phrase "cessation of hostilities" is employed with equivalent significance.

In the communiqué issued by the Ministry of Foreign Affairs on the same day that the agreement was signed, reference was made to this in the following terms:

"The Executive Power announces that at noon today there was signed in the Ministry of Foreign Affairs the agreement celebrated between the government of Panama and the government of the United States of America by which Panama gives in rental to the United States certain areas of land within the Republic of Panama destined for the defense and effective protection of the Panama Canal DURING THE PRESENT EMERGENCY."

It is clear that the word "EMERGENCY" used in this communiqué refers to the war emergency, that is to say, to the period of the existence of active hostilities, which period definitively ended for all the belligerent powers upon the effectuation of the unconditional surrender of the Japanese aboard the *Missouri*.

Further on the Ministry said in the same communiqué:

"The government of Panama has taken all the necessary caution in order to make clear, in definitive and indubitable manner, that these territorial concessions do not extend further than the period OF THE ACTUAL EMERGENCY, that is to say, that the lands given in rental for defense sites, will be occupied only for the NECESSARY TIME THAT THE PRESENT WAR EMERGENCY REQUIRES."

The United States manifested in the course of the negotiations its wish that the occupation of these lands could last "until such time as the two governments agree that the causes for said occupation have ended." Upon proposing this formula the United States manifested that it was not its intention to occupy the lands in question for any time greater than would be required while there reigned a state of international insecurity as that which actually confronts us. The government of Panama preferred to propose another formula that expressed with greater precision and exactness the period of occupation, which formula was accepted by the United States. The formula proposed by Panama establishes that these lands shall be occupied for one year after the date on which the definitive treaty of peace which brings about the end of the war shall have entered into effect, it being understood that if the circumstances should require the two governments would consult anew and would enter into a new agreement.

It would be erroneous to think that this definitive peace treaty is the possible treaty that the United Nations have to enter into with the Axis powers by means whereof normal relations would be reestablished with those countries. That interpretation is conducive to the absurd because such peace treaty, if it is ever signed, may not be signed for one or two generations, perhaps within one-quarter or one-half century when the United Nations shall have completed the task of reeducating the German and the Japanese people in a manner that qualifies them for a democratic and peaceful life within the international community of States and when the last vestiges of nazism, fascism, or political aggression of any kind shall have disappeared forever.

Finally, as I will say further on in my reply to questions No. 2 and No. 3, what was always in the minds of the negotiators was the period of emergency, that is to say, that active period of hostilities that characterize the state of war. This state of war must be understood in the general sense and it is obvious from the words that they meant the existence of hostilities and the prosecution of armed battle.

In his lengthy and detailed replies to the other two questions, Foreign Minister Alfaro reiterated the stand of his government that the Defense Sites Agreement terminated on September 1, 1946, and that the government of the United States would have to abandon all bases in the Republic of Panama on that date, and he explained that fifty-one bases had already been abandoned.

Former Foreign Minister Octavio Fabrega, who had completed the negotiations and had signed the Defense Sites Agreement, followed Alfaro and addressed the legislators. He added some cogent details to Minister Alfaro's interpretation of the agreement.

As the embassy of the United States insisted once again in the formula suggested by it, I wrote the following note to Ambassador Wilson on March 6, 1942:

"As I have had occasion to state to Your Excellency on various occasions, it is impossible for the government of Panama to accept any clause which, in referring to the period of occupation of the lands destined for defense sites, permits, or leaves in doubt, the fact that these lands may be occupied for an indefinite period even after the actual war emergency has ended. The occupation of Panamanian territory that exists in fact today by military forces of the United States is so vast that it covers zones of lands situated, without exception, in all the provinces in which the Republic is divided. This occupation on such grand scale can be supported by the government as a painful necessity during the period of the present war emergency and as a sample of its wish to cooperate in the defense of the Panama Canal but it interferes seriously with our territorial integrity, with our life as a free and sovereign nation, and gives place, with much frequency, to disagreeable incidents, injurious to the good name of our Republic.

"This government has not vacillated in lending its full and decided cooperation in the fact of the actual war emergency. But it has to respond, at the same time, to its patriotic duty not to auhorize this occupation for an indefinite period later than the termination of the present war.

"This is so vital a point for my government that I must state to Your Excellency that the formula contained in the first clause that my government now proposes represents the maximum of our concessions as regards the duration of the mentioned occupation and is, therefore, our definitive proposal."

As the embassy insisted once again in the original formula, a conference was held in the presidency of the Republic between the President, the Ambassador of the United States, and the Foreign Minister, who was myself at the time. And upon discussing the point, President de la Guardia stated to Ambassador Wilson that that note expressed the final and definitive criterion of the Panamanian government and that upon not being accepted by the government of the United States, the Panamanian government would see itself in the painful necessity of declaring the negotiations suspended. The Ambassador of the United States stated that he would confer urgently with his government, and he did and notified us very shortly that his government did not accept the formula proposed by the Panamanian government. Then, in a memorandum that he presented to the Panamanian foreign office, Ambassador Wilson proposed the insertion of the word "definitive" to the phrase used by us about the treaty of peace.

I asked him what was the intention of the government of the United

States upon suggesting the introduction of the word "definitive"; he replied more or less in these words: "This war is a *sui generis* type of war; it is a war which commenced with a treacherous attack and in which we must be prepared for all kind of surprises. It is possible that during the war an armistice of a doubtful nature might be suggested that in reality has the nature of a truce; it is possible that the Japanese may sign an armistice when in reality they are preparing for an unexpected attack like that of Pearl Harbor, which occurred precisely when Japan was undertaking negotiations of peace and friendship with us. It is for this reason that the government of the United States wants to include in the agreement that the treaty must be final and definitive."

In view of this clarification and in view of the fact that the clause was sufficiently clear in order not to permit other interpretations and that the government of the United States had abandoned its previous position and acceded to the formula proposed by the government of Panama, the government [of Panama] accepted the formula proposed by the United States.

The only thing that I have to add is that there can be no other treaty of peace that has brought about the end of this war than that signed aboard the *Missouri* and this is deduced by means of these considerations: It is true that in the past war an armistice was conditional. The beaten powers stated that they accepted the armistice on the basis of the fourteen points enunciated by President Wilson. In the present war the surrender has been unconditional; no subsequent treaty is necessary to end the war emergency; the future treaties that may be signed are not treaties that are designed to end the state of war or to promulgate peace, but they will be treaties whose purpose will be to take preventive measures against wars.

Following the addresses by both Alfaro and Fabrega, the constitutional assembly passed a resolution referring to Article III of the new constitution which read in part: "That in any case we go on record as saying that in accordance with the point of view expressed today by Dr. Ricardo J. Alfaro in behalf of the Executive, the date when the United States must abandon the lands which have been rented as military bases ends the 1st of September of 1946." This meant, therefore, that according to Panama's interpretation of the agreement, eighty-three sites had to be vacated by that date.

On November 7, 1945, Secretary of State James F. Byrnes told a press conference in Washington that the United States would fulfill its agreement with the Panamanian government on the withdrawal of American forces from the defense installations there. He added that, although he was not familiar with all the details of the agreement, he could assure Panama that the United States would observe them.

Immediately the constitutional assembly reacted on November 8, 1945, with another resolution proposed by Deputy José Isaac Fabrega which read:

1. That the questioning of Minister of Foreign Affairs Dr. Ricardo J. Alfaro in connection with the abandonment of the defense sites was not due to any doubt about the fulfillment by the United States of its obligations, contained in the agreement of May 18, 1942, for the Panamanians entertain the established conviction that the aforementioned nation is, in peace, the worthy executor of the same principles of international morals for which it fought heroically in the war.

2. That the aforementioned questioning based exclusively on the necessity of obtaining from the Panamanian Executive, for the purposes of interpretation of one of the articles of the bill of the constitution, an accurate report for the date on which said total abandonment must be carried out.

3. That the National Constitutional Assembly, in its own name and as spokesman for the Panamanian people, is pleased to go on record as saying that the spontaneous and categoric statement of the Secretary of State of the United States, Mr. James Byrnes, in which he said that the defense sites will be abandoned in the periods stipulated in the corresponding agreement, is a new and decisive manifestation of the policy of sincerity, consideration, and mutual understanding that the United States of America has been following with the other states of the hemisphere, and especially with the Republic of Panama.

It was requested that the Minister of Foreign Affairs forward a transcription of the present declaration to the Secretary of State of the United States, Mr. James Byrnes.

Foreign Minister Alfaro dispatched the contents of the above resolution to the embassy of Panama in Washington for transmittal to the Department of State. There the matter ended until August 30, 1946.

The unilateral interpretation by the government of Panama was not challenged by our Department of State. On August 30, 1946, former

Foreign Minister Octavio Fabrega wrote the following letter to President Jiménez which was published the same date in the *Panama American*:

DEAR MR. PRESIDENT:

As a Panamanian citizen and as the former Minister of Foreign Affairs who signed the Agreement for the Lease of Defense Sites entered into by Panama and the United States, I respectfully suggest that it is advisable that the Panamanian people be informed of the position which will be taken by the government of Panama on September 1, 1946, on which date all of the defense sites leased to the government of the United States should be vacated by the U.S. forces.

It is of public knowledge that said agreement established a term of occupation which should be extended to one year after the definitive covenants of peace which put an end to hostilities, and that the term of one year, as was opportunely explained to the constitutional assembly by Foreign Minister Dr. Ricardo J. Alfaro, began to run at the time of the signing of the unconditional surrender on board the *Missouri*—that is, on September 1, 1945, and consequently expires on September 1, 1946.

It is true that the agreement provided that within that term of one year after the "cessation of hostilities" the two governments could enter into a new agreement if imperative circumstances of international insecurity should be required. But the government of the United States has not initiated new negotiations in this matter, nor will it have vacated the above mentioned sites on September 1, 1946.

Undoubtedly, then, from that date the unauthorized occupation of the defense sites will create a new *de facto* situation with serious repercussions on the sovereignty and territorial integrity of the Republic.

Respectfully yours,

OCTAVIO FABREGA

On the same day that the above letter was sent to President Jiménez, Ambassador Hines delivered in person a note to Foreign Minister Alfaro in which the United States requested that consultations be undertaken to ascertain whether or not the then existing state of international insecurity "justifies an extension of time for the use of any or all of the defense sites existing on Panamanian soil."

On the morning of August 31, President Jiménez issued the following communiqué:

The Minister of Foreign Affairs has informed the press that at noon yesterday the Ambassador of the United States personally delivered a note in which the government of the United States invoked Article I of the Agreement on Defense Sites, signed May 18, 1942, and requests the government of Panama to enter into immediate consultations for an exchange of views to determine whether the existing international situation justifies an extension of time for the use of any or all of the defense sites within the term of one year. The Ministry of Foreign Affairs further said that the Ambassador's note was considered at a cabinet meeting held Friday night and that it will be replied to today in a note which will define the position of the government of Panama with regard to the matter.

On the afternoon of August 31, Minister Alfaro delivered his government's reply to Ambassador Hines, in which he pointed out that during the past twelve months the United States made no representations to Panama regarding the need for a new agreement, or did it object to any of the statements made by him in his interpretation of the agreement before the constitutional assembly on November 8, 1945. Here is the text of the note:

Mr. Ambassador:

I have the honor to refer to Your Excellency's courteous communication No. 259, which you handed to me personally at noon yesterday, and in which you make reference to the defense sites or areas, the use of which was temporarily ceded to the government of the United States of America in pursuance to the terms of the May 18, 1942 agreement between the two governments.

I begin by thanking Your Excellency for the terms of praise for the Republic of Panama with which reference is made to the cooperation it gave to the war effort of the United Nations during the last World War, which cooperation the government of Your Excellency considers to be of inestimable value and to have contributed in incalculable proportion to the happy termination of the war.

Your Excellency invokes Article I of the aforementioned agreement on defense sites and states that your government considers as being in the common interest of both countries that the matter of the defense bases be discussed anew, including it in the agenda for discussion in the round-table conference, and that, under present circumstances, it is considered of vital importance that the use be continued of certain of the defense sites, and also that the need for a limited number of new sites be studied.

In this regard, it is my duty to state to Your Excellency in behalf of my government, the following:

Article I, Section I, of the Agreement on Defense Sites mentioned in the note to which I am replying states the following:

"The Republic of Panama grants to the United States the temporary use for defense purposes of all the lands referred to in the memorandum attached to this agreement and forming an integral part thereof. These lands shall be evacuated and use thereof by the United States of America shall terminate one year after the date on which the definitive treaty of peace which brings about the end of the present war shall have entered into effect. If within this period the two governments believe that, in spite of the cessation of hostilities, a state of international insecurity continues to exist which makes vitally necessary the continuation of the use of any of the said defense sites or areas, the two governments shall again enter into mutual consultation and shall conclude the new Agreement which the circumstances require."

Article V of the agreement strengthens this stipulation in the following terms:

"The Republic of Panama and the United States reiterate their understanding of the temporary character of the occupation of the sites covered by this agreement. Consequently, the United States, recognizing the importance of the cooperation given by Panama in making these temporary defense sites available and also recognizing the burden which the occupation of these sites imposed on the Republic of Panama expressly undertakes the obligation to evacuate the lands to which this contract refers and to terminate completely the use thereof at the latest within one year after the date on which the definitive treaty of peace which brings about the cessation of the present war shall have entered into effect. It is understood, as has been explained in Article I, that if within this period the two governments believe that, in spite of the cessation of hostilities, a state of international insecurity continues to exist which makes vitally necessary the continuation of the use of any of the said defense bases or sites, the two governments shall again enter into mutual consultation and shall conclude the new agreement which the circumstances require."

The interpretation of this article brought about three questions made to the undersigned in the constitutional assembly during the session held November 6 of last year. The first of these questions was:

1. What is the interpretation given by the Executive Power to the

following expression contained in the first paragraph of Article I of the Agreement on the rental of Defense Sites, signed by Panama and the United States on May 18, 1942: "These lands shall be evacuated and use thereof . . . shall terminate one year after the date on which the definitive treaty of peace which brings about the end of the present war shall have entered into effect"? In other words the Minister of Foreign Affairs must report as to what the Executive Power holds to be "the definitive treaty of peace."

To this question the undersigned replied as follows: "The Executive Power is of the opinion that the expression 'definitive treaty of peace' refers to any pact, agreement, act, or instrument agreed upon among the belligerent countries by virtue of which the hostilities inherent to the state of war shall have ceased definitively. Therefore, the Panamanian government considers the following to be covenants which, successively, have ended the war: (1) the various instruments signed by the German military commanders and the Allied commanders in various parts of Europe and by virtue of which there were surrendered unconditionally the land, naval, and air forces in Germany and in some of the occupied countries; (2) the instrument of unconditional surrender signed aboard the battleship *Missouri* in Tokyo Bay on September 2, 1945 by the representatives of the Emperor of Japan and the military and naval commanders of the United States, Britain, China, France, Russia, Australia, Holland, and New Zealand.

"Now then, since the capitulation aboard the *Missouri* was the last to be agreed upon, and it was therefore the treaty that ended the hostilities between the Axis countries and the United Nations, that capitulation must be correctly regarded as the definitive treaty of peace which ended the war."

The second question referred to the naval base on Taboga Island which already has been returned, and, therefore, there is no point in dealing with it.

The third question was couched as follows:

3. When is the date of expiration for the authority granted to the United States to utilize the section of the national highway which traverses the Rio Hato region for aerial activities in connection with the base of the same name and to stop traffic over that section when required by such activities?

With regard to this question, the answer given by the undersigned was as follows:

"The terms of the agreement contained in the exchange of notes are so clear that they require no additional comment. No reference is made to a period of one year following the cessation of hostilities, as in the general agreement. Reference is made only to the period of the war emergency. The emergency has ceased and, therefore, so has the period for which authority was granted relative to traffic over the section of the highway which is traversed by the main runway of the Rio Hato landing field."

Since this is a matter already settled, there is no reason for my extending myself in this regard.

The statements by the undersigned before the National Assembly never have been contradicted or objected to in any manner by the government of the United States. On the contrary, that government gave them tacit consent by expressing its willingness and disposition to comply with its obligations with Panama as reported by the Associated Press in a dispatch published in the local press on November 7, 1945, which reads as follows:

"WASHINGTON, Nov. 7—(AP)—Secretary of State James Byrnes at a press conference today said that United States will fulfill its agreement with the Panamanian government on the withdrawal of American forces from the defense installations there.

"The question arose when the Secretary was asked to comment on the statement by Panamanian Foreign Minister Ricardo J. Alfaro that the United States is bound to vacate eighty-three defense sites by September, 1, 1946. Secretary Byrnes said there was a written agreement on this subject and that although he was not familiar with all the details, he could assure Panama that the United States would observe them."

The final portion of Article I of the Agreement on Defense Sites states the following:

"If within this period (that of one year aforementioned) the two governments believe that, in spite of the cessation of hostilities, a state of international insecurity continues to exist which makes vitally necessary the continuation of the use of any of the said defense bases or areas, the two governments shall again enter into mutual consultation and shall conclude the new agreement which the circumstances require."

Now then, it was not until yesterday that the government of Panama learned that Your Excellency's government deems that in spite of the cessation of hostilities there still exists a state of international insecurity which makes imperative the continuation of some of the defense sites. Panama, on its part, is not charged with the direction of military operations or the formulation of strategic plans which may require use by the armed forces of the United States of certain defense sites in its territory, or has it had a basis to arrive at the conclusion that there exists a situation of international insecurity which demands the continuation of certain of the defense sites; and up to the present time, on the last day of the period of one year, during which the government of Panama has considered that the aforementioned defense sites should be returned, there has been no development by virtue of which the government of Panama has acquired, through self-perception, the knowledge and the conviction that there is a need for negotiating a new agreement on defense sites. There has not arisen, therefore, the condition which is required by the second paragraph of Article I of the agreement quoted below for the negotiation of the said agreement:

"If during this period THE TWO GOVERNMENTS believe that, in spite of the cessation of hostilities, a state of international insecurity continues to exist . . . the two governments shall again enter into mutual consultation . . ."

The government of Panama, which always follows closely the world events, cannot help but feel grave apprehensions with regard to world peace. It considers, likewise, that we are in an era of uncertainty, and, consequently, of international insecurity, which does not allow any conscientious statesman to rest in the pleasant certainty that we have attained the era of a true and effective peace, based on law and justice.

This means that the Republic of Panama is ready today, as it was yesterday, not only to defend its own soil, but to cooperate with all the means at its disposal in the defense of the Canal, of the continent, and of the democratic cause in the entire world. But at the same time, the Republic of Panama, which is not a military power and which has no plans of its own of continental or of world projection to develop in a future war, cannot determine by itself that the functioning of certain defense sites in its territory is a military necessity.

From this point of view, the government of Panama is ready to listen to and to consider the representation of an international nature and the evidence of a technical nature which the government of the United States may submit for the purpose of determining whether there has arisen the case foreseen in the final portion of Article I of the 1942 Agreement, namely, the negotiations of a new agreement on defense sites, as required by circumstances.

In this connection, I wish to set forth that the government of Panama would not consider negotiating a new agreement on defense sites under conditions which would be more onerous than those stipulated for defense sites which exist or have existed in some of the other sister republics, and that any future agreement must take into account the principle of the fullest respect for the sovereignty and jurisdiction of Panama, and for the principal of juridical equality of the states, which the Republic has always warmly defended. But since the Agreement of May 18, 1942 has virtually fulfilled its purposes and the period for the return of the existing defense sites expires tomorrow, and there has been no development or circumstances to prevent its execution, the government of Panama, fully mindful of its international responsibilities but acting to safeguard its sovereignty and its rights in the compliance with the said agreement, considers that the government of the United States should proceed, as of tomorrow, to return and deliver the defense sites which it still is using.

I reiterate to Your Excellency, the assurances of my most distinguished consideration,

(*Signed*) RICARDO J. ALFARO,
Minister of Foreign Affairs

The foregoing note, it will be deduced, did not contain either a demand or an ultimatum that the bases be returned immediately but stated in careful yet unmistakable diplomatic language that the United States "should proceed . . . . to return and deliver" the sites which it was still using. A more hostile administration would undoubtedly have couched its diplomatic reply in stronger and more forceful terms. The bases, of course, were not returned. However, Lieutenant General Willis D. Crittenberger proceeded with plans to abandon another twenty-seven sites before the end of September. But both a domestic and an international political storm began to brew in Panama over this question.

On September 1, *El Panama America* published an editorial, which Foreign Minister Alfaro declared "correctly and accurately" expressed the position of the government of Panama on the bases question. Pertinent extracts of this editorial follow:

Evidently, the term fixed for the return of the defense sites has expired. The position of our country should be perfectly clear. Panama has already given ample proof that it is interested in contributing to the upholding of democratic ideas in the world, and to a just and permanent peace. Further, logically, Panama should defend its own interests with dignity. If a new agreement is absolutely necessary we should preceed toward it; but without further sacrifices and on a basis of equity and understanding. In other words, Panama is entitled to proper consideration.

The fact that the day fixed for the surrendering of the bases or defense sites should have arrived without the initiation by the government of the United States of the discussion of the points included in Article I of the agreement should bear no influence whatever on the results of the negotiations. It is known that to justify a new agreement for the occupation of the defense sites at least two factors must concur: (1) "a state of international insecurity" must continue to exist; and (2) that state of insecurity should render of "imperative necessity" a continuation of the occupation of the defense sites.

In view of the attitude of the Soviet Union, the government of Panama must realize—we believe—that peace is in the balance. What cannot be determined too easily is whether this situation of insecurity renders of "imperative necessity" the maintaining of defense sites in our Republic.

Certainly the government of Panama, conscious of its responsibility and of its rights, will study these delicate questions serenely and with the spirit of cordiality which inspires our relations with the government of the United States.

Patriotic national pride rose to explosive heights in Panama but it also brought forth violent denunciations of the United States that may never be erased from the record books of international relations or from the minds and hearts of Panamanians. On September 2, 1946, in the National Assembly, forty-six deputies present unanimously adopted a resolution in which they went on record "categorically expressing the view that, in support of the close harmony, reciprocity, and mutual consideration that exists between the Republic of Panama and the United States, and of the spirit of cooperation and confidence that has been attained among the nations of the Continent, it is indispensable that the government of the United States proceed to return the defense sites whose jurisdiction was granted to it through the Agreement of May 18, 1942, and which it has not yet evacuated despite the fact that the term fixed therefor has expired."

During the debate on the above resolution, former Foreign Minister José Isaac Fabrega criticized the manner in which the United States had acquired the Rio Hato air base. He asserted that what had started out as an officer's club long before the war had been turned overnight into a powerful military installation. He emphasized that there was no record in the Panama foreign office of any advice regarding the occupation of Rio Hato and pointed out that it was highly significant that the United States had insisted on including Rio Hato in the defense sites agreement drawn up in 1942. He added that if the State of California were turned over temporarily to Argentina for improving the wine industry, or the State of Virginia to the British to improve cotton raising, he was certain there would be an immediate nationwide protest on the part of the American people. No reference was made to the fact that it was former President Harmodio Arias who had privately helped find the Rio Hato formula for Major General David L. Stone in 1939.

Socialist Deputy José A. Brouwer then added that the situation heralded the return of the "big stick policy" and that the continued occupation of the defense sites beyond the deadline already expired was "an imperialistic outrage" on Panamanian sovereignty.

On the night of September 2 the United States Embassy issued the following statement:

> Ambassador Hines stated last night that he expressed sincere appreciation for the frank and clear outline of Panama's views as set forth in the Foreign Minister's note of August 31, 1946 which the Ambassador said he interpreted to mean that Panama is ever mindful of its desire to cooperate in the effective defense of the Panama Canal.
>
> The Ambassador referred to the "appreciable number" of defense sites which have already been returned and said that others will shortly be turned over to the Panamanian government. He said, however, that in conformity with the obligations of both governments to insure the future defense of the Isthmus, careful planning will be carried out which will be to the mutual benefit of both countries. Ambassador Hines said that these deliberations may require considerable time but that he is ever mindful of the need of an agreement that will be advantageous in the defense of the Isthmus.
>
> Ambassador Hines added that some sound principles of the highest respect for the sovereignty and the economy of Panama as has always existed between the two countries are uppermost in the minds of those entrusted with the problems.

The Communist party, known as the "Partido del Pueblo" (People's party), had a field day. "Today more than ever," it said in a lengthy statement published in *El Panama America* on September 3, "the Partido del Pueblo reaffirms its opinion that the military bases that the United States of North America has occupied in our territory must be returned to our country in fulfillment of the agreements signed between the governments of both countries. . . . The Partido del Pueblo today raises that flag of the Atlantic Charter which established that participation in the war would not bring forth territorial ambitions or aggrandizement once the war was over. . . . And it affirms that the dilatory and reticent deportment of the North American government in returning the bases and fulfilling its given word constitute a factor of discredit for any future agreement that it may tend to enter into in our country with our government."

On the night of September 6, Dr. Arnulfo Arias returned to Panama City from a political tour through the central provinces and addressed the nation over the radio on the issue of the day. He underlined the fact that his administration had, during the discussions of the rental contract, "reiterated insistently its sympathy for the cause of democracy and the United Nations and its live and fervent desire to cooperate in the defense of the Canal and of the hemisphere, up to the point where its territorial integrity and its political independence permitted. "We considered then, and we consider today," he said, "that in an emergency, that places in serious and effective danger the security of the Canal and of the Continent, as in the past, Panama should lend her firm and decided support in the common defense, but watching that the great sacrifices that this cooperation demanded would not be planned for the future of the country in the shape of permanent mortgages on the sovereignty and territorial integrity of the nation. This has been our constant determination so that the clauses of the rental contract would elevate the good friendship and harmony that should govern the relations between the United States and Panama. The lack of vision of the rulers in 1942 has given rise to the crisis that we contemplate presently and which must not be repeated. All the defense sites occupied by the United States in the recent emergency must be returned to Panama. And any future agreement should be negotiated with 'open doors' in order that the people may know it beforehand, and amply and later it should be submitted to a popular referendum before being ratified by the Executive Organ. The health of the nation demands it that way."

On September 4, Ambassador Hines flew to Washington for consultations with the State Department. Upon arrival he told the press that there was a difference of opinion of interpretation of the Defense Sites Agreement between the United States and Panama. This was the first such challenging statement by the United States since November 6, 1945, when Foreign Minister Alfaro had given his interpretation to the constituent assembly. Alfaro expressed complete surprise when this news reached Panama. It had served, of course, to increase the nationalistic resentment of the Panamanians against the United States.

On September 7, 1946, the State Department formally challenged Panama's interpretation for the first time. The failure to have challenged in November, 1945, contributed to the emotional buildup of fire and hate against the United States, because the statement made then by Byrnes was interpreted as acquiscence to Panama's point of view. But a feeble effort was made to challenge that interpretation, and, according to information furnished me later, it was done as soon as Dr. Alfaro had answered the question before the constitutional assembly. A cable was dispatched to Ambassador Hines in which he was instructed to convey to Foreign Minister Alfaro that the United States held a different view from that of Panama regarding the interpretation of when "a definitive treaty of peace" was signed. Hines acknowledged the cablegram, but notified the State Department that if he presented that view to the government of Panama it would jeopardize the effectiveness of his mission, because he had only just presented his letters of credentials. The State Department dropped the matter.

"That is where we made our mistake," Ambassador Ellis O. Briggs, who at the time was deputy to Spruille Braden, then Assistant Secretary of State for Latin American Affairs, remarked to me in a conversation on the subject in his embassy in Montevideo, Uruguay. "We should have issued categoric orders to General Hines to present our point of view forthwith. We failed to do so."

The Communists were busily engaged in inciting the people to demand the immediate withdrawal of the United States from the bases.

They had been holding "flash meetings" for some weeks, both in Panama City and in Colón, to generate enthusiasm for their drive. Celso Nicolas Solano, a lawyer and Secretary General of the Partido del Pueblo was in direct touch with Blas Roca, Secretary General of the Partido Socialista Popular of Cuba and a director of the Cominform, on the issue.

In his weekly press conference on September 10, President Jiménez took the situation in hand to calm the inflamed spirits of his countrymen. He issued the following statement:

> It is no diplomatic phrase when I say that the relations between the United States and Panama have developed lately in an atmosphere of cordiality and complete harmony. I am certain that the existing problems will be solved in that atmosphere. Referring specifically to the problem of the return of the bases, it is gratifying to my patriotism to see a unanimous opinion in all parts of the Republic in support of the viewpoint of our Foreign Ministry. . . . To mention only the three dailies of largest circulation, they have oriented public opinion to create the certainty that Panama is assisted by the right that it proclaims so patriotically. Naturally, neither the United States nor Panama can set aside the international reality nor can they ignore the juridical duties which arise from the treaties binding the countries, and for that very reason we strongly hope to continue relations with that great country on the foundations of mutual understanding and mutual respect.

On September 11, Ambassador Hines conferred with President Truman about the entire Panama question. The next day a joint announcement was made by both governments which read:

> Mindful of the objectives of the 1936 Treaty of Friendship and Cooperation, and of the Defense Sites Agreement of May 18, 1942, and, conscious of the recent improvements in weapons and methods of warfare, the governments of Panama and the United States have agreed to consult on the most effective means for assuring the defense of the Panama Canal.
>
> Consistent with the aforementioned agreement of 1942, the United States has already returned to the Republic of Panama seventy-one defense sites and is preparing to return, immediately, twenty-seven more.
>
> It is the desire of both governments to fulfill their joint responsibilities for the adequate protection of the Canal.

The two governments have reiterated their unqualified endorsement of the traditional friendship and the sovereign respect existing between them and the vital role which the Panama Canal plays in the defense of this hemisphere.

The statement did not alter the position of the government of Panama, which maintained that the bases should have been returned on September 1.

Just before the above announcement was made, a National Committee for the Return of the Bases was established in Panama. The committee contained representatives from known native and foreign leftist groups in Panama.

The nationalistic emotions of Panamanians were so aroused, that on the eve of Panama's independence day an extreme nationalist burned an American flag in Santa Ana Plaza. For this he was sentenced to fifteen days' imprisonment. The next day, November 3, 1946, no American troops marched in the Independence Day parade in the city of Panama for the first time since November 3, 1904. The diplomatic excuse was that no band was available in the Canal Zone. The real reason was that the American authorities dared not assume the risk of American troops being abused by an irate sector of the Panamanian public.

Despite Panama's insistence, the United States did not return the bases or sites. The United States position was that no definitive treaty of peace had been signed, and although there had been a cessation of hostilities, outposts were still required for the defense of the Canal. The State Department complained privately that it had been pressing the Pentagon for a decision on its needs for bases in Panama, but that the military staffs were dilatory in submitting their postwar requirements. This made it impossible, so the complaints indicated, to present an agreed upon and acceptable position to the government of Panama.

It was not until October, 1947, that Ambassador Hines delivered a note to the foreign office in which a twenty-year lease was sought for the Rio Hato air base, and a five-year lease for thirteen radar sites, one of which was eliminated.

The base negotiations were to continue for fourteen months. Alfaro took the opportunity, in August, 1947, to discuss the problem with

General George C. Marshall, Secretary of State, at the Quitandinha Conference at Petropolis, Brazil, while the Rio Treaty was being drafted. The base negotiations had been broken off May 14, 1947, because Panama had demanded at least a symbolic return of those sites still occupied by the United States within the Republic. The United States refused. Alfaro told Marshall that Panama was willing to sign a treaty which would permit the occupation of the bases for possibly not more than five years.

"No foreign minister, no president, no Panamanian congress will ever sign, approve, or ratify a treaty which will grant the United States permanent occupation of military bases in my country." Alfaro told Marshall.

On that premise, the State Department instructed Hines, in October, 1947, to reopen negotiations. Alfaro was busy at the United Nations General Assembly as Foreign Minister and Panama's chief delegate in the final stages of the negotiations, but he was consulted constantly by President Jiménez and his views were honored until almost the eve of the signing of the pact. He resigned in protest after the pact was signed.

On December 1, 1947, Governor Joseph C. Mehaffey of the Canal Zone completed his comprehensive study for a sea-level canal and other likely alternatives. The study had been ordered by Congress. The prospect of a $2.5 billion investment for a sea-level canal and a ten-year economic boom mellowed the Panamanian opposition in high government circles.

Meanwhile, it had not been entirely coincidental that Paul Robeson, the Negro Communist singer, had been sent to Panama by the United Public Workers of America (CIO), then a Communist-dominated union, to sing at rallies for the organization of 17,000 Panamanian workers in the Zone in May, 1947. Neither was it entirely coincidental that, at about the same time, the Communist-dominated Student Federation invited former Vice President Henry A. Wallace to travel to Panama "to address their student conference about the problem of the defense sites, internationalization of the Canal, discrimination against Panamanians in the Zone, and any other topics which may be of his predilection." Wallace declined the invitation.

On the premise enunciated emphatically by Foreign Minister Alfaro in his conference with General Marshall, the State Department sent new instructions to Hines in October, 1947, to renew negotiations. Alfaro agreed, but the issue was stalemated over the tenure of the lease for the Rio Hato air base. The United States insisted on a twenty-year lease. Alfaro considered that too long. He had no objection to the five-year lease for the other twelve bases.

The prospect of the construction of a sea-level canal in Panama, which was included in the comprehensive study sent to Congress, had not served to mellow Alfaro. On December 9, 1947, he resigned as Foreign Minister in protest over a compromise solution that President Jiménez had proposed for the Rio Hato lease. Jiménez offered a ten-year lease with an option to the United States for renewal for another ten years. Jiménez accepted Alfaro's resignation with regret and named his senior cabinet member, Francisco A. Filos, a lawyer and Minister of Government and Justice, to complete the negotiations.

The next morning the postwar defense bases pact was signed in the foreign ministry by Hines and Filos. Witnessing that ceremony were Carlos C. Hall, Counselor of the American Embassy; Octavio A. Vallarino, Minister of Public Works; and Henrique Obarrio, Comptroller General of the Republic of Panama.

The United States agreed to pay an annual rental of $28,015 for thirteen bases. In addition it agreed to pay $137,500 a year to Panama for the maintenance of its roads. President Jiménez informally asked, after the signing, for the United States to build a three hundred-mile highway for Panama to the Costa Rican border as additional compensation, in order to have a weapon with which to bargain with the legislators to insure ratification of the pact. The National Assembly had, under Panama's constitution, to ratify the Defense Base Agreement. The Senate of the United States did not have to because it was an executive agreement and not a treaty under international law. The United States did not honor Jiménez's request; even though the price may have been right and tempting enough, there was still no certainty that the special session called by the President would have ratified it had we promised to build the road.

All the bases agreed upon had been occupied during World War II. The land totaled 28,838 acres, which meant that we obtained the lease just under one dollar per year an acre. The bases were:

1. Rio Hato air base. Its 16,872 acres, sixty air miles southwest of the Canal, are in the cattle and sugar cane belt in the province of Coclé. The Pan-American Highway crosses the center of the macadam runway, which is 8,000 feet long and 200 feet wide—one of the largest built in World War II. The base fronts on the Republic's most beautiful Pacific Ocean beach, at Santa Clara. During the war it also served as an artillery and infantry training area through which were processed 100,000 troops. (By virtue of the 1955 treaty it is still being used as a training area.)

2. San José Island. This is one of the Perlas Islands group, sixty miles from the Canal. It was a privately-owned property on which very few natives lived. It was occupied in 1944 for a top secret chemical warfare experimental project. Its 9,812 acres were exclusively used for biological warfare and associated experiments. An area near the beach was cleared to permit the construction of a landing strip for twin-engine aircraft to ferry supplies and personnel.

3. Toboga Island. Located ten miles from the Pacific entrance to the Canal, ninety-one acres around its hilltop were leased for a radar station which served as a checkpoint for all pilots approaching the Canal. There was a PT-boat base there during World War II. This island was the one from which Francisco Pizarro sailed to conquer Peru and was the point from which the California settlers embarked a century ago after crossing the Isthmus via the Panama Railroad.

4. Rey Island. Two hundred acres of this island in the Perlas group were an aerophare (directional radio beacon) and radar station. A runway 4,200 feet long by 170 feet wide was built on it for use during World War II.

5. Taboguilla Island. This lies very close to Taboga and was used as an anti-aircraft and coast artillery outpost. Its 951 acres were cleared for a radar station and high-velocity weapons, some of which were carefully hidden from observation by air.

6. Pocri, a town eighty-five miles southwest of the Canal in the province of Las Tablas. On the 346 acres of land leased it had a radar station and an abandoned fighter strip.

7. Jaque, in the province of Darien, south near the Colombian border. On its 310 acres there was built a World War II fighter landing strip 3,800 feet long. The field has a river on the north and a mountain

to the south, with jungle to the east and the Pacific Ocean to the west.

8. Salud, twenty miles southwest of Colon on the Caribbean coast. A radar station was built on the 110 acres which was in continuous operation, with barracks for a complement of officers and thirty troops.

9. San Blas, or Mandinga. Fifty-three acres were leased here on the Caribbean coast for a radar station. Flanked by the colorful islands of the San Blas Indians, the station had the same facilities as Salud but only covered twenty-four acres of land despite the fifty-three-acre lease.

10. Isla Grande. This is an island off historic Porto Bello, where Sir Francis Drake is buried. Twelve acres were leased for a radar station with facilities identical to the other stations. It is located twenty miles south of Colón.

11. Cape Mala. One of the first radar stations built for the Canal in World War II was on the forty-four acres of this cape, 110 miles southeast from the Canal. It was used as a checkpoint for both aircraft and steamship pilots. Swamplands cover most of this point, which is in the epicenter of an active earthquake belt. The area is also noted for storms and high winds.

12. Las Margaritas. This is a five-acre station site located on a hilltop near the 3,000-foot-high El Valle Mountain resort. It served as a radio relay point in the event land lines were down between the Zone bases and Rio Hato.

13. Victoria. This is located only a few miles east of the Zone, midway between Albrook Air Force Base and Fort Clayton. Its twelve acres contained a radar station and there were clearings made for a supply road.

Panama was on the eve of its 1948 presidential campaign when the new agreement was signed. Jiménez called a special session of the National Assembly for December 12, and appointed Florencio Arosemena Forte, a lawyer who was attorney for the Panama Railroad at the time, as Foreign Minister. There was a political motive, naturally, behind this appointment. Arosemena's brother, Harmodio Arosemena Forte, was certain to be elected President of the National Assembly, and Jiménez apparently thought that the appointment would provide an unbeatable leverage to expedite ratification. Certain to be elected as First Vice President of the Assembly was Gil Blas Tejeira, who devoted his spare time to the writing of a column for local newspapers. To be elected as Secretary was Domingo H. Turner, a Socialist, whose sons David and Jorge were in coming years to figure prominently in the Castro-Communist activities in Panama. The international Communist plans were all in motion to coordinate effectively with those of the extreme nationalists to defeat the ratification of the bases agreement.

The Communists had successfully penetrated the National Institute, the country's major high school in the capital. In the year 1946 the Ministry of Education, responding to a request from teachers and students at the school and without the knowledge of President Jiménez, approved an authorization by the Government Printing Office to produce *ACLA*, a slick 75-page magazine, for educational purposes at government expense. The teachers who sponsored the publication were Hugo Victor and Cesar A. de Leon, both members of the Communist party. The editors, Romulo Escobar Bethancourt, Isaias Garcia, Everardo Ernesto Tomlinson, Moises Chang Marin, Moises Garcia, and Adolfo Benedetti, were all members of the Communist Youth movement. The flaming torch of the red fire of the Communist conspiracy to set Latin America ablaze colored a map of Latin America on the cover with the following caption: "Our cover indicates that the working class, and only the organized working class, is capable of carrying the torch of the economic, social, and political liberation of all Latin America."

A headline over an article on one page read: WE COMMUNISTS DO NOT BELIEVE IN FALSE LEADERS. WE BELIEVE IN THE MASSES.

Although the magazine had been printed by the government free of charge, each student at the institute was required to pay ten cents a copy. The remainder of the supply was distributed to newsstands, which were told to sell them at twenty-five cents a copy. The proceeds went to the treasury of the Communist party. The Minister of Education had already approved requisitions for the printing of subsequent issues of *ACLA,* but Jiménez ordered them canceled and fumigated the Ministry without delay.

The "mobilization of the masses," as ordered by Blas Roca from Havana, was under the direction of Celso Nicolas Solano, then Secretary General of the Partido del Pueblo, and of Ruben Dario Souza, then its Secretary of Organization. The day on which the negotiations were resumed, May 14, 1947, Souza had instructed Felicia Santizo Garcia, Provincial President of the party and teacher at the Abel Bravo High School in Colón "to start a fight of national scope, asking that the negotiations be immediately suspended and that the Panama government demand the return of the bases or that the case be referred to the United Nations in the event that the United States refuses. Comrade, this is the occasion to move large segments of masses to an anti-imperialist question of patriotism in which no Panamanian, except agents of imperialism, agrees that more should be granted. Therefore, there exists a great opportunity for the party to draft into the fight all the vast sectors of malcontents."

On December 12, 1947, Hugo Victor and Cesar A. de Leon marched the students of the National Institute, carrying their school flag of Panama, out of their classes to stage a demonstration against the bases agreement. With them in the front column was Solano. The students were encouraged to fight a pitched battle with the national police, which, under Colonel José Antonio Remon, was ordered by Minister of Government and Justice Filos to force them back into the institute. A riot erupted in which several students were wounded, one of them seriously. He was Sebastian Tapia, seventeen, who caught a bullet in his spine that crippled him. Again the Communists had produced the martyr they wanted. Now they could instigate further anti-Yankee demonstrations and attempt to discredit Panama's only armed force. Tapia was sent to the United States for surgery at the expense of the Panama government, and returned home.

As was to be expected, the encounter between the students and the police was whipped up by the now-cementing Communist-Nationalist alliance to roll the ball of agitation and opposition against the bases agreement with greater speed. Natividad Carreño, the principal of the Girls' Normal School in Panama City, the country's largest, had registered as a member of the Partido del Pueblo on March 26, 1947. She ordered her students to participate in the almost daily demonstrations that were to follow. Arrests were made of students and adults.

When the Assembly convened, in the midst of the emotional reaction to the student riots, its President appointed a committee to hold hearings as soon as his brother, the Foreign Minister, delivered the Defense Bases Agreement and a presidential message in which Jiménez asked that it be approved and that all political or partisan interest be discarded in considering it. The committee appointed to conduct the hearings was composed of Luis Enrique Garcia de Paredes, Chairman; Manuel Pino, Vice Chairman; Jacinto Lopez y Leon, Secretary; and José Maria Herrera, Gregorio de los Rios, Manuel Valera, Jr., and José Dominador Bazan. The committe met for six days and also held night sessions. The first hearings were on Saturday, December 13. They were resumed on December 15, 16, 17, 18, and 19, on which afternoon majority and minority reports were submitted.

Among the witnesses heard were former Presidents Ricardo J. Alfaro and Harmodio Arias, Foreign Minister Florencio Arosemena Forte, Undersecretary Mario de Diego, Dr. J. J. Vallarino, Ambassador in the United States, and authorized representatives of civic associations. These included four from a new Nationalist organization, the Frente Patriotico de la Juventud, which also had a Communist-infiltrated wing. Four young lawyers testified for this Patriotic Youth front. They were Eloy Benedetti, Rodrigo Arosemena, Cesar Quintero, and Erasmo Escobar. Seventeen years later, Benedetti was to figure prominently in the formulation of policy.

The Frente Patriotico opposition to the bases pact was predicated on these seventeen points:

1. It violated Article X of the General Treaty of 1936, because there did not exist danger of aggression to the Republic of Panama or to the security or neutrality of the Panama Canal.

2. Because almost all of its articles, especially III, IV, V, X, and XII are prejudicial to Panama sovereignty.

3. Because Article III designates the sovereignty of Panama to the local commander of the United States Army or to the person in whom he delegates his representation.

4. Because Article X permits the occupation of all the Republic of Panama by the Army of the United States, permitting it to block all the highways and roads of the Republic.

5. Because Articles VI, VII, IX, and XII permit the United States to occupy the sites for the installation of radio communications services, which are not specified in the Annex to the agreement. There is no stipulation in the agreement that establishes that only the specified sites in the Annex will be occupied.

6. Because Article III exempts all civilian employees, including

contractors, who work in said defense sites, from the payment of taxes and this despite the fact that the agreement says that Panama conserves its sovereignty over the sites in question.

7. Because Articles III and IV do not insure the opportunity for work for the Panamanians in said sites.

8. Because it does not insure a market for the national products that could be sold there.

9. Because Article XIII permits in said sites the importation and sale of all kind of articles without the existence of the obligation to pay any contribution or tax; there only exists the obligation to repress contraband.

10. Because Article X allows the United States, at its discretion, to reroute the national highways.

11. Because the Annex of the sites to be occupied permits the occupation of a site that not even in time of war was considered necessary for the defense of the Republic or of the Canal.

12. Because Article X will compel the national government to spend greater sums than the United States would have to pay for the maintenance of the highways and roads used by its troops, which would in no way benefit Panama.

13. Because Article V only gives criminal jurisdiction to Panama over the Panamanians who may commit a crime or an offense in the defense sites; the foreigners, on the other hand, accused of crimes or offenses, will be tried and punished in accordance to the laws of the United States by the corresponding authorities of the United States.

14. Because it neither establishes that the 1942 agreement terminated September 1, 1946, nor that it has ceased to be in effect.

15. Because even though there might be a threat of aggression against Panama or against the Canal it does not stipulate that said agreement is in development of Article X of the General Treaty of 1936.

16. Because if the principle of a threat of aggression is accepted it will open the doors for future occupations of national territory in conformity with Article X of the General Treaty of 1936.

17. Because the Hines-Filos Agreement only imposes obligations on Panama; none of its defenders has been able to point out a solitary convenience for the interests of the country.

The above arguments were a distorted and biased interpretation by the young lawyers of the fifteen articles and the Annex of the agreement.

Hugo Victor, a Communist, testified in the hearings in his capacity as Secretary General of the Students' Federation. His ten-page prepared statement was not only boastful but was indicative of the Communist plans.

"The Students' Federation," he said, "considers it only fair that it be given an opportunity to be heard, because it has been the most important motive power behind public opinion in defense of the sovereignty and the national integrity. The Students' Federation states that its password is the rejection of the defense bases pact. It maintains that our country should not grant to the United States, to any foreign power, one centimeter of its territory."

Another Communist witness, Humberto E. Ricord, a lawyer, testified as the representative of the Association of Graduates of the University of Panama. He also urged the legislators to reject the pact.

Even before the committee reported to the floor of the Assembly it was a foregone conclusion that the pact would be rejected. The bases pact had already become a political football for the 1948 Presidential campaign. Hugo Victor ordered a students' general strike for December 15, to pressure the Assembly into rejecting the pact, and there was virtually unanimous response throughout the country. The Communists called a general strike for noon of December 22, and three hours later marched on to the French Plaza where the National Assembly was to be in session.

Deputy Gil Blas Tejeira, Vice President of the Assembly, gave these reasons in his column in the newspaper, *La Nacion*, as to why the pact would be rejected:

Its rejection is above all due to failure of the United States diplomacy. The attitude of the masses has a clear explanation. The dispute over the bases is but an episode in the long history of resentments incubated in the Panamanian people by the erroneous policy carried out here by the North Americans and especially the Zone administration since the start of the Canal.

When students, workers and women shout: "We don't want the pact" they compress into one phrase all their resentments against racial prejudices which our predominantly *mestizo* and colored people have experienced, against the resistance shown by the United States when we have discussed economic matters relating to the Zone, and against all that has hurt us in forty-four years of residence alongside the Canal.

Ten thousand students and workers marched on the Assembly shouting and demanding the pact be rejected. That did not deter the majority of the committee from submitting a report in which it recommended the approval of the pact with six modifications and reservations. The principal modification was to lease the Rio Hato air base for five years with an option for renewal for another five years, provided Panama agreed.

There was a two-man minority report, signed by Rogelio Robles and José Dominador Bazan, in which they proposed the rejection of the pact and its renegotiation by both governments. The minority recommendation was amended and a motion was introduced by Deputy Felipe O. Perez, a former President of the Assembly, to reject the Defense Bases Agreement "because it was not subjected to the norms of international law and to the spirit of the Inter-American defense system."

The session had started at 4:00 P.M. The Assembly had summoned former Presidents Alfaro and Harmodio Arias, former Foreign Minister Octavio Fabrega, and Dr. J. J. Vallarino to be available for questions from the floor during the debate. The leftists had two certain allies in the assembly. They were Deputies Diogenes de la Rosa and Brouwer, and they made the most of their opportunity during the debate.

Harmodio Arosemena Forte, the President of the Assembly, also forecast the rejection when he said in a brief speech: "Do you think I am going to vote for the approval of this pact with 10,000 youths outside with sharpened knives?"

Alfaro made one well-known contribution to an important footnote to history when, in extending his reply to one question, he revealed that President Franklin Delano Roosevelt had personally overruled the State, War, and Navy Departments in 1936 and ordered that the United States relinquish its treaty rights to acquire additional land for the defense of the Canal. In 1940, the State Department found it necessary to ask Panama, according to Alfaro, for a 999-year lease of defense bases within the Republic of Panama.

"Article II of the Treaty of 1936," Alfaro said, "was the result of a personal conference I had with President Roosevelt, early in 1936. I told him that according to the treaty of 1903, there was no part of Panama territory that wouldn't be subject to occupation by the United States at one time or another, and that Panama could no longer live under such a mortgage. President Roosevelt understood the Panamanian point of view. He made the observation that we are joint fiduciaries of the Canal. He asked me whether in case an earthquake should alter the course of Gatun Lake we would give the United States additional land for the Canal. I replied in the affirmative."

At 9:30 P.M. the President of the Assembly called for a vote on the minority report and its amended resolution. The majority report was ignored. Fifty-one deputies present answered the roll call. All voted "Yes," to reject the pact. The last vote was recorded at 9:55 P.M. I was present. The galleries cheered, the doors were forced open by the crowd that had already heard the news, and they invaded the hall, cheering the deputies and singing the Panama national anthem.

The United States had suffered its first postwar diplomatic and military defeat in Latin America on the night of December 22, 1947, less than four months after the signing of the Rio Treaty on September 7, 1947.

On December 23, 1947, Lieutenant General Willis D. Crittenberger, Commander in Chief of the Caribbean, ordered his Chief of Staff, Brigadier General Lemuel Matheson, to coordinate plans for the immediate evacuation of the bases. Major General Willis H. Hale, commanding the Caribbean Command, was called up to headquarters at Quarry Heights to collaborate in the planning. The next morning, the day before Christmas, the evacuation of all the bases began with unprecedented military precision, without waiting for any further request from Panama that it be done.

Resistance against the lease of modern warfare defense sites made itself felt again in April, 1956. The State Department, acting on a request from the Defense Department, notified the government of Panama that two sites for the establishments of Nike bases were needed within the Republic to defend the Canal. Panama rejected the request, and the matter lay dormant for nearly two years. It was reopened by the American Embassy in 1958, again in response to a request by the Defense Department to the State Department.

Foreign Minister Aquilino Boyd issued a statement in which the public was informed that the government had consented to an inspection of land for two possible defense sites, and that Panama representatives would accompany United States Army staff officers. The statement emphasized that this in no way indicated that negotiations were about to begin for the sites, and that the public would be properly apprised when and if such talks were initiated. The survey was completed, but the Nike defense-site issue was quietly dropped because of "Operation Sovereignty" and subsequent student riots. The time was considered most inappropriate to negotiate for those needed sites.

11. The Basic Treaties

What Gil Blas Tejeira had written had some substance of fact, but what few, if any, Panamanians were willing to admit, and much less to accept, was the fact that the Communists had greatly contributed, as Hugo Victor had boasted at the hearings, toward the immediate inflammation of the emotions and animosity of the people, which undoubtedly influenced the unanimous rejection of the postwar defense bases pact.

The archives of the Panama foreign ministry bulge with protests sent to our State Department of alleged arbitrary actions, discriminatory practices, and commercial competition in the Canal Zone. Invoking the treaty which granted us "power and authority which the United States would possess and exercise if it were the sovereign of the territory, to the entire exclusion of the exercise by the Republic of Panama of any such rights, power, and authority," Lieutenant George W. Davis, United States Army, was ordered to assume control of the Canal Zone on May 19, 1904. This was done without any prior delimitation of the boundaries and without compensating the owners of the private land that was included within the ten-mile strip. It took years to settle that protest, but every one of the landowners finally received compensation that was set by a joint United States-Panama claims commission.

The United States abolished the mixed courts where native judges sat to try their nationals and discarded the use of Panama postage stamps that were surcharged for the Canal Zone. Under the provisions of Article II of the Treaty of 1903 our government used to grab additional land and tell the Panamanians about it afterward. Those days are gone now. No longer do we prevent the Panamanians from building a railroad or a highway within their own country—although we have defrayed most of the costs for highways and roads in recent years—or from erecting and operating radio broadcasting stations, as we used to. We insist no longer in disarming their police, as we did in 1916, nor do we intervene in their elections, as we did on several occasions.

The United States refusal to allow Panama to build railroads, except within the province of Chiriqui, a restriction which lasted from 1909 to 1919, is little known. In 1909, American engineers surveyed a three-hundred-mile railroad from Panama City to David, capital of the province of Chiriqui. The Panama National Assembly enacted legislation to authorize its construction at a cost of $10 million. The authorities in the Canal Zone objected to the project, on the grounds that branch lines would have been opened in the central provinces, and Panama was forced to abandon it. Today it would cost more than $150 million to build the same railroad.

Our legation in Panama then demanded the right from the government to veto any concession to build a railroad in the Republic. On December 30, 1912, Basil Burns Duncan, an American, obtained a contract to build a railroad from the west bank of the Chagres River, near the Caribbean entrance to the Canal, southwest for thirty-five miles, to include branch lines. Colonel George Washington Goethals, Governor of the Canal Zone, objected to a clause in the contract whereby Duncan would have been permitted to build piers at Chagres, because their construction would have required a revision of the Canal defense plans. Panama was compelled to cancel the contract, and the railroad never was built.

Again, in 1917, Duncan sought to build a railroad from the mouth of the Chagres to Chiriqui Lagoon in the northeastern province of Bocas del Toro near the frontier of Costa Rica, skirting the Caribbean all the way, and to extend a branch line to Penonomé, 125 miles northwest of Panama City in the province of Coclé, near the Pacific Ocean.

Our legation objected to the construction of the branch line to Penonomé "because it might prove detrimental to the Canal defenses." Panama was forced to rescind Duncan's contract, and to this day no railroad has been built.

In 1919, Panama granted a concession to a manganese mining prospecting company to build a fifteen-mile narrow gauge short line from Nombre de Dios to the Boqueron River in the province of Colón, not far from the Caribbean (or Atlantic) entrance to the Canal, despite repeated protests by the United States Legation. Since then the United States government has never interfered with Panama's right to build railroads within its own country, and the Chiriqui Railroad was constructed in 1928.

The Panama Canal Company, easily the largest single business enterprise in the country, for long refused to employ Panamanians in any but the lowest-paid jobs, with but a few exceptions, and then paid them wages far below those paid to United States citizens for identical work. This type of discrimination against local citizens in their own country was the same mistake the British made at the Suez Canal. The discriminatory practice was corrected but it took years of negotiation, as well as pressure by the AFL-CIO in the highest circles in Washington, to help to end it.

All these and other incidents—including the color line before the silver and gold segregation was abolished after World War II—built up in the Panamanians an inferiority complex to such a point that the natives even resented the use of the English language in the cities of Panama and Colón. Ordinances were enacted which required all store signs to be in Spanish. It was considered unpatriotic for a merchant to place a sign in the window of his store, to attract customers from the Canal Zone or tourists, which read: ENGLISH IS SPOKEN HERE.

The Panamanians displayed their emotional resistance against the acquisition of additional land by the United States army for the defense of the Canal. This resistance exploded into violence against General John J. Pershing in 1925, not unlike that which confronted Vice President Richard M. Nixon in Caracas in May, 1958. General Pershing's car was stoned by an angry, shouting mob of Panamanians as he left the Union Club in Panama City to return to his ship and continue southward to settle the Tacna-Arica dispute between Chile and Peru. The

United States Army had recently threatened to take some land on Taboga Island, which was the resort of the residents of the capital, twelve miles away in the Pacific Ocean.

It has already been noted that the Communists had been active in propagating the "Hate America" campaign in 1946-47 in Panama. In later years they were to work in close liaison with the agents of President Juan Domingo Peron of Argentina for the same purpose. Their link with the Peronist agents of subversion in Panama was Hugo Victor, who had played a prominent part in agitating the students of the National Institute in the defense bases dispute. Victor had been accepted into the Communist party of Panama in 1943. On February 23, 1944, he flew to Montevideo to attend Vicente Lombardo Toledano's CTAL Congress in the Uruguayan capital. He left there on March 13, 1944, by plane for Bolivia to deliver, as he reported to the party, "financial aid of the American workers to the Bolivian workers." Victor held nearly every office in the Party, including that of Secretary General.

In 1951 the Peronists began to try to undermine the morale and the loyalty of the Panamanian workers in the Canal Zone. Another presidential campaign was about to begin on the Isthmus. Colonel José Antonio Remon had been drafted by a coalition of parties that supported the regime of President Alcibiades Arosemena, who was sworn in when Arnulfo Arias was blasted out of the palace on May 10, 1951. The Communists considered Remon a mortal enemy and openly supported the candidacy of Roberto F. Chiari, nominated by the Liberal party opposition. In November, 1951, blatantly displaying the flag of the hammer and sickle, they appeared on the same platform with Chiari at a political rally in Santa Ana Plaza. Remon and his campaigners made political capital out of this, also exploiting the fact that Communists had mobbed and almost strangled me while I observed that meeting. Panamanian spectators saved me from them and broke their choking stranglehold on my neck.

The Peronist labor attaché in Panama cultivated a stooge in the Canal Zone. He was Juan Vicente Spiazzano Urriola, an employee in the Motor Transportation Division in Ancon. Early in 1952 Spiazzano flew to Asunción, Paraguay, to attend a preparatory meeting of what was to become Peron's hemisphere-wide ATLAS Confederation of Labor. There a declaration of principles was adopted which called for a "relentless war against Yankee imperialism."

As soon as Spiazzano returned to his job, he began an intensive campaign to apply that principle among his co-workers. The authorities in the Canal Zone refused to tolerate any more of his anti-American activity and fired him. He distributed a pamphlet that carried a sketch of President Truman lynching a Negro from the Statue of Liberty. The cartoon had appeared on the cover of a pamphlet printed by Peron's General Confederation of Labor. That prompted violent reaction by the Peronists and every controlled newspaper in Argentina published a statement by Peron's CGT which was issued through the presidential press office. It read in part:

> Imperialism has committed another outrage, which, although expected, nevertheless causes indignation. The Panamanian labor leader, Juan Vicente Spiazzano Urriola, has been fired by authorities in the Canal Zone because he refused to disown the obligation accruing from the recent Labor Unity Conference that was held in Asunción. Imperialism has responded to the manly attitude of this worthy labor representative, tending to starve him. This is the typical maneuver of imperialism: to reduce to misery and desperation everyone who does not bow to its miserable designs.

Handbills of the above were distributed throughout Panama. Remon won against Chiari by a landslide, because the well-oiled governmental machinery, his anti-Communist platform, and the strength of the coalition parties gave him a wide advantage. Fearing Remon's strong hand, the Communists effected a strategic withdrawal after his inauguration on October 1, 1952. Remon declined an informal invitation to visit the United States before his inauguration, largely because President Truman never made it formal enough for him to accept. President Eisenhower was to invite him the following year.

Remon also enunciated a policy that advocated the revision of existing treaties with the United States to eliminate old grievances that marred Panama-United States relations. The State Department was most reluctant to negotiate any revision of the treaties. Remon did not need to press the matter for political reasons; he was firmly in the presidential chair. But he elected to make an attempt. He appointed two Special Ambassadors to travel to Washington to represent Panama in the negotiations. They were Octavio Fabrega and Carlos Sucre, both of whom had served as Foreign Ministers. They were to join Ambassador Roberto Heurtematte in Washington to meet with United States negotiators for a revision of the 1903 and 1936 treaties.

On August 27, 1953, the Panamanians were asked to turn out for an "appointment with the fatherland" to herald the departure of the Special Ambassadors for Washington. Thousands of Panamanians from all walks of life marched down Central Avenue in Panama City in the biggest demonstration in the Republic's short history. Parading with them was the late Monsignor Francisco Beckman, Archbishop of Panama. Remon was flanked by six former Presidents; the only former President who did not participate was Dr. Arnulfo Arias, whose civil rights had been canceled by the National Assembly in 1951. The paraders included cabinet ministers, legislators, government officials, governors, mayors, provincial delegations, high-school students, and university students. The demonstration had been sponsored officially and organized by the presidential palace. The appearance of former Presidents Harmodio Arias and Daniel Chanis on the speakers' stand in front of the Panama Railroad station in Plaza Cinco de Mayo had its touch of political drama. Both were among Remon's principal adversaries, and both had figured prominently when he ousted Chanis four years earlier, during the political turmoil when Panama had three presidents in less than a week. One student group carried a placard which read: NEGOTIATIONS WITHOUT SURRENDER. The two Special Ambassadors spoke; Fabrega reviewed the history of the signing of the 1903 treaty:

Fifty years of the Bunau-Varilla treason will soon be observed, fifty years in which the people have been the yoke of an enslaving treaty. No Panamanian signed that treaty, no Panamanian seal was affixed to it. The treaty was signed twice by the United States. Panama gave away the monopoly of the treasure of its geographic position in that treaty. Panama has not received adequate compensation for the sacrifices it has made and is making here at the Canal. The people of the United States are making great and noble sacrifices for the defense of freedom in the world against the Communist menace. With all due respect for that tremendous undertaking, the Panamanian people are here demanding justice from the fair-minded people of the United States. Through our hands will not pass, nor will President Remon sign, any treaty which is harmful to the interests of the Republic.

The assembled thousands cheered him. They sang their national anthem, and a motorcade of several hundred automobiles raced across the Trans-Isthmian Highway for fifty miles to Colón where another farewell demonstration awaited them. Fabrega and Sucre sailed the next day for New York.

Remon was invited by President Eisenhower to visit the White House in September, 1953, to discuss the problem. Upon his return home he was accorded a virtual hero's welcome, and then undertook to direct the negotiations. He called in as advisers his hitherto arch-enemy, former President Harmodio Arias, and former President Ricardo J. Alfaro. Their experience and knowledge were a priceless asset to him.

Panama submitted twenty-one demands to the United States for revisions to the existing treaties. The reaction at the State Department was adverse. The demands, contained in documents labeled "A to U," were:

A. Limitations and restrictions on commercial and manufacturing activities of the Canal Zone to enable Panama to receive benefits from the Zone market as follows: (1) Only articles of primary need will be sold in the Zone; (2) said articles will be procured in the Panamanian market when: (3) their prices are not higher nor their quality inferior to those of the United States; (4) articles originating in Panama will enter the Canal Zone freely (elimination of the "Buy American" Act and other restrictions); (5) limitation of the volume of individual sales in the Zone establishments to a percentage of the wages of the employee; (6) the Zone stores should be situated at least 3,000 yards from the boundary line between Panama and the Canal Zone; (7) only the government and official dependencies will be able to import things into the Canal Zone; (8) only liquors, beer, and soft drinks bought in Panama may be imported into the Zone (the Zone will have no establishments to sell liquor or beer); (9) the Zone will be able to sell surplus material only to official institutions of the Panama government; (10) the Zone will not engage in manufacturing, industrial, agricultural, or cattle activities; (11) the articles that cannot be obtained in Panama will be imported only when they are produced within the continental territory of the United States; (12) the mechanical and repair services for ships will be supplied preferentially from Panama; (13) the supply of ships in transit through the Canal will correspond to Panama.

B. Preferred opportunity will be given for work in the Zone to the Panamanians and North Americans; equal pay for equal work; pension equality; equality of treatment that will extend to private contractors and employees. There will be a mixed commission of workers' representatives.

C. Powers for the Panamanian government to extend its tax system to: (1) all the residents in its territory who work in the Canal Zone; (2) the Panamanian citizens who live in the Zone; (3) the firms and contractors who reside in the Zone. Cooperation of the Canal Zone authorities for the compliance of the foregoing. The government of the United States will recognize and credit its citizens for the taxes that they pay to Panama.

D. The Panamanian flag will fly jointly with the North American flag in the Zone and on ships that transit the Canal. The official languages in the Zone will be English and Spanish.

E. The railroad will function only within the Zone. The property of the Panama Railroad Company, of the government of the United States and official dependencies situated outside of the Zone will be returned to Panama free of cost.

F. Measures for the protection of the civilian population of both territories.

G. Only the persons with *exequaturs* issued by Panama will be able to exercise consular functions in the Zone.

H. Preferential quotas will be given to Panama for the export of the following products to the continental market of the United States: sugar (500,000 tons annually); alcohol and liquors; coffee; meat; hides; fish products; cacao; vegetable oils; copra; vegetable fibers; cashew nuts.

I. Increase of the annuity of the Canal to 20 per cent of the gross revenue of the Canal that will not be less than $5 million annually.

J. Construction of a breakwater and pier in Colón by the United States at its expense and privileges for the use of same.

K. Measures for the exploitation by Panama of its geographical position by: (1) free access to the ports and waters of the Zone; (2) the Zone will not receive any commission for passages or freight for Panama or that originate in Panama; (3) cooperation with the free Zone in Colón; (4) tourism for Panama will be exempt from all tax. The Zone employees and North American tourists will be able to introduce freely into the United States merchandise up to a sum of $500 that is purchased in Panama.

L. The capital and activities of North Americans in Panama will not be taxed by the United States.

M. The monopolies granted by Panama in 1903 will be reduced to the present Canal. There will be no monopoly regarding the railroad nor interoceanic highways.

N. Corridors under Panamanian jurisdiction and sovereignty through the Canal Zone on the Atlantic and on the Pacific sides to be built and maintained at the expense of the United States.

O. Mixed courts in the Canal Zone for controversies in which a Panamanian may be a party.

P. The sanitary jurisdiction of the United States will be confined to the Zone and the cost of water supplied to Panama will be reduced.

Q. Use in the Zone of Panamanian postage stamps.

R. Panamanian jurisdiction over its flagships in Zone waters and over the ships of other countries that carry passengers and merchandise for Panama or originating from Panama; customs houses in the Zone under Panamanian jurisdiction.

S. Panama sovereignty over the Zone. Restrictive definition of Article III of the Treaty of November 18, 1903.

T. The two countries accept the obligatory jurisdiction of the International Court of Justice.

U. The period of duration of the treaties between Panama and the United States will be reduced to ninety-nine years.

The above aspirations were outlined to Secretary of State John Foster Dulles at the first meeting of the negotiators that was held at Blair House on September 11, 1953. First Vice President and Foreign Minister José Ramon Guizado presented Panama's case assisted by Heurtematte, Fabrega, and Sucre. Dulles replied that the State Department did not want to review the old treaties but preferred to confine the negotiations to a discussion of interpretation and compliance of existing pacts. The Panama delegation refused to accept this, and when Remon visited the White House he appealed to President Eisenhower, who broke the stalemate and directed the State Department to discuss all the demands.

The demands were submitted in detail at subsequent sessions, and the presentation of them was completed on October 6, 1953. The State Department requested time to study them for preparation of replies, which took several months to accomplish. There was one facet of the demands on which the State Department was inflexible. It would not agree to any of the points dealing with the sovereignty in the Canal Zone.

During the session of February 2, 1954, the State Department flatly rejected Documents D, G, O, Q, S, and U on the grounds that these would produce an impression of divided authority in the Canal Zone and that we could not accept any proposal that would limit the ample and comprehensive interpretation given to the rights granted under Article III of the Treaty of 1903. This empowered the United States government to exercise in the Canal Zone all the rights, power, and authority that would be exercised if it were sovereign thereof. The Panamanian negotiators recorded their objection to this position and expressed their "great surprise and disillusionment upon being treated like that by a powerful and friendly country to which Panama had made such vast concessions." They rejected the United States interpretation of Article III of the Treaty of 1903 and reiterated Panama's long-standing "juridical, moral and historically just interpretations of this treaty which denotes that Article III of the 1903 treaty does not have the effect given to it by the United States but, on the contrary, the legal, moral, and historically just interpretation of that treaty denotes that the United States can only exercise in the Canal Zone the right, power, and authority that is required in relation with the maintenance, operation, sanitation, and protection of the Panama Canal."

The Panama delegation also recorded its "firm and irrevocable position regarding the sovereign rights which our nation reserves for herself in the Canal Zone" and threatened to pursue the matter before the International Court of Justice at The Hague should the United States "insist in its position to assume for itself greater rights in the Canal Zone than those lawfully granted."

The negotiations proceeded slowly and then broke down when the State Department submitted a draft treaty to Panama. Article I of that draft stipulated that Panama agree never again to request a revision of the Canal treaties. This was an entirely new approach in international diplomacy, and Panama balked at it. Remon dispatched former President Harmodio Arias to Washington to seek audiences with Dulles and with President Eisenhower. After those audiences the objectionable article was stricken from the draft treaty. Then Ambassador Selden Chapin was summoned to Washington for consultations.

On December 17, 1954, negotiations were concluded to the satisfaction—begrudgingly, and by no means universal, on the part of Panama —of both parties. The approved language of the treaty was duly prepared in Spanish and English and it was ready for signature at the start of the new year, when Remon was assassinated on January 2, 1955.

Panama received eleven major concessions in the new treaty. The United States was granted seven rights. The concessions to Panama were:

1. The annuity was increased from $430,000 to $1,930,000. (The State Department assumed the obligation to include the additional $1,500,000 in its annual budget although there was no need so to stipulate in the treaty).

2. Subject to certain general conditions, Panama was allowed to levy income taxes on the following categories of personnel employed by Canal Zone agencies: (1) Panamanian citizens irrespective of their place of residence, and (2) citizens of third countries who reside in territory under the jurisdiction of Panama.

3. The United States renounced the monopoly with respect to the construction, maintenance, and operation of trans-Isthmian railroads and highways, with the provision that no system of interoceanic communication by railroad or highway within territory under Panamanian jurisdiction may be financed, constructed, maintained, or operated directly or indirectly by a third country or nationals thereof unless in the opinion of both parties such action would not affect the security of the Canal.

4. The United States renounced the treaty right to prescribe and enforce sanitary measures in the cities of Panama and Colón.

5. Certain lands, with improvements thereon, previously acquired for Canal purposes (including Paitilla Point and the Panama Railroad yard and station in the city of Panama), but no longer needed for such purposes, were to be transferred to Panama and there was to be a gradual transfer to Panama of the New Cristobal, Colón Beach, and Fort de Lesseps areas in Colón.

6. Canal Zone commissary and import privileges of non-U. S. citizen employees of Canal Zone agencies, except members of the Armed Forces of the United States, who do not reside in the Zone were to be withdrawn.

7. The U. S. Congress was to be requested to enact legislation authorizing the establishment of a single basic wage scale for all United States and Panamanian employees of the U. S. government in the Canal Zone and providing for uniform application of the Civil Service Retirement Act to citizens of the United States and citizens of Panama employed by the U. S. government in the Canal Zone.

8. The United States was to afford equality of opportunity to citizens of Panama for employment in all U. S. government positions in the Canal Zone for which they are qualified and in which the employment of U. S. citizens is not required, in the judgment of the United States, for security reasons.

9. Citizens of Panama were afforded opportunity to participate in such training programs as may be conducted for employees by U. S. agencies in the Canal Zone.

10. Articles, materials, and supplies that are mined, produced, or manufactured within the Republic of Panama, when purchased for use in the Canal Zone, were to be exempted from the provisions of the Buy American Act.

11. The U. S. Congress was to be requested to enact the necessary legislation for the construction across the Canal at Balboa of a bridge.

The rights received by the United States were:

1. Exclusive use without cost, for a period of at least fifteen years, of a military training and maneuver area (approximately 19,000 acres) in the Rio Hato region.

2. Panama waives the right, under Article XIX of the 1903 convention, to free transportation over the Panama Railroad of persons in the service of the Republic of Panama, or of the police force charged with the preservation of public order outside of the Canal Zone, as well as to their baggage, munitions of war, and supplies.

3. Panama waives certain rights in order to enable the United States to prohibit or restrict the use of a contemplated new strategic highway within the Canal Zone by commercial trans-Isthmian traffic.

4. Panama waives certain treaty provisions in order to enable the

United States to extend limited post-exchange privileges to military personnel of friendly foreign countries visiting the Canal Zone under U. S. auspices.

5. A lease for a period of ninety-nine years without cost to two parcels of land contiguous to the U. S. Embassy residence site in the city of Panama.

6. Panama was to reserve permanently as a park area certain land in front of the U. S. Embassy office building site in the city of Panama.

7. A reduction of 75 per cent in the import duty on alcoholic beverages which are sold in Panama for importation into the Canal Zone.

The National Assembly ratified the treaty with little opposition, although the deputies voiced their dissatisfaction, as well as their disappointment, that the sovereignty demands had not been honored and announced that they considered them still to be pending. After the United States Senate ratified the treaty, Panama pressed the State Department for early enactment of enabling legislation to implement the above concessions, but congressional roadblocks were to cause delays.

The 1955 treaty, while benefiting Panama's businessmen, and, to some extent, its national treasury, hit the affected Canal Zone employees where it hurt them most—right in their pocketbooks. This engendered a wave of resentment against the coalition of political parties that had sponsored it and was to make itself evident in the 1956 presidential campaign when President-elect Ernesto de la Guardia, Jr., a graduate of Dartmouth College, barely squeezed through to victory over Victor Florencio Goytia, former Chief Justice of the Supreme Court, former Minister of Education, and a respected and prominent attorney.

While President Eisenhower was in Panama in July, 1956, for the first conference of American presidents, he invited President Ricardo Manuel Arias Espinosa and President-elect de la Guardia to the American Embassy where he signed a bill in their presence which authorized the construction of a bridge over the Canal Zone at Balboa. It was not until 1958, though, that the appropriation was passed to build that $20 million span.

Congress gradually enacted the enabling legislation to implement the commitments made in the 1955 treaty. The single-wage scale bill was signed in time for Dr. Milton Eisenhower to arrive in Panama in July,

1958, so that he would hear one less complaint on a fact-finding tour for his brother that was to include every Central American republic.

The students had already showed their teeth of revolution shortly after school opened in May, 1958. (The school term in Panama runs from May through December. The Canal Zone term runs from September to June.) On May 2, 1958, they were ready with a preconceived plan. The Union of University Students sent seventy-five of their members into the Canal Zone in what they had named "Operation Sovereignty." Fifty-nine Panamanian flags were placed in the soil within the zone at different points from Panama to Cristobal at ten o'clock that morning. The American Embassy and the Canal Zone authorities were caught by surprise by that operation. The flags were collected by the Canal Zone police and were returned the next day to Lieutenant Colonel Raul Arias, aide-de-camp to President de la Guardia. The students paraded to the presidential palace with two of the university's perennial students, Cleto Manuel Souza and Bolivar Davalos, leaders of the Communist party, directing the march. They were received by the President who assured them that "Operation Sovereignty" had not ended with the return of the flags by the Zone authorities, that he would pursue the campaign for the Panama flag to fly in the Zone.

The Panama press and radio were unanimous in their praise of the deed by the students. While American authorities appeared to be inclined to laugh off the incident as a student prank, it was no joke as far as the Panamanians were concerned. This was to become indelibly impressed upon their minds in the next year, and, more tragically, in 1964.

The Communist-dominated students led a movement to try to overthrow the de la Guardia government in mid-May, 1958. The National Institute had been mobilized to join the university students for a march on the palace, to present demands for better schooling throughout the country. This was but a pretext, and de la Guardia knew it. He refused to receive them. The students rioted in the streets and, while they were being dispersed by force, one was killed. Street fighting continued for several days. On May 22, 1958, nine persons were killed and nearly one hundred were wounded as the perennial students incited them to continue the battle and converted Panama City into a battleground against the *Guardia Nacional*. This battle was to be confused by some wire services in January, 1964, when the initial stories on the flag war that erupted on the Canal Zone boundary inaccurately reported almost identical casualties in the flag riots of November 3, 1959. That was not so. Nobody was killed in the 1959 riots, and much less by American troops.

The students entrenched themselves in the National Institute and in the National University. The government suspended constitutional guarantees for thirty days and imposed censorship of the press and the radio. After this occurred, the high school students were, by agreement, moved out of the National Institute and into the redoubt that had been established in the autonomous university campus. There I saw the rifles and machine-gun emplacements that the students had erected on the rooftops of several of the faculties. The *Guardia Nacional* established a cordon around the university where one thousand students, male and female, were holed up, and cut off the students from all but telephone communication with the outside. Two of the leaders who were inside the university were, of course, Cleto Manuel Souza and Bolivar Davalos. Davalos appeared to be in command of the shock brigades there, for he operated officiously with a blackjack always visible in his hand. When I asked him what his role was in the student leadership of the rebellion against de la Guardia, he replied that he was something like a "minister without portfolio." He volunteered the information that he did not want to have an official title "because of the accusations against me that I entertain certain political beliefs."

The students, as they had done in the past, demanded the dismissal of the commanders of the *Guardia Nacional*. This de la Guardia refused to do. It took another week of negotiation before the rebellion was settled and the students returned to classes, but their weapons were not surrendered. The Communist perennial students had to retreat, because public opinion had already begun to turn against them. They had succeeded in advancing two steps in their goal toward total subversion, so now it was convenient to back up one step. The retreat, though, was to be but a temporary interlude for the bigger objectives in November, 1959, when flag riots would attract the attention of the world.

For this it was both necessary and convenient to establish a working alliance with the Nationalists. It was an easy, made-to-order arrangement. President Gamal Abdal Nasser had nationalized the Suez Canal in Egypt and gotten away with it. Panama, which had the fourth largest registered merchant fleet in the world, was incensed because it had not been invited to the 1956 Suez Canal Users' Association Conference that was called in London after Nasser seized the Suez Canal. Talk of finding a Nasser for Panama began to circulate.

The embassy of the United Arab Republic became very active along that line, and with money and intrigue it helped to stir up the passions of the Nationalists in which the Communists joined to undermine the United States' hold on the Canal. Just before the arrival of Milton Eisenhower in July, 1958, someone tossed two concrete bricks through the large plate glass window of the United States Information Service on Avenida Central in Panama City. Attached to one of the bricks was a note which exclaimed: THE CANAL ZONE IS OURS!

With the climate that had preceded his arrival, Milton Eisenhower was welcomed at Tocumen Airport on July 12, 1958, but he made no public appearances except those of an official nature. Still fresh in the minds of U. S. officials was the disgraceful discourtesy promoted by the Communists in Peru and Venezuela when they attacked Vice President Nixon and desecrated the American flag. Eisenhower had invited the university students, who let it be known that they wanted to see him, to meet him in the American Embassy residence but they refused. They demanded that the President of Johns Hopkins University hold an open forum with them in the auditorium of their university. Eisenhower would not accede to that demand, and no meeting was held. The students, though, made public a list of "minimum aspirations," for the information of Dr. Eisenhower. These included:

1. Express reaffirmation by the United States of the sovereignty of the Republic of Panama over the Canal Zone territory.

2. Equal share of the economic benefits (tolls revenue, etc.) from the Canal enterprise.

3. Express recognition of Panama's civil, penal, fiscal, and labor jurisdiction over nonmilitary affairs in the Canal Zone.

4. Elimination of United States postage stamps and exclusive use of the Panamanian postal service in the Canal Zone.

5. Flying of the Panamanian flag in the Canal Zone and recognition of Spanish as the official language therein.

6. Cessation of provocative and offensive acts on the part of Canal Zone residents and members of the United States Congress against the national dignity.

When Dr. Eisenhower's official talks with the government had concluded, Panama issued a statement in which it said that among the points presented by President de la Guardia and his cabinet to the Special Ambassador was one concerning the "creation of a better moral climate of cooperation between the people of Panama and the United States, the flying of the flag of Panama in the Canal Zone, and the adoption of Spanish as the official language there."

Eisenhower, on the other hand, very cautiously announced that there had been nothing in his talks with the Panamanians which "implied any change in the traditional treaty relationships between the two countries," especially regarding sovereignty.

But as far as the Panamanians were concerned, there remained pending the demands that had been rejected during the negotiations for the 1955 treaty, and, as was noted above, Panama, in its statement, emphasized Document D of the demands that were rejected then and now confined its desire for the official language in the Zone to be Spanish exclusively.

Dr. Milton Eisenhower left for Costa Rica in July, 1958, well convinced that there was definitely danger over Panama.

We have previously noted the rights received and the concessions made by the United States in the 1955 treaty. Better to understand the background for danger, although it has already been somewhat outlined, it may here be of benefit to make a comparison of the rights and obligations of both the United States and Panama under the basic treaties of 1903 and 1936.

Under the Hay-Bunau-Varilla Treaty of 1903 the United States made the following concessions to the new Republic of Panama:

1. Guaranteed the independence of the Republic of Panama.

2. Granted the right to have official dispatches of the government of Panama transmitted over any telegraph and telephone lines established for Canal purposes and for public and private business at rates not higher than those required from officials in the service of the United States.

3. Granted Panama $10 million in gold coin of the United States and an annual payment of $250,000 in gold, beginning nine years after the date of the exchange of ratifications.

4. Granted the Republic of Panama the right to transport over the

Canal its vessels and its troops and munitions of war at all times without paying charges of any kind. The exemption was extended to the auxiliary railway for the transportation of persons in the service of the Republic of Panama, or of the police force charged with the preservation of public order outside of the Zone, as well as to their baggage, munitions of war, and supplies.

5. The United States assumed the costs of damages caused to owners of private property of any kind by reason of the grants contained in the treaty or by reason of the operations of the United States, its agents or employees, or by reason of the construction, maintenance, operation, santitation, and protection of the Canal or of the works of sanitation and protection provided for in the treaty.

6. After fifty years, the system of sewers and waterworks constructed and maintained by the United States shall revert to and become the properties of the cities of Panama and Colón.

The rights received by the United States in the 1903 treaty were:

1. A grant in perpetuity of a zone of land and land under water ten miles in width and extending three miles into the Caribbean Sea and three miles into the Pacific Ocean, plus certain small islands in the Bay of Panama, for the maintenance, operation, sanitation, and protection of a canal across the Isthmus of Panama.

2. A grant in perpetuity of the use, occupation, and control of any other lands and waters outside of the Zone which may be necessary and convenient for the construction, maintenance, operation, sanitation, and protection of the Canal.

3. All the power and authority within the Zone and within the limits of all auxiliary lands and waters which the United States would possess and exercise if it were sovereign, to the entire exclusion of the exercise by the Republic of Panama of any such sovereign rights, power, or authority.

4. All the rights of the New Panama Canal Company and the Panama Railroad upon purchase of the Company's rights, privileges, properties, and concessions.

5. At all times and at its discretion to use its police and its land and naval forces, or to establish fortifications for the safety or protection of the Canal, or of the ships that transit it, or the railways and auxiliary works.

6. To use the rivers, streams, lakes, and other bodies of water in the Republic of Panama, for navigation, the supply of water, water power, or other purposes as may be necessary and convenient for the construction, maintenance, operation, sanitation, and protection of the Canal.

7. A grant of a monopoly in perpetuity for the construction, maintenance, and operation of any system of communication by any means of canal or railroad connecting the Caribbean Sea and the Pacific Ocean across Panamanian territory.

8. To acquire in the cities of Panama and Colón, by purchase or by the exercise of the right of eminent domain, any lands, buildings, water rights, or other properties necessary and convenient for the construction, maintenance, operation, and protection of a canal and of any works of sanitation, such as the collection and disposition of sewage and the distribution of water in said cities of Panama and Colón, at the discretion of the United States.

9. To impose and collect water rates and sewerage rates which shall be sufficient to provide for the payment of interest and the amortization of the principal of the cost of such works within a period of fifty years, upon which time the system of sewers and waterworks shall revert to and become the properties of the cities of Panama and Colón.

10. To enforce in perpetuity sanitary ordinances prescribed by the United States in the cities of Panama and Colón and the territories and harbors adjacent thereto in case the Republic of Panama should not be, in the judgment of the United States, able to maintain such order.

11. Authorization in perpetuity to maintain public order in the cities of Panama and Colón and the territories and harbors adjacent thereto in case the Republic of Panama should not be, in the judgment of the United States, able to maintain such order.

12. To make use of the towns and harbors of Panama and Colón as places of anchorage, and for making repairs, for loading, unloading, deposition, or transshipping cargoes either in transit or destined for the service of the Canal and for other works pertaining to the Canal.

13. Freedom from taxation upon the Canal, the railways and auxiliary works, tugs, and other vessels employed in the service of the Canal, storehouses, workshops, offices, quarters for laborers, factories of all kinds, warehouses, wharves, machinery, and other works, property, and effects appertaining to the Canal or railroad and auxiliary works,

or their officers or employees, situated within the cities of Panama and Colón, and freedom from taxation upon officers, employees, laborers, and other individuals in the service of the Canal and railroad and auxiliary works.

14. To import at any time into the Zone and auxiliary lands, free of customs duties, imposts, taxes, or other charges, and without any restrictions, all materials necessary and convenient in the construction, maintenance, operation, sanitation, and protection of the Canal and all provisions necessary and convenient for employees in the service of the United States and their families.

15. The right to purchase or lease lands adequate and necessary for naval or coaling stations on the Pacific coast and on the western Caribbean coast of the Republic of Panama at certain points to be agreed upon.

In the Treaty of 1936 the United States made the following concessions to Panama:

1. Renounced the guarantee of Panamanian independence.

2. Renounced the right to expropriate without restriction additional land for Canal use. Henceforth, in the event of some unforeseen contingency, should the utilization of lands or waters additional to those already employed be necessary for the maintenance, sanitation, or efficient operation of the Canal, or for its effective protection, the two governments will agree upon such measures as may be necessary to take.

3. Renounced the right of "eminent domain" in the cities of Panama and Colón.

4. Renounced the right to intervene to maintain public order in the cities of Panama and Colón.

5. Renounced the unlimited right to defend the Canal. In the event that the security of the Republic of Panama or the Canal is threatened, the matter will be the subject of consultation between the two governments.

6. Increased the annuity from $250,000 gold to $430,000 in standard currency.

7. Persons not connected with the operation or administration of the Canal were barred from renting dwellings in the Canal Zone belonging to the government of the United States or to reside in the Zone.

8. Sale of goods imported into the Zone or purchased, produced, or manufactured there by the government of the United States was limited to persons employed by the United States in the Canal Zone and members of the Armed Forces of the United States and their families. Contractors operating in the Zone and their employees and persons engaged in religious, welfare, charitable, educational, recreational, and scientific work may purchase such items only when they actually reside in the Zone.

9. All private business enterprises in the Zone, with the exception of concerns having a direct relation to the operation, maintenance, sanitation, or protection of the Canal, other than those existing at the time of the signature of the treaty, were prohibited.

10. The United States extended to merchants residing in Panama full opportunity for making sales to vessels arriving at terminal ports of the Canal or transiting the Canal.

11. The United States agreed to permit vessels entering at or clearing from ports of the Canal Zone to use and enjoy the dockage and other facilities of the ports for the purpose of loading or unloading cargoes and receiving or disembarking passengers to or from territory under the jurisdiction of the Republic of Panama.

12. The Republic of Panama was given the right to collect tolls from merchant ships in the ports of Panama City and Colón, even though they later pass through the Canal.

13. The United States agreed to furnish free of charge to the Republic of Panama the necessary sites for the establishment of customs houses in the ports of the Canal Zone for the collection of duties on importations destined to the Republic and for the examination of merchandise and passengers consigned to or bound for the Republic of Panama. Panama was given exclusive jurisdiction to enforce the immigration or customs laws of the Republic of Panama within the sites so provided.

14. The Republic of Panama was given the right to determine what persons or classes of persons arriving at ports of the Canal Zone shall be admitted or excluded from its jurisdiction.

12. The Bridge plus the Flags

As work on the $20 million suspension bridge across the Canal from La Boca (near Balboa) to the west bank, to connect with the Pan-American Highway and link the cities of Panama and Colón with the rest of the Republic, was about to get under way, the first flag riots broke out in the Canal Zone.

The bridge construction was a commitment that had been made to Panama, and, it will be recalled, President Eisenhower had signed the enabling legislation for its construction at the American Embassy when he visited the country in 1956. The United States proved to be about the only country in the world that would favor foreign manufacturers over her own industries in purchases for the Canal. The bridge was constructed with steel purchased from West Germany, whose mills underbid United States Steel by no more than $20,000. Then, in 1960, the Panama Canal Company placed a purchase order in Japan for what was ultimately to be a contract for fifty-nine electric towing locomotives for locks, and three cranes, because here, too, the Japanese were able to underbid American manufacturers.

When former Foreign Minister Aquilino Boyd had his eye on a possible presidential nomination in the 1960 campaign, he led a "sovereign-

207

ty" march into the Canal Zone on November 3, 1959, the anniversary of Panama's independence. He was allowed to head a column, carry a flag, and withdraw peacefully, after making certain he would get his desired advance publicity for the demonstration. But Communist-led students, who gathered along the Canal Zone boundary, had no intention of acting in a peaceful manner. They picked a fight with the Canal Zone police and attempted to commit vandalism. The Zone police were unable to cope with them, and Major General William E. Potter, Governor of the Canal Zone, requested Army support to control and disperse the mobs. Troops assumed positions abreast of 4th of July Avenue and contained the mobs. There were no deaths and only minor injuries.

This did not deter a mob from marching on to the American Embassy, and Aquilino Boyd was not far behind it. The mob rushed to the flagpole, lowered the United States flag, and desecrated it. Offices of American businesses were stoned and some looting took place before the *Guardia Nacional* restored order. American Ambassador Julian Harrington, who had recently returned from a visit to Washington with a personal letter from President Eisenhower for President de la Guardia, was at the palace for the Independence Day reception when the violence erupted. He had already requested an appointment with the President for November 5, with the intention of delivering the letter. The missive was to inform de la Guardia of some concessions the United States was making to Panama. Dr. Milton Eisenhower had recommended a nine-point plan in 1958, including the recognition of Panama's "titular sovereignty" in the Canal Zone by flying the Panamanian flag in selected locations, at least on ceremonial occasions. He had obtained agreement from the State Department on this, but the Congress, the Secretary of the Army, and the Governor of the Canal Zone protested, expressing fear that Panama would then demand complete jurisdiction in the Zone. A White House decision was to resolve this conflict.

Following violent disturbances on November 3, 1959, in which the students from the National Institute were in the limelight at the Canal Zone boundary, clamoring for sovereignty, flags, and other issues, President Eisenhower dispatched Deputy Undersecretary of State Livingston Merchant to Panama as his personal troubleshooter to confer with President de la Guardia. On November 24, 1959, Merchant said:

"During the course of our discussions, in response to a question by the President of Panama, I assured him that the policy of the U. S. government with respect to the status of the Canal Zone remains as it had been stated more than fifty years ago to the effect that the United States recognizes that titular sovereignty over the Canal Zone remains in the government of Panama."

Further demonstrations, including some violence against the Canal Zone, occurred again on November 28, 1959. Subsequently, the Panamanian Ambassador to the United States, former President Ricardo Manuel Arias, presented a formal request for, among other things, the flying of the Panamanian flag in the Canal Zone.

On December 2, 1959, President Eisenhower stated in a press conference that he did "in some form or other believe that we should have visual evidence that Panama does have titular sovereignty over the region." Also in a press conference, on December 10, 1959, Secretary of State Christian A. Herter stated that sympathetic consideration was being given to the proposal that the Panamanian flag fly in the Canal Zone.

President Eisenhower directed, on September 17, 1960, that the United States flag and the Panamanian flag be flown together in a single place in the Canal Zone known as Shaler Triangle. This action was announced in a White House release which read as follows:

Last December the President stated his belief that there should be visual evidence of Panama's titular sovereignty over the Panama Canal Zone. The President has now, as a voluntary and unilateral decision on the part of the government of the United States, approved and directed the flying of the flag of the Republic of Panama together with the United States flag on a daily basis in Shaler Triangle in the Canal Zone. The President has authorized the American Ambassador Joseph S. Farland, to make a public statement to this effect.

The President hopes that his decision will demonstrate the continuing close bonds that exist between the people of the United States and the Republic of Panama and their governments.

The U.S. note transmitted to the Panama foreign office on September 17, 1960, (Department of State Bulletin, October 10, 1960, Vol. XLIII, No. 1111, p. 558) stated:

I am pleased to state that, after the highest consideration by my government, I am instructed to inform you that as a further reflection of the genuine friendship existing between our two governments and peoples, my government has determined that as a voluntary act on the part of the United States, and in recognition of the titular sovereignty residing in the Republic of Panama with respect to the Canal Zone, the Panamanian flag will hereafter be flown together with the United States flag on a daily basis in the area known as Shaler Triangle in the Canal Zone. This determination is in no wise to be considered as modifying in any way the treaties and agreements in force between the United States and Panama.

On September 21, 1960, the two flags were first flown at Shaler Triangle, and they have flown there daily since then.

The fact that the flag was already being flown from the poles at Shaler Triangle and more dual sites were to be added failed to resolve the problem, for there were sinister forces at work to see that it remained insoluble. President de la Guardia told me that he did not accept an invitation that was extended to him by Ambassaor Farland to raise the Panama flag at Shaler Triangle because, despite three hours of pleading by Farland with him at his home: "I told Farland the flying of the flag at Shaler Triangle alone would not by itself solve the problem." He was present at the ceremony, but the flag was hoisted by a soldier of the United States Army. A Panamanian civilian broke through the security lines and stabbed an American Army sergeant just as the ceremony came to a close. The sergeant was not, happily, fatally wounded.

The arrival on the Isthmus of Ambassador Farland and new commanders in the Zone brought a new look to the scene. "Operation Friendship" was launched to try to abolish the "Hate America" campaign that had been in the ascendancy. Gradually, the people-to-people diplomacy of Farland, and closer contact established by the military commanders, especially Major General Theodore F. Bogart, United States Army Caribbean, began to reduce the tensions that had tended to widen the breach between the two peoples. Major General Robert J. Fleming, Jr., Governor of the Canal Zone, also sought to attain better relations, while Mrs. Fleming organized the Panama Canal Women's Welfare League for the same purpose.

But the undercurrents that were to breed future trouble failed to fade away with the advent of Operation Friendship. Nobody was more aware of that than Farland, yet his cultivation of Thelma King, who considered him a good friend, bewildered many Panamanian friends who were very familiar with her background and her activities.

President Eisenhower was ready to announce the nine-point program for improvement of relations between the United States and Panama on April 19, 1960, from his holiday White House in Augusta, Georgia. The text of the press release that was distributed by James C. Hagerty read:

The President today approved a nine-point program for improvement of relations between the United States and Panama in reference to operations in the Canal Zone. The program calls for substantial employee benefits, including pay increases and improved housing for Panamanian employees, the expansion of the apprentice program to train more Panamanians in skilled trades, and support of legislation to increase the pensions of disabled former employees.

The program also calls for the installation of a new water main to serve the city of Panama, and a reduction in the rate charged for water sold to the government of Panama for distribution within that country. The President also directed that jobs in the Canal Zone be continuously reviewed with a view to employing the maximum number of Panamanians.

Nearly all of the items in the program will be made effective immediately.

The complete program includes the following points:

1. A 10 per cent increase in the wage-rate schedules of unskilled and semiskilled employees.

2. The Panama Canal Company's apprentice program will be expanded to afford an opportunity to twenty-five Panamanians each year to begin three- and four-year courses leading to qualification as skilled workmen in various trades. This is a marked expansion of opportunity for Panamanians to learn those skills that are useful both in the Canal Zone and in the Republic of Panama. This program, in implementation of assurances given in the treaty, will provide to Panamanians upon graduation access to more positions, the pay rates of which are based on those in the United States.

3. Substandard housing occupied by Panamanian employees in the Canal Zone will be replaced by modern construction. Construction of

approximately five hundred units of modern rental housing is planned. Construction of the first houses in the program will be commenced immediately.

4. The Panama Canal Company will also pursue a course of action leading to the construction of five hundred houses in Panama for sale to Panamanians employed in the Canal Zone but living in Panama.

5. The Panama Canal Company will proceed with the construction of a new water main at a cost of $750,000 to supply the rapidly expanding suburbs of the city of Panama.

6. The Panama Canal Company will also substantially reduce the rate at which water is sold to the government of Panama for distribution in the cities of Panama and Colón.

7. The Panama Canal Company and Canal Zone government will support legislation now pending in Congress to increase the gratuity paid to employees who were not within the civil service retirement system and who were terminated because of physical disability.

8. Teachers in the Latin-American schools in the Canal Zone will receive a 10 per cent pay increase.

9. All agencies in the Canal Zone have been directed by the President to review the list of jobs reserved for citizens of the United States with a view to placing more Panamanians in skilled and supervisory positions.

The above concessions served to lessen tensions but nothing more. Despite all the grants made therein, the Panamanians still were dissatisfied and the same sinister forces were at work to keep them that way.

On June 13, 1962, the White House issued a joint communiqué between President John F. Kennedy and President Roberto F. Chiari, following their two days of meetings in Washington. The text of the communiqué read:

The meetings of the President of the Republic of Panama and the President of the United States of America during the past two days have been marked by a spirit of frankness, understanding, and sincere friendship. During their talks the two Presidents discussed general relations and existing treaties between their two countries, their mutual interests in the Panama Canal, and topics of world-wide hemispheric concern. They emphasized the close and friendly ties on which have been established a mutually advantageous association through partnership in the Panama Canal enterprise. On the conclusion of these talks, they agreed to publish the following joint communiqué.

They reaffirm the traditional friendship between Panama and the United States—a friendship based on their common devotion to the ideals of representative democracy, and to their determination that both nations should work as equal partners in the cause of peace, freedom, economic progress, and social justice.

The Presidents recognize that their two countries are bound together by a special relationship arising from the location and operation of the Panama Canal, which has played such an important part in the history of both their countries.

The President of Panama and the President of the United States agreed upon the principle that when two friendly nations are bound by treaty provisions which are not fully satisfactory to one of the parties, arrangements should be made to permit both nations to discuss these points of dissatisfaction. Accordingly, the Presidents have agreed to appoint high-level representatives to carry on such discussions. These representatives will start their work promptly.

As to some of these problems, it was agreed that a basis for their solution can now be stated. Accordingly, the two Presidents further agreed to instruct their representatives to develop measures to assist the Republic of Panama to take advantage of commercial opportunities available through increased participation by Panamanian private enterprise in the market offered by the Canal Zone, and to solve such labor questions in the Canal Zone as equal employment opportunities, wage matters, and social security coverage.

They also agreed that their representatives will arrange for the flying of Panamanian flags in an appropriate way in the Canal Zone.

In order to support the efforts of the government of Panama to improve tax collections in order to meet better the needs of the people of Panama, President Kennedy agreed in principle to instruct his representatives to work out in conjunction with the Panamanian representatives arrangements under which the U.S. government will withhold the income taxes of those Panamanian and non-United States citizen employees in the Zone, who are liable for such taxes under existing treaties and the Panamanian income tax law.

The President of Panama mentioned a number of other practical problems in relations between the two countries of current concern to his government, including the need of Panama for pier facilities, and the two Presidents agreed that their representatives would over the coming months discuss these problems as well as others that may arise.

The Presidents reaffirmed their adherence to the principle and commitments of the charter of Punta del Este. They agreed on the need to execute rapidly all steps necessary to make the Alliance for Progress effective; they recognized that the Alliance is a joint effort calling for development programing for effective use of national as well as external resources, institutional reforms, tax reforms, vigorous application of existing laws, and a just distribution of the fruits of national development to all sectors of the community.

The two Presidents declared that political democracy, national independence, and the self-determination of peoples are the political principles which shape the national policies of Panama and the United States. Both countries are joined in a hemisphere-wide effort to accelerate economic progress and social justice.

In conclusion the two Presidents expressed their gratification at this opportunity to exchange views and to strengthen the friendly and mutually beneficial relationship which has long existed between Panama and the United States. Their meeting was a demonstration of the understanding and reciprocal cooperation of the two countries and strengthened bonds of common interests and friendship between their respective peoples.

Ambassador Farland and Governor Fleming were appointed by President Kennedy as his high-level representatives, and President Chiari designated Foreign Minister Solis and Dr. Octavio Fabrega to represent him.

The flag question was the first substantive matter which they discussed. Governor Fleming, with the concurrence of Ambassador Farland, developed a list of fifteen sites at which the United States and Panamanian flags would fly together in the Canal Zone, including Shaler Triangle where the dual flags had been flying since September 21, 1960, by direction of President Eisenhower. The list of site locations was presented to Panama at a meeting on July 20, 1962, for discussion purposes and was forwarded to Washington for review by the Department of State and other departments. Panama acquiesced in the selected sites, and they were approved in principle by those who reviewed the matter in Washington. The original sites selected did not include any schools. At no time did Panama or any one in Washington, according to Governor Fleming, object to the specific list of civilian areas where the flag was to be flown or suggest any additions or deletions or raise a question about the schools.

The Bay of Pigs invasion of 1961, to try to end the Communist dictatorship of Fidel Castro in Cuba, was to dip American prestige in Latin America to an all-time low, not because it was attempted but because it was a failure. This deterioration was to become all too evident in Panama in 1962, just ten days before the Cuban missile crisis, with the new bridge across the Canal to be both the cause and the effect.

On October 8, 1962, the Honorable Clarence Cannon of Missouri, distinguished and respected Chairman of the Appropriations Committee of the House of Representatives, said this about the bridge on the floor of the Congress:

> MR. CANNON: Mr. Speaker, on October 12—Columbus Day—the Thatcher Ferry Bridge across the Panama Canal, on the site of the Thatcher Ferry—which it will supersede—will be formally dedicated. An appropriate program has been arranged, to be concluded by a talk by Maurice H. Thatcher, who will thereupon cut the ribbon and permit traffic to begin. Governor Thatcher is the sole surviving member of the Isthmian Canal Commission, the body which had supervisory authority over the construction of the Canal.
>
> The ceremonies of dedication will be carried out in the forenoon, and Undersecretary of State George W. Ball will deliver the principal address. Doubtless, Governor Robert J. Fleming, Jr., of the Canal Zone, President of the Panama Canal Company, will preside. The President of Panama, Honorable Roberto F. Chiari, and other prominent Panamanian and Canal Zone officials are expected to be present, together with the Panamanians and U.S. citizens.
>
> The bridge—from all accounts—is a splendid structure, and, aside from its utility, will symbolize—in the largest degree—the ideal of unity between and among the American nations.

The Thatcher Ferry, and connecting Thatcher Highway on the west side of the Canal, were provided under congressional legislation enacted years ago while Governor Thatcher was a member of the House from Kentucky. Since its establishment the ferry has carried across the Canal nearly 100 million passengers and nearly 24,000 vehicles.

Indeed, in the more than thirty years of its operation, toll free, it has performed for the Canal Zone and the Republic of Panama indispensable services; and the name given the bridge by the Congress retains the ferry's historic designation, and at the same time honors Governor Thatcher for his long-continued and most useful service for the Canal enterprise, and its employees—U.S. citizens and non-citizens—and for all the Isthmian people. In specific legislation, in addition for that establishing the ferry and highway, was the Act of 1928, which he introduced and sponsored to enactment, which authorized the establishment, in Panama City, of the Gorgas Memorial Laboratory, which through the years has come to be one of the outstanding institutions of the world dealing with research involving the cause and prevention of tropical disease; and since his retirement from Congress he has served as Vice President and General Counsel of the supervisory authority, the Gorgas Memorial Institute of Tropical and Preventive Medicine, without compensation, as is true of all the officers of the institute. Governor Thatcher had also been chiefly responsible for congressional legislation granting benefits of annuity and retirement character for both U.S. citizens of the Canal construction, and noncitizens, both of construction and maintenance service.

For considerations thus involved the Congress, by unanimous action of the two Appropriation Committees and the two Houses, wrote into the Appropriations Act for the Panama Canal for 1962 the formal designation for the bridge, thus specifically honoring Governor Thatcher; and following bridge nomenclature in the United States in carrying on bridge names, where the structures succeeded historic ferries, the names of ferries superseded—as, for instance, Harpers' Ferry Bridge across the Potomac River, the Eggner's Ferry Bridge across Kentucky Lake, and many others. The Thatcher Ferry Bridge will be free of tolls; and its construction costs have been—as its maintenance and operations costs will be—borne entirely by funds provided—directly or indirectly—by or under congressional authorization.

A Thatcher Ferry Bridge stamp, symbolic in character, 500,000 four-cent, was issued the day of dedication.

The bridge has been constructed by the Panama Canal Company—the official organization now authorized by law to maintain and operate the Canal. To its officers and agents, and to the contractors and all others who have contributed to the building of the structure, the thanks of all are due. The bridge, and its two miles of approaches, are wholly within the Canal Zone. It should symbolize the spirit and purposes of Pan-Americanism, and the labors of all those who have participated in the construction, maintenance, operation, and defense of the great Isthmian waterway: this, in addition to the specific honor conferred and the historic utility perpetuated. All of which the Congress evidently had in mind, and the man thus honored has emphasized.

Panamanian public opinion voiced its objections to the naming of the bridge by the Congress of the United States in honor of Thatcher. He had, as Representative Cannon had pointed out, previously been honored by the naming of the now obsolete ferry service for him. When I reached Panama several days before the dedication ceremony, I was able to observe that the campaign against the name of the bridge, which had been waging for months, had reached uncontrollable proportions and was certain to produce unpleasant incidents in the Canal Zone. Farland had been so concerned about the emotional buildup that was prevalent in Panama that he made a special trip to Washington to consult with the State Department. Representative Daniel J. Flood, member of Congress from the 11th District, Wilkes-Barre, Pennsylvania, wrote to me on August 16, 1963, after reading my chapter on Panama in *Operation America*: "With regard to your statement on page 112 that the naming of the new bridge at Balboa was done by the Congress 'over the protests of the State Department and the Department of the Army,' I can categorically state that no such protests were made by either, although there was ample opportunity to do so. Nor was any such protest made by the Republic of Panama." Governor Fleming told me in an interview in his office at Balboa Heights on January 18, 1964, that Farland discussed the problem with President Kennedy, who directed him to confer with Thatcher and urge the Kentuckian to request the Congress not to name the bridge after him. Farland was unable to persuade Thatcher. Although the Congress officially named it the Thatcher Ferry Bridge, the Panamanians insist on calling it the Bridge of the Americas.

A joint United States-Republic of Panama Thatcher Ferry Bridge Dedication Committee was organized. Fleming appointed Will G. Arey, then his information officer, to represent the Canal Zone, and

Panama designated Camilo Levy Salcedo, Director of Protocol, to represent the foreign office. Because of the command set up and the division of responsibility that prevailed in the area, the American Embassy had no primary role in the arrangements. Riding the crest of the wave of public opinion in Panama, though, the diplomatic corps, after consulting the foreign office and receiving an inconclusive reply to a question as to whether the government was extending an official invitation to attend the dedication ceremony, elected to boycott the occasion. There were weak pretexts offered, such as that it was beyond their dignity to ride in Zone buses to the bridge. The envoy of the United Arab Republic was among the prime movers of the boycott and now the entire corps solidified itself behind this obvious slap against the United States. The French ambassador remained away, as did all but two Latin-American diplomats—the Colombian, who had presented his credentials to Chiari the day before, and the Peruvian *chargé d'affaires*. The Panama foreign office also considered it an affront against President Chiari who was a guest of honor, but it did not pursue the issue, apparently realizing that its own inconclusive reply to the representatives of the diplomatic corps contributed to it. That it was intended as a slap against the United States there was absolutely no doubt, for when the members of the corps decided to boycott the ceremony they excluded Farland from the invitations to attend their meeting. Every living former President of Panama, with the sole exception of Dr. Harmodio Arias who was ill at the time, was present at the dedication ceremony on the bridge.

As often has been the case in recent years in some Latin-American countries, the Christian Democrats, who had formed a new party in Panama, quickly jumped on the bandwagon of public opinion to try to capture, and capitalize on, the bridge issue. But these political novices were to prove no match for the highly-trained Communists, who refused to let them steal their show. The Christian Democrats organized a demonstration to be held at the bridge dedication and the Communists were there right on their heels. The Canal Zone police had blocked the ramp approach from the Panama City side to the general public, but they were ordered to allow a small delegation of Christian Democrats to proceed through and display their Panama flag and a giant banner that read: BRIDGE OF THE AMERICAS, and other protest banners

across the width of the bridge. The Christian Democrats were orderly
and respectful of the orators, but not so the Communists.

Undersecretary of State George W. Ball was delivering a major
policy speech regarding relations with Panama. He had important news
for the Panamanians. The United States was going to make more concessions: Panmanian flags would be flown at additional sites and Panamanian postage stamps would be used, with overprints, in the Canal
Zone. The impact of those announcements was destroyed by the Communists, who scuffled with the police at the ramp barricade. The scuffle
graduated into a near riot. Communist activists climbed over the heads
of spectators, jumped the barricade, both human and wooden, and
then broke the police lines wide open. The police did not try to club
any one and treated the lawbreakers with kid gloves. The Communists
advanced towards the vicinity of the speakers' platform where Chiari,
visibly dismayed over the comportment of his countrymen, was seated.
The police halted them before they could reach the stand but they
shouted epithets and interrupted the orators constantly. The disturbance, which was getting completely out of hand, induced Governor
Fleming to cut short the program. Thatcher never got an opportunity to
deliver his speech. Neither was it possible for the motorcade, which was
to have been led by President Chiari, Ball, Thatcher, Fleming, Farland,
and other dignitaries, to make the scheduled official first trip across the
bridge to the west bank of the Canal. Five thousand Panamanians, led
by the Communist activists, streamed through and took command of
the bridge while the dignitaries and guests were quickly whisked away
by automobiles and buses to safety through a Zone exit from the bridge.
The Panamanians marched in force across the bridge and back, and
before they were finished they had pried loose the commemorative
plaques on each end which bore its name: THATCHER FERRY BRIDGE.

Since Chiari's return home from his White House visit, a joint high-
level United States-Panama commission had been meeting weekly to
discuss and try to iron out problems that continued to mar relations.
As has been previously noted, President Kennedy named Farland and
Fleming to represent him and Chiari appointed Foreign Minister Solis
and former Foreign Minister Octavio Fabrega as his delegates. When
Chiari and Solis left Washington they were under the misapprehension
that the joint-commission discussions were going to include treaty

negotiations. That was the impression that they conveyed to me when I interviewed them as they left for Panama. No such commitment had been made, but they had elected to give their own hopeful and wishful interpretation to the formal but inconclusive presidential meeting at the White House. Panama had repeatedly made public what it desired in a revised treaty and what it planned to add to the previously rejected demands. Chiari told the nation at the end of the year 1962 that if the United States planned to build a new canal it would have to negotiate a new treaty with the Republic.

The year 1963 found the joint commission still meeting weekly but making no headway toward treaty negotiations. There was much political criticism of Chiari in the press and over the radio because his administration was making no progress toward a new treaty with the United States. Then the bombshell exploded. In mid-August the joint commission declared its work terminated, and Farland, the most popular ambassador ever to serve in Panama since a fellow Republican, Roy Tasco Davis, Sr., was American Minister there thirty years earlier, resigned. He had become exasperated with disappointments, the bureaucratic bungling in Washington, and with other roadblocks that he encountered in the performance of his mission. The State Department had offered him a transfer assignment in the same rank, but he declined it.

Farland submitted his resignation to President Kennedy on August 25, 1963, but he did not depart for a while. He had many farewells to say. He traveled the length and breadth of the country to bid goodbye to the people—a people for whom he had done much good and whose cause he had tried to help. He had been chosen "Ambassador of the Year" by the Panamanians in 1962, an unusual, although much deserved, distinction. The Panamanians showed sincere respect, affection, and admiration for this American who had stumped the hinterlands to meet them on a people-to-people level hitherto unmatched. He was accorded the biggest farewell ever given an American Ambassador, which brought protests from the Communists who had burned him in effigy in the province of Veraguas in 1962, and from the chauvinists. Both groups complained that honors were being accorded to Farland that never had been tendered to their own officials in their sixty years of independence. Panama was to remain without an American Ambassador for many months.

The bridge incident of October 12, 1962, was a direct slap in Uncle Sam's face. The Zone police could have driven back the demonstrators, who were trespassing and were guilty of disorderly conduct, but higher authority considered it impolitic to take such action. Also, Undersecretary Ball's speech was to produce a repercussion among some American employees in the Zone that was to create the flag issue.

The official publication of the Canal Zone, the Panama Canal *Spillway*, summarized the background of the flag issue in its edition of January 27, 1964, as follows:

While the list of civilian sites was not in itself controversial, Panama sought also to have her flag flown in military areas and on transiting ships. And some members of Congress and many U.S.-citizen residents in the Canal Zone felt strongly against the flying of the Panamanian flag at all in the Canal Zone. The House of Representatives had passed House Resolution 459 on February 2, 1960, against flying the Panamanian flag. The pertinent 1961 appropriation act contained a rider prohibiting the use of Canal Zone government or Panama Canal Company funds to install a flagpole for flying a Panamanian flag in the Canal Zone (Public Law 85-451, May 13, 1960). Nevertheless, the September, 1960 action by President Eisenhower followed, and the dual flags were established in Shaler Triangle, using special funds.

When the new Thatcher Ferry Bridge was dedicated on October 12, 1962, United States and Panamanian flags were flown at each end of the center span. These flags, the first dual sets to be flown since the Shaler Triangle action, have flown twenty-four hours a day ever since.

On October 29, 1962, in further implementation of the agreement, dual flags were flown at the Administration Building at Balboa Heights, and on November 1, 1962, at the Administration Building at Cristobal. This followed public announcement of the agreement on flags by President Chiari in an address to the Panamanian National Assembly on October 1, 1962.

On January 10, 1963, the joint commission created by Presidents Kennedy and Chiari issued a joint communiqué, the first paragraph of which reads as follows:

"1. It has been agreed that the flag of the Republic of Panama will be flown together with the flag of the United States of America on land in the Canal Zone where the flag of the United States of America is flown by civilian authorities. Private organizations and persons in the Zone are free to display flags at will over their places of residence or business. Other aspects of the flag question will be discussed later."

On October 26, 1962, a Panama Canal Company employee, Gerald Doyle, had filed suit against the governor of the Canal Zone seeking to enjoin the flying of the Panamanian flag in the Canal Zone. This action received substantial support from many Canal Zone residents and from some members of Congress. While the suit was pending the Governor refrained from initiating any further dual flags at the remaining sites. Panama, apparently understanding the situation, did not press for action to further implement the flag agreement during the litigation, despite adverse press comment in Panama concerning the litigation.

The flag suit was dismissed by the U.S. District Court in the Canal Zone on July 8, 1963, the court opinion holding that the matter was one of executive discretion. The time for appeal expired on September 27, 1963, without an appeal having been filed.

Thereafter, the Governor directed that the dual flags be flown at the remaining selected sites. This was carried out in accordance with a schedule which would permit completion of the installation of all poles by February 7, 1964. As each set of poles was erected the two flags were immediately flown thereon, without publicity or ceremony. In the meantime the list of fifteen locations for the two flags had increased to seventeen by reason of the Governor's addition of sites at two cemeteries, which had been mentioned but not specifically included at the time of the original list.

During the course of the year, some flagpoles at locations not selected for dual flags were removed, such as at the Governor's residence which is a block or so from the Administration Building where the two flags were already flying. The removal of flagpoles drew some adverse press comment. In general, the sites for the dual flags were selected to provide for such display in each major population area plus special locations such as the locks and governmental administration buildings.

In November, 1963 the Governor considered flying the dual flags at the four high schools. This question was discussed informally with the Canal Zone civic council leaders and with the senior officials of the Panama Canal Company and Canal Zone government. The civic councils felt strongly that such dual displays at the schools would lead to major flag incidents. Senior agency officials generally agreed with the civic councils. This position was consistent with the informal opinion received from school officials in 1962 when the question of flags at schools was first considered by the Governor. The original decision not to fly the dual flags outside the schools, and therefore no flag, under the agreement, was reaffirmed by the Governor in December, 1963.

By the end of December, 1963, eleven of the dual flag installations were in operation, with five more scheduled for January and early February, 1964, and the final site set for new Gorgas Hospital when construction would be completed late in 1964.

During the Christmas holidays it was decided by the Governor that full implementation of the agreement with Panama would be put into effect on January 2, 1964, at which time the Panamanian flag would be flown wherever the U.S. flag was flown by civilian authorities. This meant that no U.S. flags would be flown outside the schools and at about four other locations where single U.S. flags were still flying on December 31.

On December 30, 1963 the following press release was issued by the Governor:

"On and after January 2, 1964 the Panamanian flag will be flown together with the flag of the United States on civilian land areas in the Canal Zone where the U.S. flag is flown by civilian authorities.

"This action implements the understanding made public in a joint communiqué issued by the two governments earlier this year which stated that 'the flag of the Republic of Panama will be flown together with the flag of the United States of America on land in the Canal Zone where the flag of the United States of America is flown by civilian authorities. Private organizations and persons in the Zone are free to display flags at will over their places or residence or business.'

"For some time the Panama Canal has been erecting dual flagpoles at selected sites. Work has been completed and the two flags are now flying at eleven of the sites. Dual flagpoles will be erected at five additional sites between now and the early part of February. One further location at which the two flags will fly will be the new Gorgas Hospital addition when it is completed later this year.

"The eleven locations where the two flags are now flying are Shaler Plaza, Thatcher Ferry Bridge, the Administration Building in Balboa and also at Cristobal, Miraflores and Gatun Locks, Coco Solo and Corozal Hospitals, Palo Seco, Margarita, and Coco Solo. The five remaining locations in addition to the new Gorgas Hospital addition are Gamboa-Santa Cruz, Rainbow City, Paraiso, Mount Hope Cemetery, and Corozal Cemetery. Locations at which the U.S. flag has currently been flown alone and at which no flags will be flown on or after January 2, 1964, are the schools; the Ancon District Court Building; the Industrial Division, Cristobal; a site in Gamboa, which will be replaced by the site for the two flags; and the present Gorgas Hospital.

"In accordance with law and customs requiring the U.S. flag to be displayed in or near schools, the U.S. flag will continue to be displayed in classrooms or elsewhere within the schools as at present. The Panamanian flag will continue to be displayed with the U.S. flag in all Latin-American schools and in certain other schools as appropriate, following present practice."

Schools reopened on Thursday, January 2, 1964, after the Christmas holiday. The U.S. flag, which formerly had been raised in front of each school on school days was no longer flown, in accordance with the commitment to Panama to fly two or none.

During the first few days of the new school period, students at Balboa High School began to generate feeling in protest against the discontinuance of the U.S. flag outside the school. A U.S. flag is displayed in every classroom, but the outside flag became an object of current significance. By Monday, January 6, it was known by school officials, some parents, and others that some of the students intended to go to school early on Tuesday, January 7, and to raise the U.S. flag on the outside pole at Balboa High School. On Friday, January 3, a petition to President Johnson protesting the discontinuance of the U.S. flag outside the Balboa High School was circulated at the school and signed by 400 to 500 students.

Balboa High School has an enrollment of 1,851. Of these 1,777 are U.S. citizens. Nine hundred twenty-seven, or 50.1 per cent of the students at Balboa High School, are children of military or civilian personnel of the U.S. Armed Forces; 639, or 34.5 per cent, are children of employees of the Canal Zone government and Panama Canal Company; 136, or 7.3 per cent, are children of American businessmen and other non-government personnel in Panama and the Canal Zone. Seventy-five, or 4.1 per cent, are children of U.S.-citizen employees of the U.S. Embassy, AID, USIS, and the Federal Aviation Agency. Seventy-four, or 4 per cent, are non-U.S.-citizen tuition students, principally Panamanians.

By 6:45 A.M. on Tuesday, January 7, about 25 students had gathered on the lawn in front of the high school with a flag. The halyards were locked on the pole. Attempts were made to climb the pole, but efforts to get the flag aloft were at first not successful. By 7:25 some 200 to 300 students, mostly observers, were present and a group of 50 to 80 were around the pole itself. The few actually working at it finally worked the halyards loose so that, despite the lock, the flag was raised at 7:25. School officials were present, and a couple of policemen were in the area. A dozen or so adults, presumably parents, were on the sidelines.

Classes started at 7:45, and nearly all students attended. Absenteeism during the day was nearly normal. A dozen or so adults and students remained in the area across the street from the campus. At 8:20 the Acting Superintendent of Schools, the Principal of the high school, and the Civil Affairs Director, within whose Bureau the schools operate, lowered the flag, which was taken to the Principal's office.

The first class period was over at 8:38 A.M., and at 8:40 six college students and one high-school student put up another small flag. About 150 students were on the school steps or lawn, and they pledged allegiance to the flag. A number of adults were in the area. School officials were present. No police were in the immediate area.

No effort to prevent the students' action was taken because of a policy decision approved by the Governor that an incident involving physically preventing these American students from raising the American flag outside their school and pledging allegiance should be avoided, in the expectation that the protest demonstration would have achieved its purpose and the flag could be lowered quietly later. No laws were broken, and it was considered that the demonstration by the students did not constitute a flying of the flag by "civilian authorities."

It was understood that the active ringleader group of students intended to require authorities to use force if an effort were made to prevent the raising of the flag, or to take it down once up, or to remove the flagpole. School officials urged students to return to classes, which nearly all did. Photographers, professional and others, were present at all actions described.

During the morning a small group of students kept watch from just off the campus. Between classes large numbers appeared to see what had happened, there having been rumors that the authorities intended to remove the pole or halyard. At noon the students substituted a larger flag on the pole. After school about 100 students, with adults, remained around the area until late evening to prevent action to remove the flag or pole. About 25 remained on watch all night and were furnished food and blankets by adult sympathizers.

At 6:00 P.M. on Tuesday the flag was lowered by six high-school boys. At 7:30 A.M. on Wednesday it was again raised. The situation was about the same on Wednesday. In the afternoon some 200 students marched around the flag with placards demanding that the flag stay up. Ringleaders told school officials that students would continue in classes so long as the flag was up. It was understood that if the flag were taken down the fire alarm would be used to signal a student rush to prevent the action. The Principal put out written bulletins assuring that there was no intention to remove the flagpole, and cautioning against any improper use of the fire-alarm system.

On the Atlantic side similar action was taken on Wednesday by large numbers of students at Cristobal High School with substantial parental support. Groups went to several elementary schools also and put up flags, on both the Atlantic and Pacific sides.

On Wednesday, January 8, the Governor issued a statement appealing to the public for cooperation. He reviewed the background of the dual flag program and said:

> I believe that it is unnecessary for me to dwell at length on the responsibilities of U.S. citizens to abide by the official commitments of their government. I would, however, like to emphasize that we have a particular responsibility here in the Canal Zone where our actions are subject to direct view by citizens of other countries.
>
> I request the cooperation of all U.S. citizens at this time in honoring our country's commitments and in showing our good faith by our own actions. We must set the example and some recent actions have not been good in view of an international commitment of the United States.
>
> At the same time, I will say that the list of official locations at which the two flags are to be flown is not final and absolute. Should the various communities desire dual flag displays at other locations, it is possible that we can make appropriate additions in consonance with our international commitment. In this regard, I would look to the civic councils for advice as to the wishes of the communities.

On Thursday morning, January 9, the Governor pre-taped and film-recorded an address to the public. This statement was presented by by Canal Zone radio and television at 6:15 P.M. It revealed the discussions with Panama during the preceding two years with particular reference to the flag issue. The Governor explained the commitment to Panama, the selection of the sites for dual flags, and the issue as to flags at the schools. He stated that "the flag agreement is a valid commitment of our government. We Americans in the Zone have an obligation as citizens to support that commitment regardless of our personal beliefs. I hope that we Americans will conduct ourselves with reason, and in an emotional situation successfully avoid emotionalism."

13. The Flag Issue

The already mentioned communiqué of the Farland-Fleming-Solis-Fabrega joint commission, which was issued on January 10, 1963, showed that some of Panama's demands that had been flatly rejected during the negotiations for the 1955 treaty now had been conceded by executive fiat of President Kennedy, and thus they would not require ratification by the Senate of the United States of America. The full text of the revealing communiqué read:

> The representatives of the governments of the Republic of Panama and of the United States of America, appointed to discuss points of dissatisfaction in United States-Panamanian relations with regard to the Canal Zone, have periodically met during the past four months. Various aspects of pending questions have been discussed up to the present, with the following results:
>
> 1. It has been agreed that the flag of the Republic of Panama will be flown together with the flag of the United States of America on land in the Canal Zone where the flag of the United States of America is flown by civilian authorities. Private organizations and persons in the Zone are free to display at will over their places of residence or business. Other aspects of the flag question will be discussed later.

2. Foreign consuls, on the basis of exequaturs issued by the government of Panama and, in accordance with procedures and understandings which have been agreed upon by the government of Panama and the government of the United States, may function in the Canal Zone. Subject to these procedures and understandings, the United States government will cease issuing documents of exequatur.

3. The representatives of both governments have discussed labor problems relating to Panamanian citizens who work in the Canal Zone. Special attention has been devoted to the subjects of wage scales, equal opportunities for Panamanian and United States citizens at all levels, and social security benefits. All these problems continue to be under discussion.

4. The representatives of Panama submitted for discussion the question of using Panamanian postage stamps in the Canal Zone postal system. The United States government has proposed the use of Panamanian postage stamps in the Zone in accordance with technical arrangements now under consideration and in conformance with international postal standards.

5. In accordance with instructions, the representatives have discussed Panama's need for pier facilities and have visited the present pier facilities in Cristobal. This subject continues to be under discussion.

The representatives of the governments of the United States of America and of the Republic of Panama will continue their present discussions aimed at finding solutions to other problems which remain unresolved.

The discussions are continuing in the spirit of the joint communiqué issued by the President of Panama and the President of the United States of America at the end of the visit which the President of Panama made to Washington in June of last year. From time to time additional joint communiqués outlining the program of the discussions will be issued.

The above communiqué was to produce most serious repercussions. There were American employees of the Canal Zone who were unalterably opposed to any extension of the dual flag policy because they envisaged, as Dr. Milton Eisenhower had been forewarned by Zone authorities and by the Secretary of the Army in 1958, that it would result in further encroachment of the jurisdictional rights therein. The fight in the Zone was led by Gerald A. Doyle, Jr., an architect, and he made known his views publicly in letters published in "The Mail Box" column of the Panama *American*, the only afternoon English-language newspaper. The paper was owned by the heirs of former President Harmodio Arias, who died December 23, 1962, and its executive editor was Edward William Scott, a New Zealander. Scott also acted as stringer for NBC.

The flag suit that was referred to in the preceding chapter was filed by Doyle during the height of the Cuban missile crisis and before the above communiqué was issued. As I consider the memorandum opinion of Judge Guthrie F. Crowe, which received little or no detailed publicity, of considerable historic importance, I record it in full herewith:

UNITED STATES DISTRICT COURT
FOR THE DISTRICT OF THE CANAL ZONE
BALBOA DIVISION

GERALD A. DOYLE, JR.,

Plaintiff,

vs

ROBERT J. FLEMING, JR.,
Governor of the Canal Zone   CIVIL NO. 5456
Government and CYRUS R.
VANCE, Secretary of the Army
in his supervisory capacity for
the administration of the Canal
Zone Government,

Defendants.

MEMORANDUM OPINION

The plaintiff, Gerald A. Doyle, Jr., began this action by filing a complaint against the defendant, Robert J. Fleming, Jr., Governor of the Canal Zone government. The complaint was filed on October 26, 1962 and prayed for a temporary restraining order and a perpetual injunction to restrain Fleming from displaying on or about any public building in the Canal Zone, on a daily or permanent basis, any national flag or banner except the national flag of the United States.

Doyle alleged that Fleming's proposed act of displaying the Panamanian flag on or about the Administration Building of the Canal Zone and numerous other places at an equal height with the flag of the United States is contrary to the laws of the United States, would place the sovereignty of the United States in the Canal Zone in jeopardy, and that the plaintiff and other taxpayers of the United States would suffer irreparable damage thereby and he has no adequate remedy at law.

Plaintiff filed with his complaint a list of Points and Authorities in compliance with the Canal Zone Code and among other things stated that he relies on 36 USC 175 (c).

The temporary restraining order was denied by this court on the ground that irreparable injury would not accrue to the plaintiff, and leave to amend was granted.

On November 23, 1962, the plaintiff amended his complaint and included therein Cyrus R. Vance, Secretary of the Army in his supervisory capacity for the administration of the Canal Zone government.

The amended complaint asserts that "The Governor" since October 12, 1962 has caused the United States flag and the Panamanian flag to be flown at equal heights on the Thatcher Ferry Bridge in the Canal Zone, that since October 29, 1962, the flags have been caused to be flown equally by "The Governor" at the Canal Zone Administration Building and other places and that he intends to display the two flags simultaneously at equal heights in numerous public places daily in the Canal Zone.

Plaintiff states that "The Governor" intends to abolish the use of Canal Zone postage stamps approved and issued by the United States Post Office Department for the Canal Zone postal system and to substitute therefore stamps supplied by the Republic of Panama and that he intends to recognize in the Canal Zone the exequaturs issued by the Republic of Panama to foreign consuls to the same extent that such exequaturs are recognized in the Republic of Panama.

Plaintiff prays for a final injunction to restrain the defendants for he says that Fleming's acts and contemplated acts are done or to be done with the consent or at the direction of Vance and that such acts are contrary to the laws of the United States and that the sovereignty of the United States in the Canal Zone will be placed in jeopardy or tend to be relinquished without due process of law to the irreparable damage of plaintiff and other citizens and taxpayers of the United States and residents of the Canal Zone.

An attempt was made to serve summons upon defendant, Vance, as Secretary of the Army, by leaving a copy of the summons and complaint with the Governor of the Canal Zone. A motion to quash the service and return of service was made by the District Attorney as counsel for the defendants on the ground that the Governor of the Canal Zone is "neither an agent nor a representative of the said defendant authorized by appointment or by law to receive service of process" and the motion was sustained.

A further amended complaint was filed by the plaintiff which reiterates the facts alleged in the first amended complaint and sets out additional matter descriptive of the United States interests in the Canal Zone. This pleading delineates the acts complained of more fully but asks for the same relief previously prayed and further requests that defendants, their employees, agents, or successors in office be restrained from committing or omitting any act reasonably tending to relinquish or derogate the sovereignty of the United States in the Canal Zone.

Process was thereafter served on Secretary Cyrus Vance as defendant by Gerald A. Doyle whose affidavit states that he sent to Vance at his Washington address a copy of the alias summons and amended complaint by "registered mail."

The defendants through their attorneys of the Department of Justice moved to quash the purported service upon Secretary Vance and moved to dismiss the complaint on the grounds that plaintiff lacks standing to sue and that the court lacks jurisdiction of the subject matter.

I

Motion to Quash

An attempt to have service upon the defendant, Vance, was made by the plaintiff by sending him a copy of the summons and amended complaint by "registered mail" in an attempted compliance with 28 USC 1391 (e) (Supp. 1962), which is as follows:

"(e) A civil action in which each defendant is an officer or employee of the United States or any agency thereof acting in his official capacity or under color of legal authority, or an agency of the United States, may, except as otherwise provided by law, be brought in any judicial district in which (1) a defendant in the action resides, or (2) the cause of action arose, or (3) any real property involved in the action is situated, or (4) the plaintiff resides if no real property is involved in the action.

"The summons and complaint in such an action shall be served as provided by the Federal Rules of Civil Procedure except that the delivery of the summons and complaint to the officer or agency as required by the rules may be made by certified mail beyond the territorial limits of the district in which the action is brought."

As stated in defendants' brief, ". . . the statute, by its terms, is limited to actions brought 'in any judicial district.' " Judicial districts are defined, as used in Title 28, to mean "the districts enumerated in Chapter 5 of this title." 28 USC 4515. The Canal Zone is not included and it would follow therefore that 1391 (e) above is not applicable.

The House and Senate reports contain identical statements of the purpose of this act.

"The purpose of this bill is to make it possible to bring actions against government officials and agencies in U. S. district courts outside the District of Columbia, which, because of certain existing limitations on jurisdiction and venue, may now be brought only in the U. S. District Court for the District of Columbia." (House Report 536, 87th Cong., 1st Sess.; see Senate Report 1992, 87th Cong., 2nd Sess.)

The "United States District Court for the District of the Canal Zone" is not a United States district court within the meaning of Title 28, USC, Chapter 5. Congress has defined "district courts" to be those courts enumerated in 28 USC 81-144, and the Canal Zone court is not included.

In establishing the jurisdiction and venue of the District Court of the Canal Zone further evidence is found on the part of Congress to differentiate for in Title 3, Section 142 of the Canal Zone Code it uses the following language in conferring admiralty jurisdiction:

"The jurisdiction in admiralty conferred upon the district court and the district judge is the same as is exercised by the *United States district courts* and the *United States district judges*." [Italics supplied.]

Proper service has not been made upon the defendant, Vance, and the motion to quash is sustained.

II

The Flag

1. The first question raised is the most inflammatory and has to do with the flying of the "flag of the Republic of Panama and the flag of the

United States" in the Canal Zone at equal heights on separate flagpoles in various places described in detail in the complaint. Panama has agitated the question for some time demanding that the flag of that Republic be flown throughout the Canal Zone wherever the United States standard is flown. Riots occurred in 1959 over the question when the Canal Zone authorities rejected a "flag march" emanating from Panama.

Plaintiff's position is that this act on the part of defendants is in violation of Title 36, Section 175 (c) of the United States Code originally adopted December 22, 1942 and which is as follows:

> "No other flag or pennant should be placed above or, if on the same level, to the right of the United States of America, except during church services conducted by naval chaplains at sea, when the church pennant may be flown above the flag during church services for the personnel of the Navy. No person shall display the flag of the United Nations or any other national or international flag equal, above, or in a position of superior prominence or honor to, or in place of, the flag of the United States at any place within the United States or any territory or possession thereof: Provided, That nothing in this section shall make unlawful the continuance of the practice heretofore followed of displaying the flag of the United Nations in a position of superior prominence or honor, and other national flags in positions of equal prominence or honor, with that of the flag of the United States at the headquarters of the United Nations."

He assumes the position that the portion of the Section 175 (c) that was adopted as an amendment to the existing act on July 9, 1963 and forms the second sentence of the paragraph means that no flags of any other nations shall be flown at "equal heights" with the flag of the United States and that as it was adopted as an amendment, it supercedes any statements in Section 175 which might be in conflict with it.

A detailed and careful study of the act with its legislative history demonstrates clearly that plaintiff's position is erroneous. The language is somewhat ambiguous and without the legislative history is subject to misinterpretation.

The first sentence of paragraph (c) of course contemplates that the flags of other nations should be flown at the same height in using the words ". . . if on the same level, to the right of the flag of the United States of America . . ."

In looking at paragraph (g) of Section 175, the following language is found:

> When flags of two or more nations are displayed, they are *to be flown from separate staffs of the same height*. The flags should be approximately

equal size. International usage forbids the display of the flag of one nation above that of another nation in time of peace." [Italics supplied.]

The second sentence in paragraph 175 (c) was adopted as the consequence of a bill (S 694) introduced by Senator Edward Martin of Pennsylvania. At the time the amendment was laid before the Senate after having been passed by the House of Representatives, Senator Knowland interrogated Senator Martin concerning the purposes of the bill. The following questions and answers appearing in 99 *Congressional Record* 7280 establish without doubt that the word "equal" as used in the sentence does not mean equal height as argued by plaintiff but equal prominence or honor.

"MR. KNOWLAND: Mr. President, I have some questions which I should like to ask of the distinguished Senator from Pennsylvania [Mr. Martin].

"Would this bill require that the American flag be flown at a higher elevation or be of a larger size than any foreign or international flag?

"MR. MARTIN: No. Senate bill 694 would not require that the American flag be flown higher or be of a larger size. It simply requires that no foreign flag shall be flown in a position of equal or superior prominence or honor to the American flag.

MR. KNOWLAND: The existing law, the act of June 22, 1942, title 36 of of the United States Code, section 175 (c) specifies that 'international usage forbids the display of the flag of one nation above that of another in time of peace.' Would this bill be in conflict with that section?

"MR. MARTIN: No. This bill adds a section to that act which reinforces the provisions of that act by requiring that the American flag be given the customary place of prominence and honor when flown with foreign or international flags on United States soil.

"MR. KNOWLAND: Would this bill require that the American flag be flown in the place of prominence and honor at United Nations Headquarters?

"MR. MARTIN: This bill has a specific proviso which authorizes 'the continuance of the practice heretofore followed of displaying the flag of the United Nations in a position of superior prominence or honor at the headquarters of the United Nations.' This is because of the special agreement we have with the United Nations under the Headquarters agreement."

At the same meeting and quoted in 99 *Congressional Record* 7281, Senator Martin introduced a statement for the *Record* which among other things said:

"S. 694 is good Flag Day material, Mr. President.

"It provides that no flag shall be flown in a position equal to or superior to the flag of the United States anywhere in the United States, its territories, or possessions. If the flag of the United States is displayed in conjunction with the flags of other nations, our flag shall be given the superior position of honor. *This does not necessarily mean that the flag of the United States must be larger in size or flown at a greater height on all occasions.*" [Italics supplied.]

In United States Code Congressional and Administrative News 83rd Congress, 1st Sess., p. 1859, the legislative history of the amendment was carried in Senate Report No. 258 as follows:

"The Committee on the Judiciary, to which was referred the bill (S. 694) to prohibit the display of flags of international organizations or other nations *in equal or superior prominence or honor* to the flag of the United States except under specified circumstances, and for other purposes, having considered the same, reports favorably thereon, with amendments, and recommends that the bill, as amended, do pass." [Italics supplied.]

It is therefore quite clear that the "equal height" interpretation of the plaintiff is erroneous and the position of honor at the right of the Panamanian flag is in compliance with the statute. As plaintiff complains only of the "equal height," he has not made out a cause of action and his complaint must fail on this point.

With plaintiff's original complaint filed October 26, 1962 he attached a sheet of "Points and Authorities" which included therein a citation to PL 86-451, 74 Stat. 93 and 101, May 13, 1960 in which Congress directed that no part of the appropriation contained in Title II of the act should be used to construct a flagpole, platform, or other device for the purpose of displaying the flag of Panama in the Canal Zone.

This act as shown at page 93 of the citation was for monies appropriated for the fiscal year ending June 30, 1961 and has no bearing on the present action.

The Postage Stamps

2. Congress has imposed upon the Governor the duty of "prescribing the postage stamps" in the Canal Zone and does not limit him to place of purchase or type of stamps. The language is clear and unequivocal and leaves the matter up to his executive discretion. Canal Zone Code, Title 2, Section 1132:

"Maintenance and operation of postal service

"(a) *The Governor shall:*
(1) maintain and operate a postal service in the Canal Zone, including a money order system, a parcel-post system, a postal-saving system, and

other services necessary or convenient in connection with the postage
service;

(2) establish and discontinue post offices;

(3) except as provided by subsection (b) of this section, prescribe the
postage rates; and

(4) *Prescribe the postage stamps and other stamped paper which shall
be used in the service.*" [Italics supplied.]

Plaintiff does not attack the act itself as being unconstitutional nor
illegal and there is question as to whether he would have standing to sue
in the event he were to make the attempt as there is considerable authority to the contrary. This court does not have to decide that question as
it is not raised and the authority to prescribe the stamps for the postal
service in the Canal Zone is clearly up to the executive discretion and
judgment of the Governor. This court is bound by the well-known rule
of law that the executive branch of the government has the right to make
decision and exercise discretion without interference from the courts.
The courts will intervene ordinarily only when there is a failure on the
part of the executive to perform or not perform an act which is minis-
terial in nature and no discretion is necessary. McConanghey v. Morrow,
Dist. Ct. Canal Zone, Bal. Div. 1922, 279 F. 617, 263 U.S. 39.

The Exequaturs

3. Exequatur is defined in Webster's Unabridged Dictionary as "a
written official recognition and authorization of a consular officer, issued
by the government to which he is accredited."

As stated above, plaintiff claims that the defendants intend to recognize in the Canal Zone the exequaturs issued by the Republic of Panama
to foreign consuls to the same extent that such exequaturs are recognized
within the territory of the Republic of Panama.

This may be tantamount to relinquishing in part the position of sovereignty that the United States has assumed and maintained in the past
and may affect the plaintiff and other citizens and taxpayers of the United
States in the Canal Zone. However, the court cannot question such a
decision on the part of the executive branch of the government.

The decision to recognize the exequaturs issued by the Republic of
Panama although made as a result of an agreement made by the Representatives of the governments of the Republic of Panama and the United
States-Panamanian relations with regard to the Canal Zone, of which
defendant Fleming was member, was actually decided upon by the Department of State of the United States and implemented through a "Joint

Communiqué and *Aide-Mémoire*" issued January 10, 1963 setting forth arrangements concluded between the government of the United States of America and the government of Panama with respect to certain matters pertaining to the Panama Canal Zone. An authenticated copy of the Department of State press release, Number 17 of January 10, 1963, containing a true copy of the Joint Communiqué and *Aide-Mémoire* bearing the seal of the Department of State of the United States of America and executed by Pattie H. Field for Dean Rusk, Secretary of State, showing this to be true was filed with defendants' "Memorandum In Reply To Plaintiff's Opposition to Defendants' Motions To Dismiss And To Quash Service On Defendant Vance." (The Joint Communiqué is contained in 48 Department of State Bulletin 171 dated February 4, 1963.)

The Joint Communiqué and *Aide-Mémoire* stems directly from the acts of the President of the United States, John F. Kennedy, and President Roberto F. Chiari of the Republic of Panama, in an agreement reached in Washington on June 12-13 (1962) and is, of course, an action of the executive branch of our government.

In the field of foreign relations, the courts have little or no voice. By our system of coordinate branches of government—executive, legislative, and judicial—the burden of dealing with foreign powers has through the wisdom of the framers of the Constitution been committed by that instrument to the executive and the legislative. In Oetjens v. Central Leather Company, 246 U.S. 297 (1917), the Supreme Court said:

> "The conduct of foreign relations of our government is committed by the Constitution to the executive and legislative—'the political' departments of the government—and the pro-political power is not subject to judicial inquiry or decision."

The plaintiff has the right as a citizen to express himself at the polls in selecting those to be charged in the executive and legislative branches with the high responsibility of dealing with foreign powers but he has no right to challenge the conduct of these affairs in the courts. If this were so, our government would be hopelessly embroiled in a tangle of litigation, political in nature, instigated by disgruntled citizens who do not agree with certain foreign policies. Such litigation would only hamper and embarrass our government and would be vain when decided for it would not be binding upon the countries with whom the government was dealing.

The question of exequaturs is one that rests with the executive and the plaintiff has no standing to sue nor right to injunctive relief.

III

Conclusion

Whether or not any or all of the acts complained of by the plaintiff diminish or tend to diminish the sovereignty of the United States in the Canal Zone is a matter of speculation. What nation is sovereign is between the treaty-making powers of the nations involved and is not a question that is up to the courts.

A decision by the courts that the United States is or is not sovereign in the Canal Zone would be unilateral in effect. It would be binding on the people of the United States but would have no force on the people of other nations. Sovereignty of a nation over a given territory rests in first analysis over its agreed dominance and authority over the area and in last analysis its power to retain that control.

It may well be that the acts of defendant, Fleming, in raising the flag of Panama daily beside that of the United States, using stamps supplied by Panama and recognizing in the Canal Zone exequaturs issued by the Republic of Panama are against the interests of the United States and its citizens and taxpayers. Certainly such actions are confusing and not understood. The flying of two national flags side by side in a disputed territory for an undeclared purpose is a position of weakness that can lead but to further misunderstanding and discord.

The people living in the Canal Zone are entitled to police protection, adequate courts, orderly government, health programs, and all of the things that stem from the sovereign. When the sovereign is uncertain and in doubt, these fundamental rights are of necessity weakened and may be lost.

Defendant Fleming's actions may not be to plaintiff's best interests, but he is not acting in violation of the law and the Canal Zone Code is specific in denying injunctive relief to a petitioner against a public officer who is exercising that office in a lawful manner.

Canal Zone Code, Title 5, Sec. 322, para. (b)

"an injunction may not be granted to:

.   .   .   .

(4) prevent the exercise of a public or private office, in a lawful manner, by the person in possession."

For these reasons the plaintiff's prayer for an injunction is denied and the complaint is dismissed.

This 8th day of July, 1963.

(*Signed*) GUTHRIE F. CROWE
Judge

After Judge Crowe dismissed Doyle's suit, further sites were selected by Fleming to fly the two flags. Then, on December 30, 1963, with the schools recessed for the Christmas holidays, Fleming made the following announcement, repeating the joint communiqué of Kennedy and Chiari:

On and after January 2, 1964, the Panamanian flag will be flown together with the flag of the United States on civilian land areas in the Canal Zone where the United States flag is flown by civilian authorities.

This action implements the understanding made public in a joint communiqué issued by the two governments earlier this year which stated that "the flag of the Republic of Panama will be flown together with the flag of the United States of America on land in the Canal Zone where the flag of the United States of America is flown by civilian authorities. Private organizations and persons in the Zone are free to display flags at will over their places of residence or business."

For some time the Panama Canal has been erecting dual flagpoles at selected sites. Work has been completed and the two flags are now flying at eleven of the sites. Dual flagpoles will be erected at five additional sites between now and the early part of February. One further location at which the two flags will fly will be the new Gorgas Hospital addition when it is completed later this year.

The eleven locations where the two flags are now flying are Shaler Plaza, Thatcher Ferry Bridge, the Administration Building in Balboa and also at Cristobal, Miraflores and Gatun locks, Coco Solo and Corozal hospitals, Palo Seco, Margarita, and Coco Solo. The five remaining locations in addition to the new Gorgas Hospital addition are Gamboa-Santa Cruz, Rainbow City, Paraiso, Mount Hope Cemetery, and Corozal Cemetery. Locations at which the United States flag has currently been flown alone and at which no flags will be flown on or after January 2, 1964, are the schools; the Ancon District Court Building; the Industrial Division, Cristobal; a site in Gamboa which will be replaced by the site for the two flags; and the present Gorgas Hospital.

In accordance with law and customs requiring the United States flag to be displayed in or near schools, the United States flag will continue to be displayed in classrooms or elsewhere within the schools as at present. The Panamanian flag will continue to be displayed with the U. S. flag in all Latin-American schools and in certain other schools as appropriate, following present practice.

Doyle had already resigned from his job and had returned to the United States to work and live. Another articulate Zone employee, Arthur C. Payne, Budget Director of the Community Services Division, took up the pen and became a frequent contributor to "The Mail Box" with caustic comments about the manner in which the Zone was being managed, especially with regard to the flag issue. Fleming was cognizant of this criticism among his employees (he did read the newspapers), as he told me in his office at Balboa Heights on January 18, 1964, while he paced up and down with a swagger stick past a desk on which there was mounted a painted card that read: I DON'T HAVE ULCERS. I GIVE ULCERS:

"I asked for the advice of the school authorities and the civic councils (for more than twenty years the Zone communities had elected their civic leaders). With this dilemma of two flags or none, everybody recommended none. We have four high schools in the Canal Zone—one at Balboa, which is also a junior college; one at Coco Solo (a former naval air station), situated on the Atlantic side; one at Rainbow City, on the Atlantic side; and one at Paraiso, near the Pedro Miguel Locks on the Pacific side. The last two are called Latin-American (or Panamanian) schools.

"My idea," Fleming continued, "was that the best solution would have been to fly the flag at the schools. I didn't get any support for that. All the people I talked to didn't want it. They said that if we flew the flag at the high schools, the kids would choose up sides—between United States kids and Panama kids. We have Panama tuition students as well as American youngsters at our schools. The quietest way to do it would be not to fly the flag at the schools. We got on the horn of the dilemma and the question was to fly two flags or none; we decided on none."

El Panama America, the Spanish-language "sister paper" of the Panama *American*, published an editorial on January 2, 1964, in which it protested what it termed "discrimination" in the flag issue. The editorial was written by the newspaper's editor, Dr. Jorge Illueca, former Ambassador to the United Nations. It was translated into English and published the same day on the front page of the Panama *American*. It read in part:

> But to the general surprise, the order actually issued places more emphasis on stipulating which are the sites on which, beginning today, the flag of the United States will not continue to be flown, with the ostensible objective, of course, that the Panamanian flag will not be displayed in such places as schools; the U. S. District Court of the Canal Zone at Ancon; the Industrial Division in Cristobal; the site in Gamboa, which will be replaced by another; and Gorgas Hospital.
>
> The discrimination becomes more obvious with the official announcement that the Panamanian flag will not fly at the schools for U. S. citizens, but will be displayed at all of the so-called Latin-American schools, whose pupils are Panamanians or other non-U. S. aliens.
>
> On the other hand, in an incomprehensible manner, flagstaffs from which the U. S. flag formerly was flown at the residence of the Governor of the Canal Zone, the Balboa police station, and other places, have been demolished.
>
> There is still time to correct these incongruities, which have arisen in the implementation of the agreement with respect to the flag, with the object of avoiding that an unnecessary offense be inflicted on the sentiments of many Panamanians desirous of preserving a cordial climate, comprehension and good understanding in relations with the United States.
>
> We are confident that an intelligent and timely representation by our foreign ministry, and a spirit of understanding and foresightedness on the part of the representatives of the United States government, will make it possible that a harmonious solution to the problem will be found.

That harmonious solution was not to be found, and Illueca's emotions were to explode as violently as some of the most responsible people of the government, from President Chiari down, and he was to be among the first to demand that Panama charge the United States with aggression and to urge Chiari to break diplomatic relations. This he did on the night of January 9. The fire and brimstone of his days in the *Frente Patriotico de la Juventud* had been revived by the incidents that were to follow.

On January 6, Arthur C. Payne sent another of his frequent contributions to "The Mail Box" from Balboa. It, too, was a portent of things to come. The letter read:

SIR:

I believe by tomorrow morning, if the story that has got around today proves true, American flags will appear at Balboa High School where Panama Canal officials ordered the American flag not to be flown. Flag planting of the U. S. flag in the Canal Zone is a new twist. Since the burden of proof of United States jurisdictional sovereignty has been placed upon the shoulders of its citizens, it is not entirely unexpected. For Policeman Bell of Gamboa set an example by keeping the American flag up at the Civic Memorial in that town. [Policeman Carlton Bell defied the order not to raise the Stars and Stripes at what was first built as a civic memorial in 1939 by the Gamboa Civic Council and then became a World War II Memorial.]

No doubt this may be only a one-day appearance of the American flag at Balboa High. For without a doubt the children who were courageous enough to put it up will receive censure from school officials. But, as I recall, there were many instances of Panama flag planting in the Canal Zone over a long period of time, in 1959 specifically. Little could be done with the flag planters who, despite admonishment, continued to plant them.

This expression by our children actually puts the adult U.S. citizen to shame. It speaks more eloquently than anything else of the desires of the American people as concerns the actions of American officials at the instigation of the State Department.

I think it is unfortunate that the burden of proof of U. S. ownership and jurisdictional sovereignty to the exclusion of such expression by Panama has been placed upon the shoulders of the U. S. citizenry. But such has been the case.

However censure comes to the children gallantly expressing their voice in the flag issue, it will in all probability come by persuasion by school officials. Thus will their act be admonished.

But what can be done completely to silence this expression of their rights as United States citizens? Not very much, other than to try to remove such patriotic temptations. Thus, one would expect, removal of the flagpoles in front of the schools is the preventive measure. I do not believe I am telling the officials anything they do not already know or have not already thought of. But our children are right.

For the acts of U. S. citizens are within their rights, within their responsibilities, and within their duties as citizens. While on the other hand the acts by the officials are acts, though under direction from higher officials, that are not proper as to their duties as provided by the statutes for their official responsibilities. This could all have been prevented if Panama had not coerced our U. S. State Department and our U. S. State Department had not persuaded our President and on down the line of our governmental process.

At 7:15 A.M. on January 7, five students of the Canal Zone Junior College hoisted the Stars and Stripes to the top of the flagpole on the lawn at the Balboa High School.

At 8:15 A.M. the flag was lowered and confiscated by Bernard I. Everson, Director of the Bureau of Civil Affairs, and David H. Spier, Jr., Principal of Balboa High School, as hundreds of students and parents protested. The flag had been removed in compliance with the directive issued by Governor Fleming on December 30.

At 8:45 A.M. the same students hoisted a smaller flag to half-staff on the pole, the flag having been given them by an adult who had just bought it at the commissary. The American students gathered on the lawn, bowed their heads, and recited the pledge of allegiance. When school had opened, students circulated a petition to President Lyndon B. Johnson in which they requested that the United States flag be flown at their school. The petition was confiscated by an official of the high school but it was returned by the Bureau of Civil Affairs. A similar petition was again circulated that morning for signatures.

At 10:00 A.M. Dean Charles L. Latimer, Jr., of the Canal Zone Junior College, admonished the five students who were on the lawn and took their names while Principal Spier looked on. The students later reported that they were warned that they were trespassing on government property; that if they had classes they should go to them or else leave the grounds; that they were jeopardizing their parents' employment in the Zone.

There was a rush at the flag counters of the commissaries, and on the first day of what was to become the "flag war" one store sold 144 large U. S. flags in six hours. Many more smaller flags were sold and soon appeared on the antennas of automobiles or from windows of the school buses as the students proudly waved them.

At 7:15 A.M. on January 8, as two hundred persons watched, four Junior College students erected an improvised flagpole at the entrance to their college. The students reported that a well-known Zone union leader had donated the flag, a policeman had donated a Christmas-tree stand, and a local American contractor had donated the staff as well as bricks to support it.

As Payne had predicted in his letter, students raised the Stars and Stripes all across the Isthmus, either on flagstaffs or on improvised ones. The flags went up at Cristobal High School, Coco Solo Retail Store, and the Coco Solo, Margarita, Los Rios, and Diablo Elementary Schools. A spokesman for the students said that their protest was not directed necessarily against the flying of the Panamanian flag, but against the lowering of the United States flag. This view was not held by all and drew dissent from students who attended the Pacific Civic Council meeting that night. When they asked the question, they voiced a preference for "our flag or none."

"A North American Mother," in a letter to "The Mail Box," sensed the oncoming tragedy when she wrote:

SIR:
This is just about the saddest thing I've ever seen in my long life. American children walking with their flag, singing the "Star Spangled Banner," not loud, because the school they go to, supported by their government, is not allowed to fly their American flag—tears are in my eyes. Mob spirit is being engendered into our children instead of true patriotism and love of the United States of America.

What is the matter with you middle-aged, stuffy adults that you think you know everything? You are making ill-will between Panama and the United States instead of courtesy and love.

When I came here, I thought it was not courteous to the Republic of Panama, our failing to have their flag beside ours, at the building, but I never dreamed a farce would be perpetrated. This is serious, good sound citizens of Panama and the United States. It is just a delight to Communists. Let's put our flags where they belong, work together, play together, and live as Christians.

The editorial cartoons began to appear; and the first were published in *El Panama America* and the Panama *American*. An American citizen was drawn with U.S. and Panama flags crossed in his hands, saying in pidgin Spanish: "I am a Panazonian because I am an American but I prefer to live in the Canal Zone rather than in the United States."

The Pacific Civic Council met the night of January 8, on the eve of a trip to Washington which Fleming had scheduled to confer with Assistant Secretary of State Thomas C. Mann, who had been given command of all U.S. Latin-American policy by President Johnson. It adopted a petition to Governor Fleming in which it requested him to defer any further action on the flag issue until the matter could be resolved by joint congressional action. The civic council asked that only U.S. flags be flown at the U.S. schools and at the district courthouse; that the flag be allowed to remain at Balboa High School and not be lowered again. Students were guarding that flagpole day and night, and a collection was taken up at the meeting to buy food for them. The petition was adopted after Governor Fleming addressed a message to the council which was read by President C. A. Widell. Fleming's message read:

> As Governor of the Canal Zone, I believe that it is appropriate at this time for me to repeat to each U. S. resident of the Canal Zone certain background information concerning the flying of U. S. and Panamanian flags in the Canal Zone. It is apparent from recent events that there are some misunderstandings concerning the responsibilities of U. S. citizens in this matter.
>
> The question of flying flags in the Canal Zone has been discussed for many years between representatives of the United States and Panama. In September, 1960, President Eisenhower directed the Governor of the Canal Zone to fly the two flags on a daily basis in Shaler Triangle. President Eisenhower indicated that he hoped his decision would demonstrate the continuing close bonds that exist between the peoples of the United States and the Republic of Panama and their governments.
>
> Subsequently the question was discussed directly between President Kennedy and President Chiari, and on June 13, 1962, they issued a joint

communiqué containing the following statement: "They also agreed that their representatives will arrange for the flying of the Panamanian flag in an appropriate way in the Canal Zone."

Following instructions from President Kennedy, U. S. representatives discussed with Panamanian representatives various ways to carry out the spirit and intent of the joint communiqué. With Presidential approval, the governments agreed that "the flag of the Republic of Panama will be flown together with the flag of the United States of America on land in the Canal Zone where the flag of the United States of America is flown by civilian authorities. Private organizations and persons in the Zone are free to display flags at will over their places of residence or business."

As Governor of the Canal Zone, it then became my responsibility to establish those locations where the two flags shall be flown jointly and to ensure that, in accordance with the joint communiqué, there are no official locations where only one flag is flown. Working with senior officials of the Canal Zone government, and in discussions with members of the community, we established a number of appropriate locations to fly the two flags. This list was reviewed in Washington. Details concerning these locations were given in a press release on December 30.

He went on to discuss the cooperation of American citizens in regard to the locations of the flags (this has already been cited at the end of the previous chapter), but Governor Fleming had, by his own statement to me, been playing for time. I return to my interview with him:

"After this thing started," he told me, "we were playing for time. We were trying to get the kids convinced through the principals and teachers. We were trying to get them to agree that they would like two flags to fly. We were advancing along that road at the junior college, and if we succeeded, the high schools would have fallen in line.

"The new high school and junior college were built without a flagpole and that is why the students had to improvise one when they hoisted the Stars and Stripes. The thinking students and leaders of the student body were just getting into a position where they would come to me and say they would like to have both flags. So that was the situation when those Panama kids came in—in no mood to avoid a fight."

14. The Flag War

Governor Fleming proceeded with his plans to fly to Washington to keep his appointment with the then Undersecretary of the Army (now Secretary) Stephen Ailes and Assistant Secretary of State Thomas C. Mann, an appointment scheduled for 5:00 P.M. on January 10. Fleming had called on Foreign Minister Solis at 2:00 P.M. on January 9 and discussed with him the purposes of his trip to Washington.

"I was going to tell him [Mann]," Fleming told me, "about the insistent pressure on one side and the inflexibility on the other. I was trying to get across to him that what the United States did here could not have any influence on policy in Argentina or elsewhere but it would have a tremendous impact on Panama."

Fleming and Solis agreed that the situation in Panama was tense at the moment, and the strike of the Canal Zone buses, which had begun nearly three weeks earlier, was also adding to the tension as it threatened to set off a chain reaction of sympathy strikes in Panama City. Solis told Fleming that President Chiari was striving to help to settle the bus strike, and expressed a desire that Fleming keep his appointment with Mann. So Fleming emplaned at Tocumen Airport at 5:30 P.M. that day, as the Panama students were scuffling with Canal Zone police at the Balboa High School.

Many versions have been published about how the flag war erupted. The first reports abroad were wild and confused, and they contained lamentable inaccuracies that served to influence the initial impetuous diplomatic measures, because of emotional pressures on him, by President Chiari. One could not expect the Panama press, radio, or television to do an objective job of reporting the events that turned the Canal Zone into a battlefield. The reporting was to be influenced by distortions, emotions, a rapid regeneration of the "Hate America" campaign and, especially, by the subversives whose role was either deliberately ignored or overlooked.

The nearest approach to what was described as an "objective report" on the part played by the Panamanian students in triggering the flag war was this obviously biased eyewitness report that was published in *La Estrella de Panama* and the *Star & Herald* on January 14:

BY GUILLERMO GUEVARA PAZ
12th-Grade Student, National Institute

As a reporter for the National Institute's newspaper, *Impacto,* I went on Wednesday, the day before the events, to the offices of the Balboa High School to investigate all concerning the position of the boys in that school with respect to the flag problem.

The principal of the school referred us to the offices of Mr. Baldwin,* in the Administration Building. This official informed me that the display of the American flag without being accompanied by ours was an illegal act and that the former was still flying there only because of the stubbornness of the students, who had prevented its being taken down.

After that interview, I went to the school grounds to interview the students who were guarding the flag. They told me they did not mind if both flags flew together and that their only concern was to have their flag in front of their school. This appeared to me to be a logical position and I thus reported to my fellow students who were organizing a demonstration to the Canal Zone for Thursday afternoon at three o'clock.

Student Francisco Diaz obtained permission, in writing, as Secretary-General of the Federated Association of the National Institute, from Professor Didimo Rios, Principal of the Institute, who together with the authorization, delivered to us the flag used in the student movements of December 12, 1947, of May, 1958, and November 3, 1959. This flag

*Frank A. Baldwin, Information Officer of the Canal Zone.

is displayed only on the November 4 (Flag Day) parades, because it has a great sentimental value for us for it is stained with the blood of the martyrs of the Student Federation of Panama.

At about 4:50 P.M., a group of about 200 students of both sexes left the National Institute, singing the school anthem. When we passed Gorgas Hospital, I asked my fellow students who marched in orderly fashion behind the flag, to remain silent since we were going past a hospital.

We broke the silence when we marched past the Governor's House, singing the national anthem. By then, two police radio cars were ahead of us.

After we arrived at the Administration Building and started going down the steps, I reminded my fellow students once more that this was a civic demonstration that we were carrying out, having the fullest right and justification therefor.

Just as we were about to cross the street opposite the fire station, already in sight of the solitary American flag, we were brusquely stopped by the American police, who wielded long clubs and military-type helmets.

This, of course, upset the boys, not only because of the brusqueness of the police, but also because of the lack of justification for their action. We knew that we were not disturbing the peace.

The captain in charge of the operation asked to talk with two representatives from our group; Diaz and I were chosen. Because I speak English fairly well, it was I who carried on the conference. The captain wanted to know what we wanted, to which I replied that we only desired to sing the national anthem in front of our flag and next to the American flag. He informed us that only four students could do this and that the rest had to stay where we were.

After explaining this to the boys and convincing them that while this was not fair it was common sense to yield to the captain's imposition, we chose the four who were to carry the flag, plus a standard bearer and a fellow student who carried a sign reading: PANAMA IS SOVEREIGN IN THE CANAL ZONE.

At the suggestion of some fellow students, I asked the captain for protection for our companions from the group of "Zonians" who were on the balcony and the main entrance to the school; he replied that if any North Americans insulted or showed lack of respect for our delegates, he personally would have them arrested.

Our boys were escorted and were within a few steps from the flagpole, when hundreds of students and adults suddenly appeared on the lawn around the flagpole, surrounding our companions. We, held back by the police, lost sight of them, but did not suspect anything amiss on the part of the "Zonians" because we believed they were moved only by curiosity.

But suddenly we realized that something was wrong, because of the shouting that the "Zonians" unleashed.

What really happened? Our standard bearer, student Carranza, describes it as follows: "They closed in on us. One shouted, then another, and then everybody. They started shoving us and trying to wrest the flag from us, all the while insulting us. A policeman wielded his club which ripped the flag. The captain tried to take us to where the others were. On the way through the mob, many hands pulled and tore our flag."

In the meanwhile, still unaware of what had happened, we stood restlessly, awaiting the return of our companions. Finally they got to us, with tears in their eyes for the offense that had been inflicted.

The group of Institute students, impotent as I was, felt our eyes moist and anger rising up within us.

By that time, most of the girls in our group had withdrawn, reducing the number of students appreciably.

Nevertheless, and notwithstanding the fact that the police had been reinforced, we went forward, trying to protect the national flag. This brought on a rain of blows by police clubs on us—on a lawn that had not a stone or a stick with which to defend ourselves.

Someone shouted, pointing to the American flag at the Administration Building behind us.

We headed for that flag. Unfortunately, after the arduous climb, and as we attempted to loosen the rope holding the flag high, two radio-patrol cars came at us and in "V" formation protected the flag. The policemen unsheathed their arms.

Pursued by two radio patrol cars, we started on the way back, stoning electric lights and overturning trash cans on the street for the purpose of slowing down pursuit by the police cars.

Student Rogelio Hilton, President of the Graduating Class, and I, as Vice-President, covered the retreat of the group. As some of the group went past the Gorgas Hospital building, under construction, they tore at part of the scaffolding and threw it on the street, which led me to suppose that the noise I had heard as if from firecrackers actually was the sound of the scaffolding falling down. Later, past the Ancon school, we heard the same noise this time as if in a burst, and we realized it came from shots.

There was no shooting from the radio patrol cars which were pursuing us. The shots seemed to come from houses near the Episcopal church, where numerous adult "Zonians" were. We then crossed Fourth of July Avenue, and found a group of alarmed Panamanian citizens, at the "J" Street taxi stand, who, warned by the first of our group to arrive and the shots they had heard, awaited us.

At that moment I looked at my watch, and it was 7:20 P.M.

There had been no shooting by any American civilians in the vicinity of the St. Luke's Cathedral in Ancon. This charge was entirely unfounded and was based on no hard fact. Guevara also was mistaken when he accused the police of clubbing the flag and tearing it. No police clubs touched the flag, nor did any policeman tear it, as will be noted later. The Panamanian student also failed to mention one significant and friendly act. When his delegation arrived near the flagpole site, David Blackman, President of the Students' Association of Balboa High School, began to extend to them a cordial welcome. He was jeered by some of his fellow students and one shouted: "This is your last day as president!"

The untrue, biased, and distorted reports in the Panama press regarding the explosive flag incident at the Balboa High School were corrected in this comprehensive report that was printed on January 21 in the Panama Canal *Spillway*:

WHAT REALLY HAPPENED

This is a factual summary of the events of Thursday, January 9, plus some supplementary information, prepared and written by an experienced professional newspaperman, and printed in the Spillway *as a service to its readers. It is not an official report of either the Panama Canal enterprise or of the U.S. government.*

At about 4:40 P.M. on January 9 an estimated 200 Panamanian high-school students, boys and girls, from the Instituto Nacional in Panama City, entered the Canal Zone and proceeded up Gorgas Road carrying small Panamanian flags, the Panama National Institute Student Federation banner, and the school flag. They also carried several provocative signs such as: PANAMA IS SOVEREIGN IN THE CANAL ZONE. They proceeded in a peaceful manner to the Canal Zone Governor's Residence, where they paused and sang the Panamanian national anthem and then went to the Panama Canal Administration Building, down the stairs, and past the Goethals Memorial to an area one block from the Balboa High School, shouting "Yankee Go Home" and similar slogans. Here, they were halted by a squad of 10 Canal Zone police officers who had instructions from the Acting Governor, Colonel David S. Parker, to stop the students at this point. The Canal Zone police were instructed to use no violence, but to halt the students, so as to avoid an incident.

(Governor Fleming had left the Isthmus via Tocumen by air on January 9, 1964, at 5:00 P.M., en route to Washington for an official appointment with Thomas Mann, Assistant Secretary of State for Inter-American Affairs, and Stephen Ailes, Undersecretary of the Army. On arrival in Miami, he was informed by Balboa Heights of the situation in the Canal Zone and Panama. After consultation with Washington, Governor Fleming returned to the Canal Zone by the first available flight to Panama. He arrived at Tocumen about 3:20 A.M. on January 10, 1964, and reached the Canal Zone shortly thereafter.)

The leaders of the Panama student group informed Captain Gaddis Wall, District Police Commander, Balboa, that they wished to go to the Balboa High School flagpole for the purpose of raising the Panama National Institute flag (a Panama flag with the school emblem and name in the flag's center) on the pole beside the U.S. flag, which was flying at the time, and to sing their national anthem. After some discussion among and with the students, the group was informed that five Panama students would be escorted by police to the Balboa High School flagpole, where they would be able to have their ceremony and display this flag in front of the flagpole, if they wished. Although the leaders of the group agreed to this proposition, there was considerable opposition to the proposal among the group. The opposition was led by an adult Panamanian, reportedly a Panama schoolteacher.

The five Panamanian students were escorted by the Canal Zone police to the Balboa High School flagpole. A number of Balboa High School students were gathered about the flagpole base. The Balboa High School students and a large group of adult U.S. civilians on the school grounds, who had gathered from nearby residential areas, joined in the singing of the U.S. national anthem.

The delegation refused to have a ceremony unless they could have it on the spot occupied by the Balboa High School students, who would not move. The Panama delegation then wanted to raise the Panama school flag on the flagpole where the U.S. flag was flying, and Police

Captain Wall refused permission. The Panamanian and Balboa students at the flagpole began exchanging insulting remarks.

Recognizing the tense atmosphere, the Canal Zone police endeavored to convince the five Panamanian students to rejoin the remaining members of their group before an incident could occur, but the students resisted violently. It was necessary for the police detail to forcibly push them from the flagpole. The flag was carried by four Panama students holding it at the top edge. Captain Gaddis Wall, an eyewitness, made these two statements based on his own observations. No Canal Zone policeman tore or ripped the flag. No U.S. student tore or ripped the flag. There was a tight cordon of Canal Zone Police surrounding the Panama students and separating them from the U.S. students. Since there was scuffling, pushing, and physical struggle between the Canal Zone police and the Panamanian students, the four Panama students holding the flag apparently tore it themselves during the scuffle.

The five students with the flag and a Panama National Institute Student Federation banner joined their waiting group, which was surrounded by a cordon of police to keep them separated from the Canal Zone high-school students and adults in front of the Balboa High School. The Panamanian group shouted at the police for several minutes. At no time was there any encounter between the large group of Panama students and the students of the Canal Zone, as O'Connor Place Road separated them.

Canal Zone officials had requested the Motor Transportation Division to send buses to the vicinity of Balboa High School, to stand by and provide shuttle transportation to the Republic for the Panamanian student demonstrators. At 5:45 P.M., three large buses were dispatched from the Ancon garage. The buses were parked on Gorgona Road alongside the Balboa High School Activities Building. The Panamanian students were offered this transportation but refused it.

The Panama students, after shouting insults, turned and started up the steep bank and 129 stone steps to the Panama Canal Administration Building. They halted near the dual flagpoles from which the U.S. flag flies beside the flag of the Republic of Panama. At 6:25 P.M., a group of the Panama students made an effort to lower the U.S. flag but were prevented from doing so by several U.S. civilians. With considerable shouting, the Panama students left the area and headed back to Panama City.

As the Panama students passed the Panama Canal Administration Building, they began damaging property. The group proceeded back over Gorgas Road, and en route threw stones. Five windowpanes of glass were broken on the east wing of the Panama Canal Administration Building. Twenty street lights were broken, a sign was torn off the pole in front of the Gorgas Laboratory Building, and approximately 40 louvers were broken in the Panama Canal Treasurer's Office. All the trash cans along the road were overturned. Many automobiles were stoned, and car windows were broken.

The Canal Zone police refrained from making any arrests of the students in order to get the group out of the Canal Zone as quickly as possible.

While this Panama student group was en route to Fourth of July Avenue, the Canal Zone police contacted the Panama National Guard headquarters, and informed them of the situation.

From 6:45 until about 7:15 P.M., the Panama students milled around on Fourth of July Avenue, opposite the Panama National Institute, and large crowds started forming and increased rapidly.

By 7:30 P.M., the Panama mob, now grown to an estimated 2,000 moved north on Fourth of July Avenue and President Kennedy Avenue to a point between the Tivoli Guest House and Shaler Triangle. Many of the demonstrators attempted to climb the fence between President Kennedy Avenue and the Tivoli Guest House. A Canal Zone police detail at that location repelled them by laying a screen of tear gas along the fence. Three automobiles were turned over and burned by the demonstrators in their march from the Panama National Institute.

Only 19 Canal Zone police were on duty on the whole Pacific Side when the Panamanian students entered the Canal Zone. By 7:30 P.M. practically the entire Canal Zone police force, totaling about 85 men, was deployed along the Canal Zone border, and by 7:30 P.M. it was apparent the police could not hold the crowds. The police were authorized to use tear gas, and firearms, if necessary, to protect life.

At about 8:00 P.M., the Panama mob across from the Tivoli Guest House started to move along President Kennedy Avenue, heading for the Ancon Railroad Station and the freight house. Two Canal Zone police sergeants and eight Canal Zone policemen on duty in this vicinity fell back from the intersection of Frangipani Street and Roosevelt Avenue before the onslaught of at least 3,000. They took up position between the Panama Canal Sanitation Office and the civilian homes on Frangipani Street.

The mob upset and burned an unoccupied automobile at the intersection of Roosevelt Avenue and Frangipani Street, and some of the Canal Zone police advanced and threw all the tear gas they had. The mob was stopped temporarily at this point from advancing further into the Canal Zone, and the homes were saved from being overrun.

About two or three minutes later, part of the mob started to burn and sack the Ancon freight house. Railroad passenger cars were set on fire and windows in the passenger railroad cars were broken. Other elements of the mob started breaking windows as they forced their way into the Ancon Laundry across the street from the railroad station. Several hundred of the mob started toward the Ancon Little Theater, where a rehearsal was in progress, and toward the Ancon housing area. One policeman with a shotgun and three other policemen were sent to protect life and property in that area.

As the mob headed for the residential area on Manzanillo Street in Ancon, the police were authorized to open fire with shotguns and revolvers, shooting over the heads of the mob and on the ground in front of them.

This action, at 8:20 P.M. as nearly as can be determined, was necessary to save lives. It was the first actual firing by Canal Zone police, although by that time seven Canal Zone policemen at that location had been injured in the hail of stones and flying objects directed against them.

For the next ten minutes, the mob surged back and forth and made several efforts to penetrate the Frangipani Street residential area, but were turned back by tear gas and shots fired over their heads. Small-arms fire was heard coming from Panama during this time. Considerable damage was done to the Shaler bus terminal.

The Canal Zone police received numerous reports that "Molotov cocktails" were being thrown against the U.S. District Courthouse in Ancon. A wire fence within the Zone was torn down in front of the U.S. District Court and along Fourth of July Avenue.

Acting Canal Zone Governor David S. Parker made a personal inspection of the Canal Zone-Panama border in the vicinity of the Tivoli Guest House shortly before 8:00 P.M. His car was stoned twice in the vicinity of the Tivoli Guest House. By that time a crowd estimated between 5,000 and 6,000 was gathering along Fourth of July Avenue. Molotov cocktails were being thrown against buildings in the Canal Zone, and a number of cars had been set on fire. The Canal Zone police were having difficulty in holding back the crowds which had penetrated several hundred yards into the Canal Zone, and it was apparent that life and property were in serious jeopardy.

At 7:59 P.M., Acting Governor Parker reported to General Andrew P. O'Meara, Commander in Chief, United States Southern Command, that he was unable to maintain law and order in the Canal Zone with only the police and other civilian authorities. Acting Governor Parker requested General O'Meara to assume command of the Canal Zone.

Within forty minutes from the time the first shots were fired by the Canal Zone police, U.S. Army personnel arrived at Portobello Street in Ancon. Complete Army control in that area was assumed about twenty minutes later after Brigadier General G. L. Mabry, Jr., Director J-3, Plans and Operations, United States Southern Command, had completed an assessment of the situation. He directed that no further firing be done unless an attack was made, as the Army was ready to move into that position and take over. Sporadic small-arms fire was heard coming from Panama City.

A small group of policemen, sent to the Ancon freight house after the Army arrived, dispersed a mob armed with Molotov cocktails, which were being thrown at the freight house. A Canal Zone fire rig arrived in time to put out the fire at the freight house, caused by the fire bombs.

A Molotov cocktail was thrown through the windshield of an automobile that came out of Panama into the Canal Zone at Frangipani Street, Ancon. The car burst into flames, but the two passengers escaped.

At 9:15 P.M., upward of 1,000 Panama demonstrators proceeded from the Canal Zone-Panama limits into the Canal Zone toward Balboa on Balboa Road. They were stopped initially by an eight-man detail of policemen. The mob threw stones at the police, and gunshots were heard. The Canal Zone police fired over the heads of the mob and onto the roadway in front of them in an attempt to stop them. The demonstration continued and was still in progress when the Canal Zone police detail (which had been increased to 30 men) was relieved by a U.S. Army platoon about 10:30 P.M., after the mob had penetrated about 400 yards into the Canal Zone.

The large crowd on Fourth of July Avenue in the area of the "H" Street intersection in Panama City commenced coming across Fourth of July Avenue at about 9:35 P.M., throwing stones at the home of U.S. District Court Judge Guthrie F. Crowe. The stones broke through the screens and entered the house and were followed by three Molotov cocktails. One fire bomb landed underneath the house, against the wooden latticework; another landed on the front porch, and the third landed upstairs inside the house. Despite the continuous hail of rocks thrown by the mob, Judge Crowe and Canal Zone police personnel at the scene succeeded in throwing the Molotov cocktails out of the house and extinguished one burning underneath the house.

Shortly afterward, several more Molotov cocktails were thrown and landed about in the same places as the first. The hail of rocks now was so thick it was extremely dangerous to go anywhere near the fire. Canal Zone fire-fighters appeared on the scene, but were unable to approach the house due to the continuous shower of rocks. A small Canal Zone police detail, reinforced by a squad of policemen who fired a number of shots into the air and into the ground, dispersed the rioters, who took cover in the buildings across Fourth of July Avenue and down "H" Street in Panama City. Canal Zone fire division personnel went into action and extinguished the blaze at Judge Crowe's home, where only minor damage was done.

The rioters reappeared at 9:55 P.M. and demonstrated for about two hours. They burned automobiles that they brought out of Panama, as well as cars that had been parked on the side of the road and in garages of the apartment houses in the vicinity. All these cars were pushed onto Fourth of July Avenue after they had been set on fire.

Sporadic shots were heard, apparently coming from buildings in Panama City near the Canal Zone border. From 12:45 A.M. to 3:00 P.M., January 10, the Canal Zone police furnished support to the military. After 3:00 A.M., the Canal Zone police were removed from the border and resumed zonal police patrols. At no time during the above events did Canal Zone police enter the Republic of Panama.

During the period of attempting to control the Panama mob at various locations, many Canal Zone police officers received injuries, but none were serious.

The Atlantic side of the Isthmus was fairly quiet unitl 9:05 P.M., Thursday, January 9. When information was received by the Cristobal District Canal Zone police that rioting had broken out in the Balboa District, available personnel were called out and placed at strategic points along the boundary.

At 9:05 P.M., information was received that about twenty Panamanians were proceeding toward the Canal Zone-Panama border at Colón, carrying a Panamanian flag and shouting anti-United States insults. In little more than fifteen minutes, the group grew to about 1,500 men, women, and children. They marched down Roosevelt Avenue to the Cristobal Administration Building, where, during the day, the Panama flag flies alongside the U.S. flag on dual flagstaffs. Some of the mob went to the second floor of the building and raised the Panama flag, under the surveillance of a riot squad of police.

During the flag raising, Daniel Delgado Duarte, Mayor of Colón, accompanied by several members of the Colón Municipal Council talked to the crowd and aided in averting violence at that time. Several agitators in the mob tried to incite the crowd, but were restrained.

At 9:30 P.M., the mob removed the Panama flag they had previously placed on the Cristobal Administration Building and started dispersing, many shouting insulting remarks as they passed the Cristobal Police Station. The crowd went back to Roosevelt Avenue and, on the way back to Colón, broke windows in two cars parked on the street and the lower windows of buildings along Steamship Row. The mob broke windows on the 11th Street side of the former Cristobal Commissary building and windows in the Masonic Temple.

National Guard headquarters in Colón was advised that elements of the mob were heading for the U.S. Consulate in Colón, and National Guardsmen were dispatched to that location.

The Colón mob grew in size but was contained by the Colón National Guard until about 10:00 P.M., when some of the mob broke past and moved up to Balboa Avenue. Part of the mob moved south on Balboa Avenue into the Canal Zone, breaking windows in the Canal Central Employment Office, License Office, and in the Cristobal Railroad Station. Police held them at that location until troops arrived.

It was reported that windows were being broken at the Cristobal Y.M.C.A. and that it was being looted. A riot squad of about 10 Canal Zone policemen routed some 50 looters. Four Panamanians arrested inside the building were brought to Cristobal Police Station and charged with participating in a riot. Several policemen were injured by brickbats.

Some Atlantic-side Canal Zone police officers had been injured during the rioting prior to the time the military assumed control.

After the U.S. military assumed command most of the action on the Pacific side of the Isthmus was contained along the Panama-Canal Zone border. On the Atlantic side, the Colón mobs did intense damage. Canal Zone police and U.S. troops were subjected to rock-throwing and other attacks. Persistent sniper fire killed three American soliders and wounded many others, including civilians.

No Americans were involved, except as victims, in the burning, looting, and other violence in Panama. No Canal Zone police or U.S. troops entered the Republic of Panama. Canal Zone residents remained at their residences and did not participate in or provoke any violence.

Major damage on the Pacific side of the Canal Zone, as of Saturday night, included the following: Tivoli Guest House extensively damaged (persistent sniper fire forced evacuation of Tivoli Guest House Friday night); Ancon School damaged; one flagpole razed at Shaler Triangle, the first Canal Zone site where the Panama flag was raised to fly alongside the U.S. flag; Ancon Laundry damaged; and Canal Zone police booths at Balboa Road, the Limits, and the Ancon Gymnasium destroyed. The fence on Fourth of July Avenue was torn down at numerous places. The Shaler bus terminal was wrecked and street-light standards on Fourth of July Avenue and Thatcher Ferry Bridge approach were damaged.

In addition, windows were broken in railroad coaches at Panama Railroad Station in Ancon and one coach set afire; all light fixtures on Panama Railroad Station platform were broken, station office records were scattered in the station on the tracks, shipments in baggage rooms were pilfered, drug shipments were strewn along the tracks, office furniture and files in station office were overturned and scattered, lockers were broken open and vandalized; houses in Gavilan area were stoned; street signs were torn down on President Kennedy Avenue; some outside lights were broken at Gorgas Hospital, and ambulances at Gorgas were dented by rocks; and windows were broken in the Sanitation Division's Ancon office.

The major damage in the Cristobal area included: the Cristobal Y.M.C.A., which was gutted by fire; the Masonic Temple, which was abandoned to fire; the Sanitation office, which was destroyed by fire; the Cristobal Warehouse, which was burned. The Panama Canal Personnel Bureau offices, the Driver License Examiner's Office, and the nurses' office in the former Cristobal commissary building were left a shambles with all glass broken, furniture and typewriters thrown in the street, and papers strewn about the floor. The baggage room, ticket sellers' office, dispatchers' office, yardmasters' office, car inspectors' office, shop area, and toilet facilities were destroyed by fire, and a shelter in the Dockyard 9 outside fenced area was destroyed by fire. A dozen or more ties in the main-line track in Colon and an equivalent number of ties on the ladder track also were burned out. As a result of this damage, railroad trains were unable to operate into the Cristobal pier area.

In Panama, within sight of the Canal Zone boundary, rioting mobs, partly students but with many adults, overturned and burned cars, and burned and damaged a number of buildings in Panama, especially those occupied by U.S. firms.

By taking emergency measures, the transit operations of the Panama Canal continued uninterrupted. Thirty-one ships transited on Friday, 26 transited on Saturday, and 34 were scheduled to transit Sunday.

Canal Zone Governor Robert J. Fleming, Jr., commended the out-standing performance of duty by the police officers and personnel of the fire division, who loyally and courageously served long hours without relief. He spoke of the maturity displayed by nearly all Panama Canal employees, both United States and Panamanian, who stayed with their jobs and kept ships transiting and other essential supporting operations on schedule. Governor Fleming mentioned what a welcome sight the morning train was when it arrived at Balboa Heights Friday morning, as evidence of the organization's determination to continue on.

Background information on the Panamanian student march to Balboa High School on January 9 is given below:

On December 30, 1963, Governor Fleming issued a press release stating that, commencing January 2, 1964, the Panamanian flag would be flown alongside the U.S. flag on civilian land areas in the Canal Zone wherever the latter flag was flown by civilian authorities.

This plan was described as implementing an agreement reached earlier in 1963 between the government of the United States and the Republic of Panama.

The press release of the Governor was printed both in English and Spanish in local newspapers. It stated that both flags were flying at eleven different sites, including Shaler Plaza (near the Panamanian boundary at Ancon, Canal Zone) and at the Thatcher Ferry Bridge, and that six additional sites had been selected. It was also indicated that the U.S. flag would not be officially flown alone at certain other sites in civilian communities.

Among the places where the flag would no longer fly was outside Balboa High School. Some students, encouraged by their parents, re-sented the removal of the U.S. flag from their school.

On the morning of Tuesday, January 7, students ignored the Gov-ernor's directive and raised the U.S. flag at the flagpole on the lawn of Balboa High School. An hour later, Civil Affairs Director, Bernhard I. Everson, and the high-school's principal, David A. Speir, took down the flag and removed it.

A short time later, Balboa High School students gathered outside the school and massed for a demonstration. Some students raised a smaller flag on the flagpole and it was not removed the second time by school officials.

Students who feared the Panama Canal officials might remove the flagpole stood vigil during the night. The next day, students at several other schools also raised American flags.

The student activity with its controversial aspects was printed in detail. The majority of the Spanish-language news media twisted the story to make it appear that the Balboa High School students objected to the flying of the Panama flag.

This was the situation which led to the visit to Balboa of the students from Panama's Instituto Nacional on the afternoon of Thursday, January 9, which, as it later turned out, was the catalyst for the violence which started that night.

By noon Friday, January 10, the newspaper *La Hora* was on the streets with a chronology of THE AGGRESSION STEP BY STEP. It was published on an inside page above a five-column photo of the dismantled cyclone fence, which was erected on a part of Fourth of July Avenue to keep trespassers from penetrating into the Zone. The caption of the photo read: "THE INFAMOUS FENCE CEDES BEFORE THE PATRIOTIC FORCE OF PANAMA." *La Hora*'s chronology follows:

6:05 P.M. A group of Institute students, with a flag, on the lawn in front of the Administration Building of the Zone, insist on raising the flag on the staff in front of the Balboa High School. Captain Wall, of the Pacific District of the Zone police, gives permission to a delegation of students with the flag to proceed to the flagstaff of the Junior College in order to sing the anthem. Minutes after arriving at the flagstaff they were surrounded by Zone students supported by some adults, who shouted threats at them and prevented the Panamanian students from accomplishing their objective. The North Americans sang their anthem. Upon the insistence of the Panamanians to sing their anthem and to raise their flag, the police under the command of an aggressive sergeant, by shoving, ejected the boys from the place; in the scuffle between the students and the police to take away from them the Panama flag this was torn in several places. In view of this situation the students became indignant and shouted against the police.

6:15 P.M. The students were ejected from Balboa. The students had left the National Institute for Balboa at 4:30 P.M. Groups of students deployed along all of Fourth of July Avenue and Avenida Kennedy, destroying every car with a Zone license plate that they found in their way; all the traffic lights and some street lights were destroyed. Cars with Zone license plates 6718 and 1778 were the first ones burned. Rocks were thrown against the Masonic Temple, the Ancon Gymnasium, the residence of the Maryknoll Sisters, and the Pan American Building.

7:20 P.M. The firemen arrived; they did not try to extinguish the different fires. [This refers to the Panama Fire Department.]

7:45 P.M. Rocks were thrown and the Zone police replied with tear gas and shotgun fire. Major Urrutia (one of the Deputy Commanders of the *Guardia Nacional*), who was in the vicinity, was one of those who suffered the effects from same. A group of individuals who were not identified as students destroyed and burned the Canal Zone bus service.

8:00 P.M. The first shots of short arms, revolvers, shotguns, and possibly rifles were used by the Zone police, wounding a great number of Panamanians. The police fired from in front of the Hotel Tivoli. The students and the people who joined them made the police retreat. The people started for the railroad station [in Ancon] where at least two passenger cars were destroyed and burned. At least fifteen cars were burned along Fourth of July Avenue. [Fourth of July Avenue is all within the Canal Zone.]

8:15 P.M. Strong gunfire from the Zone police in the Ancon Station; the students made them retreat with rocks. The police returned to the charge and wounded a great number of demonstrators. The Good Neighbor Bar was destroyed. [This bar was situated on a corner of Avenida Francisco de la Ossa and the intersection of Tivoli Crossing on the Panama side.]

8:40 P.M. The first squad of soldiers, who were placed in different sectors of Avenida Kennedy, arrived. Shooting erupts, when a car of the National Department of Investigations [Panama's Secret Police], driven by the Deputy Chief and members of the *Guardia Nacional*, delivered a wounded gringo to his countrymen. The police fired against the car.

9:10 P.M. New shooting and wounded; the principal posts of the Zone are reinforced with infantry troops, armed with rifles and fixed bayonets. Some tried to prevent the newspapermen and photographers from fulfilling their duty.

9:20 P.M. A helicopter and a small plane from the Zone fly over the city. Broadcasts are made from the small plane.

9:40 P.M. Armored cars and tanks of the Army arrive and are placed along Fourth of July Avenue. Various acts of vandalism occur around the *Edificio Panamericano,* where the offices of Pan American World Airways are located. That building and the contiguous one are set afire. The offices of Pan American, Boyd Brothers, Helen Linen Center, Braniff, Varig, the Abrigo Rojo *boite,* and the Relax Cantina, and other stores are sacked by thieves. The *Guardia Nacional* and the DENI

(National Department of Investigations) detained 17 thieves. Various North American offices like All-America Cables and Goodyear are destroyed. [All-America Cables was not destroyed. Rocks were hurled through the windows but Simon Bolivar Aleman, the Panamanian manager, confronted the mob at the entrance and courageously dissuaded them from entering the office to destroy the valuable transmission and receiving equipment.]

10:30 P.M. Molotov cocktails manufactured by the people are launched against the tanks and the soldiers. New shooting occurs. At this hour the wounded are calculated at more than 100, the dead at six.

11:00 P.M. Fires and shooting occur in different places, like the Bridge of the Americas [Thatcher Ferry Bridge] and other places. The mob ransacked the America Gun Store and stole twenty shotguns and revolvers. From 11:00 P.M. on attacked and destroyed in part were the offices of the USIS, which was burned [this was totally destroyed], the First National City Bank and its branch, the Chase Manhattan Bank, Kodak, Singer Sewing Machine, and the Fuerza y Luz, the Electric Bond and Share Company, subsidiary of American Foreign Power.

4:30 A.M. to *5:00* A.M. There was a demonstration in front of the American Embassy [located on Avenida Balboa near the Santo Tomas Hospital and the Statue of Balboa that faces the Pacific], which was found to be guarded by forces of the *Guardia Nacional*. Rocks were thrown against the building. A car at the service of the embassy was set afire.

6:00 A.M. Up to this hour there were five dead reported from bullet wounds.

7:00 A.M. It was reported that five bodies had been found inside the Pan American Building, some of them had bullet wounds. Of the ten dead, six have been identified. They were Ascanio Arosemena, Teofilo de la Torre, Alberto Oriol, Gonzalo Frazer or Crance, Victor Manuel Iglesias, and Ezequiel González Meneses.

The dismantled cyclone fence already mentioned was torn down by the Panamanians but the framework uprights and the barbed wire on the top remained.

When General O'Meara assumed total command of the Canal Zone, all press releases were centralized under his Public Affairs Office. The Public Affairs Officer was Lieutenant Colonel L. J. Churchville, United States Air Force. This was his first release early in the morning of January 10, 1964:

On December 30, 1963, Robert J. Fleming, Jr., Governor of the Canal Zone, announced further implementation of the joint communiqué of the United States and Republic of Panama governments jointly to fly the flags of both nations at selected sites in the Canal Zone. At these civilian land areas where the U.S. flag is flown by civilian authorities eleven dual flags were flying and five sites were in preparation for the dual flags to be flown in February of this year.

Governor Fleming also announced that flags no longer would be flown outside schools, the U.S. District Court building in Ancon, and three other sites. Thus the U.S. flag would continue to be displayed in classrooms or elsewhere within the schools as at present. This flag decision was effective on January 2.

From January 7 to 9, students at the Zone schools on both sides of the Isthmus, disregarding the announcement that the U.S. flag was no longer to be flown outside the schools, as it had been, hoisted the flag on both regular and makeshift flagpoles and on lightning rods at the schools.

At 4:00 P.M. yesterday, January 9, a group of Panamanian students entered the Canal Zone, carrying Panamanian school flags. The students proceeded to the Balboa High School grounds and mingled with North American students near the flagpole. Five Panamanian students with Canal Zone police protection planted a school flag of Panama beside the American flag.

The Canal Zone police maintained control and directed the students back to Panama.

The Panamanian students returned to Panama City and along the route broke some street lights and overturned garbage cans.

After the students departed, and under the cover of darkness, disorderly mobs invaded the Canal Zone where they damaged automobiles, ransacked buildings, set fires, and stoned and fired on police attempting to control them. In the initial phases of the disorders, and before troops had been brought into action, police returned fire with tear gas and firearms.

When the demonstrations reached proportions beyond the scope of Canal Zone police, the acting Governor requested that General Andrew P. O'Meara, Commander in Chief, U.S. Southern Command, assume command of the Canal Zone.

At 8:00 P.M. last night, 9 January 1964, General O'Meara issued the following proclamation: QUOTE: Upon request of the Acting Governor of the Canal Zone I have assumed command of the Canal Zone.

All persons not working or living, or attending school in the Canal Zone are hereby directed to leave the Canal Zone immediately. All residents of the Canal Zone not engaged in official duties will return to their place of residence and remain there until further orders. Upon return to a normal situation, announcement will be made over the Southern Command Network, 790 kilocycles on your radio and Channels 8 and 10 on your television. UNQUOTE.

A U.S. Air Force aircraft, equipped with a public address system, was ordered into the air last night (January 9) to broadcast in Spanish and English General O'Meara's proclamation to all concerned.

The aircraft was an Air Force Commando U-10A from Howard AFB and was airborne for more than an hour broadcasting the proclamation. The broadcasts appeared to have a quieting effect on the demonstrators.

Troops of the U.S. Army Forces, Southern Command, were ordered to secure the Canal Zone and disperse all demonstrators. When troops ordered demonstrators to disperse, the groups fell back in an orderly fashion.

At 11:00 P.M. last night (January 9), General O'Meara announced that the incidents that occurred earlier yesterday were under complete control and that to prevent recurrence of the disturbances, all personnel not living or working in the Canal Zone had been ordered out of the Canal Zone. Residents of the Canal Zone not involved in official duties were ordered to remain in their residences.

In the fire which troops received in making initial contact and in subsequent sniping at U.S. troops, three U.S. soldiers were killed and thirty-four soldiers have been wounded.

Schools will be closed in the Canal Zone today, and all residents of the Canal Zone not engaged in official duties will stay in their homes.

As troops of the U.S. Army Forces Southern Command's 193rd Infantry Brigade arrived in positions to assist the beleaguered Canal Zone police, they took up riot-control formations and effectively moved the rioters from the Canal Zone.

First soldiers on the border were U.S. Army military policemen who arrived at 8:30 P.M. last night (January 9) in squad strength at the Curundu Gate, which borders on Panama. There they restored order, moved traffic past overturned vehicles.

Colonel Henry J. Richter, Commanding Officer of the 193rd Infantry Brigade, closed the Canal Zone border from the Curundu Gate to and along Fourth of July Avenue. Elements of the brigade stationed on the Atlantic side of the Isthmus closed the border at Colón.

Persistent sniper fire at soldiers protecting the Canal Zone in the vicinity of the Tivoli Guest House resulted in casualties to the U.S. Army infantryman. As the casualties mounted to four wounded, the order was given to return the sniper fire. The Army selected trained marksmen for carefully directed return fire. A fifth soldier was seriously wounded in the head and a sixth was wounded before the sniper fire ceased.

Ship traffic through the Panama Canal was not affected.

There was one obvious error in the above release, which I ascertained when I made by own on-the-spot investigation in the Canal Zone and Panama. It was the statement that the Panamanian students "planted" their flag. They did not. They were halted before they reached the flagpole.

General O'Meara and the American military forces in the Zone became the immediate target of a vicious and vulgar smear campaign that was exploited by Panamanian Communists, Nationalists, and chauvinists in the press, over the radio, and on television. Unaware of this because of the exigencies of his command functions in the emergency, General O'Meara held an historic press conference in the theater at Quarry Heights on January 12. This transcript of the conference furnishes a full report of the military action during the flag war and corrects the biased reports disseminated on the other side of the line:

Gentlemen, if you are ready, I am. I'm General O'Meara. I'm prepared to answer your questions for the next few minutes on the matters on which I am a competent witness, that is what has occurred from the time I assumed command of the Canal Zone and all operations and civil concerns with the Canal Zone. This was at 7:59 P.M. on Thursday, the ninth of January. Up until the present moment anything that has occurred in that interval is my responsibility. I will not attempt to answer any questions as to political or other types of developments prior to the time that I assumed full responsibility. There are many more competent witnesses than myself on those matters. I will, of course, not speculate on any military plans or developments for the future. I will not speculate on any political developments for the future. There are many more competent people than I to discuss these items with you.

Q.: General, will you please tell us what your mission was, and is, when you assumed command?

A.: Well, I went over this with a number of you before, but you weren't all here so I think I'll go over it briefly. About 6:50 in the evening of Thursday, the ninth of January, my headquarters called me and said that the Acting Governor, Lieutenant Governor Parker—the Governor was on an airplane on his way to Miami to report to Washington at that time in connection with his official duties, having nothing to do with this matter—had called. However, the Lieutenant Governor said that there was a disorderly group of students in the Canal Zone, that he felt he could handle it with his own resources, his Canal Zone police, but that just in case it got out of hand he requested that we alert some troops in case he should have to ask me to take command and assume full responsibility for the Canal Zone. About 7:10—I didn't look at my watch at this time, of course, it could be five minutes off—Colonel Parker, the Acting Governor, called me on the telephone and stated that he had made this request to my headquarters. I said that I was aware of it and that he was glad to say that the students had left the Canal Zone, that there had been some disorder, there had been some breakage of windows, overturning of garbage cans, other disorderly conduct, but there had been no violence other than this, and that the students had left the Canal Zone and he was very happy to say that the incident was concluded relatively peacefully. Within ten minutes he called me back.

At 7:59 Lieutenant Governor Parker, the Acting Governor of the Canal Zone, came into my operations center and said, "General, the situation is completely beyond the control of the police. There are large mobs at the border of the Zone, there are a large number of men of all ages who had forced their way into the Zone in numbers. The police are trying to hold them back. It is completely out of my control. Will you please assume command?"

I said: "Dave, I am assuming command as of now."

I then immediately ordered the troops which I had told to move to the forward area, but which of course had not reached there, to move to the Zone boundaries in the Ancon area, to evict all disorderely personnel and to seal the Zone boundary. At that time I of course became responsible for all United States government authority in this area, military or civilian. The police came under my command, but the police were widely separated, were a very thin line. There were only about thirty policemen in the Ancon area against several thousand rioters. They were without communication between each other, of course. They don't have tactical communication like military forces do. I could communicate with them only after the military troops came and made contact with them and took over from them, but responsibility was mine of course from 7:59 on.

Q.: Reports published at home said you had established martial law. Did you?

A.: I said I had assumed full responsibility. You can legalize this as you will because that statement stands. I am responsible for everything. We have not established military courts to try the civilian personnel. I would like to say that there have been a good many false reports circulating from whatever source. Some of you who spoke to me yesterday have been exposed to some of these reports. I would like to emphasize some of the remarks I made then. There has been no machine-gun fire on the part of any United States personnel, either police or military. The police aren't equipped with machine-guns. Before I took over, and of course in the brief time before my troops relieved the police, the police were equipped with shoutguns, their .38 caliber pistols, and with some tear-gas grenades. All too few I would say, but the police organization didn't have time to get the tear gas that could have been very usefully used at that time in the hands of the police. This resulted in the use of weapons by the police under the exigency of the situation and this resulted in the Panamanian casualties of rather large numbers, including a substantial number of deaths, which all of us regret.

Not only were no machine guns fired, no machine-gun ammunition was issued to the troops at any time. As you probably all realize, though, the caliber of the machine gun is the same as the caliber of the M1 rifle, .30-caliber machine gun. It will fire the same individual round. Machine-gun ammunition is quite distinctive from rifle ammunition in that it must be belted in order to fire. No belted ammunition has been issued. No belted ammunition is in the hands of the troops nor has it been since this thing started. There are also reports that .50-caliber rounds had been fired against the legislative palace. No .50-caliber weapon has been fired and no .50-caliber ammunition has been issued, no .50-caliber ammunition has been on the scene of the action in the hands of the United States forces at any time, or, as far as I know, in the hands of the Panamanians.

Let me tell you a bit about the casualties that have occurred on the United States side. I have heard reports of casualties on the Panamanian side, some of which came from what I think are quite authentic sources, but they were early in the day. I have no later information which I would consider authentic.

I will give these casualties cumulatively between Thursday, the time

I assumed command, the time the forces were committed to action, up until 6:00 A.M. on Friday morning. There were troops killed, United States soldiers killed by gunshot, 3; wounded by gunshot, 10; wounded by other means, either sticks, stones, bottles, when they were in close contact with the mob and forcing the mob back out of the Zone boundaries and other wounds, 51. From six o'clock Friday until six o'clock Saturday: wounded by gun shot, 4, which is sniper fire; wounded by other means, 7. From six o'clock Saturday morning until six o'clock Sunday morning: wounded by gunshot, 6, five soldiers and one United States civilian employee; wounded by other means, either bottles, Molotov cocktails, rocks, sticks, what have you, 10. Since six o'clock this morning: wounded by gunshot, 2, both of those have been since noon today, and both of them have been on the Atlantic side. These are troops. All of these figures I have given you are troops, except that one civilian employee who was wounded by a gunshot yesterday and he was in the area performing his duties as a civilian employee of the United States government.

Now, it's a little harder to tell you how much incoming fire we've sustained. Between midnight on Thursday and midnight on Friday we have no estimate of how much firing was done between the time that I assumed command and midnight; there was some firing. But, on the Panamanian side, not a great deal, some shotguns and small arms, but not a great deal, and the confusion at that time was great. You realize considering how far off the troops were when I took command it was some time before they were able to take over, for the police were under very great pressure trying to contain this mob down near the freight house in Ancon, for instance, and the laundry in Ancon there was a mob in excess of [Here, as aside.] "George, you were there. How many in excess of 400?" "Considerably in excess, less than 1,000, probably between 800 and 1,000."

By the way, I have called from time to time on my Operations Officer, General George Mabry, who is a very competent observer, having been in more combat than most of us are given to experience and recognized by the United States government with one Congressional Medal of Honor, one Distinguished Service Cross, one Silver Cross, and a lesser assortment of medals. I sent him down there right after I took command, to observe the situation for me on the scene. He took with him several highly experienced senior officers who he used as his deputies to assist in seeing that the troops were deployed to the places where they were most needed as soon as they arrived on the scene and to report back to me since he had communication with me when he went down there, radio communications. Opposing this mob, which was at least 800, it might have been a thousand, were 6 policemen, 4 in another location, and the penetration at this point was . . . [Another aside.]—"How many yards?" "One hundred fifty yards in the Zone right in the Zone right up against the civilian housing area at that point." The police were there. The police fired shotgun ammunition and then .38-caliber pistol ammunition. They say into the air and into the ground, frequently on concrete, and if they fired into the ground, it would have undoubtedly ricocheted. Whether any of their fire went directly into Panamanians from their weapons without going into the ground, I'm in no position to say. Certainly, those policemen were under very great stress. They fired large amounts of ammunition. The handful of men against a very large mob. They felt that the mob was breaking windows, setting fire to buildings, setting fire to a railroad coach. It was a very ugly mob— sticks, stones, bottles.

You and I might have done better than those men. You and I might have acted with more restraint, maybe we would have been able to contain the mob better than the policemen did, they did have some success in containing it. Several times the men fell back and then surged forward again. It did not enter the housing area, the civilian housing area. They did approach the Commissary Building down there, the Little Theater Building, in which there were a group of civilians at that time carrying on their own activities. As soon as the troops came, as soon as there were troops, General Mabry rushed down there. First point of issue was the Tivoli Hotel which was where the pressure was greatest, here the mob was greatest. General Mabry committed the troops there first and they evicted the mob from the Zone at that point and they then took a handful of men and went down to the next point of danger which, however, where the mob was smaller at that point, was the point of deeper penetration. This was where a good deal of firing was going on. He stopped the firing and with . . . [Aside.] "How many?" "Four troops first." Four of them came in first and then two others blocked off the mob and the mob responded very well to the application of military authority and they withdrew before the soldiers. Later we got more soldiers down there.

Now, there was a lot of firing going on in front of the Tivoli Hotel, where the troops were first committed, the first troops to arrive were committed. Police were using shotguns and again .38 caliber pistols. When the troops moved in, they moved in promptly; the mob started to fall back. There was a lot of close contact. This was where many of those fifty-one casualties other than gunshot wounds occurred. Some of the first troops committed to action though the orders were very strict that a minimum of force would be used. The policemen were firing both shotguns and pistols when some of the first troops went into action. They also fired with their shotguns. General Mabry believes that less than twelve rounds were fired by the troops with their shotguns before their officers brought them under complete control and they ceased all firing. They then simply used their weapons at the high parts and they were generally in wedge formation or close formation and moved the mob back and the mob fell back in reasonably good order, if you consider reasonably good order being the inflicting of something approaching fifty casualties.

The other place there was a deep penetration in the Zone at the time that the troops arrived there—and the troops didn't arrive there until much later because it was the second contingent which we had to commit there—was on Balboa Avenue. There the penetration was to a depth of between three and four hundred yards. Balboa Avenue is the street which runs from the Fourth of July Avenue where the first exit from the bridge approach comes at the big traffic-light complex. . . . [Aside.] "At least three hundred people, George? You had gone down there in case, didn't you? How many people did they think were inside the Zone?" "I would estimate four hundred to four hundred fifty." Four hundred to four hundred and fifty men in the mob which had penetrated to a depth of between three and four hundred yards; this is something of a defile; the police falling back firing over their heads and firing into the ground. Our estimate is that few if any Panamanian casualties occurred from this firing but it may have.

When the troops did move in here they didn't use any firearms whatsoever. They had two armored personnel carriers, which have been frequently referred to as tanks. They are not tanks. They are armored infantry carriers; they are track vehicles; they have one-quarter-inch armor all the way around; they have a machine gun mounted on top of them; as I said, no machine guns have been used. Neither have any machine guns been in place anywhere; nor have any machine gun emplacements been prepared. One reporter, I know quite honestly, told me yesterday he had seen a machine-gun emplacement up on one of the upper stories of the Tivoli Hotel. What he saw was sandbagging behind which a trained marksman was emplaced to try to aim fire on the snipers who were causing the casualties which I have enumerated here on a day-by-day basis. I might say that at least half a dozen of these gunshot wounds were suffered by our trained marksmen. We took them from our competition marksmanship team, our trained marksmen who were using 30-30 rifles, high-powered rifles, with telescopic sights on them, trying to pick off the snipers who were causing the casualties. They themselves suffered casualties in the course of it. They needed the sand-bags which we put around the windows to give them the maximum protection while they were doing their duty. As I say though, there were very few, if any, casualties on the part of Panamanians on the Balboa Road. When the troops arrived there with their personnel carriers they moved the two personnel carriers forward. The infantry were outside the personnel carriers on foot, sending the line to the right or left. They moved forward slowly. The mob withdrew before them in reasonably good order. Of course, throwing rocks and stones and sticks as they withdrew.

When the troops had cleared the area, they sealed the area. They put up concertina barbed wire which you can spread out and closed it to all traffic. There was one area near St. Luke's Cathedral which probably was seen where a great deal of the fencing was knocked down. There were some penetrations there. Molotov cocktails were thrown against the house of a federal judge, which is fairly close to the boundary. Three small fires were set but the commander on the scene got a few troops over there very quickly. The mob was pushed out in that area with relative ease and the policemen and firemen then put out the fires. Now, have I given you the estimate of incoming rounds as yet which caused these casualties?

These are estimates, mind you, and since beginning on Friday, auto-matic weapons have been brought into it, which have been firing in bursts. You can't expect the men who are doing the counting to get a very accurate count. But this is the best figure we've been able to obtain. From midnight on Thursday until midnight on Friday, on the Pacific side, 600 rounds were fired at United States troops. On the Atlantic side 130 rounds were fired. From midnight on Friday until midnight on Saturday, during this time the automatic weapons were brought into play, more than 750 rounds were brought in on the Pacific side. Some of the estimates are much higher than that on account of the automatic weapons fire, but I prefer to use what I consider a reasonable estimate, though it may be somewhat low, of 750 rounds, with 50 rounds being fired on the Atlantic side. From midnight on Saturday up until the present time, approximately 850 rounds were fired on the Pacific side and approximately 172 rounds on the Atlantic side. I think this is a good time to open it to general questions between General Mabry and myself. We'll try to answer them to the best of our knowledge.

Q.: Where was the heaviest fighting?

A.: [General Mabry]: Mainly around the Tivoli area, a great many of them from the Legislative Assembly Building. There were men up there with automatic weapons and they were fired in bursts as high as twenty-five at a time; this is from Friday night until midnight yesterday, midnight Saturday, that's right. From about midnight on I don't think there was any automatic weapons fired but there was some pistol fire, there was some high-velocity .22 and some low-velocity .22. I was down there myself the last time about two o'clock in the morning and there would be periods of quiet and then there would be three, four, five, six rounds fired and then a period of quiet for five or ten minutes again.

Q.: In that automatic firing were any of them taken? Any of the automatic rifles captured or identified?

A.: I don't think they were, properly speaking, automatic rifles, they were Tommy guns and carbines which can also fire automatically. You can turn a carbine to automatic and fire first or fire fast.

Q.: I understood, perhaps incorrectly, that you said that from Saturday midnight to the present there were 850 rounds fired, the present being mid-Sunday afternoon.

A.: No. Wait a minute, yes, that's right. It was from Friday midnight to Saturday midnight, 750; from Saturday midnight to the present, approximately 850.

Q.: So this morning would be down at the Tivoli section from the Legislative Building.

A.: That was mainly between midnight and 4:00 A.M., and most of it fairly close to midnight when there was considerable automatic fire. Some of that automatic fire as I recall, George, was from two men down in Shaler Triangle itself. I think they were trying to draw fire on themselves. One of them was firing first with a Tommy gun. He fired first the first ten, then fifteen. Then he put in a new clip and fired perhaps all twenty-five. You can run up high numbers rather fast that way. With him was a man with a carbine who was generally firing in bursts of ten. During this time we did not suffer any casualties. They were shooting at the Tivoli Hotel building or on the ground around it. As I say, our instructions in all of it, my instructions from the first was to use the minimum of force, to use tear gas, except when we were taking casualties from snipers and at that time they could aim fire by designated riflemen at the sniper, provided the sniper was not in a crowd or in a place where innocent people were going to be injured by the fire.

On the Atlantic side where we had the three men killed we have taken a fair number of sniper casualties from gunfire. No major caliber weapons have ever been used. If you know the Atlantic side, the streets are narrow there, the distances we are talking about are shorter, and the military commander therefore, in keeping with my instructions, said he would use the minimum of force in responding to the fire which is placed on them, using nothing but machine guns, excuse me, nothing but, you've got machine guns on my mind, that's not a joking matter for me, use nothing but shotguns and the only type of shot that he used was number four and number seven and a half, these are both bird shots, you know. Those of you who are hunters know that number four is a standard-size shot when you are shooting at ducks; it's too small to use on geese unless the goose is awful close to you; I use number two when I try to shoot geese. Seven and a half is what you use on very small birds, like doves. This is what is being used on the Atlantic side. This is the only type of ammunition that has been fired by any United States troops on the Atlantic side. Before the troops were committed and again when the police, and a few police, were on line over there, the police did use their own shotguns and their tear gas guns.

Q.: Could you tell us about the exchange of shots between our troops and the *Guardia Nacional* this morning?

A.: Yes, I will. I'll tell you what we've been able to determine about it. We really don't know the facts because we haven't been able to investigate it as we would like. I'd been in bed about thirty or thirty-five minutes, I would say, and when General Mabry called me on the phone; General Mabry was on duty in my operations center at that time, and he said, "General, we have just received word that there has been an exchange of fire between the *Guardia Nacional* and our troops in Cristobal; that a *Guardia Nacional* truck pulled out rapidly around the Masonic building just at the time that some fire was being placed on the Masonic building from the Colón side across the street and that our troops returned the fire and wounded some *Guardia Nacional* personnel in the truck. This is certainly far from the intent of anyone on the American side. Let me speak for a moment of the *Guardia Nacional*. I'll say what I said yesterday, that I think for a very small force, a force entirely too small for the very large responsibilities which it carries. For those of you who don't know much about Panama, there are 3,000 men in the *Guardia*

Nacional it's the only type of security force this republic has. It is responsible for all police and security service of any type from traffic control to constable in the little isolated villages down in Darien. It's spread over what is not a large country, but is a hell of a lot of difficult land to police and it has responsibility for the security of two large cities, Colón and Panama, and of several other fair-sized cities, such as David, Chitre, Santiago, a number of others. They are spread very thin, their equipment is very limited, and considering their resources, I have the greatest respect for what the *Guardia Nacional* has been able to accomplish under very trying circumstances in the last three and one-half days. All of my commanders, and I think all of my men, bear my sentiments. I know all of my commanders do, of course, I can't say for all my men; therefore, this is a very regrettable incident.

I called General Bogart and asked him to please get in touch with Colonel Vallarino, the Commandant of the *Guardia Nacional,* and tell him we'd heard this report, we regret it very much that any incident of this type could have happened, and suggesting that we have a joint investigation at daylight today. Colonel Vallarino agreed and said that he regretted it too. We've named our man to conduct the investigation. When I left my headquarters about 12:30 and went home to get a bowl of soup and get thirty minutes sleep before I came over here, Colonel Vallarino was still asleep. The officers in the *Guardia* said they were not going to awaken him, and so the *Guardia* representative has still not been designated.

However, General Bogart had a senior officer of his own on the scene make an investigation immediately which he followed up as best he could at daylight, and the story which we get is that there was fire being placed on the Masonic Temple, both shotgun and large caliber fire from Colón. When this three-quarter-ton truck appeared on the scene, moving rather rapidly, a bullet hit a rear tire and stopped it. Remember, bullets were not being fired by United States troops. When this bullet hit it, however, two men immediately dismounted from the truck and, one on each side, went around to the rear of it, took a rolling fall up against the tire, where they'd get the maximum protection, and opened fire with their pistols on the Masonic Temple building, where they apparently thought the fire had come from. Two soldiers in the Masonic Temple each returned that fire with a shotgun. Each fired one round, and re- member, there was no larger shot than number four available. Fire continued to come from Colón, both shotgun fire and large calibre fire, rifle fire. Both men were hit. A policeman, a *bombero,* came out to assist them and he collapsed. Someone else ran out from the other side of the street, reached into the driver's compartment, grabbed a pistol, fired one, perhaps several rounds at the Masonic Temple, and ran back into the city again. This was the end of the action which lasted, according to not only two men who were there, but men who were on the upper floors of the Masonic Temple as well, it lasted perhaps forty-five seconds in all, a real fast-breaking action. The Panamanians then came out and took the two men back. One of them has died. The Captain of *bomberos,* the Captain of the fire department, went out to assist. We understand he collapsed because of a heart attack, but he seems to be all right now. We understand and we hope that Colonel Vallarino will wake up and name his man pretty soon so we can look at it. We understand from a source that of course we can't corroborate, maybe some of you gentlemen can, that the *Guardia Nacional* man who died has a hole the size of a silver dollar in the front of his chest. I'm just telling you this last one is an unconfirmed rumor that has gotten to us from across the lines so I can't verify that anyway. The rest of it is obtained by a senior officer questioning every soldier, every man who was on the scene who was in a position to witness it. It's the best thing we've been able to put together so far. We'd like very much to have the combined investigation which General Bogart and Colonel Reilly agreed to about 3:15 this morning.

Q.: *Luis A. de Leon, Channel 4, RPC, radio and television* [General O'Meara requests translator]:

Translator: His first statement was, sir, that they [his channel] would like to have a brief résumé in Spanish of your opinions of what has occurred in the short days of the trouble. He also said that his channel feels that you will give him a complete rundown because they feel you are still a very good friend and could they be provided a person who could translate for them into Spanish the things they need.

General O'Meara: I will be very happy to have the opportunity to do so; what I am saying now is being taped. I have always had and have today the greatest respect and the greatest warmth of feeling for the people of Panama. No one is more burdened by what has happened than I am. I will provide a most expert translator that I know of, and he's one of the best in either language. English or Spanish. He'll transpose my words to you this afternoon into Spanish on another tape and you can carry it away with you.

[General O'Meara explains to Colonel Moura that he (O'Meara) would like Colonel Moura to be the official translator for the rest of the session and to translate his answer "word-for-word" to Leon on tape. Colonel Moura is introduced to the audience and General O'Meara calls him "the best master of the two languages that I know."]

Moura: They say that's fine sir, but they also are interested in asking you specific questions, special questions.

General O'Meara: Translate to him what I first said to all of the group that this afternoon I am going to answer questions on the things on which I am a competent witness. In other words, what happened from the time I took command from 7:59 P.M. on Thursday the ninth until the present moment.

[Translation made by Colonel Moura to Leon.]

General O'Meara: I will not talk about any matters political or otherwise which occurred before that time because many people are much more competent than I.

[Translation made by Colonel Moura to Leon.]

Colonel Moura translating for Leon: They are not interested in political matters either, General. They're merely interested in getting opinions of authorized U.S. spokesmen to the Panamanian people without mixing politics into those opinions.

General O'Meara: Exactly, and for that reason, I will also not speak of anything in the future since I'm a responsible military commander on the scene, I will not speak of any military action which could or might occur in the future. Even less so would I speculate on any political developments in the future.

Colonel Moura (translating Leon's question): His question is related to a UPI dispatch out of New York which states that you informed the press here in Panama that your troops fired only nine shots. How do you relate that to the fact that there were over 200 people wounded in Panama?

General O'Meara: I'll answer that very briefly. I said that in the initial contact there were about nine shotgun rounds fired. After that, against the sniper fire, several hundred rounds of fire were fired against the snipers, but this is not when the large number of casualties occurred. The large number of casualties occurred, dead and wounded, before the troops were committed, when we had three and four and six policemen and very angry mobs who were forcibly advancing against the housing areas and civil population which those police were charged with protecting.

[Translated to Leon by Colonel Moura.]

General O'Meara: Colonel Moura, may I suggest that you tell the gentlemen that this translating here in the midst of our limited time uses up a good many minutes that some of these other people I'm sure would like to ask questions on too. I would be happy for you to bring the gentlemen from the Panamanian radio up to my office for about ten minutes after this is over and the three of us can then continue it.

[Translated to Leon by Colonel Moura.]

General O'Meara: I would be happy to have the other members of the Panamanian press come with him.

[Translated by Colonel Moura.]

Q.: Could you tell us whether any steps have been taken to pull troops back from the border of the Zone in this area?

General O'Meara: Yes. At five o'clock on Friday morning, remember this thing broke out Thursday night, General Mabry, at my direction and after my consultation by telephone with the representative of the Commandant, a senior officer at the *Guardia Nacional* conferred as to the state of order at that time. And we agreed that if there was a reasonable degree of order obtained at that time, I would withdraw the troops from immediate contact, I would open the entrances into the Canal Zone to peaceable traffic with only a pair of military police at each entrance to verify that the people who wanted to come in had peaceable and authentic intentions. And this has occurred each day since then. As long as people were peaceable the crossing points are open to anybody who wants to go through. When mobs start forming they've been closed. The troops push up to a crossing point or to a danger area only when that area is threatened. The rest of the time they pull back out of sight. These are my orders. And I verified them in person on the scene that they are being obeyed.

Q.: General, there was a release given out earlier today which said something along the lines that there had been no agreement reached on whatever the phraseology was, pulling back or withdrawing troops from the border area. It said it referred to erroneous press reports, and I wonder if you could clarify what you just said now in the light of this?

General O'Meara: This report did not come from me, either the report itself or the one which it was refuting. But I can tell you what I understand the facts to be. There was a press report that the troops were leaving the border area and the *Guardia Nacional* was assuming control and that there had been an agreement between the Panamanian authorities and the United States authorities with respect to this. This was denied. I have not been approached with this proposal. It has been discussed at a political level. No agreement with respect to this has been told to me, and, therefore, a press release was made saying "no, this was not true." Until law and order prevailed or I received other orders from higher authority, I would discharge my responsibilities of maintaining law and order in the Canal Zone using troops as necessary and I'll continue my same policy of using the very minimum force.

Q.: General, just one more question. This concerns the matter of the casualties and is connected with the Panamanian gentleman's question. Is there any report or is there any knowledge of how many Panamanian snipers were killed by our aimed fire?

General O'Meara: It's very hard to tell, but not very many. [Aside.] "George, could you give any estimate on it? Killed or wounded I'll say, it's hard to tell."

General Mabry: No sir, I cannot give an estimate. The only way we could get an estimate would be from the opposition—the opposite side of the tracks.

General O'Meara: I would say this, that the men who actually engaged in the fire do not believe they were successful in hitting more than ten of the people they were shooting at then. I don't know how many less than that. Shooters are always optimistic, but even these people don't think that they've gotten as many as ten.

Q.: I wanted to know if this incident over on the Atlantic side with the *Guardia Nacional* is the first time that the *Guardia Nacional* has shot on the United States Armed forces.

General O'Meara: Has what?

Q.: Is it the first time that they have fired on the United States armed forces during the incident?

General O'Meara: It certainly is, yes.

Correspondent: Thank you.

General O'Meara: It's certainly also the first time the United States armed forces have ever directed any fire against anybody in the *Guardia Nacional*.

Q.: General, could you give us a picture of the situation more or less at present as applies to this end and what's happened since this morning on the other end, because most of us are out of touch with Colón.

General O'Meara: Well, it's very quiet on this side. On the Colón side there is some sniping; two rounds were fired between noon and the time that I came over here just before two o'clock. And besides that, there are a good many bottles of gasoline, Molotov cocktails, being heaved at the Masonic Temple over there, in an attempt to get it burning again. There is not a large mob, there is a crowd, but it's not what you'd call a large disorderly mob, on the Colón side. When I left to come over here there were just a few small groups of people on the Pacific side. One more short question because we've got something else we want to show you. No lady has asked questions yet, let's give her a chance. I'm sorry, my apology, my sincere apologies.

Q.: Last night, Panamanian domestic employees working in the Zone, not last night but the night before, were turned back at the guard posts because soldiers and policemen there said the firing from Panama was so indiscriminate that it was against *Guardia Nacional* and other Panamanians. Is this true? Do you have any indication of indiscriminate firing in the mobs in Panama?

General O'Meara: We have observed firing in Panama which was not directed toward the Canal Zone. I'll say no more than that. It is my short memory and nothing else. Okay, this is the last question and then I want to tell you something else I think will be of interest.

Q.: I want to get this straight in my own mind, sir. At five o'clock tomorrow morning you make the decision, at five o'clock, whether or not your guards are to be left at their posts or to be pulled back, is that correct?

General O'Meara: We made the decision the first morning at five o'clock only. Since then that has prevailed throughout. The entry points are open day and night now for anybody to come through who wants to come through on legitimate and peaceful business. Anybody comes up here in his private automobile and says, "I want to go through," they look who's in there and say, "You got an ID card? Any identification?" If he's got any kind of identification that looks recognizable he goes right on through.

Q.: There was some shooting last night they tell me; the guards at the number two post, and they pointed out the house where they said the shooting was coming from. Why don't you call the *Guardia Nacional* in Panama and tell them that there's a sniper in a certain building?

General O'Meara: I've not only called the *Guardia Nacional* about it, I have called the Foreign Minister on it. Some of the senior delegation that came down here from Washington have talked to senior officials of the government of Panama. General Bogart has talked repeatedly to the *Guardia Nacional* headquarters and several times the *Guardia* has been very successful in getting these people. Numerous times they have attempted to follow up on their leads and have gotten them, and we know of a number of instances, certainly a dozen, maybe more than a dozen, where the *Guardia* has picked up these snipers. But not all of them, and it hasn't stopped our casualties.

At the outset I was unable to document as to who fired the first shots, whether from the Canal Zone over into Panama or from Panama into the Canal Zone. I did verify that there had been no firing by either police or civilians in the vicinity of the St. Luke's Cathedral (Episcopal) in Ancon, as was alleged by the student, Guevara. United States District Judge Guthrie F. Crowe was able to set the record straight in an unsolicited letter dated January 13 which he wrote to E. S. Shipley, Canal Zone Police Chief. The letter read:

DEAR CHIEF SHIPLEY:

I am writing to express my appreciation for the fine work that was done by the courageous men under the direction of Lieutenant Richards at my home and the courthouse on Thursday night, January 9, when the rioting took place on the border between the Canal Zone and Panama City.

The rioters succeeded in breaking down the storm fence which separated my house and the courthouse from Fourth of July Avenue, and a howling mob of four or five hundred were storming up the hillside and burning my house when a small group of your men came down and went in the house with me and fought the fire and assisted the Fire Department in extinguishing it.

At the time the mob was attacking the house, it was impossible to get the fire truck and equipment up to the front because the rioters were shooting and throwing rocks, and your men repelled the mob by opening fire and shooting a few bursts of ammunition over their heads. This permitted the fire truck to operate in the house and all of our personal effects were saved. The men performed with the greatest of courage as they were hopelessly outnumbered and very lightly armed.

I have had many years of experience with police officers, first as Commissioner of the Kentucky State Police and later here in the Canal Zone as Judge of the District Court, and I have never seen men act with more restraint and composure in the face of extremely hazardous duty than the group of men assigned to this area Thursday night. I think you should be extremely proud of them and so should the civil authorities of the Canal Zone. I am forwarding a copy of this letter to the Governor of the

Canal Zone and to the Director of Civil Affairs so they may be apprised of the splendid work that you and your men performed.

With kindest personal regards and again expressing my great appreciation, I am,

Yours sincerely,
(Signed) GUTHRIE F. CROWE
U. S. District Judge

The pattern that had been employed followed definitely defined Communist strategy and tactics. These facts will be documented in a subsequent chapter, although some have already been recorded in this one.

As soon as Secretary Vance directed Fleming to fly dual flags at all schools, the Governor issued orders for flagstaffs to be erected as quickly as possible. The reopening of the schools was delayed until Wednesday, January 15, in order to allow the completion of the construction of the staffs and to insure the resumption of the Canal Zone bus service which would release teaching mothers from their household chores during the day as their maids and cooks would be able to report for work.

On the eve of the reopening of the schools, Fleming called a meeting of the civic council officers and read the flag riot act to them as follows:

As Governor of the Canal Zone, I believe that it is appropriate at this time for me to give to residents of the Canal Zone certain background information concerning the flying of the U. S. and Panamanian flags in the Zone.

The question of flying flags in the Canal Zone has been discussed for many years between representatives of the United States and Panama. In September, 1960, President Eisenhower directed the then Governor of the Canal Zone to fly the two flags in Shaler Triangle. President Eisenhower indicated that he hoped this decision would demonstrate the continuing close bonds which then existed and still exist, between the peoples of the United States and Panama, and between their governments.

Subsequently, President Kennedy decided to extend further this gesture of friendship to the Republic of Panama, and acting under his directives, U. S. representatives discussed with Panamanian representatives various ways to carry out the spirit and intent of what was desired by both governments. With presidential approval, the governments agreed that the flag of the Republic of Panama will be flown together with the flag of the United States of America, on land in the Canal Zone where the flag of the United States of America is flown by civilian authorities. Private organizations and persons in the Zone are free to display flags at will over their places of residence or business.

As the Governor of the Canal Zone, it then became my responsibility to establish those locations where the two flags were to be flown jointly and to insure that in accordance with the joint communique, there were no official locations where only one flag is flown. Working with senior officials of the Canal Zone government, and in discussions with members of the community, we established a number of appropriate locations to fly the two flags. Details concerning these locations were given in a press release on December 30. Schools were not included in the list of locations for exterior display of flags, but the very unfortunate events of the past week have focused much attention on the question of flags at Canal Zone schools. As you know, it was necessary for Secretary of the Army Cyrus R. Vance to visit the Canal Zone as a representative of the President of the United States. During his visit, the following announcement was made:

"After consultation with Governor Fleming, Secretary Vance announced tonight that the Canal Zone government will continue to fly the United States flag outside public schools in the Canal Zone and that in accordance with the existing agreement between the Republic of Panama and the United States, the Panamanian flag will be flown alongside the U. S. flag at these locations."

Accordingly, when Canal Zone schools reopen, dual flags will fly at public schools as indicated in Secretary Vance's statement.

It should not be necessary for me to dwell at length on the responsibilities of U. S. citizens to abide by the official commitments of their government. I would, however, like to emphasize that we have a particular responsibility here in the Canal Zone where our actions are subject to direct view by the citizens of other countries.

I therefore request the cooperation of all Americans at this time in honoring our country's commitments and in showing our good faith by our own actions. As far as the United States is concerned, the recent events have not modified the commitment which we entered in good faith, and we intend to live up to it scrupulously. We must remember that ours is a "government of laws, not men."

And those laws will be enforced.

15. The Communist Role

I was scheduled to deliver an address at DePauw University at Greencastle, Indiana, at 10:00 A.M. on January 10, which found me in Indianapolis that morning. At 7:15 A.M., I telephoned President Chiari. Our conversation was in Spanish. I asked Chiari for details of what had occurred, and he replied that they were all in the newspapers, which, of course, they were not. So I lost no more time and asked what steps he had taken.

"I have suspended diplomatic relations with the United States," he said, "and they will not be resumed until all of our pending problems are resolved."

"Can you please tell me what specific problems you have in mind?"

"You know them better than I do," he snapped back in an irritated voice.

"Then the whole works?"

"Yes. Everything."

"May I call on you tomorrow in your office?"

"Certainly. I will expect you."

I knew what he meant by everything: a revision of the basic 1903 Treaty and the abolition of the perpetuity clause, among other things.

And, of course, he knew that I knew it and that was why my direct question so irritated him.

Efforts to talk to General O'Meara or to Governor Fleming proved futile, but I was finally connected with Major Egon Friedman of the Public Affairs Office of the United States Southern Command. He read to me the press release that appears in the preceding chapter.

My lecture at DePauw was to end Latin-American Week which was organized by the student senate. Ambassador Juan Ignacio Plate of Paraguay spoke the night before. I kept my commitment but I threw my prepared text into the wastebasket and confined the major portion of my lecture to an improvised exposition of the Panama Crisis. I emphasized particularly the fact that Chiari had employed the word "suspension" and not "broken" when he referred to his diplomatic move against the United States.

While I was delivering my lecture at Greencastle, President Johnson made an unprecedented move in our diplomacy with Latin America. He telephoned President Chiari, who agreed to receive a personal representative from Washington. President Johnson designated Assistant Secretary of State Thomas C. Mann, his expert on Latin America, for this delicate assignment. It was to be the first test for both of them under the fire of a Latin-American crisis since Mann was wisely picked for the post before Christmas.

As Mann was boarding a jet transport at Andrews Air Force Base with Secretary of the Army Cyrus R. Vance (now Undersecretary of Defense), Ralph Dungan of the White House, Assistant Secretary of State for Public Affairs Robert Manning, and Ambassador Edwin M. Martin, who had been Mann's predecessor, Foreign Minister Solis was cabling Secretary of State Dean Rusk the formal notification that Panama was breaking relations with the United States. The distortion of the facts, as previously recorded herein, will be clearly discerned in this text of Solis's cable:

MR. SECRETARY OF STATE:

In the name of the government and people of Panama, I present to Your Excellency a formal protest for the unmerciful acts of aggression carried out by the armed forces of the United States of America stationed in the Canal Zone against the territorial integrity of the Republic and its undefended civil population during last night and this morning.

The unjustifiable aggression to which I have referred, without parallel in the history of relations between our two countries, have brought to us Panamanians, up to now, a tragic toll of 17 deaths and more than 200 injured. In addition, the buildings and property situated in certain sectors of the city of Panama adjacent to the Canal Zone have suffered damage of major consequence as a result of the controllable acts of aggression by the North American forces.

The inhuman actions—such as that of the police of the Canal Zone, and later the North American armed forces which attacked a group of young students of both sexes which totaled no more than 50, who attempted to display in a calm manner the national flag in that strip of Panamanian territory—are lacking in any justification.

This incomparable incident has revived chapters of the past which we believed would never again occur in American lands.

The acts of violence which motivate this note cannot be ignored nor tolerated by Panama. My government, conscious of its responsibility, will make use of all measures at its disposal, of those of the American regional system and international organizations, with an end to achieve a just idemnification for the dead and for the injured, and for the property destroyed.

My government seeks the application of sanctions for those responsible for such damages and the guarantee that in the future neither the armed forces stationed in the Canal Zone nor the civilian North American population residing in that section of national territory will ever again unloose similar actions of aggression against a weak and unarmed people anxious to come to the defense of its inalienable rights.

Finally, I desire to inform Your Excellency, that due to the events to which I have referred, the government of Panama considers its diplomatic relations with your illustrious government broken and as a result has issued instructions to its ambassador, Augusto G. Arango, for his immediate return to his country.

I take this opportunity to manifest to Your Excellency the guarantee of my highest consideration.

The jet transport landed at Howard Air Force Base at 6:00 P. M. There had been no acknowledgment of Solis's cable, much less any reply. The United States did not break relations. Panama had made two more diplomatic moves. Ambassador Arango had requested an emergency session of the Council of the Organization of American States, and Ambassador Aquilino Boyd had left Panama by plane for

New York to request an emergency session of the United Nations Security Council to accuse the United States of aggression against Panama.

The OAS decided that the most feasible measure and the quickest action could be obtained by dispatching an Inter-American Peace Committee, which is a permanent, available instrument to extinguish brush fires. To make that decision it is unnecessary for the ambassadors to consult their governments for instructions on how to vote. Ambassador Juan Batista de Lavalle, Chairman of the Council, appointed that committee early in the evening, as Boyd was flying to New York from Miami for the Security Council session.

Mann and his party were driven to Quarry Heights where they were given a comprehensive briefing on the situation. Then he was driven to the palace with Secretary Vance. They conferred for an hour and a half with Chiari, who speaks fluent English. Also present was Foreign Minister Solis, who, too, speaks fluent English.

When Mann and Vance were sitting in Chiari's office, the death toll of the flag war had already reached 20 and there were nearly 400 wounded. Chiari had denounced the three treaties with the United States, those of 1903, 1936, and 1955, and his ambassadors were accusing our country of "unjustified aggression" before the OAS and the U. N. A Pandora's box had been opened up, and Chiari's precipitate moves against the United States presaged not unexpected further tension and trouble. Mann issued this brief statement after his conference with Chiari:

> President Johnson has already said how deeply we regret the tragic events of the last hours which have cost the lives of Panamanians and Americans alike. The President has also said that the path for us all can be that of peace and understanding, not that of violence. We are here today to do everything we can to move along that path. We should not allow violence to deter reasonable men in both countries from continuing their efforts to resolve their differences or to obscure the long history of cooperation between the people of Panama and the United States.

The Panama presidential press office issued this terse statement, one that contained overtones for domestic consumption and underscored that Chiari had given no ground:

President Chiari was precise and energetic in presenting Panama's position. The United States envoys declared that they would convey to President Johnson all that had been said by President Chiari.

That afternoon President Johnson ordered the American Embassy in Panama City to burn all classified material and official codes preparatory to evacuation of all its staff and personnel. The order was promptly carried out.

Boyd made an impassioned denunciation of the United States in his speech before the U. N. Security Council the same night, accusing the United States of aggression and mass murder. He demanded the nationalization or the internationalization of the Canal, for which, I am certain, he had no instructions, but was acting on his own volition. Ambassador Adlai E. Stevenson denied Panama's charges and pointed out that the Organization of American States had already met at 4:00 P. M. and had named an Inter-American Peace Committee to fly to Panama to end the bloodshed. On a motion by Brazil, the Security Council decided not to become involved in the Panama Crisis, at least not yet, but to let the OAS try to resolve it.

Ambassador Lavalle appointed the Inter-American Peace Committee. The Chairman was Ambassador Enrique Tejera Paris of Venezuela. Members included two former Foreign Ministers, Ambassador Manuel Trucco of Chile and Ambassador José Antonio Bonilla Atiles of the Dominican Republic. The other two members were Ambassador Alfredo Vasquez Carrizosa of Colombia and Ambassador Rodolfo A. Weidmann of Argentina. Accompanying them was Ambassador Augusto Guillermo Arango of Panama and Ambassador Hector Obes Polleri of Uruguay. The latter was Uruguay's resident Ambassador in Panama. He had been on special duty as Uruguay's representative on the Special Investigating Committee that flew to Venezuela to probe President Romulo Betancourt's charges against the direct and indirect subversion of Fidel Castro's Communist Cuba.

Castro had accomplished two objectives. He had contributed to the production of an immediate cold war victory in Latin America that Khrushchev had been demanding, and he had delayed action by the OAS on Venezuela's charges against him. For another member of the peace committee was Ambassador Weidmann of Argentina, the Chairman of the Special Investigating Committee in the Venezuela case. The Weidmann committee would be unable to complete its report for at least another month.

The Inter-American Peace Committee had no other terms of reference than to end the flag war as quickly as possible. The Panamanians mistakenly expected the committee to indict the United States as the aggressor, and more so because Betancourt's government had announced from Caracas that it was supporting Panama in the dispute. With Tejera Paris as Chairman of the committee, Panama had an automatic and certain friend in court, for he had received cabled instructions from his foreign office to support Panama. That would normally disqualify a judge and/or a juror, but the committee which he headed was acting as neither. It succeeded in warding off the pressure by Panamanian public opinion to enter into a finding on the aggression charge, which had not yet formally been invoked before the OAS under the Rio Treaty. It did attempt, though, to become involved in the matter of treaty negotiations. On the night of January 9, Deputy Thelma King, the avowed friend and admirer of Fidel Castro, grabbed the microphone of Radio Tribuna in Panama City, of which she is part owner, and incited the mobs to fight the Americans. Tape recordings of her broadcasts are a matter of record, and she admitted her role in a tape-recorded interview with me in her office in the Legislative Palace.

But even before she went on the air, the Communists were in action along Fourth of July Avenue. There were both men and women. The women carried a unique party affiliation and activist identification as they incited the mobs to burn, destroy, and pillage. Their identification was a zebra-skin handbag, and they assumed stations on Fourth of July Avenue in the vicinity of the *Edificio Panamericano*, shouting, cajoling, and ordering.

We have noted how the Panamanian officials, as well as many citizens of that country, deny vehemently that the Communists played any role in the initial riots. We believe that they are sincere in their insistence in that regard, but their sincerity is based on a lack of understanding and knowledge of Communist tactical operations. For example, it is very doubtful that emotionally angered extreme Nationalists, and/or chauvinists, would normally employ the tactics that burned the Pan American World Airways offices, no matter how disturbed they might have been by the developments and by the distorted and false reports which they heard, nor would they assume the roles of snipers.

Two automobiles were pushed onto the sidewalk at Fourth of July Avenue and through the glass show windows, which, of course, were shattered. Once inside of what were the attractively decorated sales offices, the rioters removed the caps from the gas tanks, fired a shot into each of the tanks, and the building went up in flames. A total of seven bodies was ultimately removed from that building. They were apparently those of would-be looters who were caught inside by the flames that engulfed every floor of a building located on the site where the Chagres Club once stood. The property was owned by Panamanians and not by Pan American World Airways.

Molotov cocktails were used, by the admission of the Panamanian newspaper, *La Hora*, to set fire to other buildings. Although American firms occupied those buildings, almost every one was leased from Panamanians.

The *Guardia Nacional*, which, if it had been alerted by Chiari to preserve order on the boundary and to prevent riots, could have controlled the situation, was held in reserve. The report circulated that Chiari feared the riots were part of a plan to overthrow him, and he dared not commit his only armed force. Moreover, having been the target of scurrilous smear attacks by the Communists in past years because the *Guardia Nacional* had ruthlessly suppressed Communist lawlessness, Colonel Bolivar Vallarino, the Commander, had for some time insisted on receiving written orders before committing his efficiently trained shock troops to repress such political violence. Those orders were not issued until the night of January 11.

It has already been recorded that the Panama Students' Federation is Communist-dominated. The students from the National Institute spearheaded the flag parade into the Zone. The University Students' Union was to take over the main activist roles on the boundary, led by Victor Avila, Secretary General, Adolfo Ahumada, former President, and Cesar ("Tuto") Arosemena, Secretary—all Cuban trained. I saw Arosemena lead a flag march on the boundary on the afternoon of January 11, as he and other comrades began to mobilize 2,000 students and adults for another demonstration of violence against the troops. Before the afternoon was over the Communists had lowered the Stars and

Stripes from one of the flagstaffs at Shaler Triangle, sawed off the tall pole, and carried it away.

They had already changed the name of Fourth of July Avenue to that of *Avenida de los Martires* (Avenue of the Martyrs), which they painted on the retaining wall that separated Shaler Road from Fourth of July Avenue. They also painted another sign beside it, which read: *"Abajo el Gobierno"* (down with the government), but were quick to erase it when Chiari announced his hard line against the United States.

Nicolas D'Anello, the Corregidor, or town magistrate, of San Francisco de la Caleta, a suburb of Panama City near the Panama Golf Club, with gun in hand, personally led the attack against Americans in his jurisdiction. This included the burning and damaging of their automobiles and the sacking of their apartments and homes. Many of the 3,000 married American soldiers and their families who were evacuated lived in that area. D'Anello, a Communist, was arrested by the *Guardia Nacional* and jailed pending trial. He was dismissed from his appointive post.

The *Guardia Nacional* escorted the American troops and their families, who were innocently caught in the middle of the riots, to safety to the Curundu Gate at the Panama City side of the boundary. Panamanian neighbors and friends helped in this unprecedented rescue operation. Many Panamanians saved the automobiles of some of these families by removing the license plates that identified them as connected with the Zone, and either leaving them without a plate and driving the cars to the Curundu Gate for delivery to the owners, or substituting their personal plates on the cars in a shuttle service.

This did not prevent one American youth who was born in Panama from becoming an innocent victim of the fury on the boundary. He was Robert ("Bobby") Sander, son of Harold W. and Frances Sander of Madison, Wisconsin. Bobby's father was a former President of the American Society of Panama. They have lived there for thirty-three years. Bobby, twenty-one, had been to a movie with his fiancée and was driving her to her home in the Zone when he was caught in the middle of the rioting on Fourth of July Avenue. Despite the fact that his automobile had a Panama license tag on it, the car was attacked by a mob, which tried to halt it and assault the passengers. The mob smashed the rear windshield with iron bars and rocks, and dented the sides of the car. They hurled rocks through the front windshield. Bobby's fiancée hid herself from view as best she could. One large rock flew through the front windshield right into Bobby's left eye. Bleeding painfully and profusely, he stepped on the accelerator and forced the mob to break while he managed to turn into the Canal Zone and stop near the old Ancon Post Office. With his financée he left the car and raced as quickly as he could up Ancon Hill to Gorgas Hospital.

Bobby was operated on on Friday and lost his left eye. When I saw him with his father Harold afterward, he was in excellent spirits. He had taken the misfortune very well. I felt a personal distress in his misfortune because I have been close friends of the Sander family for years. Also, Bobby had been the battery mate and pal of my son Victor on a Little League baseball team in the Canal Zone for several years. Both attended St. Mary's Parochial School in Balboa, and Bobby was an excellent southpaw pitcher and a good hitter, while Vic was his catcher.

The riots and arson continued. Even the KLM offices on Fourth of July Avenue were sacked; thus, the assault was not only against American companies. KLM happened to be located in a building adjacent to the Braniff International Airways offices and the Royal Dutch Airlines was included in the terrorist plan. The building is owned by a Panamanian, and KLM rented the space.

Thelma King is forty-two years old. She has four children, three born out of wedlock and one recently adopted. She is a resident of Colón, where she says she was arrested during World War II as a Nazi-Fascist sympathizer. She blames the late American Ambassador Avra Warren for the accusation. She didn't spend a week in jail. She was, as has already been mentioned, suspected of having been the finger girl in the assassination of President José Antonio Remon. She denies that she is a Communist, although she admitted in response to my insistent questioning that she has had long-standing ties with the Party. She confessed that were it not for the fact that she enjoyed parliamentary immunity in her capacity as a deputy of the National Assembly she would have been in jail for her role in the flag war. She harangued the people in her broadcasts over Radio Tribuna. She marched to the presidential palace with a mob that demanded Chiari give them weapons with which to fight the American troops. She called out the mob to march on the *Guardia Nacional* headquarters to demand they be given arms. Here is an extract from my tape-recorded interview with her:

Q.: Did you call out the troops and the people in Panama City?

A.: I called on the *Guardia Nacional* to leave its barracks and defend the Panamanian people. When I did it, I was complying with my duty as a deputy of the National Assembly. It was the obligation of the Panamanians to go out and fight because the constitution said so.

Q.: I understand that you went to the palace to ask for arms for the people. Is that true?

A.: I told the President of the Republic—and I said so over the air—that if he did not want to use the *Guardia Nacional* please to give the people arms so that they would not be massacred with empty hands.

Q.: What did he answer?

A.: The President told me that if the *Guardia Nacional* went into the streets the massacre would have been greater, which I do not believe.

Q.: Then the President did not wish to order the *Guardia* to act?

A.: The President of the Republic considered at the moment—and I believe that he still considers it—that the *Guardia Nacional* is not equipped to oppose the American troops. I believe the Commander of the Guard thinks the same. I asked myself then, why do we have it? To defend ourselves against whom?

Q.: Aren't they here to defend the borders and the country?

A.: To do that a police force is enough.

Q.: Then you would revert it to a police force?

A.: I would devote all my efforts to that. I have been fighting for that a long time. I never have understood why the Americans want such a strong force as our guard here. I am absolutely sure that we can defend ourselves with our own means, as we now have proved. That error, that mistake that communism is coming here, is false.

Q.: You deny you are a Communist, yet you are accused of being one because you are an admirer of Fidel Castro and you have visited Cuba three times and also Moscow. How do you reconcile that?

A.: I have visited Cuba much more than three times under Castro and Moscow only once. Now I admire Castro even more.

At 2:20 A.M. of January 10, Thelma King was again at the Radio Tribuna microphone.

People of Panama, we have always believed that in the difficult moments of the country there should be a unity of destiny, of ideals and of struggles. That is why we, on request by the groups which were present in the Fifth of May Plaza facing the bullets of the North American troops, went to the Presidency of the Republic to tell Roberto F. Chiari, our political adversary, but President of the Republic of Panama, that in this moment of pain and crisis for the republic, he could count on the small but sincere support which we could give the national government.

President Chiari said that in spite of his superhuman efforts to hold talks with the diplomatic representatives of the United States in the Republic of Panama, it was impossible, according to the U. S. officials, because they could not leave the U. S. Embassy since it was surrounded by Panamanian citizens. The President, by means of telephone calls, obtained the promise that troops would withdraw 150 meters and that fire against the inert mass of Panamanian people would come to a halt. The President told us solemnly that Panama will not resume relations with the United States until our situation in the Canal Zone is decided in a definite and permanent manner.

Aquilino Boyd departed tonight for the United States on a special mission of the Panamanian government to present to the OAS the complaints of the smallest nation, which has been attacked in a cowardly manner by the most powerful nation of the world. We have always asked from this tribune and through our column in the papers: Where is the free world about which the North Americans brag? Today they have demonstrated what the free world is, that their democracy is one which takes aim at and assassinates the defenseless people.

Panamanian people cannot continue to be massacred. Panama has no arms with which to face the blondes of the Canal Zone. But the Panamanian people wrote today the most beautiful page in our history, because they showed the North Americans that before the force of the bullets, the force of reason will triumph. And tomorrow, or the day after, only one flag will fly in the Canal Zone. It will be the Panamanian flag!

Earlier, at 10:00 P.M., Minister of Education Manuel Solis Palma, one of the *Frente Patriotico de la Juventud* leaders of 1946-47, broadcast this message over Radio Mia:

I address the Panamanian people and the students who have shown their patriotism with great sorrow. But I am sorry that they are acting in a way which will not take us anywhere. The President will take measures, and he will act with patriotism. I call on the students to stop this, for we are heading toward some sacrifice. I do feel proud of being a student leader, for they have shown patriotism for our country. I ask you to act wisely.

His appeal, of course, found little response. Fifteen minutes before Thelma King had made the above address, Ruben Reyna Pupo, President of the National Directorate of Union Coordination, read a communiqué over Cadena Universal in Panama City. Reyna was a naturalized Panamanian of Cuban birth. He had been an insurance salesman and in a business promotion enterprise. The Panama Chamber of Commerce had to evict him from his office in the building for nonpayment of rent. He suddenly appeared in the limelight in the top union post in the country, after having no known previous record of labor activity. His defenders vouch for him, asserting that he is a devout Roman Catholic who has the support of Bishop Mark McGrath. The text of his communiqué follows:

COMRADES: The National Directorate for Union Coordination, considering the cowardly attack of the U. S. Army on our defenseless people is an armed invasion of our national territory, calls on each of its members to become a soldier of our country. We ask the President to order the opening of recruiting offices and to put arms in the hands of the people so that they may recover our lost sovereignty. In the same way we demand that the matter be denounced before the International Courts of Justice on the grounds that all treaties between us and the aggressor have been disregarded.

For fifteen years or more Carlos Francisco Chang Marin had been the chief organizer of the Communist party activities in the central provinces, with headquarters in his home town of Santiago, capital of the province of Veraguas. He had been trained in Moscow and Peking in the early 1950's. He was one of eleven Panamanians who attended the Conference of eighty-one Communist and Labor parties in Moscow in 1960. He had risen in the Party ranks and continued to rise to become chief of all agitation and propaganda operations in those central provinces. On the night of January 9, 1964, the fine red hand of Chang

Marin was active in prodding a town meeting to declare war on the United States. It was claimed that more than 1,000 signatures had been affixed to the resolution, the text of which follows:

The people of Santiago, in an open town meeting [*cabildo abierto* in Spanish] declare:

WHEREAS, The United States Army stationed in the Panamanian territory of the Canal Zone is cowardly massacring Panamanian people for the sole reason that they love their country and steadfastly maintain their sovereignty; but Panama is, and always will be, sovereign in all its territory in spite of the savagery, economic power, and the great brute force of the United States Army,

Resolve, 1. That the people of Santiago declare war on the United States government.

2. To protest the vile aggression of which they have been victim.

3. To declare a sitdown strike tomorrow, 10th of January.

4. To back the government in the stand it has taken of severing diplomatic relations with the United States government.

5. To demand that said relations not be renewed until the 1903 Treaty is totally abolished, particularly the clause that grants the use of the Panamanian territory of the Canal Zone in perpetuity.

6. To demand from the Panamanian government the immediate cessation of the use of the national highways by vehicles and units of the North American Army.

The above resolution was dated in Santiago, January 9, 1964.

By 3:00 A.M., President Chiari decided to halt the independent radio broadcasts because of their incendiary overtones and ordered his press secretariat to establish the national network under control of the presidential palace. While this action curtailed the harangues of people like Thelma King and her associate, Homero Velasquez, it did not serve to contribute toward any reduction of the hysteria that swept the country. Instead, it furthered its development by broadcasting all the messages of support that poured into the presidential palace from the entire country and from abroad, in which "the Yankee aggressor" was constantly condemned. The wave of patriotic, nationalistic hysteria that was being whipped up was all too reminiscent of the brainwashing that had been administered to the people of Cuba against the United States. Chiari and the highest officials of his government were too busy with their duties to be able to listen long to the official broadcasts. Anyway, they were in full agreement with the nature of the messages that were received, and appreciated them because they bolstered what had been denounced as a weak government, assuring it of virtually unanimous support. The agitators appeared on the streets with sound trucks on January 10 to continue the incitement.

Chiari decreed official mourning and ordered a state funeral for the victims of the flag war. Panama flags were flown at half-staff officially until after the state funeral that was held on January 12.

Yet, on the morning of January 10, some significant handbills were distributed in the cities of Panama and Colón. There were two in particular. One was by the Panamanian Committee for the Defense of the Cuban Revolution, whose officers include David Turner and his brother Jorge Enrique Turner. The other was by a new front organization which called itself *Izquierdista Socialista Istmena* (Isthmian Socialist Leftist). The latter's handbill linked what had happened in the early morning hours of January 10 in Panama with the anniversary of the assassination of Julio Antonio Mella, a Cuban Communist in Mexico in the late 1920's.

"The Socialist blood of Cuba is the same that has been shed by the anti-Imperialist blood of Panama," the handbill said.

Both groups claimed credit for the flag war on the boundary. The text of the handbill of the Panamanian Committee for the Defense of the Cuban Revolution, read:

> The Panamanian Committee for the Defense of the Cuban Revolution declares that it was present in the heroic protests of the Panamanian students against the troops of Yankee imperialism in the Canal Zone. It addresses itself to the Panamanian people through this means in order to make known that the generous blood spilled by the students and worker youth will not have been spilled in vain.
>
> Panama will be very soon like Cuba, a Marxist-Leninist state, and will have leaders of the stature of the comrade Fidel Castro, great captain of the Second Latin American Independence.
>
> Then the Canal Zone will be Panamanian, as in effect it is, and there will be no mass assassination of students and men and women of our people. Very soon the supreme revolutionary movement will arrive. Everything is ripe for the reconquest of our fatherland.

Panama will be a Socialist country that will count, as Cuba now counts, with the atomic, economic, and moral support of the Fatherland of the Proletariat, which is the U.S.S.R.

Panamanians: Let us not allow the government to yield in the national demands and in the protests of the country against the dilatory maneuvers of Yankee imperialism. Let us follow the example of Cuba: to every Yankee demand, a Panamanian demand. To every Yankee outrage, a Panamanian protest. To every Yankee assassination, a Panamanian act of vengeance. Let us confiscate the Yankee properties in the entire national territory. Out with all the Zonians and other gringo Imperialists from Panamanian national territory.

This Committee for the Defense of the Cuban Revolution, which led and seconded the students from the Eagle's Nest [this is the nickname that was given to the National Institute—*Nido de Aguilas* in Spanish— after the students first confronted the United States troops on the Zone boundary in 1959], toward the heroic anti-Imperialist battle, reports to-day to all the Panamanians that Socialist Cuba is on our side, corresponding to our cause as we correspond to theirs. Castro will send us more arms and more experienced leaders so that we can make revolutionarily viable the demands of our government. For that it is indispensable that President Chiari break relations with the United States and reestablish them with Cuba. Also it is necessary that our government denounce the treaties of 1903, 1936, etc.

With the support of Socialist Cuba we will have support from the Socialist world.

Let us be faithful to the mandate of our martyrs. Let us make ourselves worthy of their memory as fighters for the territorial integrity of the fatherland, expelling all the Yankee assassins from Panama.

The mimeographed handbill carries the date of January 10, 1964. When I showed it to Lieutenant Colonel Julio E. Cordovez, an officer on the staff of Colonel Vallarino, he remarked: "In addition to that one there were many more that were distributed."

The same afternoon, Foreign Minister Solis sent his long cable to Secretary of State Dean Rusk in which he advised that Panama was breaking relations with the United States. There were rallies throughout the Communist bloc announcing support of Panama.

New "front" organizations began to sprout up to campaign along the lines of the demands already recorded here. When the government noted that the Communists had the upper hand, especially in the newly organized Committee for the Recovery of National Sovereignty, it called on anti-Communist friends to try to pack the auditorium of the *Sindicato de Periodistas*, where this group was going to meet so they could outvote and outtalk them. The Communist infiltration in Panama was much greater than the government officials would care to admit or would even want to believe, even though their numbers were infinitesimally small.

On the morning of January 10, a motorcade of more than fifty vehicles, each with a large Panama flag, began its two-hundred-mile trip toward Panama City. When they learned the bridge across the Canal was closed, most turned back. Violence had erupted in Colón the previous night, and three soldiers were killed by sniper fire, one of them a Puerto Rican, Luis Cruz Jiménez. Panamanians tried to convince me that he was killed by American soldiers because he had refused to shoot at any natives. I checked their version and found it to be inaccurate. Cruz Jiménez had been issued no ammunition. He was killed by a .22-caliber bullet. The army does not use that caliber. The story, of course, was an obvious plant and an invention designed to develop more sympathy and solidarity among Latin Americans as well as further to smear the United States.

When Foreign Minister Solis held his news conference at the presidential palace on the night of January 13, and before he was able to make his opening statement, Escolastico Calvo, Editor of *La Hora* and President of the *Sindicato de Periodistas* (Newspapermen's Association) complained that the Panama Embassy in Rio de Janeiro had refused to issue a visa to Vadim Poliakovsky, *Pravda* correspondent in Brazil, who had cabled an appeal for help to his organization. Solis announced that he would issue orders for the visa to be given to the *Pravda* man the next day. When Poliakovsky arrived in Panama a few days later, Calvo became his escort. Two weeks later, Solis turned down another request by the *Sindicato de Periodistas*, this time for visas for two correspondents from Communist China's New China News Agency.

The Socialist party of Panama issued a communiqué on January 16, signed by its Chairman of the Central Committee, Carlos Ivan Zuñiga, another veteran of the *Frente Patriotico de la Juventud* organization of 1947-48. The text, as follows, contains most revealing paragraphs, as will be noted:

The Socialist party of Panama, which took its position on the firing line repelling aggression and defending our sovereignty, denounces to public opinion the turn which the government has given to the announced policy in moments of crisis, and appeals to the Panama people to block the way to any betrayal of national dignity.

The present government promised the country to break diplomatic relations with the United States of North America, and not having broken them in accordance with the best international practice, announced the resumption of these relations before the funeral of our martyrs was over.

The present government said that it would denounce the Treaty of 1903 and the subsequent agreements signed with the United States of America. And now it officially announces that it has not denounced these instruments and does not intend to do so for the present.

The present government committed itself to the country to denounce aggression before the O.A.S., and the fact is that such a denunciation has not been made formally.

As for the accusation presented to the Security Council, the spectacularly poor and deficient manner in which it was managed, omitting the gravity of the armed oppression of which the Panamanian people were the victim, has attracted much attention.

The present government has devoted itself to the persecution of the popular elements who carried out the heroic action of the 9th and 10th of January and is keeping in arrest members of the Socialist party, who distinguished themselves in defense of national sovereignty. Among them were several persons who were wounded.

The Socialist party of Panama is ready to support the fulfillment of the policy originally announced by the President of the Republic, but it is also ready to combat, as it does through this communiqué, any deviation from that policy.

The above communiqué was signed by Zuñiga for the Central Committee of the Socialist party. Zuñiga had been acting as attorney for the Communist-dominated Banana Workers Union at the United Fruit Company operations at Puerto Armuelles, in the province of Chiriqui.

The United Fruit Company had evacuated 103 Americans to Costa Rica on January 11, because the previous night a mob tried to attack the residence of Royce A. Holcomb, General Manager of its Tropical Divisions, at Puerto Armuelles. The mob, naturally, was Communist-led. Only a skeleton force remained there, as a ship was due to load 65,000 stems of bananas on January 13. But it didn't load them. The workers were called out on strike, and the ship sailed empty to Golfito, Costa Rica. It was significant that Humberto E. Ricord, the Communist lawyer, had flown to Puerto Armuelles, to direct that agitation, and must have drafted, or at least instigated the drafting of, a resolution which the Municipal Council of the District of Baru, which includes Puerto Armuelles, adopted the same day. The 65,000 stems of bananas were a total loss, because there was no refrigeration shed in which to store them, nor could they be moved to one if it were available. The District of Baru resolution read:

> The Municipal Council of the District of Baru:
> WHEREAS, The civilian and military authorities in the Canal Zone are directly responsible for the massacre of numerous compatriots, wounding and murdering our brothers because of their peaceful protest against the disrespect and trampling upon our sovereignty;
> WHEREAS, The North American civilian and military authorities in the Canal Zone, present, with each passing day, a greater danger to Panamanians, and,
> WHEREAS, Before the tragedy mounts in scope, it is necessary once and for all to extirpate, at the cost of any sacrifice, the threat and jeopardy that any jurisdictional act taken by the United States constitutes; and
> WHEREAS, It is the duty of this council, as part of the nation, to cooperate with the national government in order to attain social well-being;
> *Resolves:*
> 1. To declare hereby the United States civilian and military authorities stationed in the Canal Zone *persona non grata.*
> 2. To request from the Executive Branch and the National Assembly the nationalization of the canal called the Panama Canal.
> 3. To request, as well, from the rest of the municipal councils of the country their support for any move destined toward the nationalization of the Panama Canal.
> 4. To send copies of this resolution to His Excellency, the President of the Republic, to the National Assembly, to the press, and the radio.
> Puerto Armuelles, 13th day of January, 1964.

Ricord, the same Communist lawyer who testified at the National Assembly hearings in 1947 to drive the United States from the defense bases in Panama, had more party work to accomplish in Chiriqui. Before he returned to Panama, the Province of Chiriqui's Chapter of the National Bar Association adopted this four-point resolution:

1. That the new treaty to be discussed by Panama and the United States include a clause declaring Panama's absolute sovereignty over the Canal Zone.

2. That the new treaty set a term of at least ten years for the duration of the treaty, and establish the ultimate nationalization of the Canal and its neutralization.

3. That the Canal Zone be demilitarized, and the annuity the United States pays Panama for the Canal be increased.

4. That the United States pay reparations to Panama for the damage caused by the United States Army.

That resolution was dated January 15, 1964. The Baru maneuver was a very slick one, a prelude to the convening of a National Conference of sixty-three municipal councils in Panama City for the week end of January 18-19.

Meanwhile, Victor Avila, Cuban-trained Secretary General of the University Students, called a general assembly of the students in the university auditorium for January 15. The teamwork and coordination of the Communist machinery proved to be well-oiled and working to perfection. There were five speakers at the general assembly, all Communists. Besides Avila, they included Cesar Carrasquilla, Humberto Harris, Honorio Quesada, and Eligio Salas. The *Guardia Nacional* was accused by the students of applying pressure on Chiari to give in to the United States. Those charges were untrue; Colonel Vallarino was strongly supporting Chiari's position. The students adopted a resolution that called for Chiari to demand:

1. Recognition of Panama's sovereignty throughout the national territory.
2. The elimination of the "in perpetuity" clause in the Canal treaty.
3. The demilitarization of the Canal Zone.
4. The neutralization of the canal.

Then the students began a march toward the presidential palace. I followed their route in a taxi and parked at strategic intersections that enabled me to ascertain their mood and their plans. The banners were typical Castro-Communist slogans against Yankee imperialism, including one which read: OUT WITH THE GRINGOS! The banners were carried by the students and were painted in giant letters. There were also shouts of: *"Arango paredon!"* (Arango to the Execution Wall!). The Communists were out to get Ambassador Arango. He was considered to be too pro-American. Others were also out to get him. From Fifth of May Plaza I made my way to Santa Ana Plaza, and as they marched by each one of them—I estimated about 1,500 and not more than 2,000—I would proceed to the next plaza before catching up with them at the palace. At Cathedral Plaza, where the old Hotel Central still stands, they turned toward the palace. There was definite Communist organization of the parade. It was orderly and effective. Also marching, in addition to the orators already mentioned, were Adolfo Ahumada, Cesar ("Tuto") Arosemena, Alberto Calvo, Rafael Merida, Ricardo Iglesias, Gonzalo Menendez Franco, Carlos Carrasquilla, Humberto Carrasquilla. There were many girls, and the faculties identified were those of law, engineering, humanities, and public administration. Humberto Bruggiati was not at the meeting or in the parade, for he was wounded in the fighting at the boundary.

Chiari talked to the students from the balcony, probably without being aware of the ideologic affiliations of all of their leaders, and Avila gave a report of the meeting over Union Radio immediately afterward.

"About 2,000 to 3,000 students left the university," Avila said, "and by the time we reached the presidency there were more than 5,000 persons accompanying us who backed our proposals." That was untrue. The crowd did not grow in size. "At the entrance," Avila continued, "President Chiari received the students and declared he firmly held to his position of negotiating for a new treaty. We informed him that as long as the government stood for a fair treaty which embodied the nation's interests, the students and the people would support that position, but that as soon as any attempt was made to negotiate a treaty which disavowed the popular claims, we students would lead the popular protest to block a new mockery of the people. We also declared that it was impossible to conduct patriotic negotiations with the United States while our ambassadors were people like Ambassador Arango, who betrayed the country's interests to sell out to the North Americans.

"In that respect we asked the President that there should be included in the Panamanian committee of negotiators intellectuals, professionals, laborers, students—in one word, representatives of the people who with their blood have made new negotiations possible. We students will insist on that position, for it is high time the people had a hand in directing the affairs of the nation. The students also have decided to take to the streets again on Friday and have called for a huge mass meeting of patriotic forces in Santa Ana Plaza to reaffirm the manifesto approved by the university students."

On Friday night, January 17, the meeting was held in Santa Ana Plaza but it proved to be a fizzle of Communist claques and Communist oratory. Present at this meeting was Floyd Britton, another Cuban-trained Communist, who was very active in the May, 1958, fight against the *Guardia Nacional* and the constitutional government of President Ernesto de la Guardia, Jr. Britton, with some of his fellow Party members, had also been active on the boundary during the flag war of the previous week. Orators at this meeting included Ceferino Torres, representing the Union of High School Students; Bolivar Cerrud, of the National Institute; Sergio Otelo, of the Labor Federation; Ruben Reyna Pupo, of the National Labor Committee; Eligio Salas, President of the Union of University Students; and Victor Avila, for the Panama Federation of Students. The anti-Yankee placards were present again, as was the Communist claque that occupied the ringside below the bandstand. This time there were two placards which attacked the two principal American wire services. The Associated Press was labeled anti-Panama. The United Press International was labeled *Union Periodistas Infames* (Union of Infamous Journalists). There was a large banner which read: NOT ONE STEP BACKWARD—NEW TREATY.

Attending the meeting, standing against a wall of a building next to the French Bazaar, was Dr. Jorge Illueca, Editor of *El Panamá America* and former Ambassador to the United Nations. Youths were selling both Panama flags and banners commemorative of the flag war. Those banners were a revelation because they were either preplanned or designed and printed with extraordinary speed. I bought both a flag and a banner, paying twenty cents for the flag and seventy-five cents for the banner. The banner was printed on taffeta in four colors on a white background. The colors were red, white, blue, and black. At its widest part the banner was 8½ inches deep and it was triangular in shape, coming to a point. Also at the widest part, the banner showed a man holding the staff of a tattered Panama flag, kneeling in a pool of blood, looking toward one of the locks of the Canal, which were opening to allow a warship to pass through. A ring and spots of blood encircled the locks and the warship. At the top left-hand corner above the flag staff was printed (in Spanish) January (in red) 9-10-11-12 (in black) to signify the days of the flag war. To the right of the lock were the words *Sovereignty* (in blue) or *Death* (in black). At the point was a triangular Panama flag. The entire banner was bordered in mourning black. Being thoroughly acquainted with the printing and publishing facilities available in Panama, it was very obvious to me that there was expert planning, either in advance of, or during the flag war to produce the artwork and to have a printer provide a finished product in those colors.

Chiari was visiting his daughter and grandchildren when the students were on their way to the palace after their rally. Only about 1,000 students marched to the palace; the rest of the crowd in the plaza went home. They had had enough of agitation and demonstrations for the week. Among the 1,000 were the hard-core Party members. Avila kept the students entertained with some ad-libbing over a microphone by the palace gates. He was flanked by Floyd Britton and Eligio Salas, as well as other Party members, male and female. Chiari arrived on foot after alighting from his limousine half a block away, and the students cleared an opening for him to pass through the gates. He climbed the flight of stairs that leads from the inner patio where the white herons strut during the day (the palace is called *El Palacio de las Garzas*, the Palace of the Herons) but the birds were already in their newly-built cages in the front left-hand corner of that patio. He appeared on the balcony to the cheers of the students.

Chiari reassured them that he would not budge one iota from his determined stand not to resume relations with the United States until and unless he got an airtight commitment that a new treaty will be negotiated. Chiari gave the students a boxer's clasped hand salute and shouted: *"Viva Panamá!"* The students replied *"Viva"* and dispersed.

The next day, the sixty-three municipal councils met at the Panama City Municipal Council Hall. Resolutions were introduced identical to those which had been adopted the previous Monday in Chiriqui. They were approved. All the communities of the country had now demanded what the municipal district of Baru was the first to ask for. The wheels of pressure, once they started to roll, spun very fast.

The Committee for the Recovery and Defense of the National Sovereignty had already adopted similar resolutions, including one calling for the printing of Panama flags with the inscription, NATIONALIZATION OF THE CANAL, to be displayed in all stores and on all buses. It also called for the negotiations for a new treaty to be conducted in Panama and not in Washington.

Alvaro Menendez Franco, the Cuban-trained former President of the Municipal Council of Panama, was active in meetings of both of the above groups. Also active in the defense committee were Jorge Turner, and the Souza brothers, Cleto Manuel and Ruben Dario, all of whom had participated as activists in the flag war. The Souza brothers were veteran Communists, having played a role in the 1947 defense base riots and subsequent flag riots, while Cleto Manuel Souza was one of the eleven Panamanians who were delegates to the Conference of eighty-one Communist and Labor parties in Moscow in 1960.

Menendez Franco made the closing speech of the conference of the municipalities. He demanded repudiation of the Canal treaties and asked: "What better way is there to do so than the bloodshed of the ninth of January?" He also urged Chiari to seek support of the Socialist (Communist) and neutralist nations, and, still ostensibly speaking in the name of the sixty-three municipalities, he demanded the removal of United States troops from the Zone and that the presidential elections scheduled for May 10 be postponed "until something positive is done regarding negotiations." The latter demand was an admission of fear that Dr. Arnulfo Arias, the only candidate who had publicly attacked the Communists, might win.

Radio Tribuna had evinced a similar fear on January 17 when it took Arias's *Panameñista* party to task for a statement it had made.

"The *Panameñista* leaders," the noon commentary said, "are echoing the coarse accusations of the North American papers which claim that the deeds of the 9th of January were inspired, directed, and organized by elements of international communism. With this anti-patriotic attitude, the *Panameñista* party is providing ammunition and arguments for the enemies of the cause of Panama in the entire world. The *Panameñista* party is the only political party that has echoed these infamies and in a reckless manner it is repeating them in search of applause from foreigners. All Panama knows, and we do not have to convince anyone, that the movement of the 9th of January was a rebellious movement against injustices imposed upon us by the United States. For this reason, to accept the insinuation and proclaim that agents of international communism actively participated in the patriotic movement of the Panamanian people is to convert oneself into an ally of that sector of the North American press which, to be able to justify the massacre of Panama, uses the pretext of international communism."

Chiari, too, emphatically denied similar charges when he was interviewed over his own television station by Mario Velasquez, a brother of the part-owner of Radio Tribuna. Here is the question and answer as I taped the broadcast:

Q.: Mr. President, the international North American press and news agencies are trying to assert that the civil movements which took place in Panama during those days were directed, encouraged, and promoted by Castro-Communist agents. What can you say to these assertions, Mr. President?

A.: I would give them a most hearty denial. It is not possible to conceive that a nation could have acted in the way it did in face of the aggression and the insult to our flag because forces of absolutely foreign ideologies, which will never have force here, moved them to act in that way. That is the most brazen lie I have heard and seen in a press which is misconstruing the truth and which, knowing that it is acting that way, still wishes to maintain that position. We know that there is social unrest in this country, and movements and leaders of ideologies alien and foreign to democracy will try to take advantage of it. But the just and great causes, as is the Panamanian cause, cannot always be said to be directed by those elements. Impossible. If they would have given a greater role of participation and a greater sense of responsibility to the Panamanians in the operation, protection, and maintenance, the situation would not be different. These statements of Senator Morse in connection with colonialism, with those privileges existing in the Canal Zone, as I said before, regrettably have come precisely forty years too late.

Foreign Minister Solis was quoted in *Pravda* in Moscow on January 22 as ridiculing "the slanderous fabrications of American propaganda about the events in Panama having been organized by Communists."

"Panamanian Communists," Solis was quoted by Tass as having told the *Pravda* correspondent in Panama, "like members of other political parties in Panama, were with the people in the streets of the city during the January events. But this certainly does not mean that they direct, or, as the American press writes 'manipulate' the developments in Panama. This contention is a base lie, and it is being spread to distort the true meaning of the broad patriotic movement of protest against injustice, a movement that is entirely Panamanian, without any prompting from the outside."

Fidel Castro returned from his mission to Moscow on January 23, and the next night he confidently offered to send Panama "all the economic aid" it needed without any strings attached. He changed the line that had been used by his agents on January 10 by adding that Panama did not even have to resume diplomatic relations with him to get that aid. There was no comment from official quarters in Panama on this offer from a man who needed all the aid he could get for his own mismanaged economy.

The flag war of January 9, 10, 11, and 12 gave the Communists their greatest victory on the banks of the Panama Canal since they were successful in driving us from the defense bases sixteen years earlier. The 1964 triumph was even more resounding, for overnight they had accomplished the following:

1. Forced a protracted confrontation of American troops with armed Panamanian civilians.

2. Succeeded in provoking Panama to break diplomatic relations with the United States.

3. Produced a public denunciation by Panama of all existing treaties with the United States, although the government later withdrew the denunciation as an illegal act.

4. Promoted a demand for a new treaty that will give Panama sovereignty in the Canal Zone.

5. Produced a combined death toll of 21 Panamanians and 4 Americans, and nearly 400 wounded, mostly Panamanians.

6. Created civilian martyrs and a military martyr for the Nationalist cause and produced an exchange of gunfire between American and Panamanian troops for the first time in history.

7. Blackened the image of the United States throughout the world.

8. Projected Panama's charges of aggression against the United

States to the world through a special meeting of the United Nations Security Council.

9. Inflicted millions of dollars worth of damage on American businesses and property through fires and looting.

10. Depressed the economy of Panama by enforced unemployment at the business establishments destroyed and by frightening both native capital and private investments.

11. Stimulated "Hate America" agitation in all quarters, causing ransacking of homes of American citizens and destroying their automobiles and other personal property.

12. Forced the evacuation of all Americans from the United Fruit Company tropical operations headquarters at Puerto Armuelles, in Chiriqui, the northwesternmost province. (They later returned.)

13. Advanced in their campaign toward the nationalization and/or internationalization of the Panama Canal.

14. Flouted law and order and defied constituted authority, demonstrating that political leaders can opportunistically fail to take measures to repel rioting and looting and attacks against the Canal Zone.

15. Forced the evacuation of 3,000 Americans (mostly troops and their families) from Panama City, thus emptying many apartment houses owned by Panamanians.

16. Wrecked the winter tourist trade by their "Hate America" campaign, causing cancellations of cruise ships.

In order better to appreciate the manner in which the Communists were able to spark the flag war, leaders of the Vanguardia de Acción Institutora (Vanguard of Institute Action or VAI), a Communist-oriented group at the Instituto Nacional took over the demonstration at Balboa High School. Among the leaders were identified Napoleon de Bernard, Guillermo Roberto Mas Calzadilla, Rinsky Sucre, Francisco Diaz, Sergio Quiros, Otto Gonzalez, Eligio Carranzo, and Toribio Manuel Espino.

Having set the stage for the flag war, those students were displaced in the leadership at night on the boundary by the leaders of the Vanguardia de Accional Nacional (Vanguard of National Action or VAN). This is a Marxist-oriented political group that advocates a Castro-type revolution which cooperates closely with the illegal Partido de Pueblo (Communist Party) that was outlawed by the National Assembly in

1953. Alvaro Menendez-Franco, thirty-one, who formerly presided over the Panama City Council, is the leader of VAN.

The above are only two of the more than twenty Communist-front organizations that were active in the flag war. The Partido del Pueblo (PDP) has about 600 hard core members, of whom about twenty have been trained in Russia, Red China, and Cuba. In addition there are an estimated 5,000 sympathizers, useful idiots, and fellow-travelers who respond to the beck and call of those twenty.

Hugo Alejandro Victor, fifty, who still heads PDP, was rewarded with a trip to the Soviet Union a month after the flag war, as was Cesar Carrasquilla, twenty-three, an activist in the Communist Youth Movement.

That VAN played a major role in the flag war at the zone boundary there is no doubt. Among the VAN leaders were Jorge Enrique Turner, forty-two, and his brother David Francisco Turner, forty, both lawyers who joined the Communist Party in Mexico. David Turner was in Moscow in July, 1962, for the World Peace Congress, and Jorge Turner was in Mexico in March, 1961, for the Conference of Solidarity with Cuba. From there Turner flew to Havana on a visit and a year later returned there for guerrilla training. In February, 1963, thoroughly indoctrinated and trained he returned to Panama.

Another activist on the boundary was, of course, Floyd Britton, twenty-seven, who graduated from the National Institute in 1958. After participating in the guerrilla uprising in Cerro Tute in the Province of Veraguas in April, 1959, Britton obtained refuge in the Guatemalan embassy. Given a safe conduct, he was flown to Guatemala where, oddly enough, he got a job with the police force and underwent police training there. Returning several months later to Panama, he was a leader in the flag riots of November 3 and November 28, 1959. Having been accepted as a member of the PDP in 1960, he was assigned to agitate in the University of Panama, where he enrolled as a student. Late in 1961 he began guerrilla and sabotage training in Cuba, finishing his course in March, 1962. He has been active in the university ever since.

Two other VAN leaders are Andres Galvan, thirty-three, and Jack White Bailey, thirty-eight, both of whom have undergone guerrilla and sabotage training in Cuba. The Panama Secret Police (FBI equivalent) records show that in addition to the above other Panamanians trained in subversion in Cuba include: Rolando Ernesto Carrasquilla, Miguel Antonio Porcell Peña, Alfredo Almengor Borbua, Leonidas Alveo, Garcilaso de la Rosa Aguila, Victor Manuel Lombardo Rodriguez, Anastasio Rodriguez Batista, Felix Gonzalez Santiago, Inocencio Garibaldi Gondola, Gilberto A. Velasquez, and Francisco Pitti Castillo, all of whom were in operation at the boundary in Ancon and Cristobal.

The Communist-front organizations that played the major roles included:

Partido Socialista (Socialist Party), heavily infiltrated with PDP members. Professor Carlos Ivan Zuñiga, leader of the radical wing, controls the party.

Federación de Estudiantes de Panama (Panama Students' Federation or FEP), which claims to dominate all students except those who attend Roman Catholic schools. Victor Avila, twenty-six, is the Secretary General and heads the seventeen-member Comite Ejecutivo Federal (Federal Executive Committee). It is worthy of note that in 1947, during the Defense Bases Fiasco, Hugo Alejandro Victor held the same post as Avila.

Union de Estudiantes Universitarios (Union of University Students), which claims official representation of the University of Panama students. Rolando Armuelles, president of the UEU, is a member of the PDP.

Frente de Reforma Universitaria (University Reform Front or FRU). This group, which is the most powerful student political party at the university, sets the policy, through its Communist leaders, for the FEP and the UEU as well as for many secondary schools. It practically controls the seven faculties at the university.

Comite Pro Rescate de la Soberania Nacional (Committee for the Recovery of National Sovereignty or CRSN), which group of ultranationalists, leaders of the Socialist Party and known Communists handpicked Professor Ricardo Arias Calderon, a Christian Democrat and scion of a socially prominent family whose deceased father was a graduate of West Point, to preside over the meetings as their front man.

Agrupacion Columna Literaria (Literary Column Group or ACL), composed largely of University of Panama students, Marxist-oriented writers, and poets.

Circulo Cultural Universitario (University Cultural Circle or CCU), a group which indoctrinates university students in Marxism-Leninism.

Accion Reformista (Reformist Action or AR), an affiliate of FRU in the Faculty of Humanites at the university, which contains the largest number of frustrated leftists and Communist agitators.

Circulo Cultural Femenino (Feminine Cultural Circle or CCF), which is the women's section of CCU.

Frente de Unidad Revolucionaria (United Revolutionary Front or FUR), an affiliate of the VAN.

Impulso (Impulse), an affiliate of FRU at the Faculty of Engineering of the University of Panama.

Impulso Reformista de Arquitectura (Reformist Impulse of the Faculty of Architecture or IRA), an affiliate of the FRU.

Grupo Jose Dolores Moscote (Jose Dolores Moscote Group or GJDM) named after the deceased Rector of the Instituto Nacional whose Communist leaders virtually dominate the Faculty of Law at the University of Panama.

Renovación Autentica Universitaria (Authentic University Renovation or RAU), affiliate of FRU at the School of Public Administration and Commerce at the University of Panama.

Also active in the riots and agitation was Alberto Calvo, twenty-five, former student at Tulane University, who turned Communist after he returned home from New Orleans where he had been involved in an accident case that caused his withdrawal from school.

16. The Treaty War

Immediately after World War II the strategists of the international Communist conspiracy devised a sinister maneuver in the United Nations which was designed further to inflame Panamanian passions against the United States. At that time they were already ablaze over our refusal to withdraw from the defense bases. The maneuver was a subtle one to try to expedite plans for the internationalization of the Panama Canal.

Alger Hiss, as Director of the Office of Political Affairs of the State Department, included, on August 19, 1946, the Panama Canal Zone in a list of nonautonomous territories of the United States in a report to the United Nations as was required by Article 73 of the UN Charter. The Panama Canal Zone was officially included in the report of Secretary General Trygve Lie in Document A/74 of October 21, 1946, that he submitted to the Political Committee of the United Nations General Assembly.

Hiss had failed to coordinate his action with Spruille Braden, then Assistant Secretary of State for Latin-American Affairs. Braden first learned of it, much to his concern, when he read the news in the Washington newspapers. Hiss's maneuver, though, was speedily supported by John Zilliacus, an extreme left-winger who held a Labour party seat in the House of Commons. Zilliacus took advantage of the news of the United States report on the Panama Canal Zone to demand that Great Britain deliver control and operation of the Suez Canal and Gibraltar to the United Nations and that the United States should do likewise with the Panama Canal.

Braden protested Hiss's uncoordinated action to Acting Secretary of State Dean Acheson without avail. Panama, though, had no intention of allowing Hiss's contribution to Moscow's plans to go unchallenged. Foreign Minister Ricardo J. Alfaro addressed the Political Committee of the United Nations on November 14, 1946.

"The inclusion of Panama among the territories and possessions of the United States and among the territories about which a report would have to be submitted under the UN charter," Alfaro said, "is a manifest error that the Republic of Panama expects to be corrected through the appropriate means."

Alfaro, who became a Vice President of the International Court of Justice at the Hague (popularly known as the World Court), summed up in his speech the international status of the Panama Canal Zone and the rights of the United States therein with the following conclusions:

1. That the Republic of Panama is and never has ceased to be the sovereign of the strip of land known with the name of Canal Zone.

2. That the United States only has acquired by treaty "the use, occupation, and control" of the Canal Zone.

3. That said "use, occupation, and control" has been granted for the specific purposes of the construction, the maintenance, the operation, the sanitation, and the protection of the Canal.

4. That the Canal Zone is not a possession nor a part of the political domain of the United States.

5. That the Panama Canal Zone is a territory without native, permanent, and homogeneous population.

6. That the inhabitants of the Canal Zone do not have interests linked with the land and do not have nor can they have political aspirations for independence or self-government.

7. That the Canal Zone only can be administered as a strip of land exclusively destined for the purpose to maintain, to operate, and to protect the Canal.

Alfaro included in his exposition to the UN Political Committee a legalistic interpretation of the sovereignty question in the Canal Zone that deserves to be registered here. He claimed that Article III of the Hay-Bunau-Varilla Treaty "establishes in unequivocal terms that Panama retains its sovereignty over the Canal strip."

Amplifying the above in a review of Articles II and III, Alfaro added:

> In effect the articles referred to establish that the United States is granted "the rights, power, and authority that the United States would exercise *as if it were sovereign of the territory*." [The emphasis was supplied by Alfaro.] The phrase "as if" signifies, clearly and indubitably, that they *are not* [again Dr. Alfaro's emphasis] the sovereigns, and, therefore, that the United States acquired solely the power of administration and jurisdiction inasmuch as the supreme attribute of sovereignty belongs to the original sovereign, the Republic of Panama.
>
> This interpretation of the treaty is supported no less than by the juridical authority of William H. Taft, former President of the United States and later Chief Justice of the Supreme Court.

The full text of the above speech was used by Dr. Alfaro from 1948 on as a text when he occupied the Chair of International Public Law at the University of Panama and also when he lectured at the School of Diplomacy—which was established there later. It has been used as a primary text ever since at both the Faculty of Law and at the School of Diplomacy.

Spruille Braden was prepared for the Panama answer. The State Department notified Panama that the United States would no longer include the Canal Zone in the "occupied territories" report under Article 73 of the UN Charter. But the damage had already been done, and more fertilizer had been poured on the blossoming seeds of Nationalist-Communist agitation in Panama.

The Alfaro thesis has been Panama's unalterable and inflexible position regarding the Canal Zone. The United States recognized this in 1960 when Panama was notified that, as evidence that it held "titular sovereignty" over the Canal Zone, the Panama flag would be flown jointly with the United States flag at a selected site within the Zone.

As soon as the flag war ended with the agreement reached before the

Inter-American Peace Committee in the El Panama-Hilton Hotel, the treaty war began. Even before that, Chiari had already found himself in a juridical jam because he had publicly denounced the treaties of 1903, 1936, and 1955, without consulting his National Council of Foreign Relations, which he had not summoned into session. Foreign Minister Solis called a news conference for the night of January 13 to try to clarify some points of confusion that arose during a news conference held earlier in the day at the palace by Fabian Velarde, presidential press secretary, and previous statements made by the latter allegedly in behalf of Chiari. Solis's hour-long news conference contained these observations:

1. Panama has not denounced the Canal treaties. To denounce a treaty is not like tearing a piece of paper. The Canal treaties are still in force. Panama wants them to be revised so that it can obtain a new treaty. If the United States does not want that, then Panama will have to resort to the international courts. That would be done as soon as all peaceful means are exhausted through the Organization of American States and the United Nations Organization.

2. Although diplomatic relations have been broken with the United States, consular relations, which are of a commercial nature, will continue their normal course.

3. When diplomatic relations are broken, the diplomatic officers lose their status and must leave the country. If they remain in the country they do so only as private citizens.

4. The decision to fly the flags at the schools in the Canal Zone does not give Panama sufficient satisfaction, but it did contribute toward the lessening of tension caused by the events of the last week. But Panama would not abandon its claims for indemnification to which it has right because it had been the object of aggression.

5. In the entire world there is no situation of agitation in which the Communists are not involved or do not infiltrate. But this does not signify that the Communists generated or dominated the Panama events.

6. The current position of Panama is that there will be no renewal of diplomatic relations until the United States gives the assurance that it will initiate immediate conversations for a new treaty. In the past, the United States has taken the position that, each time situations similar to the present crisis arose, it would not negotiate under pressure.

As soon as Solis finished, Fernando Eleta, local cigarette manufacturer and television and radio network tycoon, invited foreign newsmen to meet a group of representative men of industry, business, and banking who were convened in the Executives' Club in the new Hotel Continental. Eleta, a member of the National Council on Foreign Relations, kindly invited me to accompany him in his automobile. This group was having its organizational meeting and had not yet given itself a name. While we were there the name was chosen: Committee of National Reaffirmation. Joaquin José Vallarino, Jr., son of the former Ambassador to Washington, presided protem. I taped the proceedings on my recorder.

"We bring to your attention," he said, "the complete backing that this group is giving the nation with respect to negotiating an entirely new treaty with the government of the United States of America. We consider that this is a just and long-held aspiration of the Republic of Panama; that it is misleading to infer that it is a Communist movement. We are here to show you that this is not a Communist movement and we want to give you the full impression of our understanding and our full support of the government attitude at this moment and we are here to answer any questions that you have and we have also requested Dr. Octavio Fabrega, on my right, to express to you the point of view of this meeting."

Octavio Fabrega, the former Foreign Minister who negotiated the 1942 defense bases agreement, was at the time Chairman of the National Council on Foreign Affairs, an advisory body to President Chiari. He had also been a member of the negotiating team for the 1955 treaty, accompanied Chiari to Washington on his official visit to President Kennedy in 1962, and was one of Panama's two high-level members of the joint commission that carried on discussions for more than a year with Ambassador Joseph S. Farland and Governor Robert J. Fleming, Jr., as agreed upon between Kennedy and Chiari. The other Panama member was Foreign Minister Galileo Solis. Fabrega was a graduate of Harvard Law School, and in fluent English he presented what he clarified were his personal views which "I don't think that you are going to find that the views that I express are different from the views of the government because we work together in this. And at the same time I don't want them to be branded as official because they are not." His explanation of Panama's grievances and aspirations, as I recorded them, follows:

Now this group is composed essentially of members of Industry, Banks, individuals of, you might say, the leading ones in carrying the wheels of commercial and industrial activity in Panama. It is not a political group. It's an objective group. Of course a group of Panamanians. But this is a group that is not seeking any gain for any particular section of the community or representing any special interest. This is a group that is active solely as Panamanians and you will find, and that is one of the main characteristics of the whole present situation, that you will find the leading men in the capitalist group, you might say and industry, banking; you'll find them identified with the liberal economic class. You'll find them identified with the students, identified with the lower class of people, on this general question of the Canal Zone problem.

Now after the preliminary explanation let me state to you that we really have two problems. One that you might call the immediate problem and the other the mediate problem, but as I shall develop them later on you will find them so closely connected that the solution of one problem wouldn't mean much if you don't solve the other problem, too. The immediate problem of course is that we have had an explosive situation here in Panama. It is apparently calm now, it's calmer in a few degrees, but we cannot say that tension has been totally reduced. The situation continues to be, although with less passion, continues basically and fundamentally to be at least potentially explosive for the future. And, of course, the immediate situation as you all know was caused by this matter of the raising of the flag in the Canal Zone which, in turn, led to the destruction, the violation of the flag, by civilians and that, in turn, led to demonstrations that went into the Canal Zone and that led to fighting on the part of the Canal Zone police, and then fighting on both sides and the arrival of army forces to the Canal Zone border, and a number of twenty dead and over four hundred injured. And all the international repercussions that you are all aware of.

Now, of course, the immediate problem as I say is what has been Panama's reaction to that situation. Panama has considered that it has been the victim of an aggression; that the aggression was not provoked by Panama, but provoked by the attitude of the Canal Zone with regards to the flag initially. Civilians in the Canal Zone, and then by the initial firing from the Zone police, and Panama considers that the U.S. has been the aggressor and Panama has charged the U.S. as aggressors before the Security Council of the United Nations, and before the O.A.S. . . . Panama also broke relations with the U.S., and President Chiari has said that the relations will continue broken unless and until a new treaty is negotiated that will replace the original 1903 treaty and all other treaties relating to the Panama Canal. Of course, as you know, President Johnson called President Chiari and an envoy of President Johnson, Mr. Mann, arrived and has had interviews with President Chiari. But there is a little anomaly there in having had interviews with President Johnson's envoy and President Chiari when there were no relations between the two countries, relations having been broken.

Of course, in these days of excitement you find that things are not always 100 per cent consistent. Then you also know that a committee from the O.A.S. has arrived here, has interviewed the Panama government, has interviewed the Canal Zone authorities; has viewed the scenes here and, of course, we don't know what the report of the committee is or will be. So as to the immediate problem the U.S. stands charged now by Panama as aggressors before international bodies. Of course, that carried with it the demand by Panama that the aggressor be condemned as an aggressor, that the reparations be paid to Panama; that guarantees be given to Panama that there will be no further aggressions at the point. And to that President Chiari has added: not before the international bodies, but we have added as a public statement that he doesn't consider that the situation will be permentally solved unless and until we have a new treaty that will settle the relations of the two countries vis-à-vis the Panama Canal on a totally new basis. So as to that I understand the Security Council of the United Nations has held in abeyance all action until after the O.A.S. takes the proper decision, or makes the proper recommendations, or takes the action that it thinks proper. And that has not yet happened; those things take some time.

Now whether that attitude or that reaction on the part of the authorities of Panama has produced a lessoning in the tension among the Panamanian people for the time being, I think it has to a great extent. I think that that action, that attitude of the government has proved to the people, the masses here, a complete identification on the part of the government with the attitude of public opinion and the masses of Panamanian people, and it is that identity of purpose which has contributed to relative lessening of the tension, because, otherwise, I'm sure that those same masses of public opinion would still be in a violent state. In other words, it is the hope on the part of the masses of people that something will be done, that some basic redress will be obtained, that has produced a lessening of the tension. But then the other thing that I called the mediate, the not so immediate problem, but which I say is intertwined with the immediate explosion is the question of the revision of the treaty situation between the two countries, because it is the feeling of Panamanians, of all adults of all classes, that you gained very little by solving the immediate explosion and even paying reparations to Panama, or giving immediate redress. You solve very little by that unless we do not get to the root of the problem and don't solve the basic problem of the revision of the treaty relations.

Now let me speak about that. Our treaty relations with the United States basically are governed by a treaty that was signed in 1903 under which the Canal was built. There have been modifications of parts of that treaty in certain aspects, but Panama feels that the basic ills of that treaty of 1903 are still there. They are still the source of friction and resentment on the part of Panamanians and that resentment that grows with every generation until now at the present time it has reached the point where no longer that matter is being handled by means of discussion or persuasion, but now the masses of public opinion wants action; and they have so demonstrated. Now it is the feeling of Panama that the United States should have long ago replaced that treaty and changed it by a new treaty with an entirely new complex, new concept. We have always felt that the treaty of 1903 was negotiated under very unfortunate conditions; in fact it wasn't even negotiated; in fifteen days it was signed.

I have a very distinguished friend from Colombia here next to me, and it was in the days of the independence of Panama from Colombia, and Panama knew that if it didn't sign the treaty the Colombian government would put down the revolution in Panama so it was signed on the very unfortunate pressure of the part of Panama, practically no negotiation, and we feel, I'm sorry to have to say this, because there are some Americans here I think, but we feel that the United States took advantage of the position of Panama at that time and obtained the treaty which was purely a unilateral thing, all the rights, all the concessions for the United States and very little for Panama, and very little consideration for Panama's dignity and sovereignty as a nation. Now, of course, I don't think we should feel too sinful about that because those were the times, those were the days of the "big stick policy." I mean the standards of relations and the morals of international relations have changed considerably since that time.

Now the feeling in Panama has been that it is clear by treaty and it has been even admitted by the United States that Panama never did make a sale, a transfer of the Canal Zone to the U.S. The U.S. is not territory which was transferred to the U.S., as was Louisiana or Florida, but it is a piece, a portion of Panamanian territory on which Panama, that is the U.S., was given a concession to operate, maintain, and defend the Canal. It was given jurisdiction of rights for that purpose. Ample rights, but for that purpose. That has been the position of Panama. And from the early days of the signing of that treaty the highest authorities in the U.S., including President Teddy Roosevelt, said to the Panamanians, "Don't worry, we don't want to set up an independent colony in Panama, we just want to build the Canal and operate the Canal." But the facts have been otherwise. The U.S. has established a colony in the Canal Zone just as much a colony as French Algeria or any one of that type, and Congress but eight or ten years later took legislative powers over the Canal Zone and has been legislating over the Canal Zone just as much as if it were U.S. territory; U.S. judges impart justice in the Canal Zone. English is the language of the Canal Zone so they have made that a colony within the territory of Panama with a civilian population governed by U.S. laws, having many privileges and exemptions and exonerations and no duty and things which have brought collision with economic interests of Panama, and the fact of having that civilian legislation, that civilian community there, has created a community with a mentality which is typically the mentality of the Colons. A mentality which is even something foreign to the U.S. citizens who come from the U.S. And, as you know, with the Vietnamese in the French situation they found that they were more French than the Frenchmen in the capital. So they have been more nationalistic, more U.S. nationalistic than the continental U.S. And they act and they think and they speak as though the Canal Zone was U.S. territory, as though every plea, no matter how small, that Panama makes for a small concession is as though Panama were trying to take something from their personal heritage, and it is that Vietnamese attitude that I speak of that has been increasing and increasing and finally, resulting in protest.

Then the U.S. agreed that the Panamanian flag should fly alongside the flag of the U.S. in the Canal Zone. Well now, the first thing that hurt Panama, as I say, is the creating of this civilian Zone there, then Panama feels that many other basic injustices are in the treaty of 1903. Panama feels that the sovereignty of Panama has not been properly respected in the Canal Zone. That if the U.S., if Panama, granted the concession to operate the Canal then in all other respects not related to the operation of the Canal, Panamanian sovereignty should have been visible, effective, tangible. We should have had Panamanian courts, Panamanian language, and the U.S. should have left that Zone be Panamanian territory for all other purposes not immediately connected with the operation of the Canal. Then Panama has also felt that there has been a great injustice done to Panama in the sense that Panama doesn't get from the Canal Zone the benefits that it should get and has been getting. Now to some individuals especially not familiar with the situation, you might have called them 100 per cent Americans, they would say well, why should Panama get more benefits?

Our position has been that what we call our geographic position, the fact that our land is the land that lends itself for the benefit of the Canal, that the geographical position is our main treasure, is our main natural resource, and that we should be the beneficiaries, the main beneficiaries, of that main natural resource that we have. That that is just a source of natural resource, as oil is to Venezuela or tin to Bolivia or any other natural resource, and, of course, you all know the United Nations last year adopted a resolution saying that the sovereign state has a right to the full benefit of its natural resources. Now then, we don't get that at all, we get an annuity which comes pretty close to $2 million a year for the U.S. operation of the Canal. Now we have private companies here with smaller concessions which pay to Panama more than that. I mean moneywise it's a pittance, you know. And somebody was telling me the other day that the Suez Canal gives to Egypt a net of something over $100 million a year. Now Panama, which is a poor country, with the full economic benefit of our geographical position we would have progressed more, we would have no need of asking now for loans and many other types of aid because that would have been our main resource. Now, on that, Panama has made efforts to get more benefits out of that, but as I say we have only been getting very mild concessions like increasing the rent from $500,000 to $1,900,000. Just a pittance, I mean to be colloquialwise.

Then, another basic point on which Panama feels that the whole treaty is unjust and unfair is in the so-called perpetuity clause. The treaty of 1903, which was exacted from Panama under pressure, provides this treaty in perpetuity. Now Panama feels that it is unfair and unjust and it is not compatible with the sovereignty and dignity of Panama to have a piece of its territory subject to foreign jurisdiction in perpetuity. If that, if there had been a transfer of territory, a sale of the land, O.K., all right. But that was not the case, and that being Panamanian territory it should not be encumbered in perpetuity in that sense. So Panama wants with whatever new treaty comes in to have four points:

1. To have a limit, time limit.

2. To have the sovereignty of Panama respected, defined in a clear and tangible way.

3. That Panama should get the main benefits, economic benefits from the Canal. And the fourth point, which I haven't mentioned yet, is that:

4. As a source of labor and employment, Panama should get the main benefits of the Panama Canal as a source of labor and employment. And not to have the situation which we have today in which 90 per cent of the highly-paid jobs are held by American and then Panamanians only hold 90 per cent of the low-paying salaries.

Those are the basic points, and Panama wants a new treaty to write history beginning from now, because we do not only think that the treaty was unjust and unfair but we also think that times have changed; that the relations between countries have changed; that the deals with the different countries do not respond today to an imperalistic concept, but rather to having honest and fair and good relations between the countries. We really want to have peace on a stable basis as times have changed and this is very important. This is very important, I cannot stress this too much: that we feel that history shows that the treaty was signed originally, or rather the Canal was built orginially by the U.S. as a military establishment, for strategic purposes, because it was necessary to the defense of the U.S., and today it has been said in the highest official sources in the U.S. that the Canal no longer has any military value, any strategic value, it is purely a commercial exploitation, and we Panamanians feel that if that is a commercial exploitation, it is our main richness. Our main natural resource, the commercial exploitation should mainly be in favor of Panama, and that for the U.S. to continue exploiting for itself this commercial situation, being such a rich country, and Panama being so poor, is a piece of colonialism, is a piece of colonialistic policy which is the very policy for which the U.S. criticized England and France in the case of the Suez and brought pressure on England and on France so that France would abandon that colonialistic policy. And that's what the newspapers are saying today, editorials as of yesterday say well why does the U.S. continue to hold this colonialistic territory when they told us in the Suez situation that the big powers should abandon that policy, and they have abandoned that policy?

So times have changed and Panama feels that there should be a new treaty, a new deal from that basis. To some people the attitude of Presi-

dent Chiari of having broken relations and saying the relations would not
be restored until a new treaty is negotiated, to some people that might
seem too drastic, but the state of public opinion here has been saturated
to such a point that unless there is a cessation of that situation we are
going to have more and more trouble and periodical bloodshed and violence as we have seen here. And so there is no sense in trying to do a
cover-up job and trying to solve just this tragic outrage of these days, but
we should solve the problem at the basis of it. Of course the situation has
been aggravated by what we consider to have been arbitrary and improper interpretations of the existing treaty. I would be speaking all night
here as I would be giving you examples of where Panama says: "Well,
you're not living up to the treaty as where the treaty says that Panamanian and American employees should be treated equally and without
discrimination." We have shown the facts and figures where there is discrimination so there have been all sorts of arbitrary interpretations.

The Inter-American Peace Committee was occupied in trying to
extinguish the boundary brush fire. It met with Mann and Martin, on
the one hand, and Foreign Minister Solis and Ambassador Arango,
on the other. Also sitting in on the Panama side was Eloy Benedetti,
the legal counsel of the foreign ministry. The committee obtained an
agreement to appoint a Joint Cooperation Committee composed of two
Panamanians, two Americans, and one Chilean. Ambassador Trucco
was to preside. The American members were Brigadier General
George L. Mabry, Jr., the J-3, or Operations Officer, of the United
States Southern Command, and Minister William Belton, a career diplomat and Political Advisor on General O'Meara's staff. The Panama
members were Eloy Benedetti and Lieutenant Colonel Julio E. Cordovez, a member of Colonel Vallarino's staff. The mission of the
Joint Cooperation Committee was to safeguard the security of the
boundary with Ambassador Trucco acting as the top peacemaker and
the channel of communication between representatives of two governments and two armed forces that had been deprived of direct diplomatic
relations.

The flag war had thus been successfully brought to an end, but
the solution produced a most uneasy truce in what was very soon to
erupt into a treaty war. Mann, Vance, Dungan, Manning, and others
of the Washington party flew back to the capital to report to President

Johnson. Mann left Martin behind as his personal representative to continue conversations with the peace committee with the rank of Special Ambassador. The talks were carried on in the El Panama-Hilton Hotel in both the Spanish and English languages, for Martin had not yet acquired a proficiency in Spanish. His interpreter was the capable Colonel Moura. Although the committee worked from a Spanish document, Martin insisted before the committee that he be allowed to work from an English document, and his request was granted in the presence, and with the acquiescence, of the Panamanians.

The emotions of the Panamanians were scorched, and their tempers exploded when the White House announced after Mann's two hours and twenty minutes with President Johnson that night that the American forces had "behaved admirably" in the Canal Zone. The Panamanians had an exclusively one-vision view of the flag war. The right, according to them, was entirely on their side.

"Mr. Mann emphasized," the White House statement said in part, "that United States forces behaved admirably under extreme provocation by mobs and snipers attacking the Canal Zone. The President continues to believe that the first essential is the maintenance of order. For this reason, the United States welcomes the establishment of the Joint Cooperation Committee through the Inter-American Peace Commission."

The Panamanians were also told by the White House that the U. S. had no intention of retreating from the insistence of retaining full power over the Canal.

Nevertheless, the OAS group in Panama accepted Panama's plea to try to get the United States to agree to negotiate a new Canal treaty. Ambassador Tejera Paris of Venezuela, who had instructions from his government to support Panama, had earlier in the day appealed to Panamanian reporters to be patient with his commission, "because everything is going to work out right for you." The local press had been attacking the commission, and Tejera Paris and his associates gave the Panamanians a private briefing, which was a rather unusual procedure for what was supposed to be an impartial commission from the Organization of American States.

The peacemakers met all afternoon with Martin and Solis, the latter assisted by Arango and Benedetti. There had to be frequent high-level consultations by both sides as the talks became bogged down in a battle of semantics. The high-level consultations usually took at least an hour, for Martin had to be escorted by a Panamanian officer from the hotel to the Curundu Gate in an official limousine of the Panama government, and there transfer to an army vehicle for the trip to Quarry Heights to telephone Washington. The drive was usually twenty minutes each way, while Solis had to spend another twenty minutes to drive to the palace to confer with Chiari. The United States refused steadfastly to give any prior commitment to Panama that we would negotiate a new treaty. The Panamanians insisted on the employment of the word "negotiations" in the official Spanish text that was being drafted because, it was argued, the translation of the word "discussions" which the United States insisted on had an entirely different connotation in Spanish than the word desired by Panama. After a near-midnight consultation with Washington, Martin returned to the hotel and accepted "negotiations" in the Spanish text, but made it clear for the record that it was so done because of the difficulty to find an acceptable translation of "discussions," and added that the United States considered the English text as its official position.

At 1:40 A.M. of January 15, the commission opened its doors to make the announcement of an agreement. Ambassador Tejera Paris, the Chairman, stood and read a document that was titled *Communiqué Number 3*. He prefaced his reading of the communiqué with the remarks that he felt certain that everyone would agree that the document would show that the blood that had been shed had not been in vain. Tejera Paris first read the Spanish text and followed immediately and read the English text as both were approved by the parties. I recorded the texts of both communiqués as he read them, and the tape reposes in my journalistic library.

For the benefit of the political scientists, lawyers, diplomats, students, and the general public, whose interest in Inter-American Affairs includes familiarity with the Spanish language, I record the Spanish text herewith first:

Comunicado No. 3

La Comisión Interamericana de Paz, con base en su Estatuto que la faculta para ofrecer sus buenos oficios a los Estados que los requieran, ha

*proseguido las conversaciones con los Representantes de la Republica de
Panamá y los Estados Unidos y ve con satisfacción el restablecimiento
de la paz que es condición indispensable para el entendimiento y negocia-
ción entre las partes.*

*En consecuencia la Comisión Interamericana de Paz ha invitado a las
partes que restablezcan sus relaciones diplomáticas a la mayor brevedad.
Las partes han acordado aceptar esta invitación y han convenido en que,
treinta días después de haber sido restablecidas sus relaciones diplomáticas, iniciarán negociaciones formales, por medio de representantes
que tendrán poderes suficientes para negociar sin limitaciones todas las
cuestiones de cualquier naturaleza existentes que afectan las relaciones
entre Panamá y los Estados Unidos.*

Panamá, 15 de enero de 1964.

The text in English as read by Tejera Paris follows:

Communique Number 3

The Inter-American Peace Commission, based on its statutes which
authorize it to offer its good offices to the States requesting them, has
arrived on conversations with Representatives of the Republic of Panama
and the United States and notes with satisfaction the reestablishment of
the peace which is an indispensable condition for understanding and
negotiation between the parties.

As a consequence, the Inter-American Peace Committee has invited
the parties to reestablish their diplomatic relations as quickly as possible.
The parties have agreed to accept this invitation and, as a consequence,
thereof, have agreed to begin formal discussions which will be initiated
thirty (30) days after diplomatic relations are reestablished by means
of representatives who will have sufficient powers to discuss without limitations all existing matters of any nature which may affect the relations
between the United States and Panama.

Panama, January 15, 1964

It was immediately apparent to me that all that had emerged
from the meeting was a most precarious truce in the treaty war; that
two different interpretations would be given to the communiqués that
were read; one by Panama, which would insist that the Spanish text
was the official working document and therefore the United States had
committed itself to "negotiate" a new treaty, and the opposite by the
United States that we had only agreed to "discuss" and made no com-

mitment to "negotiate," but left the door open for a possible revision of the existing treaties.

As Ambassador Martin left the conference room with Colonel Moura, his interpreter, I asked him please to clarify the issue for me. This is how our conversation went:

Q.: Ambassador Martin, could you give me an interpretation? The Spanish text refers to negotiation in the body and we come up with discussion.

A.: There is a difference between discussion and negotiation in Spanish and we have used negotiation in the Spanish text and discussion in the English.

Q.: Yes, I know. But, we're not going to negotiate a new treaty.

A.: The discussion will be without limitation.

Q.: Without limitations. That means we might negotiate a new treaty?

A.: We might.

Q.: We might?

A.: We might, we have to agree.

Q.: O.K., thank you. That's what I wanted to get straight. I thought you told me earlier tonight that we wouldn't do that.

A.: No I didn't say that. I said that we would review the treaty. We have no advance commitment.

Q.: No commitment in here?

A.: We will review the treaties, we will review everything and then . . .

Q.: There's no commitment in here?

A.: No commitment.

Q.: But we may at a later date?

A.: Yes, if in negotiations we see that we will need to reach agreement.

Q.: In other words, as it is right now, we do not have any commitment to Panama to negotiate a new treaty?

A.: No. We have a commitment to negotiate about the problems. That's all we have right now.

That was the United States position, but Panama held a different view. In the meantime, the OAS commission clamped down a censorship on statements by both sides regarding the flag war and future intentions. Each side was asked to guard its official tongue in order to dampen the explosive potential of what was now to become the treaty war. This was because Foreign Minister Solis protested to the committee that Panama objected to President Johnson's praise of the manner in which the Army had acted in the Canal Zone. Panama had wanted President Johnson to admit the United States was the aggressor. Martin agreed to the censorship on official statements.

But on the morning of January 15 Chiari was the first one to break that agreement. Ramon Periera telephoned him from Radia Mia and asked Chiari to explain the OAS communiqué.

"Within thirty days," Chiari said, "negotiations will be intiated, without limitations of any sort, in regard to all relations governing Panama and the United States—relations which for many years were motives for the events which we saw just three or four days ago. I do not claim for myself any glory in all these happenings. I do not claim for myself any merit. Everything which has happened, everything which has been achieved, and everything which will be achieved in the future when the Panamanian plenipotentiaries go to Washington to discuss the relations between Panama and the United States, should be done as a tribute rendered to the heroes who fell on the ninth of January."

> *Q.*: Mr. President, tell me, will diplomatic relations be resumed with the American government in order to discuss this matter?
> *Chiari*: Because there is the formal promise, agreed on with them, that conversations start rapidly and quickly. I repeat again: negotiations without limitations of any sort regarding relations between Panama and the United States.

Washington was quick to react to this, and an official statement was issued about the same time Chiari was making his second speech within five hours on the same subject, in which it was denied by Richard I. Phillips, State Department spokesman, that the United States had made a commitment to negotiate a new treaty.

"I promised the nation," Chiari said in his 12:45 P.M. broadcast, "that diplomatic relations would not be reestablished with the United States until that country consented to begin negotiations for the drafting of a new treaty, and this promise has been obtained through the mediation of the Inter-American Peace Commission.

"Panama will resume its diplomatic relations with the United States in line with this declaration by the Peace Commission with the determination that the negotiations which are to be initiated as a consequence of that declaration shall be held with the purpose of substituting for the existing treaties a new treaty which will eliminate for all time the causes which have given rise on more than one occasion to such dolorous events as those which have occured." Chiari concluded, "From this position I shall not retreat a single instant. I shall maintain with firmness and without vacillations my stand of defending the national cause. This decision by my government commits me to choose a group of fellow citizens of all sectors of public opinion so that, with deep patriotic sentiment, they may take the responsibility before the Panamanian nation for negotiating and signing a new treaty in which the rights which belong to Panama as a participant in the work of the Canal shall be clearly established."

That night the students marched on the presidential palace from the university and demanded that Chiari stand firm against the United States and not resume diplomatic relations. Chiari assured the students that he would not resume diplomatic relations unless and until he received assurances from Washington that it would negotiate a new treaty. Fabian Velarde, his press secretary, later released the following statement for Chiari:

"The government of Panama will not resume diplomatic relations with the United States while the government of the United States does not give to the Panamanian government assurances that negotiations will begin to reach an agreement on a new treaty to replace the existing ones."

Velarde assured me that Panama had not repudiated the Peace Commission agreement, but it was, implicitly, to be so. Ambassador Manuel Trucco of Chile, who had been left behind to act as OAS troubleshooter, was shocked when he learned of this action. The Nationalist-Communist alliance had chalked up another victory.

For the first time since the crisis erupted on January 9, Chiari called a meeting of his National Council of Foreign Relations to discuss the problem and to enlist their support for his hard line against the United States. He got their unanimous support.

The fact that the Panama flag was raised over the schools in the Canal Zone that morning to fly jointly with the American flag, and the additional fact that General O'Meara and Governor Fleming issued a joint proclamation in which they decreed a day of mourning for January 17 in the Canal Zone to pray for the victims of the riots of the previous week made no impact on the Panamanians. O'Meara returned control of the Zone to Fleming the morning of January 16.

The Communists, who had demanded the scalp of Ambassador Arango, scored still another victory. Arango resigned on January 17 as Ambassador to the United States and Ambassador to the Organization of American States. Arango became the political and diplomatic scapegoat as Chiari accepted his resignation and promptly appointed former Foreign Minister Miguel J. Moreno, Jr., one of the seven presidential candidates, as Ambassador to the OAS to keep a channel of communications open through that organization with the United States.

Trucco made a final effort on the morning of January 17 to bring the United States and Panama together on the treaty question. He met with Martin and Solis in the El Panama-Hilton with inconclusive results. American *chargé d'affaires* Wallace Stuart, immediately after luncheon, ordered all American Embassy staff and affiliated personnel and their families to move forthwith into the Canal Zone, in expectation of Panama's order to close the embassy to complete the diplomatic break. Seventy families gathered in the Balboa Theater and were processed quickly. James Shirley, Superintendent of the Housing Branch of the Canal Zone government, was in charge of the reception center. The theater canceled its scheduled movie for that night. As soon as Zonians or armed forces officers telephoned to advise they had room for a family, one was dispatched to those quarters.

There already had been 3,000 American refugees from Panama in the Zone, most of them families of service men, and there was a premium on quarters' availability. One-third of the service families elected to be evacuated back to the United States and were shipped out in an emergency airlift. All praised the help that they had received from the Panamanians who had escorted them to safety into the Zone when the flag war erupted and the mayhem was committed in Panama.

At about 4:15 P.M. of January 17, Arturo Morgan Morales, Chief of the United States Section of the Panama Foreign Ministry, called on Stuart at the embassy and formally ordered the embassy to be closed.

Stuart moved into the Zone, while Henry Taylor, of Seattle, Washington, the Political Officer of the embassy, who had also been accredited to Panama as a consul when he reported for duty there a year and a half earlier, remained and reassumed the duties of consul. Consular relations had not been severed. Panama also closed its embassy in Washington, but Moreno was to use it for his mission.

With the diplomatic break completed, the Communist students cheered the development at their rally that night. Then Chiari met successively for two days with his National Council on Foreign Relations to draw up a plan of action and instructions for Moreno. On January 21 Moreno flew to Washington to take his seat in the Council of the Organization of American States. The members of the Peace Commission, meanwhile, had been seeking a conference with President Johnson, and he finally received them with Secretary of State Rusk, Assistant Secretary Mann, and Ambassador Ellsworth Bunker present. On January 23, after meeting with the members of the Peace Commission, President Johnson issued an unequivocal statement in which he reiterated the position of the United States as follows:

> I want to take this opportunity to restate our position on Panama and the Canal Zone. No purpose is served by rehashing either recent or ancient events. There have been excesses and errors on the part of both Americans and Panamanians. Earlier this month actions of imprudent students from both countries played into the hands of agitators seeking to divide us. What followed was a needless and tragic loss of life on both sides.
>
> Our own forces were confronted with sniper fire and mob attack. Their role was one of resisting aggression and not committing it. At all times they remained inside the Canal Zone and they took only those defensive actions required to maintain law and order and to protect lives and property within the Canal itself. Our obligation to safeguard the Canal against riots and vandals and sabotage and other interference rests on the precepts of interntional law, the requirements of international commerce, and the needs of free world security.
>
> These obligations cannot be abandoned. But the security of the Panama Canal is not inconsistent with the interests of the Republic of Panama. Both of these objectives can and should be assured by the actions and the agreement of Panama and the United States. This government has long recognized that our operation of the Canal across Pan-

ama poses special problems for both countries. It is necessary, therefore, that our relations be given constant attention.

Over the past few years we have taken a number of actions to remove inequities and irritants. We recognize that there are things to be done and we are prepared to talk about the ways and means of doing them. But violence is never justified and is never a basis for talks. Consequently, the first item of business has been the restoration of public order. The Inter-American Peace Committee, which I met this morning, deserves the thanks of us all not only for helping to restore order, but also for its good offices. For the future, we have stated our willingness to engage without limitation or delay in a full and frank review and reconsideration of all issues between our two countries.

We have set no pre-conditions to the resumption of peaceful discussions. We are bound by no preconceptions of what they will produce. And we hope that Panama can take the same approach. In the meantime, we expect neither country to either foster or yield to any kind of pressure with respect to such discussions. We are prepared, thirty days after relations are restored, to sit in conference with Panamanian officials to seek concrete solutions to all problems dividing our countries. Each government will be free to raise any issue and to take any position. And our government will consider all practical solutions to practical problems that are offered in good faith.

Certainly, solutions can be found which are compatible with the dignity and the security of both countries as well as the needs of world commerce. And, certainly, Panama and the United States can remain, as they should remain, good friends and good neighbors.

After the White House meeting and Johnson's statement, the Inter-American Peace Committee renewed its task to attempt to mediate, this time with the treaty plea of Panama in mind. Moreno had his instructions: either an airtight commitment from the United States to negotiate a new treaty or to proceed with a request to convoke the Organ of Consultation of the OAS under the provisions of the Inter-American Treaty of Reciprocal Assistance, which is popularly known as the Rio Treaty. No progress was made, and Moreno asked for a special meeting of the Council of the OAS on January 31.

At that meeting the council heard Moreno make fourteen accusations against the United States in detailing the charges of aggression. With extreme care I analyzed the original Spanish text of Moreno's speech and found that it contained fourteen falsehoods and distortions. The manner in which he delivered his speech, the tone of his accusations, and the knowledge among the ambassadors that Moreno was one of the seven presidential candidates produced a wave of silence among the envoys when he finished that was more eloquent than the Chinese proverb that a picture tells more than 10,000 words.

Moreno based his case on the fact that the flag march into the Zone was so spontaneous that the students had to borrow the school flag from the rector of the National Institute. We have already seen in a previous chapter the eyewitness report of Guillermo Guevara Paz, the twelfth-grade student at the Institute, in which he reported that the march was planned ahead of time the previous afternoon. Other charges included:

2. "That Americans in the Zone insulted and tore the Panama flag." False. The Americans taunted the Panamanian students when they reached the flagpole at Balboa High School. No American ever touched the Panama flag.

3. "That the Panama students were forced to return to Panama City pursued by civilians and Zone police." False. In a previous chapter we have also seen the correct report of events.

4. "That the students who gathered at the Canal Zone boundary after they learned of the Balboa incident only tried to enter the Zone to raise their flag." False. Their advance guard carried flags as a cover but behind them were the trained Communists with Molotov cocktails, iron bars, and rocks.

5. "That the combined fire of police and civilians halted them." Distorted. There were no civilians who fired on any Panamanians.

6. "That new groups, after hearing the news over the radio, flocked unarmed to the Zone boundary to try to raise the Panama flag and were fired on by Zone police and civilians." Distorted. The same situation obtained here as in No. 3 and No. 4 above.

7. "That there was machine-gun fire and rifle fire constantly between Central Avenue and Kennedy Avenue." Distorted. If there was it must have been firing by the Panamanians because that area, up to Kennedy Avenue, is in Panama and is several thousand yards from the Zone boundary.

8. "That U.S. troops used automatic weapons to repel citizens of Colón who were peacefully trying to enter the Zone to raise the Panama

flag." False. Three soldiers and a civilian were killed by rifle fire by the allegedly "peaceful" Colón invaders before any fire was returned as we have seen by General O'Meara's report. No automatic weapons were issued to U.S. troops.

9. "That tanks were used by U.S. troops." False. An armored personnel carrier was moved into a reserve position at the Tivoli Guest House in Ancon; tanks were alerted and held in reserve deep back inside the Zone.

10. "That the students responded only with rocks to all firing by police and soldiers and had no weapons." Distorted. The police and soldiers were fired on from Panama City and Colón. There were Cuban-trained snipers in action and the *Guardia Nacional* arrested ten of them before the fighting ended January 12.

11. "That economic aggression was committed when the Thatcher Ferry Bridge across the Canal at Balboa was closed, thus cutting off all traffic with the interior, and when the Colón Corridor was blocked." False. Both actions were taken as security measures to prevent the transit of would-be saboteurs and armed agitators. They were only closed temporarily.

12. "That the blockade of the Colón Corridor cut off the only connecting route between Panama and Colón and prevented the dispatch of medical teams and plasma that were needed in the Atlantic side city." False. The railroad was operating from Ancon to Cristobal. There is also a landing field at Colón and had Panama desired to get medical teams or plasma to Colón it could have flown them there. Moreover, no request was made to the Zone for a safe conduct for such teams and supplies while the corridor was blockaded.

13. "That young students who entered the Zone were welcomed with bullets and death." False. No student was killed inside the Zone. The deaths occurred as a result of retaliatory fire when shot at by Panamanians from across the line.

14. "That the aggression was preplanned by the United States and unprovoked by the Panamanians." False. The evidence that disproves the charge is contained in the foregoing and in preceding chapters.

Ambassador Bunker flatly rejected Moreno's accusations and the council adjourned until February 4 so the envoys could consult their governments. The United States had made it clear that no objection was entertained to the naming of an investigating committee as requested by Panama.

On February 4 Moreno renewed his attack against the United States, and this time Bunker replied in forceful language, emphasizing the falsity of the charges. The council established itself as a Provisional Organ of Consultation under the Rio Treaty, with Chile voting against it. The council Chairman, Ambassador Juan Batista de Lavalle of Peru, appointed a five-man investigating committee to fly to Panama. He named Ambassador Juan Ignacio Plate of Paraguay as Chairman. Other members were Ambassadors Ilmar Penna Marinho of Brazil, Gonzalo J. Facio of Costa Rica, Vicente Sanchez-Gavito of Mexico, and Emilio N. Oribe of Uruguay.

The committee conducted its investigation in Panama and at the same time tried to pursue mediation efforts. Ambassador Martin was still there and Deputy Assistant Secretary of State for Inter-American Affairs Sterling J. Cottrell also flew down to help his former chief. Cottrell virtually began his foreign service career at the American Embassy in Panama and was familiar with the situation there.

The Communists called a rally for February 9, which was the first month's anniversary of the eruption of the flag war. They burned in effigy Ambassador Manuel Trucco of Chile because, acting on instructions from his government, he had voted against Panama's motion at the OAS. His speech at the special meeting of the Council of the OAS on February 4 was a devastating rebuttal of Panama's charges of aggression against the United States. He said in part:

> When a state presents a claim based upon Articles 6 and 9 of the Inter-American Treaty of Reciprocal Assistance, as Panama has done on this occasion, another state is being accused of the crime of aggression, another state is being classified as an international criminal on which the entire weight of the force and punishment of the hemisphere must fall. . . .
>
> To put the machinery of the Inter-American Treaty of Reciprocal Assistance into operation the acts referred to in Article 9 must be evident, patent, and impugnable. It is not enough, in our judgment, and in this thesis we follow the most famous treaty experts of modern American international law, that one state unilaterally classify an act of aggression. It is the council that is responsible for declaring whether or not the qualification of aggression is valid, and whether there is or is not process of law. . . .

But, Mr. Chairman, it is all too clear that the case of aggression claimed by the Representative of Panama is not one of these evident, patent, and impugnable acts, since the claimant has not been able to formulate precisely the crime committed by the accused nor to frame that crime, also precisely, within the terms of the penal statute it asks be applied. . . .

My government believes, Mr. Chairman, and has so informed the government of Panama, that the crisis that developed on January 9 and 10 might have justified, at the very time, the application of the Inter-American Treaty of Reciprocal Assistance, on the basis of the terms of Article 6. But it is also the firm belief of my government that that situation was mitigated and superceded by the intervention of the Inter-American Peace Committee and that, as a result, there is not now a situation that endangers the peace of the hemisphere.

I was a member of the Inter-American Peace Committee. In the minutes of the meetings held by the committee in Panama, and as each of my distinguished colleagues and the representatives of both parties will remember, I am sure, there was sufficient evidence that the emergency situation that existed in Panama on January 9 and 10 was completely solved forty-eight hours after the Inter-American Peace Committee, with the collaboration of both parties, took action. . . .

I can also say that, from January 13 to the 29 of the same month, on which date Ambassador Moreno stated to the Inter-American Peace Committee that he had instructions from his government to put an end to its action before that autonomous agency of the Organization of American States, the members of the committee never heard any discussion between the parties as to the existence of an aggression. In the innumerable meetings the committee held, day and night, for more than two weeks, with the representatives of the United States and Panama, all the conversations referred to the need for quickly reestablishing diplomatic relations between the two countries. All the exchanges of points of view of the parties were limited to the question of stipulating the terms under which negotiations should be undertaken later with a view to solving the problems existing between them, as a consequence of the existence of the Panama Canal. . . .

I can also state emphatically that, when the meetings of the Inter-American Peace Committee with the representatives of both parties were resumed here in Washington, for more than a week both parties continued to search, among themselves, with the assistance of the committee, for a formula that would permit them to establish their diplomatic rela-

tions and later begin direct negotiations with a view to the solution of
the problems that separated them. Those problems did not include, nor
was there any discussion of, a presumed aggression. . . .

My government maintains, Mr. Chairman, that what in truth exists is
a dispute between the United States of America and Panama. This dispute, which concerns other matters, can only be resolved through understanding between the parties, with the good faith of the parties, with the
devotion of the parties to the peaceful means of settlement that constitute
the most valued tradition of the Inter-American system. The settlement
of this dispute can be obtained only through good and normal relations
between the parties and not by the application of the punitive machinery
of the system.

Naturally, even the above abridged text of Trucco's speech was
not published by Panama's press, much less broadcast over its radio
and television stations. More will be said later about those media.

A group of about twenty of the participants in the rally of Sunday,
February 9, tried to march into the Zone, but the *Guardia Nacional*
had been deployed to prevent that. All but one of the group were dispersed before they could reach the boundary. One youth managed to
slip through the lines and plant a flag in the Zone. He and the flag were
returned unharmed to Panama City. But before the Communists closed
their shop of agitation for the day they stoned the headquarters of a
Cuban exile organization and demanded that all anti-Castro Cubans
be expelled from Panama.

Familiar signs, similar to those that had appeared in Cuba, made
their appearance on the walls, both outside and inside, of churches.
One Roman Catholic priest refused to paint out the slogans, and the
hammer and the sickle, telling his parishioners that he wanted them to
become aware of the vivid evidence of the spread of atheistic communism among their fellow citizens.

Just before the special investigating committee departed for Panama,
Moreno distributed to the members of the Council of the OAS what
was purported to have been a secret memorandum in which the State
Department promised Panama a revision of the Canal treaties. Moreno
then leaked the story to the press, referring to "a secret agreement."
There was no such secret agreement. The copies that Moreno had circulated were of a lower-level memorandum of conversation of June

15, 1962, between some Panamanians and an officer of the State Department, after the Kennedy-Chiari talks. The memorandum described "certain conditions that could arise in the future which might entail treaty revision." This is believed to have had reference to the possibility of the building of a sea-level canal through Panama. It is very strange that Panama never had previously made public that alleged "secret agreement." The State Department was quick to issue a categoric denial that any secret agreement had been made with Panama for a revision of the treaties.

A curious footnote to history was the fact that the grandfather of Ambassador Gonzalo J. Facio of Costa Rica, who was a member of the special investigating committee, was the same Francisco Antonio Facio, Undersecretary of Public Instruction of Panama, who signed the ratification of the 1903 Canal Treaty. The Facio family later moved to Costa Rica.

After one week of collecting information and attempting futilely to bring about an agreement for a satisfactory formula to end the dispute, the special investigating committee flew back to the snows of Washington without revealing any findings at the time.

Other efforts were made to mediate, among them those of President Francisco J. Orlich of Costa Rica, who met with Chiari at the Panama frontier. Nothing substantial emerged from the talk. On February 27, Assistant Secretary of State Mann said that no progress had been made but the United States still hoped for the best. Orlich dropped his mediation efforts because of their futility.

17. The Zonians

"They are Ugly Americans!"

"Who?"

"The Zonians!"

"Why?"

"Because they are the most privileged people in the world!"

"Any resemblance between them and the Americans who reside in the continental United States would be purely coincidental; the Zonians are an entirely different breed."

"They are more American than the Stars and Stripes."

"They think they own the Canal Zone and Panama."

"They have the same mentality of the Algerian colonials."

"They buy everything cheaper in the Zone than they can in the United States and they live like kings over there."

"They get a 25 per cent pay differential while the Panamanians are discriminated against."

"All the best jobs over there are reserved for the Zonians and their sons."

"The Panamanian is on the low end of the totem pole."

"The Zonian pays only $6 a month rental to anchor his boat at the Balboa Yacht Club."

"The Zonian gets his gasoline much cheaper than we do in Panama."

"The United States pays an annuity to Panama which amounts to about one-quarter of the sum that is paid annually to us by the United Fruit Company in taxes for its operations in our country."

"Our quarrel is not with the Americans who are in business here in Panama or who work here. It is with the Zonians. They are to blame for all of our troubles."

Those are but some of the complaints that are poured into the ears of correspondents who arrive in Panama during any crisis with the United States. The complaints would be fed to them largely by Panamanians from all walks of life. As one who has worked and lived, on and off, during twenty-three years of his adult life in Panama and who studied law at the University of Panama, I am not ready to accept, and much less condemn, all of the Zonians after listening to the above. The perspective is not that one-sided. Moreover, the majority cannot be blamed for what might be done by a minority.

Again I refer to the Panama Canal *Spillway*, which in its issue of January 20, 1964, explains the typical Zonian. I find the description objective as well as factual. It should be pointed out, though, that it was not until 1951 that the Zonian was required by an Act of Congress to pay U.S. income tax. Here is the description:

What is the typical Zonian like?

The typical Zonian is a U.S.-citizen employee of the Panama Canal. He is *not* a second generation Zonian, but has come from the North Atlantic, Middle Atlantic, or East Central States. He is married and has two children. He has thirteen years of education and sixteen years' federal service. Of this service, thirteen years have been with the Panama Canal organization.

He pays U.S. income tax just like persons working in Washington, D.C., and U.S. citizens in any part of the United States. If he owns property in the United States, he pays property taxes on it in the United States.

The typical Zonian is certainly no less than a typical employee of Uncle Sam anywhere in the States, whether in a naval shipyard on one of the coasts or in any of the federal facilities scattered throughout the nation. Some observers have asserted his skills' level for his job is markedly higher than that of his counterpart on a similar job in the States.

He has the same normal economic and educational aspirations for his family and himself as any other employee of the U.S. government.

The typical Zonian, however, has an education problem for his children. And his children recognize that when their schooling is completed, employment opportunities in the Zone are strictly limited. Upon graduation from their schools here, sons and daughters of the average Zonian accept employment in the United States.

The typical Zonian enjoys a relatively high standard of living which was imported into the Canal Zone from continental United States. The employment office recognizes the fact that there would be difficulty in recruiting employees for this area unless prospective employees had assurance of a comparable standard of living. Canal Zone housing is no better, and in many instances, far less adequate than the housing at Cape Kennedy, Florida.

The typical Zonian and his family have shopped in Panama, attended cultural and social functions in Panama, attended the country fairs, and made visits to towns and cities throughout the land. Some of the Zonians have established homes in Panama and when they retire plan to spend the remainder of their lives in the Republic. Others returned to the home areas from which they came.

According to statistics compiled from personal information sheets, only 15½ per cent of the U.S.-citizen employees are second generation. Many of these employees accompanied their parents to the Isthmus at a young age, and their parents have since left the Isthmus.

Many of the typical Zonians are married to Panamanians. The typical Zonian dances the traditional folk dances of Panama, eats Panamanian food, and can make pretty good *seviche* himself. [*Seviche* is a fish delicacy that is made by partly boiling fish or shrimp and seasoning it with hot peppers, onions, and lime juice.]

The typical Zonian is a man (or woman) of many hobbies: painting, skin diving, fishing, sports, arts and crafts work (with emphasis on Panamanian themes), gardening, rock hounding, stamp collecting, folklore study, and charity or welfare work. In many of these fields, in many instances, he participates with Panamanians individually or in groups.

Nevertheless, there developed a gradual void that was to curtail the hitherto close relationships between Zonians and Panamanians. Of course there was natural resentment because segregation was practiced in the Zone, where there was a Gold Roll and a Silver Roll, white and colored, respectively. It was connected only with the pay scales when, at the start of the construction of the Canal, white Americans and foreigners were paid in gold while Panamanians and imported laborers from the West Indies were paid in silver. The segregation was complete and included the residential communities, the schools, and the rest rooms. For almost forty years there were no, or very few, signs in Spanish in the Canal Zone. The Panamanians were compelled to understand the English language, which, of course, was an utter impossibility for all of them. Some Zonians injured the sensibilities of colored Panamanians by their overbearing and superior manner, which created a fear complex among some of the latter that frightened them away from the Zone.

The void was to show its first trends as far back as 1940 when Arnulfo Arias began to implement his *Panameñismo* in his first term. Laws and ordinances were passed. As has previously been recorded here, shopkeepers had to remove their signs in the English language and replace them with those in the Spanish language. The inviting placards, ENGLISH IS SPOKEN HERE, had to be removed from show windows. Telephone operators at hotels had to answer calls in Spanish and no longer acknowledge in English. Panama had become too Americanized for the National-Socialist wave that Arnulfo Arias and his most ardent supporters mistakenly thought was going to sweep the world because of the guns, planes, and tanks of Adolf Hitler's military might. This chauvinism not only startled the Zonians but also irritated Americans who had resided in Panama for many years.

Because of the Volstead Act, which was made applicable to the Canal Zone, there were built in Panama three social clubs that used to be frequented, in the majority, by Zonians and, also, by Americans in business in Panama. These were the Century Club, the Chagres Club, and the Miramar Club. The first two were right near the Zone boundary, and the latter was on the ocean front at Bella Vista. The Chagres Club in later years was replaced by the *Edificio Panamericano*, where Pan American World Airways had its offices and which was burned on January 9. The street-floor offices of the old Century Club, a very few yards away, which later became the Ministry of Health and Sanitation, were also sacked the same night. The Miramar Club was sold to a Roman Catholic order for a school and then was demolished.

Some Zonians had been admited as members of the Union Club, which was the gathering place of Panama society, and overlooks the Pacific only a block away from the famous Flat Arch, which assured the engineers that the Canal would never be destroyed by an earthquake. In addition, as far back as 1922, Zonians were invited by Panamanians to help found the Panama Golf Club, the only course available until links were built near Gatun Locks in the Zone shortly after. Also there was the Hotel Central in downtown Panama, and such places of diversion as the Hotel Metropole at Santa Ana Plaza, where the French Bazaar now stands, and the famous Kelley's Ritz, the Happyland and the Hotel International on Fifth of May Plaza, as well as an assortment of cantinas like Guy Hancocks, which served free lunches with your beer. Zonians used to flock to them and, in the course of those visits, used to mingle with Panamanians.

In Colón there was the Strangers' Club, jutting out into Limon Bay, and the Hotel Washington, as well as Max Bilgray's famous Tropic Bar and a varied complex of other cantinas. Zonians were admitted into membership at the Strangers' Club, and there was close association with Colónites on many levels.

Every time the United States fleet arrived at Balboa or Cristobal, the doors of the Union Club and the Strangers' Club and the other clubs always had the welcome sign out for the officers. Army officers stationed in the Zone on the Atlantic side used to patronize the Strangers' Club, to which they were invited with membership privileges. On the Pacific side, some of them joined the clubs already mentioned but they also established one of their own in Panama City. They rented a floor of a building at a corner of the presidential palace and established "The Alibi Club." On its door there was a most descriptive sign that was meant for all members and guests from major generals down to second lieutenants. It read: HE WHO ENTERS HERE LEAVES ALL RANK OUTSIDE.

As each weekend approached, Zonians would flock to Panama and to Colón to buy lottery tickets, and many of them won big prizes. This indirect tourist trade meant much money for the Panamanians. After

the Volstead Act was repealed and the officers' clubs in the Zone
opened their bars, there was less fraternizing on that level across the
line. But the Zonians had nothing comparable, for no liquor was served
in the clubhouses, although they could patronize the Tivoli Hotel bar
and dine in its restaurant, which many did. There was a steady drop
in membershop of the Century, Chagres, and Miramar Clubs. The
breweries had opened beer gardens within a block or two from the
Zone boundary and these became popular places for both Zonians
and Panamanians who could not enjoy club memberships, or who
preferred them to the clubs. There was drinking, dancing, and good
food.

Not many Zonians ever undertook to try to learn how to speak
Spanish, largely because there was no need for them to do so. The U.S.-
educated upper strata of Panamanians, moreover, preferred to associate with the top brass in the Zone and would look down their noses
on the average Zonians as being below their own social status. Most
Zonians, likewise, would not associate with the lower class of Panamanians for the same reasons. A middle class did not begin to make
its emergence in Panama until after World War II, and then it appeared
mostly as a body of resentful Panamanians who felt they owed Uncle
Sam nothing and, on the contrary, that the bewhiskered, Star-Spangled
Giant of the world owed them everything.

With this state of mind fast becoming predominant—as evidenced
by the defense bases agitation of 1946-47—the Zonian felt that an air
of hostility had been erected around his presence in the midst of the
land where he was working and residing, so his trips into Panama became less frequent. This was especially so when the Communists
undertook to propagate the post-World War II "Hate America" line.

There was continued, direct, and apparently friendly contact on the
official level, but one could sense a steady erosion of what had hitherto
been a togetherness. Besides, there was a new breed of Zonian brought
down from the States after World War II, and this was a breed who
were largely misinformed about the background of the Republic and
the people.

I was sufficiently concerned about this evident erosion in 1947 that
I ventured to suggest to the then Governor, Brigadier General Joseph
C. Mehaffey, to begin orientation lectures in the Canal Zone for the

benefit of the employees. I suggested that such lectures could be held once a week in the theaters, and English-speaking Panamanians would be pleased to have the opportunity to explain to the Zonians what they considered the relationship should be between both people, and also to explain the historical, cultural, and customs and traditions background of the Panamanians. The suggestion was made orally, but it was never translated into reality. I envisaged, on the other hand, that Americans from the Zone could participate in similar orientation programs in Panama. Up to that time Panama was one of the very few countries in Latin America where there had not yet been established a United States-Panama Binational Center. It was utterly impossible to find Panamanians with stature and courage enough to undertake its organization, while the Communists worked very hard to prevent it.

Then in 1951 the Congress included the Canal Zone in the income tax law and there was much grumbling—not entirely without reason—of taxation without representation. The Zonians, in this case, had been placed on equal rights with all American citizens but failed to enjoy all of the privileges. When our government insisted in the negotiations for the 1955 treaty that the Zonians be given a 75 per cent tax discount on the purchase of liquors within the Republic of Panama, we helped to contribute toward the virtual isolation of the one people from the other. The Zonians purchased their alcoholic beverages at these reduced prices and consumed them within the Canal Zone, very few finding it desirable, and much less necessary, to continue to patronize old haunts across the line.

The prelude to the eruption of the flag war has already been narrated. With each protest that was published in "The Mail Box" of the Panama *American* against the flying of the dual flags, Panamanian tempers flared and the press and radio vented their caustic criticisms against the Zonians. For a city with a population of only 250,000, like Panama, and not more than 75,000 in Colón and its environs, there were six daily newspapers, and two weeklies, besides new periodicals that had appeared exclusively for the duration of the presidential campaign.

There was a time when governors of the Canal Zone, operating under the authority given to them by what is known as the Panama Canal Act, enacted by the Congress in 1914, kept a tight rein on the employees and refused to tolerate any dissension within the ranks or any building of fires that could be fanned into general conflagrations by the chauvinistic press and radio of Panama. Newspapers were never allowed to be established as competitive commercial enterprises in the Zone, and they were barred completely by treaty provisions of 1936 and 1955, wherein our government conceded that no businesses competitive with those of Panama would be permitted to be established in the Zone.

The Zone government published its own newspaper for the Canal diggers at its Mount Hope printing plant. It was called the Panama Canal *Record* and carried no advertising, only news of the Zone and the progress of the construction work. The only newspaper published in Panama at the time was the *Star & Herald*, founded in 1849 by an Irish immigrant to the United States, who halted between ships in Panama en route to California to seek riches in the gold fields. His name was Boyd, the grandfather of Ambassador Aquilino Boyd. José Gabriel Duque purchased the newspaper years later and made it trilingual during the French canal days. It was published in English, its founding language, Spanish, and French, all in one package. His son, Tomas Gabriel Duque, took over the newspaper after his Cuban-born father died, and maintained a pro-American policy. Duque branched out into many businesses and became probably the wealthiest man in Panama, as he held directorates in many firms and was almost permanent President of the National Brewery. On emotional national issues, though, he would find himself supporting the administration in power.

The *Star & Herald* and its sister, *La Estrella de Panamá* (after the French section was dropped with the American occupation of the Zone), had a monopoly in Panama until Nelson Rounsevell, an American, founded the Panama *American* in 1925. Rounsevell brought a more aggressive and controversial type of journalism into Panama, and later established its Spanish language counterpart, *El Panamá América*. He sold out to ex-President Harmodio Arias in 1938 and left the Zone. This was the beginning of Arias's journalism and radio empire. Arias injected a more nationalistic approach into Panama journalism, although *La Estrella de Panamá* had campaigned vigorously in 1933-34 for the revision of the 1903 treaty. Harmodio Arias established an alter-ego for *El Panamá América*. It was the midday tabloid, *La Hora*, the introduction of popular yellow journalism into Panama.

With Arias's death, the papers and radio station passed to the control of his three surviving sons and one daughter. The daughter, Mrs. Rosario Arias de Galindo, was elected President of the corporation in a family agreement in 1963. Harmodio, Jr., a Deputy of the National Assembly, became Publisher of *La Hora*, which post was formerly held by Roberto or Tito, husband of Dame Margot Fonteyn, the prima ballerina. Gilberto, who had been Finance Minister, and was a first vice presidential candidate in the 1964 campaign for the Alliance Party of the Opposition, was founder and publisher of *Critica*, a morning tabloid.

Another morning tabloid, *El Día*, was founded and owned by Marcel Penso, millionaire head of the Republican party and co-owner of the Santa Rosa Sugar Company with Max Delvalle, candidate for first vice president on the coalition ticket with Marcos Robles, and backed by Chiari. The Penso-Delvalle sugar company and Chiari's plantation and mill had the sugar market monopolized in Panama, and bid on contracts to sell sugar to the Zone.

The Chiari family published a weekly, *El Tiempo*, and as the flag war subsided they began the publication of a new tabloid daily, *La Prensa*.

To build circulation and to fan the nationalistic spirit, and because of infiltrations, these tabloids, mainly, leaped on every opportunity to undermine relations with the Zone as a popular policy. Their editorials, their biased stories, and the distortions of some of their columnists were eagerly rebroadcast by radio commentators and the journalistic novelty for Latin America, the *radioperiodicos* (radio newspapers), with additional caustic comments added over the airwaves. Some of the cartoons had viciously vulgar anti-American overtones. They were hate developers, instead of exercising the mission of a responsible press to attempt to correct ills and suggest sensible solutions rather than to aggravate the problems.

Generalities are normally unfair, but perhaps the best illustration of the professional caliber and quality of the Panama press, and a large segment of its radio and television media, is the fact that not a single Panamanian reporter from any media was present at the El Panama-Hilton Hotel at 1:40 A.M. of January 15, 1964, when the Inter-American Peace Committee was ready to announce its *Communiqué*

Number 3. It was unnecessary for the *Star & Herald* and *La Estrella de Panamá* to send reporters, because the presidential palace assumed the role of getting the communiqué to those sister newspapers before the committee released it to all the foreign correspondents who were waiting in the hotel. A foreign office aid rushed a copy of the communiqué from the hotel to the palace as soon as it had been signed, and the palace rushed it over to the newspaper. The reason given to me by the Panama authorities for this was that they had requested the newspaper to hold its deadline for the story. In doing so, the government failed to notify the editors that there were two communiqués, one in Spanish and another in English. The *Star & Herald* published its own translation of the Spanish communiqué under this eight-column banner on page 1: US AGREES TO NEGOTIATIONS. The editors were at fault, too, for failing to have a reporter assigned to cover the story, so they would have been able to have had the correct English communiqué with the word "discussions" instead of "negotiations."

This should serve as a lesson for future OAS committees so that no more releases will be issued in advance by the interested government for partisan as well as national and international political advantages.

The manner in which the Panama press treated the flag war story induced Governor Fleming to write a message to the Zone employees, which was published in the Panama Canal *Spillway* of January 21 and which read:

FELLOW EMPLOYEES,

With so much bad news reaching us these troubled days, it is cheering to have a positive report of good news each day. This good news is that the employees of the Panama Canal are continuing to transit ships expeditiously and safely. A magnificent record of sustained service to shipping is being maintained during this troubled period.

I thank the employees of the Panama Canal for their loyalty, restraint, forbearance, and dedication to duty. The lack of communication with our employees has kept them in a state of confusion and perhaps frustration. Conflicting reports and rumors have created tension and excitement.

My message to employees is this: Don't get excited about what you read in the local papers. English-language newspapers printed in Panama are Panamanian papers and in all recent reports have been slanted. News favorable to Panama is highlighted. One of these papers for months has been dedicated to encouraging the controversy between Panama and the United States.* And when the chips were down and all of us, Panamanians and Americans alike, needed objective reporting, the other one was not much better.**

When you read the local newspapers, keep cool and remember that the items you read are calculated to stir you up and get you excited. Now you may ask about the United States press. The first batch of newspapers from the States really clobbered the Zonians. I have been working with correspondents, and I believe the tide is changing. The next few days should bring stories from the United States which will be more objective. It is essential that we get the true story before the American public but it takes time and we couldn't do it during the first few days.

During the time of crisis along the borders, the Panama Canal administration could not publish, print, or disseminate news to its employees directly. It was necessary, and I am sure you know why, that only one voice should speak for the United States. Later the Peace Commission of the Organization of American States requested the governments of the United States and the Republic of Panama to refrain from discussing the events starting Thursday, January 9, in an effort to improve the climate for resumption of relations. The United States has scrupulously observed this request. Our forbearance will earn us allies in the long term.

I do not need to tell you that the American employee of the Panama Canal has been singled out for special attack by many individuals and much of the press and radio media. I have been telling, and most emphatically, representatives of the press and radio that the American employee was not responsible for what has happened. The current conflict springs from something bigger, more basic, than us Americans in the Canal Zone.

Before the existing crisis is completely resolved an examination will be made of the basic causes of the United States-Panama differences. To the extent that I am permitted to do so, I will keep the Panama Canal employee informed of what is going on. You can depend on this.

Panama Canal employees may receive more unwarranted criticism before the true facts are established and the United States public better understands the situation. In the meantime, keep your blood pressure

*This was a reference to the Panama *American*.
**This was a reference to the *Star & Herald*.

down, ignore unfair and slanted publicity, and continue to do your work to the best of your ability. This will be a major contribution from each of you. Again, I thank you for your loyalty and steadfastness.

(*Signed*) ROBERT J. FLEMING, JR.
Governor

Some representatives of news media who flew to Panama to report the flag war failed to verify the emotional complaints that were poured into their ears against The Zonians. They bought as a solid package not only "the ugly American" and the "Algerian colonialist mentality" charges—which were echoed in statements and speeches by public figures like Senator Wayne Morse, Democrat of Oregon, Chairman of the Subcommittee on Inter-American Affairs of the Foreign Relations Committee—but also the resentments that the Zonians were privileged characters because they were able to buy their foodstuffs cheaper in the commissaries (which are now officially called retail stores) than they could buy in the United States.

I was aware that many years ago the commissary prices may have been lower on foodstuffs, as well as luxury items that were manufactured in Europe and in the Orient, than those in the continental United States, but I was also aware that for some time the situation had changed radically. Yet the average American, including Senator Morse, immediately expostulated when they read the inaccurate stories sent by some correspondents of our leading newspapers and accepted as an incontrovertible truth what was not the real fact.

To substantiate the above, I obtained the Refrigerated Products Retail Price List No. 363, effective January 4, 1964, of the Panama Canal Company Retail Stores Branch, and compared it with prices for identical products advertised in the Miami newspapers on February 27, 1964. Here is the illuminating comparison:

PRODUCT	U. S. PRICE	C. Z. PRICE
Sliced bacon, 1 lb.	$ .49	$ .63
Frankfurters, 1 lb.	.49	.66
Swift, link sausage, 8 ozs.	.49	.51
Pork sausage, 1 lb.	.59	.75
Baked ham, 6 oz.	.69	.67
Muenster, sliced cheese, 6 oz.	.29	.37

Wisconsin sharp cheddar, 6 oz.	.29	.33
Shrimp, fresh, 1 lb.	.49	1.00
Filet of sole, 9 oz.	.49	1 lb. .55
Oysters, 5¼ oz.	.47	8 oz. .95
Frozen peas & carrots, for 6 10 oz. pkgs.	.99	each
		1 lb. pkg. .21
Swift hens, baking, 1 lb.	.33	5/7 lb. .47
Swift, premium canned ham, 3 lb.	1.89	2.63
Swift, premium ducklings, 1 lb.	.39	.54

As for fresh beef, the Zonians preferred the Panama product which the commissaries purchased from the native packing house after Zone inspectors were allowed, by special agreement, to inspect the quality for health reasons. The prices, per pound, with the rarest of exceptions, were much lower than stateside, as can be seen below:

PRODUCT	NATIVE	U.S. CHOICE
Porterhouse steak	$ .78	$1.30
Rib roast (1st 5 ribs)	.36	1.00
Rib roast (last 2 ribs)	.34	.70
Round roast, boneless	.58	1.08
Round steak, boneless	.60	1.08
Hamburger	.44	.60
T-bone steak	.68	
		None Imported
Steak, club	.58	1.05

The Panama fresh beef products are so acceptable that of forty-three items listed only fourteen equivalent ones are brought in from the continental United States. And the Zonian housewife gets no merchants Green or other trading stamps for those purchases.

Panama eggs and stateside eggs, for example, are identical in price: native large cartoned per dozen 54¢, medium cartoned, 47¢. The Zonians buy their native sugar, for which President Chiari and the Penso-Delvalle monopoly bid, cheaper than the Panamanians. In the Zone they pay 6¢ per pound, while the Panamanians pay 10¢ per pound. Nobody is to blame for that but the native sugar combine. The Zone also buys milk and milk products from President Chiari who has developed the largest and most profitable dairy in the country.

Besides the 25 per cent differential paid to the U.S. employees, they are given free transportation to the United States for home leave every two years. This may be by steamer, if space is available, or by commercial aircraft. Until the flag war erupted, the Panama Canal Company-Zone government used to furnish employees and their families an official car to transport them to Tocumen Airport—seventeen miles east of the Canal Zone—to board their planes. The risk was considered too great to continue this practice and Pan American World Airways was requested to provide a jitney service from the YMCA at Balboa to Tocumen.

Naturally, there were some Zonians who acted like "ugly Americans" but they were an infinite, although vocal, minority. That minority, too, might well have developed a mentality akin to that of the Algerian Colons, but the majority could not, and should not, be blamed here at home and much less by the Panamanians, for their actions. Perhaps a proper orientation program, as that which I took the liberty to suggest in 1947, might have helped to correct such a lamentable state of mind. James Jenkins, Jr., the student who was a ringleader in the flag-raising incident at Balboa High School, was a post-World War II arrival in the Zone with his family. The pamphlets that were issued to newly-contracted employees were insufficient to develop the proper psychological approach to the Panama problem. The flag issue arose from an obstinacy and from a weakness. The obstinacy was the opposition of some Zonians to the flying of the Panama flag alongside the U.S. flag at the schools. The weakness was the failure of Governor Fleming to use the powers with which he was vested by the Panama Canal Act of 1914 to make the right decision at the right time, one that would have prevented the subversive elements in the Republic from taking advantage of a situation that was handed to them gratuitously on a highly polished platter.

The original fault lay in the fact, as was pointed out by the distinguished and articulate Republican Minority Leader from Illinois, Senator Everett McKinley Dirksen, after a conference with President Johnson, that the United States had opened the door by consenting to fly the Panama flag in the Zone after nearly sixty years. But once that decision was made, and once it was amplified by the late President Kennedy, it is my opinion that it should have been enforced by Fleming with all the vigor that was at his command. The powers vested in him under the Panama Canal Act are so broad that United States statutes are inapplicable in the Canal Zone courts unless the Congress specifically orders them to be included when it legislates.

It was only natural that American students should have wanted to see the Stars and Stripes fly in front of their schools in the Zone. It was an original error, though, to have stricken the schools from the list of proposed dual flag sites, notwithstanding the energetic protests by the civic councils. The United States had entered into an obligation; the federal court in the Canal Zone upheld the right of the Governor to implement that obligation; the Congress had not seen fit, despite any misgivings that were held by some of its members, to enact any binding legislation that would have vetoed that obligation, although it banned the use of appropriated funds for the dual flagpoles. Special funds were used.

The Congress was blamed by Governor Fleming for many of his administrative difficulties. He complained that it refused to legislate for the changes that he had recommended insistently, changes that would have helped to reduce the tensions and animosities between the Panamanians and the Zonians. He also inculpated those he described as the "150 per cent Americans and the 50 per cent bourbon drinkers" for the trouble. There is absolutely nothing wrong in being 150 per cent American, for it is most evident that we need much more of that type of sincere and dedicated patriots here at home. But we also need a clear perspective that will enable us properly to implement our mutual obligations when we contract them in the Canal Zone.

Assistant Secretary of State Mann and then Secretary of the Army Vance understood the problem well enough to take immediate corrective measures after twenty-four hours in the Canal Zone. Fleming amended the dual flag order to include the schools in it, after Vance discussed it with him. Then President Johnson announced that the government would not tolerate any rebellion by Zonians against established policy. The hard line was to be applied to the conscientious objectors.

In reviewing the Zonians I have, up to now, omitted any reference to the living status of our armed forces personnel stationed in the Canal Zone. They enjoy better price privileges than do the Zonians, but no more so than in any of the overseas bases. Like the Zonians, our armed forces personnel are not able to rent or buy land or property within the ten-mile strip. They cannot plan to build any homes of their own, except within the Republic, or make investments for such in the continental United States and/or elsewhere. The armed forces personnel have been obedient, in the main, to the indoctrination which they receive over the Southern Command network and at their bases. They have been told repeatedly that they are looked upon by our neighbors as unofficial ambassadors of the United States and they should act accordingly. Some of the Zonians failed to absorb that indoctrination or pay heed to it.

On February 6, Governor Fleming announced that plans had been drawn up to include, eventually, fifty Panamanians in the Canal Zone police force. This immediately brought a public protest by Richard Meehan, President of Canal Zone Police Lodge 1790 (AFL-CIO) that it was detrimental to the security of the Zone. This was promptly refuted by Fleming as an entirely unwarranted and unfounded statement. The Panama Canal Pilots' Association also objected to this plan and cabled a protest to the Secretary of the Army. Arthur C. Payne, the Budget Director of the Community Services Division, and Meehan, continued to wage a public fight against this plan. Then Fleming cracked down on them, using his full powers. He directed Edward Doolan, Director of Personnel, to issue thirty-day notices of dismissal to each for allegedly "libelous" statements, and for failing to obtain "clearance" to issue statements regarding government policy. As this was written the battle was still waging, with the Central Labor Union expected to make representations in Washington on behalf of Payne and with the Police Union going to the aid of Meehan. The directive from President Johnson was being implemented.

Another thing that irritated the Zonians, and very justifiably so, was the fact that Panamanians who complained about the alleged privileged position which the Americans enjoyed, overlooked the fact that they (the Americans) were paying much more income tax to the U.S. government than the natives were paying to their own treasury.

Another source of irritation was Panama's constant complaint of equal pay for equal work for Panamanians in the Zone, even though much advancement had been made along this line. More so when the

Panamanians themselves paid their own workers starvation wages. The Zonians remember all too well the widespread protests by businessmen and manufacturers in Panama in 1959 when President de la Guardia insisted on the enactment of a minimum wage law that would guarantee workers 40¢ (yes, forty cents) an hour in the Republic. Rather than lose juicy profits, businesses began to reduce the number of employees so the niggardly raises would not have to be paid to all of their hired help. Is there any wonder that Zonians, as well as Americans resident in Panama, know the answer as to why communism can make great inroads?

In the year 1962 alone, the Republic of Panama received nearly $85 million in financial benefits from the Canal Zone. This sum included the $1,930,000 annuity, expenditures made in Panama by U. S. citizens employed in the Zone, net payments including retirement and disability to non-U. S. citizens employed in the Zone, direct purchases made in Panama by U. S. government agencies, contractors' purchases of goods and services for Zone projects, and purchases of goods in Panama by private organizations operating in the Zone. Also, from 1961, when the Alliance for Progress began, through 1963, Panama received from the U. S. $18.1 million in outright grants or $8.1 million more than it was paid for the Canal rights. Of that total $11.5 million were allocated for rural development. This included agrarian reform, farm-to-market road construction, self-help schools, rural health facilities, water resources, industrial development, self-help housing, mineral resources surveys, national economic planning, higher education, nursing education, government management and administration, manpower training, and advisory services for education, including the University of Panama, public safety, sewer design, technical studies for electric power development, hospital design, and program support.

The above does not include additional grants under programs sponsored by the UN, OAS, Military Assistance Program, and Food For Peace Program. Neither does it include the Peace Corps, whose presence is anathema to the Communists. The Panamanian students, in promoting their "Hate America" rally for February 9, declaimed over Radio Tribuna that: "The students and the Panamanian people must demand that the Peace Corps, better known as the espionage corps, leave our country." The one who made that demand was Floyd Britton, the Cuban-trained Communist who spoke as representative of the high school students in the program of the Panamanian Students' Federation. The Party line was familiar, as expressed by Britton and by Ricardo Aguilar, Secretary of Organization of the Students' Federation, Enrique Mendoza of the National Institute, and Alcibiades Alcedo of the Normal School of Santiago, Veraguas. Here is what they said:

> Panamanians, the people must unite against North American imperialism. At this time, when our country is struggling against North American imperialists, we must know who our friends are and who our enemies are. We must be aware that the Panamanian cause has outside and also local enemies. The enemies outside of the country are those sectors who talk about their democratic system but who in real life have shown many times that they are for slavery, for racism, and oppression. In spite of the justice of our cause, in spite of its dignity, there are groups inside our country, well-born sons of our country, who are allied with the enemy.

By the end of February, 1964, dual flag installations had been completed at twenty-nine sites in the Zone and a thirtieth was due to be added before the end of the year. Here is the list of places where the United States and Panama flags are flying together:

Location	Date Dual Flags First Flown
1. Shaler Triangle	9/21/60
2. Thatcher Ferry Bridge	10/12/62
3. Administration Building, Balboa Heights	10/29/62
4. Administration Building, Cristobal	11/1/62
5. Miroflores Locks	10/24/63
6. Gatun Locks	11/9/63
7. Coco Solo Hospital	11/15/63
8. Corozal Hospital	11/30/63
9. Palo Seco Hospital	12/4/63
10. Margarita Townsite	12/18/63
11. Balboa High School	1/15/64
12. Canal Zone College	1/15/64
13. Balboa Elementary School	1/15/64

14. Ancon Elementary School   1/15/64
15. Diablo Elementary School   1/15/64
16. Diablo Junior High School   1/15/64
17. Los Rios Elementary School   1/15/64
18. Pedro Miguel Elementary School   1/15/64
19. Paraiso Elementary School   1/15/64
20. Paraiso Junior-Senior High School   1/15/64
21. Gamboa Elementary School   1/15/64
22. Santa Cruz Elementary School   1/15/64
23. Cristobal Junior-Senior High School   1/15/64
24. Coco Solo Elementary School   1/15/64
25. Rainbow City Junior-Senior High School   1/15/64
26. Margarita Elementary School   1/15/64
27. Gatun Elementary School   1/15/64
28. Mount Hope Cemetery   1/31/64
29. Corozal Cemetery   2/7/64
30. New Gorgas Hospital   Scheduled later in 1964

18. The Sea-Level Canal

The importance of the Panama Canal to the national defense during World War II can be illustrated by statistics. From Pearl Harbor Day, December 7, 1941, to V-J Day, September 2, 1945, more than 6,400 warships and 10,300 other military craft were locked through from ocean to ocean. Naval architects long complained that the 110-foot-wide and 1,100-foot-long locks were a handicap for their plans for modern and future warship construction. The obstacle was disregarded before the end of World War II when it was decided to plan for a two-ocean Navy and the architects drafted aircraft carriers that could not be squeezed through the Canal.

Existing conventional weapons of war, before the employment of any nuclear bomb, could have destroyed the present lock canal if they had been able to penetrate the defenses. A sea-level canal, just like a lock canal, can be closed by the sinking of one or more ships in the channel, by sabotage or bombing, or by debris from a direct hit on embankments by a nuclear bomb.

Aircraft carriers and ocean liners have already been built that are too large for transit through the Canal. Also on the seas are tankers and freighters which are too large to be locked through Gatun, Pedro Miguel, and the Miraflores locks.

The Congress directed the Governor of the Canal Zone to conduct a comprehensive survey of possible canal routes and to submit cost estimates and recommendations for the possible course of action that should be adopted, and adapted, for the needs of the thermonuclear age. This was done as soon as World War II ended.

A staff of engineers headed by Colonel James H. Stratton surveyed thirty routes over the 400,000 square miles of the American Isthmus from Tehuantepec in Mexico to the Atrato River in Colombia for a site for a prospective new canal. They were aided in their surveys by aerial and ground reconnaissances, radar mapping, geological mapping, and exploratory drilling. Possible choices were finally narrowed down to eight for further studies for both lock and sea-level canals. Only five sites were then selected, but an estimate never was attempted for a sea-level canal through Nicaragua because of the astronomical cost before thermonuclear excavation was contemplated. The present Panama Canal route, of course, was also included in the estimates. All estimates were based on conventional forms of excavation and 1946 prices for material and equipment, as well as wage scales.

The basis for fixing safe excavation slopes for the new canal was established after engineering analyses and laboratory tests of soils and rocks and studies of slides during and after the building of the present Canal. Preliminary plans for harbors and port facilities were made by the Navy's Bureau of Yards and Docks. A flood control plan for a sea-level canal was developed with the help of specialists furnished by the Chief of Army Engineers. Pilots, ship owners, marine operating personnel at Panama, Suez, Houston, and Cape Cod Canals, and in the Navy Department were consulted to develop navigation requirements as they affect the dimensions and alignment of the channels and the requirements for the control of currents. Ship-model tests were made by the Navy to determine the behavior of ships, and a hydraulic model of the proposed sea-level canal was built and operated at the David Taylor Basin of the Navy to determine the effect of tide and the most favorable methods for tidal regulations. Construction machinery manufacturers and operators, such as the Bucyrus-Erie Company, the Yuba Manufacturing Company, the Atlantic Gulf and Pacific Company, Gahagan Construction Corporation, and Standard Dredging Corporation investigated deep-dredging equipment designs for the study. Deep underwater drilling and blasting tests were made in the Canal Zone. It was estimated that at peak of construction there would have been in operation at the same time: one 40-inch hydraulic dredge, one 28-inch hydraulic dredge, four ladder dredges of 2 cubic yards each, one 20-cubic yard dipper dredge, fifteen shovels of 33 cubic yards each, twenty-two draglines of 25 cubic yards each and 25 shovels of 5 cubic yards each.

General Mehaffey recommended in his report that the reconversion of the present Canal to sea level was the most practical and economic plan at the time. He also eliminated the possibility of building a ship railway across the Isthmus of Tehuantepec on the grounds that it would be too costly and too vulnerable. The sea-level canal, even in the less costly reconversion of the present lock Canal, would still be an enormous enterprise, and, based on the study submitted in 1947, its enormity can be appreciated by the following pertinent facts:

Its cost would have been seven times the original total cost of the existing Canal; it would have taken ten years to build; it would have required the excavation of 1,068,699,212 cubic yards of hard rock, medium rock, soft rock, and earth, which is just three times more than was dug from 1904-14 when the present Canal was built and opened to traffic; it would have required eight dams and three diversion channels for its flood control system compared to the present three dams; it would have required a 200- by 1,500-foot tidal lock, a 750-foot navigable pass closed by steel gates and a water control structure; two vehicular tunnels each one mile long would have had to be built under the canal; two bridges would have had to be built across the canal; five two-lane and one four-lane highway totaling 75 miles would have had to be built; new power plants would have had to be erected; new harbors would have had to be built; eight installations would have had to be relocated, among them the Naval Radio Station at Summit at a cost of $10 million, the Army Radio Station at Corozal at a cost of $2 million, Navy facilities at Rousseau at a cost of $3.5 million; there would have had to be built for 35,000 employees and their families housing, schools, recreation buildings, administration buildings, supply and service buildings, hospitals, dispensaries, aid stations, and a water supply system; by the second year 41,-360 skilled and unskilled workers would have been employed; 3.1 million barrels of cement, 178 million board feet of lumber and 117,-000 tons of metals would have been purchased.

"On the basis of excavation yardage alone," Mahaffey said in his report, "the Panama Sea-Level Canal and the Panama Sea-Level Conversion Route is definitely superior to the others. In addition a sea-level canal on the Panama Sea-Level Conversion Route would utilize the numerous existing operational, commercial, and defense facilities of the present Canal. No other route possesses characteristics that would make it superior to the Panama Sea-Level Conversion Route in capacity or security. The potential benefits of the Tehuantepec and Nicaraguan routes to shippers would, as in the case of the lock Canal, be offset by greatly increased annual charges."

Mehaffey's recommendation was approved by the Joint Chiefs of Staff, sent on to Secretary of Defense James Forestal, who also approved it, and the latter forwarded it to President Harry S. Truman, who made the consent unanimous. As the Congress had ordered the study and recommendations, President Truman directed that the entire documentation be transmitted to the Congress. It was so done, but without any request by the Administration that the Congress enact legislation to build the sea-level canal. Mehaffey's estimate, which included clearing, relocations of the radio stations, roads, railroads and minor facilities, dry channel excavation, wet channel excavation, conversion plugs, harbor improvements, flood control, tidal-regulating structures, highways, power, vehicular tunnels, operating facilities, townsites, utilities, medical facilities and sanitation, design, supervision, and inspection and overhead totaled $2,482,810,000.

The remarkable feature of the reconversion plan, if the engineers were correct in their planning, and there is no reason to suspect otherwise, is that there would have been only one week of interference with the operation of the present Canal while the transition was made to sea-level. This would have occurred while the 163½ square miles of Gatun Lake was to be drained, to lower its water surface from 85 feet above sea level. Also, the sea-level route would have been five miles shorter than the present lock Canal, and also wider, deeper, straighter, and free from navigational hazards. The Canal is now 51.2 miles long. It has a minimum depth of 37 feet in Balboa Harbor at low tide and a minimum width of 300 feet in the tortuous eight-mile-long Gaillard Cut where the minimum depth is 42 feet. There are 23 angles or changes in direction along the route. The sea-level canal would have provided a minimum depth of 60 feet at low tide, a minimum width of

600 feet at 40 feet below low tide. Plans called for it to follow the general route of the present Canal with considerable improvement in alignment to reduce angles and changes. When the navigable pass would be used, the changing 20-foot tide would flow in from the Pacific and develop a current of 4½ knots which would flow north into the Caribbean. Yes, the Canal runs south from the Caribbean into the Pacific. Operating twenty-four hours a day, the tidal lock at the Pacific would have been able to handle 86 ships, with 2¼ normal-size vessels being locked through every 40 minutes. The navigable pass, which was planned to be used safely during 16 hours daily, would have permitted 116 ships to sail through during that period.

Mehaffey emphasized in his report that the construction of a sea-level canal would not have been tossing money down a rathole. He pointed out that by fiscal year 1947 the present Canal had returned to the United States in money and free services the entire cost of maintenance, operation, sanitation, and civil government since its completion and all but $66 million of interest on the net capital investment which then was less than $515 million. Three per cent interest is paid annually on the net capital investment after depreciation into the United States Treasury. The cost estimates, of course, excluded expenditures for military, naval, and air force requirements, costs of management, medical, and municipal services, civil government, and other charges that were usually added to the annual budgets before the Congress reorganized the structure of the Panama Canal.

Congress was given an opportunity in the Mehaffey study to review three plans to improve the present lock Canal. These are still valid, despite the fact that a third set of locks, which was under construction when World War II began, was discarded because continued work on them produced an unnecessary burden in shipping and materials on our war effort. They include—again under 1946 cost estimates—the following:

Plan I. At a cost of $130 million the existing locks would be gradually modified to eliminate periodic four-month overhauls but include no improvements for increasing the security of the Canal against attack. The locks would not be made larger and the work would take ten to twelve years.

Plan II. In a ten-year job all Pacific locks would be located at Miraflores, and this project would be accomplished in two phases, but still would not provide security against attack. The first phase would cost $1,126,000,000. The second phase would cost another $506,000,000. One lock, 200 feet by 1,500 feet and with a depth of 50 feet, would be built at Gatun and Miraflores. Miraflores Lake would be raised to the 85-foot level of Gatun Lake, and the Pedro Miguel Locks would be abandoned. The channel would be widened to 500 feet at a depth of 40 feet. An additional upper chamber would be added to each lane at Miraflores Locks. In the second phase a new lock would be built at Gatun and Miraflores, and the existing locks would be abandoned. The upper operating level of Gatun Lake would be raised to 92 feet to obtain additional water for lockages. Ships would complete the transit in 7¼ hours instead of the current 8 hours.

Plan III. Similar to Plan II, with the exception that the new locks at Gatun and Miraflores would be widely separated to reduce the probability of simultaneous destruction. An attack by conventional weapons would close the Canal for at least one or two years. A thermonuclear bomb attack would render it useless for four years or more. The project would cost $2,308,000,000, or $174,810,000 less than the sea-level plan.

Four other lock-canal estimates were submitted. They were the San Blas and Caledonia routes in Panama, Nicaragua, and Tehuantepec. The costs: San Blas, $5,960,000,000; Caledonia, $4,751,000,000; Nicaragua, $3,566,000,000; Tehuantepec, $13,280,000,000.

Three other sea-level canal estimates were forwarded. These were: San Blas, $6,272,000,000; Caledonia, $5,132,000,000; and the Atrato River in Colombia, $4,594,000,000. No effort was made to estimate the costs for sea-level canals in Nicaragua and Tehuantepec because it would be necessary in the Central American nation to excavate 5,200,-000,000 cubic yards of earth and rock, while in Mexico it would be necessary to dig out 6,130,000,000 cubic yards.

Over the Panama sea-level route it would have been possible for ships of all sizes to sail through from ocean to ocean at a speed of 10 knots in 4½ hours when using the tidal lock, and in only 4 hours when using the navigable pass.

The House Merchant Marine and Fisheries Committee, which acts as the congressional vigilante over the Panama Canal, received the

Mehaffey study, but, as the Panamanians rejected the Defense Bases Agreement almost concurrently therewith, the proposals were filed in a very deep freezer.

The 81st Congress, though, in 1950 enacted Public Law 841, which is referred to as the Reorganization Act. This created the Panama Canal Company in addition to the Canal Zone government. The Governor also became President of the Panama Canal Company. The Canal had thus, in the public mind, been made a commercial enterprise by an Act of Congress. At least that was the psychological impact that the legislation produced in Panama. This was enhanced by announcements that at the time, with the Korean War on and with our country committed elsewhere around the world, the Panama Canal was accorded the lowest category of priority by the Joint Chiefs of Staff.

A statement that appears in the handsomely published annual report of the Board of Directors does not serve to dispel that psychological impact. The statement reads:

The Panama Canal Company is a corporate agency and instrumentality of the government of the United States. As sole owner of the corporation created by Act of Congress, the United States is represented by the President or his designee, referred to as the "Stockholder." The Secretary of the Army has been so designated, in his individual capacity as personal representative of the President of the United States.

In the 1962 report, Governor Robert J. Fleming, Jr., as President, submitted the following letter to Cyrus R. Vance, then Secretary of the Army, as the designated stockholder:

PANAMA CANAL COMPANY
Balboa Heights, Canal Zone
Office of The President

LETTER TO STOCKHOLDER:

Subject: Annual Report of Board of Directors:

It is very gratifying to report that a record volume of traffic moved through the Panama Canal last year reflecting the Canal's expanding role in the steady growth of world ocean-borne commerce. The average time spent by ships in Canal Zone waters during transit was reduced to 15.5 hours, compared with 16.5 hours per transit in 1961. This 1-hour reduction in transit time represents a savings of approximately $1 million to our customers.

Waterway improvements progressed on schedule during 1962, and the final contract in the channel widening program will be awarded within the next year.

For the 11th successive year since its reorganization (July 1, 1951) the Panama Canal financed within its resources, and without cost to the taxpayer, all of its operational and capital requirements.

The capital program required expenditures of $16.1 million during the fiscal year. This was the second highest annual expenditure of this nature since the reorganization. The largest single item of capital expenditure was $5.9 million toward widening of the Empire Reach within Gaillard Cut. In the 5 years through fiscal year 1962, a total of $22.8 million has been expended for the channel improvement program and additional expenditures necessary to complete this program will approximate $20.9 million. Other major expenditures in 1962 included $2.3 million on the quarters replacement program, $1.3 million for an additional electric generating plant, $0.6 million on the central air-conditioning plant, and $0.5 million on the new locks towing locomotives.

The funds provided through operations, net revenue, depreciation, etc., were not sufficient to finance capital expenditures and it became necessary to draw down cash reserves to the extent of $1.7 million.

Tolls revenue was at an all-time high of $58.3 million, for transiting 11,340 shops over 300 tons. Comparative figures for 1961 were $55.2 million and 11,054 ships. The average cost to the shipper per cargo ton was 74.9¢ (excludes vessels transiting in ballast or measured on displacement basis), as compared to 74.8¢ for the previous year. The tolls rate remains unchanged at 90¢ per laden ton under Panama Canal measurement.

On June 29, 1962, the S.S. *Ancon* was transferred to the U. S. Maritime Administration, Department of Commerce, on a nonreimbursable basis, for ultimate transfer to the State of Maine. Consequently, the equity of the U.S. government in the Company was reduced some $2 million.

Special emphasis has been given to equality of treatment of all employees. Several programs have been initiated to improve communications with our Spanish-speaking employees as well as our neighbors in the Republic of Panama.

By order of the Board of Directors
    (*Signed*) ROBERT J. FLEMING, JR., *President*

The same report explains that Public Law 841 of the 81st Congress established and provided the basic conception of the Panama Canal Company-Canal Zone government organization effecting philosophy of division between the functions normally associated with civil government and the functions which pertain to the operation of the waterway. The Company and the Canal Zone government are closely interrelated in purpose, organization, and operation, and the function of the two agencies in combination is the administration of the Panama Canal enterprise as a whole. The Governor of the Canal Zone, who is charged with the administration of the Canal Zone government, is "ex officio" a director and President of the Panama Canal Company.

The Panama Canal Company is required by law to recover all costs of operation and maintenance of its facilities, including depreciation. The Company is also required to pay interest to the United States Treasury on the net direct investment of the United States government in the Company and to reimburse the United States Treasury for annuity payments to the Republic of Panama under the 1936 Treaty ($430,000), and the net costs of operation of the Canal Zone government, including depreciation of fixed assets. The enterprise as a whole is designed to be self-sustaining, and the Company operates from its own revenues.

The Canal Zone government, differing from the Company, operates on appropriations received from Congress each year. Any revenues received by the Canal Zone government during the year are returned to the Treasury of the United States and are deducted from the gross appropriations of that year. The net cost of the Canal Zone government, after deducting these revenues, is then reimbursed by the Panama Canal Company to the Treasury of the United States.

The functions of the Canal Zone government are those normally associated with the civil government. They include police, fire, schools, courts, medical facilities, sanitation, roads, customs, immigration, etc.

Despite the original inaction by the Congress on the plan to improve the Canal's capacity, later it approved the action of the Board of Directors of the Panama Canal Company, which authorized work to begin on a long-range plan to achieve that purpose in a more economical, although stopgap, way. It was decided to widen the entire length of Gaillard Cut from 300 feet to 500 feet. If funds continue to be available for capital improvements, the widening project will be finished in 1967.

Another problem that confronts the engineers is the greatly increased demand for lockage water as well as the greater navigational depth needed to handle the new superships. This requires the maintenance of a higher than usual level of Gatun Lake. Because of the priority given to the navigation demands, the water available for hydroelectric power has been greatly reduced. There are plans to build a low head dam with overflow of 11 feet above the normal level across the Trinidad River arm of Gatun Lake. This would impound approximately 430,000 acre feet of water and increase the usable storage 44.5 per cent, thus reducing the necessity for drastic draft limitations of transits because of low lake levels in very dry years.

While commercial emphasis was placed on the canal by virtue of Public Law 841, the Canal Zone became an increasingly important place in the strategic plans of the United States for the defense of Latin America against Communist subversion and guerrilla warfare to full-scale war. The late President Kennedy authorized the establishment of the United States Southern Command, with headquarters at Quarry Heights in the Canal Zone, as one of the nine unified and specified commands that had been created by the Department of Defense in 1963. General Andrew P. O'Meara was given his well-deserved fourth star and designated Commander-in-Chief, USSOUTHCOM. His headquarters was staffed jointly by Army, Navy, Air Force, and Marine Corps personnel. His area of responsibility covered more than seven and one-half million square miles and his mission included administering the Military Assistance Program for nineteen Latin-American countries; conducting mapping and charting activities; directing U. S. participation in hemisphere defense exercises; directing disaster relief and search and rescue operations. All this covered the vast area from the northern frontier of Guatemala to the Straits of Magellan, and across the Caribbean to Puerto Rico. The primary mission, naturally, was to protect the Panama Canal. Although hemisphere defense planners operated on the theory that the most immediate threat to Latin-American countries is presented by Communist-supported insurgent actions within their boundaries, including the use of infiltrated guerrillas, the eruption on the Canal Zone boundary on January 9, 1964, tested the capability of General O'Meara's command to repel Communist-supported insurgent elements who employed their Cuban-based guerrilla training in street fighting and terrorist activities. There was more than the Canal Zone to defend that day and the days that were to follow. There was the prestige of the United States of America.

Being trained in the Canal Zone at the time were officers and non-commissioned officers from other American republics. They were undergoing an intensive ten-week course in counterinsurgency at the United States Army School at Fort Gulick, near Cristobal. In addition there were a number of mobile training teams assigned to duty with missions in Latin-American countries, at the request of those governments, to instruct their military personnel in the military, economic, sociological, and psychological features of counterinsurgency operations. Those teams were comprised of officers and men from the U. S. Army Special Forces and the Air Commandos of the U. S. Air Force. The Air Commandos trained the Latin-American crews in the techniques of aerial resupply, operations from strange fields and sod strips, low-level navigation, rocketry, skip bombing, napalm dropping, strafing, air infiltration and exfiltration, and aerial reconnaissance.

In addition there was heavy emphasis being placed on civil action projects by the standing armies, such as building new roads, new air strips, public schools, irrigation canals, dispensaries, hospital care and facilities, and the drilling of potable water wells. This program was designed to improve the image of the standing armies among the people and to counteract the Communist propaganda that constantly smears the military as being a drain on the national treasury and wastefully expending the people's money. The armies did not do this all alone, either, but employed civilian laborers, which provided much needed income for the jobless and assured them and their families of sustenance.

The above, plus combined exercises to perfect hemisphere defenses and periodic conferences in the Canal Zone of Latin-American military chiefs under the sponsorship and terms of reference of the Inter-American Defense Board, was a major obstacle in the path of expansion of the global Communist conspiracy. Much more than the Alliance for Progress, the impact of the USSOUTHCOM on the Latin-American military both frightened and angered the Communists and their fellow travelers and useful chauvinists. The successful training, which the Latin-American military men were receiving at the counterinsurgency school in the Canal Zone and under the mobile training teams at home, erected a most impenetrable roadblock in the forward march of the Communist plans quickly to take over Latin America. They feared more than anything else a solidified and unified military that was confident of its own ability to combat them and that could not be cowed by smear and invective, much less by the subversive, terrorist, and guerrilla tactics which they were taught in Communist Cuba. That is why the demilitarization of the Canal Zone emerged as one of the major campaign objectives of the Communists after the flag war erupted.

19. The Present and the Future?

The flag war in Panama gave Fidel Castro a very much desired reprieve of more than one month from a sure indictment by the special investigating committee of the Organization of American States against him, based on Venezuela's evidence of aggression to substantiate its charges. Had the attention of the OAS not been diverted by the Panama crisis, the indictment would have been handed down before the end of January. Instead it was not returned until two weeks and two days remained for President Romulo Betancourt, the accuser, to leave office after becoming the first popularly elected chief executive ever to finish his constitutional term of five years. The diversionary operation in Panama could not have been more perfectly timed to help Castro, for although the indictment was read to the Council of the OAS on February 24, as the month ended the date had not yet been set for the Foreign Ministers of the American republics to convene to try and convict Castro of the charges. Moreover, Betancourt's successor, President Raul Leoni, had to organize his coalition government in order to govern with a congressional majority that would insure stability and support his proposed legislation. And Venezuela had not yet crushed the Communist subversion and the guerrillas who had infested the country, although more intensive efforts were made by the military.

The unfortunate feature of the flag war is that it need not have occurred. The tensions were present and it was known that they were building up, yet for some inexplicable reason if the intelligence were in hand it was either evaluated incorrectly or failed to reach the people who could act on it in time for the proper authorities to take adequate precautions and to implement successful counter-measures. President Chiari could have prevented trouble at the boundary, as he did on February 9, but he elected not to order out the *Guardia Nacional* a month earlier to perform that mission. His excuse was that the *Guardia Nacional* was occupied trying to prevent violence from spreading throughout the city at the time. That excuse, however, is not supported by the facts.

The disorders had erupted on the heels of the massive demonstration of political strength by Arnulfo Arias on January 4, and amid rumors that his supporters might be involved in a plot to try to seize the government. The latter assumption was erroneous, for no one today could seize the government of Panama without the concurrence of the *Guardia Nacional*, and Arias certainly lacked that from the force that had blasted him out of the presidential palace on May 10, 1951. Yet Chiari had apparently been led to believe such was the case, and he was reluctant to commit the *Guardia Nacional* in time to prevent the invasions into the Zone. Furthermore, he, too, had been led to believe that the Zonians had defiled the Panama flag, which also was false. Emotions took precedence over reason, and when erroneous and unsubstantiated press reports were broadcast to the United States and returned by the wire services to Panama and the rest of Latin America, Chiari became further incensed.

There were two such specific reports. One was a wire-service story that Chiari had requested General O'Meara to send troops into Panama to quell the disorders. That was untrue, and the wire-service story from Washington, when read over a local radio station, fell like a bombshell. General O'Meara himself hastened to deny the report, but still that apparently did not assuage Chiari. The other was a report by Ted Scott of the Panama *American* to NBC that it was reported that two Americans had been lynched in David. A wire service picked it up in New York, attributed it to Scott and NBC, and it was received back in Panama and throughout Latin America. This, too, incensed Chiari and many already emotionally inflamed Panamanians. The report could easily have been verified or disproved before transmission, because Panama now has one of the best microwave telephone communications systems with its provinces in all of Latin America. A call could have been put through to David in a matter of minutes, and the report would have been disproved because it simply did not happen. Scott had to seek safety in the Zone, and later sailed for the United States. There were Panamanians who were looking for his scalp; besides that broadcast, they also blamed him for inciting the Zonians against the Panamanians in the manner in which he displayed the flag story in its build up stages and because of the publication of controversial letters in "The Mail Box." Although a New Zealander, he was accused of being "on the side of the gringos." The Panamanians, in any such dispute, usually maintain one vision: either you are with them 100 per cent or you are against them.

If Scott had telephoned David, he would have learned that a mob burned the newly constructed USIS cultural center. The director, Kent Harrith, was at a meeting of the Lions' Club into which he had just been initiated that night. When news of the riots arrived, the Lions' meeting broke up. Harrith sped to his house, which was located several miles outside of the city, hurriedly loaded his wife and four children into his car, left all his furniture and clothing behind, and drove up the mountain to Boquete. After a few days he proceeded over the Pan American highway to San Jose, Costa Rica.

The subversive elements had been alerted and ready to exploit the situation, and, as has been pointed out, they did just that. Yet Chiari and his friends and advisers, emotionally upset by the tragic developments on the boundary, refused to believe that and allowed themselves to be duped into contributing toward the diversion that Castro needed to save himself from speedy punitive action by the Organization of American States. Having been under fire by political opponents for a long time because he had been unable to make any headway with the United States regarding negotiations for a new treaty, and needing to make political gains at home because of the threat posed by the candidacy of Arnulfo Arias, Chiari seized upon a golden opportunity to attempt to pressure the United States to agree to revise the Canal treaties. He had an issue that would insure him national unity and enhance his popularity, but it was also an issue which the Communists could, and would, exploit to its fullest consequences. That, as has been seen, they did.

It was vehemently denied that political capital was to be made as a result of the crisis by Chiari in behalf of his presidential candidate, Marco A. Robles. Yet here, too, the facts tell a different story. A full-page political advertisement was published by Chiari's coalition in *La Estrella de Panamá* on February 24, 1964, to promote Robles' candidacy. Robles was pictured full-length in conversation with Chiari, and the text read in part: "The President of the Republic, Don Roberto F. Chiari, the ruler who will pass on into history as the 'President of the National Dignity,' converses in full interior country with Don Marco A. Robles, the future President of the Republic, about the vital problems of the man of the field."

So the problems that faced the United States and Panama as the month of February ended were:

1. We were still operating the Panama Canal under three valid treaties in the midst of a country whose President had impetuously broken diplomatic relations with us and refused to renew them until and unless we gave him an airtight commitment that we would agree to negotiate a new treaty governing our operations in the Zone.

2. That government had accused us before the OAS under the Rio Treaty of 1947 as an aggressor because twenty-one of its citizens had died and more than three hundred were wounded when they battled police and troops on the zone boundaries of Panama City and Colón.

3. A Nationalist-Communist alliance had succeeded in whipping up a patriotic hysteria against us similar in scope and impact to that Fidel Castro had generated in Cuba in the first year and a half of his revolution.

4. The Panama press, radio, and television contributed to the development, and prolongation, of the hysteria through irresponsible reporting and inflammatory commentaries, including vicious and vulgar attacks against General Andrew P. O'Meara, Commander-in-Chief, United States Southern Command, who had complied with his duty to

defend the security of the Canal Zone when called upon by the Acting Governor to assume command.

5. The persistent attacks against General O'Meara and the Armed Forces in the Zone followed a definite Communist pattern not only to discredit the U. S. military in the eyes of the Panamanians and all of Latin America but also to demilitarize the Zone and leave the Canal defenseless.

6. After he made a statement in Washington that Communists had been involved in the flag war, former Ambassador Joseph S. Farland became the target for similar smear attacks. His former friend Thelma King's Radio Tribuna had this to say: "Joseph Farland, former U. S. Ambassador to Panama, will have to be considered a spy diplomat after his statements in the United States that the events of 9, 10, and 11 January were caused by Communists. It is well known that he was a G-man, and as such was aware of everything that happened in Panama. In accordance with these statements by Mr. Farland, who was so loved in our country and upon whom the greatest honors were bestowed, he was in Panama more as a U. S. spy than as a diplomat. This is how the devil pays him who serves him well."

7. Both nations were involved in presidential campaigns, and President Johnson was not prepared to relinquish before November, 1964, any more treaty rights held in Panama, while President Chiari held to his original firm position and, despite denials to the contrary, had backed himself into an inextricable corner. He could not afford to modify his posture without endangering the stability of his government and insuring the defeat of his presidential candidate in the May 10 elections. He was assured of the full support of the *Guardia Nacional* as long as he maintained his firm demand for treaty negotiations.

8. Efforts at mediation both by the OAS and President Orlich of Costa Rica had been futile.

9. With schools scheduled to reopen after the dry-season vacation (Panama's summer) May 20, there was certain to erupt more anti-American student violence. The international Communist apparatus stepped more firmly into the picture from another area. Professor Cesar A. de Leon, who with Hugo Victor was a teacher at the National Institute and a member of the Central Committee of the Partido de

Pueblo, the Communist party, in the 1947 defense bases agitation, was sent to Panama from Chile, where he held a professorship, to contribute to the agitation. He spoke on the issues to university students after being introduced by Professor Ricardo J. Bermudez, another veteran of the Frente Patriotico de la Juventud organization. Dr. Cesar A. Quintero, Panama's alternate delegate to the UN and also a Frente Patriotico de la Juventud veteran, received an invitation to speak at the Yale Law School and denounced the Canal treaties as "void under international law." It was a foregone conclusion that the government would not attempt to apply any brakes on the anti-American violence that would be generated either just before, or immediately after, the May 10 elections, depending on when it authorizes the school year to begin.

Now the question arises: where do we go from here?

There have been suggestions that we stand firm and offer to take the dispute to the International Court of Justice at The Hague for a juridical ruling on the validity of the existing treaties with Panama. There is no doubt that an impartial tribunal will have to rule in favor of the United States. That, though, would take several years to resolve. Can we afford to continue to sit on a powder keg at the banks of the Canal, where any Communist could time a crossing over the Thatcher Ferry Bridge and drop some plastic bombs on a ship that might be sailing under it and thus easily disable it in the channel and block the Canal until equipment could be brought up to move it? Can we afford to allow our enemies to weaken our national defense by forcing us to give more concessions that would chip away the ramparts for the defense of the Western Hemisphere?

The obvious answer to the above questions is only one: NO!

Can we afford further to weaken our defenses by offering control of the Canal to the United Nations or the Organization of American States or even Panama today?

The obvious answer to that is also: NO!

Representative Daniel J. Flood, of Pennsylvania, said wisely in Congress on April 17, 1957:

"In the event of war the forces of world communism would in no wise respect the neutrality of the Canal, whether under Panamanian or international control. They would certainly seek to destroy it as a matter of their war strategy, which is characterized by unfailing defiance of every concept of freedom and international law."

We have seen in the preceding chapters how our government has, over the years, made many concessions to Panama to rectify protests over the 1903 treaty, but there has been one concession that we have steadfastly refused to make. That is the abolition of the pereptuity clause in that treaty. Now Panama insists upon that as its primary objective in any future negotiations for a new treaty. The Panama Communists have demanded a definite time limit of ten years in any new treaty and then delivery of the Canal to that government. The Panama negotiators, unless they would be cowed by pressure from the Nationalist-Communist and other alliances that might be formed at home, would probably insist on a ninety-nine-year lease and a partnership deal in the operation and management of the Canal with the shares to them free of charge.

Panama is not the only danger spot in Latin America. There will be even greater threats facing our way of life and our hopes for Western democracy south of the border in years to come. To be able to perform our mission and our responsibility to defend the hemisphere, the Panama Canal must be secured through cordial and acceptable relations between the government and the people of the United States and the government and the people of Panama. To achieve that several decisions must be made on the highest level. The major decision must be based on the following questions:

1. What is our Panama Canal policy to be?

2. Do we plan to build a sea-level canal through the Republic of Panama pursuant to the recommendations made to the Congress in 1947?

3. Do we intend to enlarge the capacity of the current lock Canal pursuant to the same recommendations?

4. Do we or do we not want, for reasons of military strategy, to keep our Panama Canal rights, as stipulated in the 1903 treaty, for perpetuity?

5. Are we disposed to grant the demands that Panama made in the negotiations for the 1955 treaty and which, with the exception of those that have since been accorded in the joint agreement of January 7,

1963, are still pending by virtue of a resolution adopted by the National Assembly when it ratified that treaty?

6. Do we plan to build a sea-level canal, or any type of interoceanic canal, on the Central American Isthmus in the foreseeable future, in a country other than the Republic of Panama?

Perhaps those questions have already been answered on the highest level of the executive branch of our government. The policy adopted in the treaty war has, in my opinion, been absolutely correct and the only course that could be followed by the United States. It was made clear to Panama that we were ready and willing to discuss every facet of the Canal problems, but Chiari, having said too much too soon and having made too many promises to his own people that he would not retreat unless and until he got a commitment from the U. S. to negotiate a new treaty, held out for more than ever could be promised under normal or even abnormal practices of diplomacy. Also, it had been made crystal clear in the minutes of the Inter-American Peace Committee meetings in Panama by Ambassador Edwin M. Martin what the U. S. position was, and, as was noted in a previous chapter, Martin also explained to me that if there emerged from the discussions the realization by the United States of the need for a new treaty, then one might be negotiated. The Panamanians, however, reacted like the schoolboy whose toy was taken away from him because he would not do his homework, and stomped about the house in tantrums refusing to do it until the toy was returned to him.

It was not the United States that severed diplomatic relations. It was Panama.

It was not the United States that repudiated the agreement signed before the Inter-American Peace Committee. It was Panama.

There has been much talk on both official and private levels in the United States about building a canal through the Tehuantepec Isthmus of Mexico, or in Nicaragua, or along the Atrato River in Colombia. The problem is not so simple as the talk would have one believe, and it is made less simple by statements like one made by Senator Mike Mansfield, Democratic Majority Leader from Montana, that the Panama Canal is already obsolete, and which was prominently published in Panama.

"If that is true," Max Heurtematte, former Minister of Government and Justice, and other Panamanians asked, "then why does the United States insist on retaining the perpetuity clause?"

Should we approach Mexico, Nicaragua, or Colombia and propose to negotiate for the construction of a sea-level canal, we shall encounter the same obstacles that we faced at the beginning of the century. Every one of those governments, despite the treaty we have with Nicaragua, would insist upon reserving its sovereign rights over the canal route and never would make a grant in perpetuity.

On January 7, 1948, Senator William F. Knowland of California introduced a bill in the Senate, after we were forced to evacuate the defense bases in Panama, in which the President would have been authorized to enter into negotiations with Nicaragua for the construction of a canal. When the ratifications of the Bryan-Chamorro Treaty for the construction of a canal through Nicaragua were exchanged in Washington on June 22, 1916, we paid that Central American government $3 million for that right. The treaty had been negotiated by William Jennings Bryan and Emiliano Chamorro in 1914. Although Nicaragua granted to us "in perpetuity" the "exclusive proprietary rights necessary and convenient for construction, operation, and maintenance of an interoceanic canal" in Article I of that treaty, the same article stipulated that "the details of the terms upon which such canal shall be constructed, operated and maintained to be agreed upon by the two governments whenever the government of the United States shall notify the government of Nicaragua of its desire or intention to construct such canal."

In Article II of that same treaty, the United States obtained from Nicaragua the lease for ninety-nine years of Great Corn Island and Little Corn Island in the Caribbean Sea, and the right to establish for the same period a naval base in Nicaraguan territory bordering on the Gulf of Fonseca on the Pacific coastal boundary with Honduras.

The employment of thermonuclear explosions will, as has been indicated, reduce the costs of construction of a sea-level canal, but the astronomical cost estimates made in 1947 practically ruled out the Tehuantepec, Nicaraguan, and Atrato routes. It is believed that Colombia is not too enthusiastic about the possibility of building a canal through its land at this time or in the immediate future. The Nicaraguan government would be pleased to have one, but the terms it would seek might not differ greatly, because of internal pressures, from those demanded today by Panama.

We must realize that our problems at the Panama Canal are not going to fade away because many of us might entertain such wishful hopes. Our enemies will not allow them to disappear. On the contrary, they will do everything within their means to aggravate them.

Therefore, we must approach the issues with a definite long-term objective that will serve to solidify and to satisfy the mutual interests of the United States and Panama. Total satisfaction is a millenium that we may never be able to achieve, but some sort of effort must be made to resolve one of the most complex of all of our current global dilemmas. This situation has become magnified ever since the Communists launched their "Hate America" offensive in Panama after World War II. And, with but few interludes, we have lost steadily in the cold war there, and now Panamanians in the highest government posts insist that the only way they are going to get what they want—and they want much more than we appear to be ready and willing to give them—is by trying to keep up the pressure of violence and by provoking us to react as we were forced to do in the flag war. They have, unhesitatingly and confidently, told me that and have emphasized that they intend to continue that form of international pressure tactics to blacken the image of the United States and compel us to concede.

Our global commitments and our interests at the Panama Canal require us to insure the military security of that waterway for the free world and the nations of the Western Hemisphere. The operation of the Panama Canal is an imperative auxiliary for that security and for the adequacy of world commerce. It is true that we acted in self-interest when we helped Panama to secede from Colombia but had it not been for the United States, the youngest Republic in the Americas might never have been born on November 3, 1903.

It would be suicidal for us and for the free world to surrender the Panama Canal. Theodore Roosevelt, with great vision, counseled against its internationalization years before the Communists displaced Kerensky and conquered Russia. The Kremlin, it will be recalled, made the internationalization of the Panama Canal one of its strategic objectives more than forty years ago. Yet we can rest assured that our enemies of the Communist bloc will do everything within their subversive capabilities, both covertly and overtly, to try to make untenable our operation of the Canal. In this regard, we cannot, and must not, ignore the designs of Nasser and his United Arab Republic, whose embassy in Panama has been most active in its promotion of the intrigue through financial, psychological, political, and diplomatic action.

In January, 1963, Abdel Hamid Abubakr, Secretary General of the Suez Canal authority, was invited by the State Department to visit the Panama Canal under its foreign leader program. He was received by Governor Fleming and escorted on a tour of the Canal. He lectured in Panama on how Egypt had seized the Suez and how it now operates it. His mission accomplished, at the expense of the American taxpayer, he left for home after having successfully fertilized the seeds that were to help the Nationalist-Communist alliance blossom against the United States hold on the Canal a year later.

The trepidations of such capable public servants as George H. Roderick, then Assistant Secretary of the Army, that any concession of "visual evidence of Panama's titular sovereignty" over the Zone would produce grave future repercussions because that was not its final objective, proved to be accurately prophetic.

Our House of Representatives was disturbed enough in February, 1960, to adopt a resolution, by a vote of 381-12, in which it insisted that any variation in the traditional interpretation of treaties with Panama shall only be made pursuant to the treaty. But when the Congress adjourned, President Eisenhower directed that the Panama flag be flown at Shaler Triangle as "visual evidence of Panama's titular sovereignty." This was the first foot in the door. When the new Congress convened in January, 1961, under President Kennedy, the legislators were so busy opening the "New Frontier" that the flag decision was not challenged and later the late chief executive ordered an expansion of the number of sites where the flag should be flown.

It is the easiest thing in the world to be a Monday morning quarterback, but our relations with Panama might never have been filled with frictions and frustrations if the flags of both countries had been flown in the Canal Zone from May, 1904, when we first occupied it.

The final objective of which Roderick warned was to be announced publicly by Minister of Finance and Treasury Gilberto Arias in a speech on July 5, 1962—only two weeks after he returned with Chiari from the latter's visit to President Kennedy—before the Panamanian Association of Engineers. This brilliant son of the late President Harmodio Arias, who was to become candidate for First Vice President on the ticket of Juan de Arco Galindo of the Alliance Party of the Opposition in the 1964 campaign, had this to say:

"In the future, upon the opening of negotiations for a new treaty, another new step toward our destiny, we will achieve, with the help of God, the political and economic conquests that the Panamanian people hope for, and we will have advanced still another step toward our final objective: a Panama Canal that will be the property of Panamanians under full jurisdiction of the Republic of Panama, maintained by Panamanians, operated by Panamanians, sanitated by Panamanians, and protected by Panamanians."

On January 17, 1964, Gilberto Arias reproduced the full text of the above speech in two pages of solid type in his tabloid newspaper, *Critica*.

A new situation arose in the Canal Zone with the disciplinary action against Payne and Meehan by Governor Fleming for making "libelous" and "unauthorized" statements regarding policy. Non-U. S. citizen employees in the armed forces, the majority of them Panamanians, who are immune from such disciplinary action today, came out a week later in full support of Chiari. The *Star & Herald* published a statement by Local 907, Union of Employees of the Armed Forces, AFSCME, AFL-CIO. The union President is José de la Rosa Castillo, an employee of the U. S. Navy, who had been nominated as candidate for Second Vice President on the Christian Democrat party ticket. The statement read in part:

> We consider the position assumed by the President of the Republic in view of the tragic incidents of January 9 was patriotic, manly, and adequate. . . . The salaries that we make constitute foreign currency which we need today to back the patriotic stand of maintaining a constructive attitude, proud and unbending in regards to the demands of justice which for sixty long years we have kept with perseverances. We are firmly convinced of the goodness and justice of the Panamanian cause and we exhort that compact nucleus of Panamanians, with whom we are contributing to ensure our nationality, to continue showing that we have

grown up and that we practice our sober and constant patriotism to bequeath to our children a morally dignified nation. . . .

We want to close, reiterating our backing to President Chiari in the Canal problem, demanding from our countrymen the necessary vigilance and loyalty to defend our legitimate rights, not only in what regards the the Canal, but also in the internal affairs, adding our voice of encouragement and hope for a more dignified and prosperous Panama.

In any review of the Panama Canal issue, our executive and legislative branches of government should carefully consider the report by the Office of the Comptroller General of the United States. That office conducted an exhaustive investigation of the services and facilities of the Panama Canal Company and the Canal Zone government and completed its audit in June, 1954. After finding that the armed services "are reluctant to relinquish control" over the Zone, the Comptroller General made these important recommendations:

1. That the Panama Canal Company and the Canal Zone government be combined into a single independent government agency.

2. That the organization be administered by a single civilian administrator or by a small civilian board or commission composed of not more than three members.

3. That the administrator or members of the board should serve full time, reside in the Canal Zone, and be selected on the basis of successful backgrounds in governmental, utility, and commercial fields.

There are many who agree with the recommendation that a civilian take over the administration of the Zone. He could and should be a competent engineer, and the job should not be made a plum of political spoils but should be given a permanence that would insure stability of management and operation. A troika commission or board would not be as practical as a single administrator, but the commission or board could serve full time and act in an advisory capacity while its members held important executive posts under the administrator. Congress would have to enact the legislation to bring about such a change in organization and administration as is contained in the first recommendation.

The concept of the United States Southern Command is the best possible answer to our military requirements at this time and should not be altered. The mission and responsibilities of the Commander in Chief would in no way be altered by a reorganization of the Panama Canal Company-Canal Zone government as recommended by the Office of the Comptroller General.

What does need a redefinition is the mission and the responsibility of the American Ambassador to Panama. Although almost any and every action that is taken in the Canal Zone affects our relations with the Republic, the officials in the Zone are not obligated to consult our ambassador about their intended moves. President Johnson had the wisdom to centralize all responsibility for Latin-American policy and operations under his fellow Texan, Thomas C. Mann, one of the most capable, respected, and dedicated men in our foreign service. That centralized diplomatic command has long been a necessity. It should be carried on into the field, especially in Panama. This does not mean that our ambassador should have power to issue orders to the Zone officials. The happiest and most practical solution would be to provide him with a mission directive that would empower him to coordinate all activities therein that affect our relations with Panama. Similar directives should be issued to the Zone officials. There should be no freewheeling that would by-pass the embassy, and neither should the embassy become a bottleneck that would curtail necessary daily liaison between agencies on both sides of the line on lower levels.

The time is definitely at hand for the National Security Council to make a thorough estimate of our present and future requirements regarding an interoceanic canal so that a positive policy regarding Panama may be approved by the President. Now that Panama has resumed diplomatic relations with us, we are going to have to sit down with that country's plenipotentiaries at a conference table and thrash out our mutual problems. This may well lead to some form of treaty revision, such as a more substantial annuity, but there cannot be any concession that could endanger the security of the Canal for the duration of the proprietary rights in the event we want to amend the perpetuity grant.

The Communists have had designs against the Canal for more than forty years; it was thirty years ago that a Communist spy ring stole the plans of the coastal defenses of the Canal at Fort Sherman, facing the Caribbean Sea. The Soviet Union has succeeded, with others who have become their allies of the moment, to generate such hatred against us on the banks of the Panama Canal that we are now faced with a hostile civilian population on both sides of us. This augments our internal security problem within the ten-mile strip that is the Canal Zone. The Soviet Union has targeted the Panama Canal to be wrested from the United States and weaken the links in the chain of hemisphere defense. Communist China is pursuing the same goal.

No treaty that we would ever negotiate with Panama will entirely satisfy all the aspirations of the ambitious politicians and people, and much less the agents of the Communist conspiracy and their Egyptian allies in this case, unless we agree to surrender the Canal to them. Nevertheless, when we do ultimately negotiate any modification of the existing treaties, reserving for ourselves all rights that insure our security and that of the nations of the Western Hemisphere, we should include in that revised treaty a clause that will establish a joint permanent high-level commission in Panama to meet regularly for a continual interpretation and review of pending problems. This will not eliminate the danger that is over Panama or the final objective as Gilberto Arias and others have spelled it out, but, at least, it could contribute to reduce the tensions and serve as an antidote to prevent another crisis like the flag war of 1964.

Neither the Plate Commission nor the special investigating group from the International Council of Jurists of Geneva could find any valid evidence to substantiate Panama's charges of aggression against the United States. Nevertheless, the Plate Commission jumped the gun with a premature announcement on Sunday, March 15, of an agreement between the United States and Panama. This prompted President Johnson to shock the Latin American diplomats in his speech the next day at the Pan American Union on the occasion of the third anniversary of the Alliance for Progress.

"Let me now depart for a moment from my main theme to speak of the differences that have developed between Panama and the United States," President Johnson said as the ambassadors and guests listened to an unprecedented and unmistakable intercalation in his prepared speech.

"Our own position is clear, and it has been from the first hour that we learned of the disturbances. The United States will meet with Panama any time, anywhere, to discuss anything, to work together, to co-operate with each other, to reason with one another, to review and to consider all of our problems together, to tell each other all our opinions, all our desires, and all our concerns, and to aim at solutions and answers that are fair and just and equitable without regard to size or the strength or the wealth of either nation.

"We don't ask Panama to make any pre-commitments before we meet, and we intend to make none. Of course, we cannot begin on this work until diplomatic relations are resumed, but the United States is ready today, if Panama is ready. As of this moment, I do not believe that there has been a genuine meeting of the minds between the two Presidents of the two countries involved.

"Press reports indicate that the Government of Panama feels that the language which has been under consideration for many days commits the United States to a rewriting and to a revision of the 1903 treaty. We have made no such commitment and we would not think of doing so before diplomatic relations are resumed and unless a fair and satisfactory adjustment is agreed upon."

With that diplomatic rebuff, the Council of the OAS met and gave a vote of confidence to its chairman, Ambassador Juan Batista de Lavalle of Peru, to attempt to bring about a meeting of the minds. Lavalle set to work on it and on April 3 a joint declaration was issued by the OAS which read:

"In accordance with the friendly declarations of the Presidents of the United States of America and of the Republic of Panama of the 21st and 24th of March, 1964, respectively, annexed hereto, which are in agreement in a sincere desire to resolve favorably all the differences between the two countries;

"Meeting under the chairmanship of the President of the Council and recognizing the important cooperation offered by the Organization of American States through the Inter-American Peace Committee and the Delegation of the General Committee of the Organ of Consultation, the representatives of both Governments have agreed:

"1. To re-establish diplomatic relations.

"2. To designate without delay Special Ambassadors with sufficient powers to seek the prompt elimination of the causes of conflict between the two countries, without limitations or pre-conditions of any kind.

"3. That therefore the Ambassadors designated will begin immediately the necessary procedures with the objective of reaching a just and fair agreement which would be subject to the constitutional processes of each country."

Johnson announced the agreement at a reception at the White House for the OAS ambassadors. Moreno was there for Panama.

"Panama can be confident, as we are confident," Johnson told the envoys, "that we each desire an agreement which protects the interests and recognizes the needs of both our nations."

Moreno resigned as a presidential candidate and accepted the appointment as Ambassador to the United States in addition to the OAS. He was accepted. Jack Hood Vaughn, a Texan, who was Latin American chief of the Peace Corps, was named Ambassador to Panama.

Johnson announced the appointment of Robert S. Anderson, a fellow Texan, who was Secretary of the Navy from 1953-1954 and Secretary of the Treasury from 1957-1961, as his Special Ambassador to hold the treaty discussions with Panama. A 1932 graduate from the Texas Law School, Anderson had served as Assistant Attorney General of Texas and as a Professor of Law at the University of Texas. He was, thus, exceptionally well qualified to tackle the intricacies of legalisms involved in the discussions with Panama on the Canal treaty and more so because of his service in the cabinet of President Eisenhower. It was while he was Secretary of the Navy that the negotiations were held in Washington for what ultimately became the 1955 treaty.

Chiari appointed another political opponent (as Moreno had been) as his Special Ambassador to deal with Anderson. His name: Dr. Jorge Illueca, the former Ambassador to the UN, the former member of the Frente Patriotico de la Juventud and at the time of his appointment editor of *El Panamá America*.

President Johnson announced that in compliance with the recommendation of the Senate Commerce Committee and with the approval of the Executive Branch of the government, he had ordered a survey team to fly to Colombia to explore the Atrato-Truando River route for a possible construction of a sea level canal there. Why the mosaics and the plans prepared in 1947 would not be suitable for that survey is a puzzle. Perhaps, as the Panamanians were to scoff, this was another diplomatic pressure play.

What caused President Chiari, on the other hand, to retreat from his intransigent stand regarding the need for a prior commitment that we would negotiate a new treaty with Panama? The flag war, followed by the treaty war, served the Communist purpose to wreck Panama's economy. The pinch was on at home, and Arnulfo Arias was almost certain to make political capital from it. Moreover, the rapid and favorable reaction by President Johnson to the successful revolution in Brazil that ousted President Joao Goulart and his pro-Communist regime, had its impact in Panama. There was a hurried meeting of the minds and hence the OAS announcement that was ratified by Johnson without delay.

Epilogue

PANAMA—This is written after the official unofficial results of the most crucial presidential elections in the history of this country had ended. The term "official unofficial" might bewilder many people, but it is the simplest manner in which to define one of the complexities of Panama's complicated electoral system. The National Electoral Tribunal is the supreme election authority, but the National Electoral Scrutiny Jury is the body that verifies the official count of the votes.

The National Electoral Tribunal, in order to provide the citizens with the results of the May 10, 1964, elections and prevent the irresponsible claims of any faction, decided to issue returns based on reports received from its representatives at each of the country's 1,134 election boards. The tribunal emphasized, however, that its returns were official figures but that they could not be considered definite until the minutes attested by each election board were verified by the National Electoral Scrutiny Jury.

The final official unofficial results gave a photo finish victory to Marco A. Robles, the candidate of President Roberto F. Chiari. Robles received a scant 11,441 vote majority and this figure could be reduced after the scrutiny mentioned above. The figures announced on May 13, 1964 were:

Marco A. Robles	134,627
Arnulfo Arias	123,186
Juan De Arco Galindo	49,818
Jose Antonio Molino	9,744
Florencio Harris	3,955
Norberto Navarro	3,832
Jose de la Rosa Castillo	2,774

Arias, of course, was the candidate of his Panamenista Party. He cried fraud and threatened violence, but he had no justifiable basis for his protests. He lost fairly and squarely. Robles came through with a Garrison finish in the campaign to nose him out, thanks to the independent vote.

Molino's small, but significant vote, made the Christian Democrat Party a new factor in Panama politics and indicated it will grow in the future.

The 3,955 votes polled by Florencio Harris, the Socialist Party candidate, do not reflect the total strength of that party because, like the Christian Democrats, they split their vote for president. They presented four candidates for deputy to the National Assembly on the Socialist (Communist) Party ticket. As this was written it was a little too early to know if any made the grade.

Nevertheless, one of the contradictions of Panama politics became evident again in the campaign. Candidates for deputy on the ticket of the Coalicion Patriotica Nacional Party of ex-President Ricardo M. (Dicky) Arias included Thelma King, once again for Colon, and Romulo Escobar Bethancourt for Panama with Bolivar Davalos on the same list for alternate. This party comprised part of the coalition that supported Galindo.

The name of Alvaro Menendez Franco also appeared on the ballot of the new Partido Istmeno Revolucionario for deputy in the Province of Panama. This party was one of the eight that supported Robles. Another party that supported Robles, the Partido Movimiento de Liberacion Nacional, which has no connection with the Communist national liberation movements, nevertheless nominated as candidates for deputy for Panama Celso Solano, ex-Secretary General of the Partido del Pueblo (Communist Party), and Carlos Calzadilla, whose militancy for those causes is well known.

In Robles the Panamanians have a man of middle class extraction. He was born in the city of Aguadulce in the Province of Cocle on November 8, 1905. He graduated from the Instituto Nacional, which was the extent of his education. Then he became a government employee at different intervals from 1929 to 1940 when he obtained employment as a truck driver for the United States Army in the Canal Zone. He resigned after the overthrow of Arnulfo Arias in 1941 to return to government service. In 1948 he was elected a deputy to the National Assembly for his native province, and Chiari appointed him Minister of Government and Justice, the top cabinet post, which he resigned when he became a candidate.

Robles has both personal courage and a mind of his own. He makes decisions after listening to all arguments and all advice. He has gone on record that he will support the policy enunciated by Chiari regarding treaty negotiations with the United States. To obtain his views on the matter, I interviewed him in his home on May 12, 1964. Here is the verbatim translation of the interview:

Q. How do you envisage your relations with the United States when you become President?

A. I hope that in my government there is observed the most cordial policy that ever existed between the United States and Panama for the benefit of both countries.

It is necessary, however, in order to achieve this purpose, that on the part of the United States government there is a spirit of justice, equity and understanding to the just demands and aspirations of the Panamanian people. If this is obtained, as I hope, the policy with the United States as much on the part of the government, as well as the Panamanian people, will be of the most satisfactory and cordial.

Q. Are you going to insist on a revision of the treaty?

A. Yes. The treaty negotiations have practically started with the visit of Special Ambassador Anderson here two weeks ago.

Q. Did you meet Ambassador Anderson?

A. No. But I hope to have the same friendly personal friendship with him that I had with Ambassador Farland.

Then a tape recorded interview for WGN, Chicago, followed:

Q. You say your hopes for the future relations between Panama and the United States are what?

A. The best ever had for both countries because I am in that temperature. And I hope that the United States officials be of the same mood.

Q. You hope that the government officials of the United States will be of the same mood. What do you contemplate that mood means?

A. It means that there be an understanding point of view of Panama.

Q. Do you think that you will be able to maintain order on the border of the Canal Zone so there will not be a repetition of the Canal Zone flag riots of last January?

A. I think that I will be able to stop any riot and any act against the United States citizens if the United States be as understanding as they should be in the points of view of Panama.

Q. Now Don Marco, you will assume the Presidency on October 1st after your credentials are given to you by the National Electoral Jury. After you become President do you intend to take energetic measures to prevent any further disorders on the Canal Zone boundary as those that occurred last January?

A. I do expect that the treaty that will be renegotiated be on so favorable a plan that it would not be necessary for a citizen, or a group of citizens, to act in that way.

Q. Now Don Marco, when you are President and if any group, any sinister group, of citizens attempts to prevent an understanding that you hoped for and tries to attack the Zone boundary again and you have information thereof, will you take energetic measures to prevent it?

A. Certainly. I will do that—prevent it—prevent any intent of riot that will overflow into the Canal Zone. I hope that case won't happen for the good of both countries.

Robles' eyelash victory over Arias was a result of many factors, the major one being the distrust of the independent voters in the demagogic promises and the instability of the man who had twice been overthrown. Antonio Isaza, who had been his private secretary in 1940, was public relations secretary of the National Electoral Tribunal. He put into perspective the defeat of Arias.

"Arnulfo," he told the author, "has not changed at all. On the contrary. You will have noted that most of us who were with him in 1940 and again in his second term will have absolutely nothing to do with him. He had some good men around him but that is no longer so. Imagine him attacking the oligarchs and the rich when he now is one of them himself."

Robles is to be faced with the tremendous problems that exist in Panama. He is familiar with them and he intends to tackle the social reforms by clearing the slums, stimulating industry, providing jobs as well as better housing for the poor masses. In this he will be supported by a new breed of Panamanians, sons of the wealthy who have progressive ideas that are designed to give the underprivileged a better deal in consonance with the times.

Yet as the Panama Canal prepares to observe its Golden Jubilee of opening on August 15, 1964, one finds that ships using the waterway still pay the same tolls that were established in 1914. This is probably the only enterprise in the world which has not raised its prices in fifty years. Why not? Because the Congress of the United States has steadfastly refused to do so.

It was the Bureau of the Budget that proposed to the Congress that the Panama Canal Company be established. The Company created the connotation of a money-making enterprise. The Congress agreed, but in doing it added kindling to the fires that were later to burn, as has previously been indicated.

With schools available in the Canal Zone, which were attended not only by the residents but also by children of Americans residing in Panama and Colon, tuition rates were so sharply increased because of the change enacted by the Congress that it became impossible for many Panamanians and United States citizens, not employed in the Canal Zone and resident of the terminal cities, to send their children to those schools.

The Congress did not see fit to utilize those facilities, and much less authorize scholarship grants to Panamanians, for the purpose of good neighborhood and possibly improved relations. The "Not Wanted" sign had virtually been hung out for Panamanians.

That action by the Congress was in dire contradiction to the farsighted policy of the armed services, which had established schools in the Zone for the advance training of officers and non-commissioned officers. That training, as has already been seen, is at no expense to the men or their governments.

What a golden opportunity was let to slip out of the hands of the United States! No matter how many millions of dollars the United States Information Agency could spend within the republic to try to improve the image of Washington, the $46 per month tuition for a Panamanian to attend the Zone high school makes those expenditures virtually worthless.

President Johnson has appointed a high level commission composed of Ambassador Jack Hood Vaughn, Governor Fleming, and

General O'Meara to meet regularly to coordinate all Panama problems and to adopt corrective measures within their respective jurisdictions and under whatever authority may be vested in them.

Coordination is also needed, and most urgently, in the handling of public relations. More than coordination, a central direction is imperative for all the government agencies that operate in Panama and in the Canal Zone.

The steamship lobbies, while defending their interests, must realize that their stubborn pressure on the Congress to maintain the archaic toll structure of the canal is of only transitory benefit to them. Tolls should be increased and with such an increase the United States can then justifiably offer Panama a larger annuity commensurate with the income from the canal.

The Congress should, too, amend the legislation that created the Panama Canal Company. Does the United States belong in such a business as a government? Did we not have a better case for our right to protect the canal as a rampart of our national defense before we announced to the world what is tantamount to a primary mercenary interest? The word company should be stricken from the canal and thus remove the justifiable complaint that our only purpose at the Panama Canal is to make money.

The Congress, too, should authorize adequate appropriations that would permit the access to the Canal Zone schools of as many Panamanians as may wish to attend so that they can get to know us better and learn that not every one inside that ten mile strip is an Ugly American.

If we are going to remain in Panama and operate a canal then, we must prepare a long term modus vivendi so that the frictions and tensions will be minimized to such an extent that any efforts by our enemies to ignite fires like those that raged in January, 1964, will never reoccur. Otherwise the danger over, and in, Panama will increase rather than decrease.

Panama City, Panama
May 15, 1964

Bibliography

Aguilera, Fito. *50 Millas de Heroicidad.* 2nd ed. Panama: Imprenta Nacional, 1949.

Aleman, Roberto R. *The Panama Canal Treaty: Text of Lecture Delivered at Louisiana State University Law School, April 21, 1959.*

Alfaro, Dr. Ricardo J. *Speech of the President of the Delegation of Panama in the Session of the Political Committee of the United Nations General Assembly, November 14, 1946, with reference to the International Status of the Panama Canal Zone. United Nations.*

————. *Medio Siglo de Relaciones Entre Panamá y los Estados Unidos.* Panama: 1959.

Arosemena, Pablo Escritos. *Panamá.* 2 vols. Panama: Imprenta Nacional, 1930.

Arrocha, Graell Catalino. "Historia de la Independencia de Panamá," *Star & Herald* (Panama), 1933.

Arrubla, Henao. *History of Colombia.* Translated by J. Fred Rippy. Chapel Hill: University of North Carolina Press, 1958.

Biesanz, John and Mavis. *The People of Panama.* New York: Columbia University Press, 1955.

Bishop, Joseph Bucklin. *The Panama Gateway.* New York: Scribner, 1913.

Bunau-Varilla, Phillipe. Panama, the Creation, Destruction and Resurrection. London: 1913.

————. *The Great Adventure of Panama.* New York: 1920.

Canal Zone. *Panama Canal Record*

————. *Panama Canal Review*

————. *Spillway*

————. *Report to the Congress on Surveys and Estimates of Possible New Sea Level and Lock Canal Routes, 1947.*

Carles, Ruben D. *Horror y Paz en el Istmo.* Panama: 1950.

Castillero Pimentel, Dr. Ernesto. *Panamá y los Estados Unidos.* Panama: 1953.

Castillero Reyes, Ernesto J. *Documentos Historicos Sobre la Independencia de Panama*. Panama: 1930.

Crespo, José D. *La Moneda Panameña y el Nuevo Tratado del Canal*. Panama: 1936.

Congress of the United States of America. *Story of Panama, Hearings on the Rainey Resolution, House of Representatives, Committee on Foreign Affairs*. Washington, 1912 and 1913.

————. *Report on United States Relations with Panama, House of Representatives, Subcommittee on Inter-American Affairs, Committee on Foreign Affairs* (86th Cong. 2nd sess.) Washington, 1960.

De la Rosa, Diogenes. *El Mito de la Intervención*. Panama: 1927.

Documentos Fundamentales Para la Historia de la Nación Panameña. Panama: Imprenta Nacional, 1953.

Dubois, Jules. *Freedom Is My Beat*. Indianapolis: Bobbs-Merrill, 1959.

————. *Operation America*. New York: Walker & Co., 1963.

Duval, Miles P. Jr. *Cadiz to Cathay*. Stanford: 1940.

————. *And the Mountains Will Move*. Stanford: 1947.

Dziuk, Augusto. *La Internacionalización del Canal de Panamá*. Panama: 1934.

Eisenhower, Dr. Milton. *The Wine Is Bitter*. New York: Doubleday, 1963.

Escobar, Dr. Felipe Juan. *Arnulfo Arias o El Credo Panameñista*. Panama: 1946.

Garay, Narciso. *Panamá y las Guerras de los Estados Unidos*. Panama: 1930.

Goethals, George W. *The Panama Canal, An Engineering Treatise*. 2 vols. New York: McGraw-Hill, 1916.

Goytia, Victor F. *La Función Geografica del Istmo*. Panama: 1947.

————. *Unidad y Poder en la Paz de America*. Panama: 1950.

Harding, Earl. *The Untold Story of Panama*. New York: Bookmailer, Inc., 1959.

Haya de la Torre. *Victor Raul, El Antiimperialismo y el Apra*. Santiago, Chile: 1928.

————. *La Defensa Continental*. Buenos Aires: 1942.

Heald, Jean Sadler. *Picturesque Panama*. Chicago: C. Teich & Co., 1928.

Hill, Howard C. *Roosevelt and the Caribbean*. Chicago: University of Chicago Press, 1927.

Mack, Gerstle. *The Land Divided*. New York: Knopf, 1944.

Marsh, Richard M. *White Indians of Darien*. New York: Putnam, 1934.

Martz, John D. *Central America*. Chapel Hill: University of North Carolina Press, 1959.

Mendez Pereira, Octavio. *Justo Arosemena*. Panama: Imprenta Nacional, 1919.

Miner, Dwight C. *The Fight for the Panama Route*. New York: Columbia University Press, 1940.

Minter, John Easter. *The Chagres*. New York: Rinehart, 1948.

Morales, Eusebio A. *El Tratado del Canal*. Panama: 1928.

Morales, Juan Alberto. *¿Un Nuevo Canal por Darien?* Panama: 1945.

Organization of American States. *Speeches of Sessions of Council, January 31, 1964 and February 4, 1964*. Washington: Pan American Union.

Ortega, B. *Ismael, La Jornada del 3 de Noviembre de 1903 y sus Antecedentes*. Panama: 1931.

Panama. *Memoria de Relaciones Exteriores (1906-1946)*.

————. *Segunda Legislativa Extraordinaria de la Asamblea Nacional*. 1947.

Rippy, J. Fred. *The Caribbean Danger Zone*. New York: Putnam, 1940.

————. *South America and Hemisphere Defense*. Baton Rouge: Louisiana State University Press, 1941.

————. *Globe and Hemisphere*. Chicago: Henry Regnery Company, 1958.

Robinson, Tracy. *Fifty Years at Panama*. New York: The Trow Press, 1911.

Sands, William F. (with Joseph M. Lalley). *Our Jungle Diplomacy*. Chapel Hill: University of North Carolina Press, 1944.

Sibert, William L. (with John F. Stevens). *The Construction of the Panama Canal*. New York: Appleton, 1915.

Siegfried, André. *Suez and Panama*. New York: Harcourt, Brace, 1940.

Stevens, John F. *An Engineer's Recollections*. New York: McGraw-Hill, 1936.

Teran, Oscar. *Del Tratado Herrán-Hay al Tratado Hay-Bunau-Varilla*. Panama: 1935.

Tomlinson, Edward. *Look Southward, Uncle*. New York: Devin-Adair, 1959.

Vasquez, Publio A. *La Personalidad Internacional de Panamá. Boletin de la Academía Panameña de la Historia*. Panama: 1933.

Westerman, George W. *Hacia Una Mejor Comprension*. Panama: 1946.

————. *Puntos Sensibles en las Relaciones Entre los Estados Unidos y Panamá*. Panama: 1952.

Williams, Mary W. *Anglo-American Isthmian Diplomacy (1815-1915)*. Washington: American Historical Society, 1916.

Index

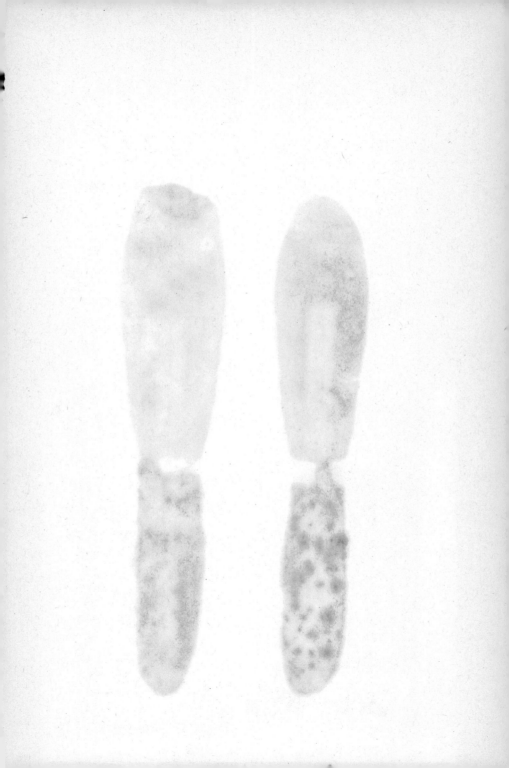

Y6/64

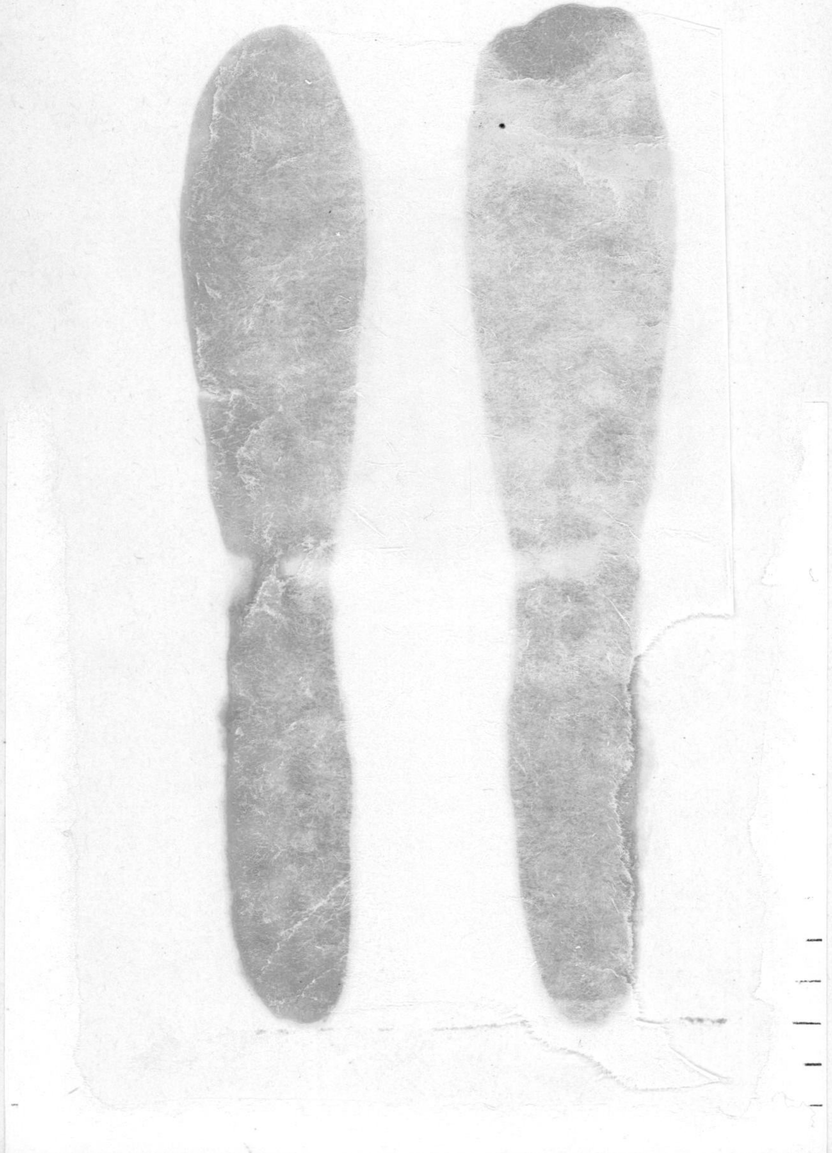